The Complete Journals of

L.M. Montgomery

The PEI Years, 1889–1900

Mary Henley Rubio

Elizabeth Hillman Waterston

OXFORD
UNIVERSITY PRESS

OXFORD
UNIVERSITY PRESS

Oxford University Press is a department of the University of Oxford.
It furthers the University's objective of excellence in research, scholarship,
and education by publishing worldwide. Oxford is a registered trade mark of
Oxford University Press in the UK and in certain other countries.

Published in Canada by
Oxford University Press
8 Sampson Mews, Suite 204,
Don Mills, Ontario M3C 0H5 Canada

www.oupcanada.com

Database right Oxford University Press (maker)

First Edition published in 1985/1987.

Library and Archives Canada Cataloguing in Publication
Montgomery, L. M. (Lucy Maud), 1874–1942
The complete journals of L.M. Montgomery : the PEI years, 1889–1900 /
edited by Mary Henley Rubio and Elizabeth Hillman Waterston.

Includes bibliographical references and index.
ISBN 978-0-19-900210-8

1. Montgomery, L. M. (Lucy Maud), 1874–1942—Diaries.
2. Montgomery, L. M. (Lucy Maud), 1874–1942—Sources.
3. Novelists, Canadian (English)–20th century—Diaries.
4. Prince Edward Island—Intellectual life—19th century.
I. Rubio, Mary, 1939– II. Waterston, Elizabeth, 1922– III. Title.

PS8526.O55Z53 2012   C813'.52   C2012-902274-8

Cover image: Photograph of L.M. Montgomery, used by permission of the
L. M. Montgomery Collection, Archives and Special Collections, University of Guelph Library.

Printed and bound in the United States of America

2 3 4 — 15 14 13 12

Contents

The Complete Journals of L.M. Montgomery

The PEI Years, 1889–1900

Acknowledgements

We happily acknowledge that many helped create this unabridged edition of L.M. Montgomery's Prince Edward Island journals (1889 to 1911). People keenly interested in both Prince Edward Island and the writings of Montgomery acted as tireless aids in our research and as eagle-eyed scrutinizers of our notes: Beth Cavert, Carolyn Collins, Betsy Epperly, Judith Fingard, Benjamin Lefebvre, Jennifer Litster, Jennie Macneill, Sandy Wagner, Christy Woster, and Emily Woster. Proofreaders who helped read this entire text against the original handwritten journals included Cadence Cook, Ciara Corbeil, and Tess Hudson. Writers in London, Ontario, and Sarasota, Florida, improved the wording of our introduction, and Theresa Lemieux bravely took on the job of scanning the images, among other work. Librarians at the University of Guelph and the University of Prince Edward Island stood by, including Kathryn Harvey, Bernard Katz, Simon Lloyd, Michael Ridley, Helen Salmon, and Darlene Wiltsie. Supportive members of the administration at these universities include Donald Bruce, Dean of Arts at Guelph, who came to our aid in funding some of the development costs, including the production of the Index. We again thank all those persons and agencies who contributed to the research and production of our 1985 publication, *The Selected Journals of L.M. Montgomery, Volume I*.

At Oxford University Press, Sherrill Chapman created the elegant new format for these fully illustrated journals, and Ariel Bourbonnais stepped up to the big and challenging job of production editor, as did editor Katie Scott. Indefatigable Jennie Rubio has done double duty as our totally involved and perceptive in-house editor, and as one of the family members (including Jennie's daughter Ruby) who helped us meet our deadlines. The encouragement of Doug Waterston and Doug Killam has carried us through the joys and sorrows that beset us, as we once again relived those that beset L.M. Montgomery when she recorded her exuberant, troubled, inspiring, and fascinating life.

Mary Henley Rubio
Elizabeth Hillman Waterston

Publisher's Note

These journals were written over a century ago. This facsimile edition is an attempt to reproduce the original text in its entirety. In the decades since it was written, society's attitudes toward Canada's First Nations peoples and indeed the very terms used to denote those societies have changed greatly. These journals are, like any creative work, an artifact of their time, and it is only fair to say that the twenty-first century reader may stumble across the occasional expression no longer in common use.

Foreword

With the appearance of this new Volume I, Oxford completes the publication of one of the great journals in our literature.

How great? Well, consider reviewer judgments about a "unique" record of one "bruised and unquiet mind," "the map of a mind struggling against madness and reaching the equilibrium which made her great novels possible. On every page the sharp twin edges of intelligence and abnormally acute senses make their impress." "It is the balance between the outer and the inner life which is unique," "an almost unequalled account of the imagination working." Consider snippets of text, chosen virtually at random: "Such is the cold today that I doubt whether I can go on with my disquisition. On such a day one would need to be of solid emerald or ruby to burn with any flame, & not merely dissolve in grey atoms in the universal grey." … "I feel Sunday clinging to my clothes like the smell of camphor." … "For some time now life has been considerably ruffled by people. … I grow wearied of 'going out to tea' & yet can't resist it."

Praise for and phrases from the *Journals* of L.M. Montgomery? The words ring absolutely true, don't they? In fact they come from a sister document, *The Diary of Virginia Woolf.*[1] Yes, an enormous gulf separated the sensibilities and cultural milieux of these two literary women, who happened to live and write, and die, at about the same time in history. But it's equally wrong to deny the ways in which they were if not kindred then certainly parallel spirits in the production of great journals and great novels, in their personal fragilities, and even in the sad endings of their lives. Is it easy to decide which of the two has had the greater influence on the minds and lives of young women around the world in the twentieth and twenty-first centuries?

Closer to home, consider an ambitious, talented, and insecure Presbyterian of Anglo-Scottish descent, born in 1874, who rises to the top of a tough, demanding profession, and in a private journal pours out page after page of anxiety and loneliness, as well as fascinating detail, while writing obsessively about leading "a very double life." It certainly could be Montgomery. In fact I'm referring to William Lyon Mackenzie King, Canada's longest-serving and arguably greatest Prime Minister. The Mackenzie King diaries, much too long for even multi-volume publication, are considered one of the most remarkable personal/political records ever written. And there really are fascinating comparisons between King and Montgomery, especially in their ability to

---

1. Reviewer blurbs from the back jackets of the Penguin paperbacks of *The Diary of Virginia Woolf*; vols. 5, 2, 4, 1; texts from January 30, 1919, vol. 1, p. 236; August 20, 1920, vol. 2, p. 61; 4 February 1920, vol. 2, 17.

compartmentalize their double lives. The comparisons extend even to the edge of comedy, as the lonely bachelor obsesses about his dogs named "Pat," while the aging writer fusses endlessly about her cats, "Luck," "Pat," and others.

After we amuse, possibly enlighten ourselves with the comparisons, what is most impressive about the Montgomery *Journals* is the uniqueness of the emergence of this wonderfully talented writer from a cramped, obscure environment in nineteenth century rural Prince Edward Island, a place where cold winters and camphor-like Sundays were only Old Country baggage brought to the struggles of everyday life in a much harsher New World. Now with the full account of Montgomery's Island years in these volumes, we become steeped in the writing of a young woman reaching out to capture time and timelessness, particularity and universality, homeliness and profundity. These are journals about the human condition written by a woman obsessed by her surroundings and the relentless passing of time, and whose madelaines are a grove of spruce trees and a winding lane.

Like all great journals, these are fodder for social and cultural, as well as literary historians. They become more fascinating even as their era, its manners, its pace, its therapies, recede from our modern lives. To understand Lucy Maud Montgomery most fully, concentrate on the love of the Prince Edward Island landscape that infuses all her journals, especially the first volume. Be pleased to know, too, that if you spend time on Prince Edward Island today, by the shore, on country lanes, in Cavendish, you will appreciate her pages even more fully.

Spend enough time on PEI and you will begin to sense how deeply this talented, tormented woman identified with what she called her "birthright— this background—this unfailing 'oneness', with the great Eternal Spirit of beauty and reality and peace." Consider the summing up she wrote, first when she was young, then wrote again, and wrote and rewrote in practically every season of her life:

> You never know what peace is until you walk on the shores or in the fields of Prince Edward Island on a summer twilight when the dew is falling and the old old stars are peeping out and the sea keeps its nightly tryst with the little land it loves. You find your soul then—you realize that youth is not a vanished thing but something that dwells forever in the heart. And you look around on the dimming landscape of haunted hill and murmuring ocean, of homestead lights and old fields, tilled by dead and gone generations who loved them—and you say, "I have come home."[2]

Michael Bliss, February 18, 2012

---

1. V, 61, April 9, 1936.

Introduction

Anne of Green Gables astonished a world of readers in 1908. The charm and humour of an energetic girl erupting into the home of two elderly inhibited people in a small, staid village created a bestselling phenomenon. Not then considered a children's book, *Anne of Green Gables* instantly delighted the famous and powerful, such as Mark Twain and Governor-General Earl Grey, as well as the notably less famous, including our own grandmothers. The cry for "more of Anne!" was answered quickly by translation into a wide swath of languages, from Swedish to Hebrew to Braille, and ultimately by a long string of further fictional works "by the author of Anne."

In 1985, another publication again astonished the reading world. L.M. Montgomery, creator of "Anne," born in 1874, had begun keeping a secret journal before she turned fifteen. From 1918 on, she had carefully recopied her entries into uniform ledgers and enriched them by inserting appropriate, evocative pictures. She intended this rich life-record to be published after her death. Although she died in 1942, it was not until forty years later that her son, Dr. E. Stuart Macdonald, knowing of our scholarly interest in his mother's work, invited us to begin transcribing, editing, and publishing her journals. Montgomery's long-hidden version of her early life story emerged into bestsellerdom as *The Selected Journals of L.M. Montgomery: Volume I, 1889–1910*.

"Selected" was a key word in that 1985 publication. Producing a book in print in the pre-"E-book" period was a very expensive business. It seemed financially prudent to offer to an unproved audience a tightly organized book with a central narrative line, emphasizing the unfolding of Montgomery's life as a writer. This decision meant setting aside many entries on her philosophical musings, her effusions over landscape, and her increasing moods of depression.

Changes in readers' attitudes and publishing possibilities since 1985 now allow us to reproduce Montgomery's early journals, uncut, as she meant them to be published.

This unabridged volume represents Montgomery's intention in another sense. An enthusiastic amateur photographer and a woman with a highly visual imagination, she embedded in the text her pictures of family and friends and of the natural world so much a part of her experience. Furthermore, as she had done in her scrapbooks, she pasted other visual elements—newspaper clippings, postcards, studio photos—at appropriate points and crafted her journals as a sophisticated multi-media experience. At the time the first volume of the *Selected Journals* was published, however, standard practice was to choose and group together a few samples of her illustrations. Now technical advances allow us to recreate the format she herself devised, fitting each illustration into the narrative. While the photographs—taken over a century ago before the days of high-quality lenses—are of varying quality, they tell us something about the world Montgomery saw around her.

Another kind of technological advance has brought changes in the end-notes which illuminate details in the text. In the 1980s, we visited faraway libraries and sent snail-mail requests to distant authorities. The internet has upended that method of research. Through the world wide web we are in quick and fruitful touch with archives and individuals in America, Europe, Asia and other places where Montgomery devotees harbour relevant information. With their help we identify more people and places, offer additional sources and comments on quotations and books cited by Montgomery, and deepen aware-ness of the political, theological and social implications of her comments.

In the future, modern technology will allow the general public to access more and more material related to the Montgomery journals. For example, in her last decade Montgomery typed an abridged and sanitized copy of the jour-nals she had been keeping over her long lifetime. Into this typescript she copied a diary jointly composed with her friend Nora Lefurgey in 1903. The playful tone of this short joint diary—and its brief glimpse of Ewan Macdonald, the new minister who caught Montgomery's eye in 1903—make it an intriguing adjunct to the handwritten journals. Someday it will be uploaded on the inter-net as a universally accessible "E-appendix" to this book, on one of the websites devoted to expanding knowledge of the author's life and work. The University of Guelph through its research centre site, www. lmmrc.ca, for instance, will make more and more material (text and pictures) available over time, as well as providing links to other useful websites.

Meantime, this uncut edition of the first parts of Montgomery's carefully handwritten life-long diaries releases a complex, illustrated, and annotated narrative. Here a skilful, passionate, perceptive woman recreates the forma-tive years before she married and moved to Ontario, where she spent the rest of her life.

It is important to remember, however, that the handwritten jour-nals covering the Prince Edward Island years were all recopied sometime between 1918 and 1922. Montgomery claimed that she changed nothing while transcribing into uniform volumes the earlier entries kept in random note-books. Nevertheless she did actually have the opportunity during the recopying process to polish, alter, expand, or embellish her earlier text. Certainly the original manuscript shows that some pages have been razored out and replacements have been pasted in. One may well suspect that while recopying she perhaps half unconsciously crafted the casual records into a storyteller's version of her life.

Indeed, this version releases not one but five stories of life between 1889 and 1911, presented with verve and wit, sometimes with careful evasive-ness, and sometimes with painful honesty.

First, here is a portrait of the artist as a young woman. A child presents her father with a bit of blank verse. ("Very blank!" he mutters.) A sixteen-year-old publishes three examples of her word-work: an essay on a prairie province, a poem on the gladness of June, and a story of shipwreck. A chilled young teacher warms her hands at an oil-lamp hours before school opens, pens a comic anecdote titled "A Baking of Gingersnaps" and mails it off to a faraway magazine, *The Ladies' Journal*, which will publish it in 1895. Away for one precious year at university, a mature student garners enough publications to console her for having to return home for another bout of country school teaching—and for another baking of publishable stories and poems: at least 286 stories and 256 poems in print by the time she is thirty-four. A successful apprentice becomes a successful—unimaginably successfu—novelist in 1908 when the first printing of *Anne of Green Gables* arrives "spleet new" on Maud Montgomery's desk.

Story number two, meanwhile: a teenaged girl discovers the fun of flirtation, moves into complex awareness of her own sexuality, and settles ultimately for strategic marriage. The unabridged journals of these early years offer a detailed anatomy of feminine response to male courtship. As a counterbalance, Montgomery finds a dearly loved kindred spirit in her cousin Frederica Campbell. She displays the cultural mores surrounding both romance and female friendship in the era.

Story number three records a spiritual voyage. A Presbyterian child sings Calvinist hymns with such intensity they will stay with her forever. A probing young explorer feels her certainties erode as she reads unorthodox books and adds them to her spiritual map. A woman who has been an intellectual adventurer ultimately dons the mask of submissive wife of an orthodox minister.

A case history of incipient bipolarity is the fourth story that appears in the early journals as prelude to a lifetime disturbance. Genetic twist? Troubled childhood? Sheer chance? Something leads to an emerging cry of psychological distress, and that something is explored with an ambiguity of openness and concealment, precision and puzzlement.

A fifth might be called the recording of readership. Living in books—experiencing the "polite and unpunishable vice, this selfish, serene, life-long intoxication," L.M. Montgomery turns her journal into a different case history, revealing the way a reader survives non-reading times by escaping, or evolving, or enlarging through the pages of Scott and Brontë, Macaulay and Gibbons, Barrie and Kipling. The end of this story is one of emergence: Montgomery herself becomes one of the grand purveyors of absorbing reading for many generations, in many worlds.

Mary Henley Rubio and Elizabeth Hillman Waterston

JOURNAL
Volume I[1]

L.M. Montgomery

September 21, 1889–April 19, 1897

---

1. This first book reproduces the first, and part of the second, of L.M. Montgomery's handwritten journals. Her first handwritten journal begins on September 21, 1889, and ends on April 19, 1897. The second handwritten journal (beginning on p. 363 below) begins on April 25, 1897, and ends on February 22, 1901.

1889

Cavendish,[1] P.E. Island
Sept. 21, 1889

I am going to begin a new kind of diary. I have kept one of a kind for years—ever since I was a tot of nine. But I burned it to-day. It was so silly I was ashamed of it. And it was also very dull. I wrote in it religiously every day and told what kind of weather it was. Most of the time I hadn't much else to tell but I would have thought it a kind of crime not to write daily in it—nearly as bad as not saying my prayers or washing my face.

But I'm going to start out all over new and write only when I have something worth writing about. Life is beginning to get interesting for me—I will soon be fifteen—the last day of November. And in *this* journal I am never going to tell what kind of a day it is—unless the weather has something to do worth while. *And—* last but *not* least—I am going to keep this book locked up!!

The Old Home

To be sure, there isn't much to write about to-day. There wasn't any school, so I amused myself repotting all my geraniums. Dear things, how I love them! The "mother" of them all is a matronly old geranium called "Bonny." I got Bonny ages ago—it must be as much as two or three years—when I was up spending the winter with Aunt Emily in Malpeque. Maggie Abbott, a girl who lived there, had a little geranium slip in a can and when I came home she gave it to me. I called it Bonny—I like things to have handles even if they are only geraniums— and I've loved it next to my cats. It has grown to be a great big plant with the cunningest little leaves with a curly brown stripe around them. And it blooms as if it *meant* it. I believe that old geranium has a soul!

---

1. Village of farmer/fishermen and their wives and children, on the north shore of Prince Edward Island, with two churches and a meeting hall, but no bank, no mills, and no doctor.

Sunday, Sept. 22, 1889
Cavendish, P.E. Island, Can

[Shoreline]

From sheer force of habit I was just going to write "a dark cold day with frequent showers of rain."

But I won't!

Last night Pensie[1] came up and asked me to go down and stay all night with her. Pensie Macneill—almost everybody in Cavendish who isn't a Simpson is a Macneill[2] and mostly they are both—is a girl who lives about a mile from here and is my second cousin. She is a good bit older than me—she is nearly eighteen—but we have always been great chums. It is fine fun to go down there to stay all night. We've had some dandy old times together—coasting and berrying and picking gum and going to the shore and playing with the cats in the barns.

Today we came up to church together and after dinner we went to Miss Clemmie Macneill's funeral.

Tuesday, Sept. 24, 1889

We have lots of fun in school these days. Mollie wasn't there to-day and I was terribly lonesome. Mollie is my greatest chum. Her real name is Amanda Macneill[3] but the boys always call her "Mollie" and me "Pollie." I liked being called "Pollie." Mollie and I have always sat together in school ever since we were teeny-weeny tots.

Cavendish School

---

1. Penzie Maria MacNeill (1872–1906), a second cousin whose name LMM consistently misspelled as "Pensie." LMM's letters to "Pensie" appear in F.W.P. Bolger's *The Years before "Anne"* (1974).

2. Among LMM's forty schoolmates, six were Simpsons and six Macneills. Their forefathers, William Simpson (1733–1819) and John Macneill (1750–1815), had been pioneer settlers in Cavendish in 1775. As was common among Scottish immigrants, some of the Macneill clan (including Penzie's family) spelled their surname "MacNeill."

3. Amanda Jane Macneill (1874–1949), daughter of LMM's third cousin William C. Macneill, lived south-west of the Cavendish crossroads, by the Long Pond (sometimes identified as the Lake of Shining Waters).

Clemmie Macneill—not the one who was buried yesterday but another—and Nellie Macneill sit behind us. They are hateful girls. I fell out with them a spell ago and we have never spoken since. I don't want to speak, either. They would like to make up again though. They told Lucy—Lucy is my cousin. She lives just across our field. *She* is a Macneill, too—that they would speak to me if I would speak first. Well, I will not! They got mad first and they can get over it first or stay mad—*I* don't care which. They are not the sort of girls I care to be very friendly with anyhow. They are not to be trusted.

Amanda and Tillie Macneill. Amanda has hat on.

Snip was in school, too, and we had some fun. Snip—dear me, if I hadn't burned all my other journals I wouldn't have to explain all over again who

"Snip's Home"

everybody is—is Nathan Lockhart.[1] He is the Baptist minister's step-son and lives in the parsonage. Mollie and I call him "Snip" and John Laird,[2] who sits with him and is *his* chum, we call "Snap." Snip is a very nice boy and we are great friends. He is crazy about books and so am I. We exchange those we've got and talk about them. And the other scholars don't like it because we talk of things they don't understand.

Wednesday, Sept. 25, 1889
Cavendish

This has been such a perfectly exquisite day that I've just got to say something about it. It was so bright and crisp, with an exhilarating air and *such* a lovely sky—brilliantly blue, with lacy trails of misty white cloud straying over it. But I hadn't much time to enjoy it. We were picking potatoes all day up in our hill field. I don't think anybody ever got to such a pitch of virtue

---

1. Nathan Lockhart (1875–1954), stepson of the Baptist minister, living in the parsonage, west of the crossroads.
2. John Laird (b. 1875) lived in the farm south of LMM's, on the road to Charlottetown.

A corner of the hill field

as to like potato-picking. I hate it! But since pick I had to I was glad it was up in the hill field because I love that field. There is such a glorious view from it—the deep blue sea, the pond as blue as a sapphire, the groves of maple and birch just turning to scarlet and gold, the yellow stubble-lands and the sere pastures. I just love to look at such things. But glory be that we are done with the potatoes! To be sure, potato-picking has its funny side. It would have made a hermit laugh to have seen Lu and me as we trudged home tonight, in tattered, beclayed[1] old dresses, nondescript hats and faces plastered with dirt and mud. But we didn't *feel* funny—no, indeed!

Friday, October 11, 1889

After school I took a basket and set off to "Sam Wyand's field." This is a lovely field away back behind Jimmy Laird's woods—now, never mind who Jimmy Laird is!—where we go to pick strawberries in summer. It is all surrounded by maple woods and it is just lovely. And we go through such beautiful lanes to get there, all trees overhead and ferns underfoot. The maple leaves are just splendid now. I picked my basket full and then just roamed around, having a fine time in spite of an impertinent little shower that came pattering down, making the maples overhead rustle like silvery music. I just love the woods and those woods in particular.

Tuesday, October 22, 1889

Oh dear, we have an examination in arithmetic tomorrow. I don't like arithmetic. I had to write a composition on Cleopatra tonight. But I like writing compositions. Miss Gordon[2] makes us write them every week. Miss Gordon is our teacher. She is a good one and I like her splendidly.

---

1. Covered with clay: a word not in dictionaries, used rhetorically for comic effect.
2. Harriet Gordon Smith (1864–1942), to whom LMM dedicated *Anne of Avonlea*, had entered Prince of Wales College for teacher training at 15; she left Cavendish school for Oregon in 1892.

Thursday, October 24, 1889

Nate brought me "Undine"[1] to-day and I read it under the lid of my desk while Miss Gordon thought I was studying history. It is delicious—"Undine," I mean, not history. You don't catch me calling history delicious! I love books. I hope when I grow up to be able to have lots of them.

I went to prayer-meeting tonight and had such fun. Topsy followed me— Topsy is my cat—and all my efforts to send her home were unavailing. She went under the church and I sat through the meeting on pins lest she should take it into her perverse little head to come in and attend the services.

Wednesday, November 13, 1889

It seems a long while since I've written in my journal but there has been nothing much to write about until last night when Rev. Mr. Carruthers[2] of Charlottetown lectured in the hall. With much difficulty I got grandpa's and grandma's leave to go. I went over to stay all night with Mollie and we went to the lecture. The hall was crowded and the lecture was splen-

The Presbyterian Church, Cavendish

did. I never laughed so much. When it ended Mollie and I began to edge our way out. We had to go slowly because of the crowd. I could see Snip behind us, pushing ahead with all his might. He appeared to be in a great hurry but when he got behind Mollie and me he stopped forging ahead and seemed content to take things a little easier. Out on the platform we met Miss Gordon and Mollie asked her if she were walking.

"Oh, no," she responded. "We have a first-class cart."

Cavendish Hall[3]

---

1. A romance by de la Motte Fouqué (1777–1843) about a water sprite in search of a human soul; first published in English 1811, it influenced Walter Scott's *Guy Mannering* (1815).

2. Rev. James Carruthers, born in Pictou, NS, was minister from 1885 to 1892 at St. James Kirk in Charlottetown, 24 miles (39 km) south of Cavendish.

3. Founded 1886 to house lectures, concerts, and a library.

Humph! A few minutes later we saw her perched in Toff McKenzie's[1] buggy, as composed as if first-class carts were never heard of. The boys tormented Toff by hanging on to his wheels to keep him from turning and all the time Miss Gordon sat there, while poor Toff, reins in hand, was vainly trying to get into the buggy and saying "Comeah, comeeah," to the plunging and terrified horse!

Mollie and I decided not to start until all the buggies had gone, because it is so awfully dark on the hall hill. When we did start Nate and Neil Simpson were just behind us. At the top of the hill Neil turned in at his own gate. Snip also turned in at his, but said to us as he did so,

"I don't suppose there will be any *white horses* on the road tonight, will there?"

"No, I guess not," I said.

"If I thought there would be I'd go with you," he said.

Mollie laughed and I said, "No necessity" but Snip said meditatively,

"I guess I'll go anyhow."

"He's coming," whispered Mollie excitedly.

And come he did, right home with us. You don't know how silly I felt, walking down that road arm in arm with Nate. We had lots of fun and rehearsed all our private jokes, for the road seemed deserted, except for our three gay selves. What was our dismay therefore, on going down the slope by Wm. Simpson's lower gate to discover two girls just ahead of us— Clemmie Macneill and Emma Tobin. Emma Tobin is Mrs. Spurr's servant girl. Mrs. Spurr is Nate's mother. These explanations will be the death of me, especially when they come at such a breathless moment.

We were furious. Clem and Em were just crawling along—on purpose, as we knew very well—and as Mollie and I could not summon up enough courage to pass them we had to fall into step behind.

"Oh dear me," I whispered "that hateful creature will have this all over Cavendish tomorrow."

"Oh, well, what's the difference?" said Snip easily. "They must have something to talk about, you know."

This was undoubtedly true but I did not relish them talking about *us*. At last C. and E. reached John Macneill's gate and had to turn in. They stood there watching us, as we walked past—gnashing their teeth, I've no doubt, for they are both crazy over Nate. We walked faster then, anxious to escape a crowd of boys coming behind, until we reached the shelter of Mollie's lane,

---

1. Theophilus Mackenzie (1843–1915), son of the Mackenzies who lived at the eastern edge of Cavendish, was a cousin of LMM's through the Woolner connection with Grandmother Lucy Woolner Macneill.

down which we sauntered at a more leisurely pace. Of course, after Mollie and I went to bed we talked for *hours* and just *couldn't* get to sleep. I suppose we were a pair of fools; but then it was the very first time we had had an escort home; and we knew Clemmie and Nellie would be wild with rage

[Amanda's home]

over it. They *were*, too. They did nothing but talk about it all day in school. Nate was not there at all; perhaps Clemmie and Emma waylaid and murdered him on the way home last night!

Saturday, Nov. 23, 1889

Last night there was a Literary concert at the hall. Miss Gordon asked Mollie and me some time ago if we would recite. I consented but I was dreadfully nervous for I've never recited in public before. But I learned a piece, "The Child Martyr,"[1] and have been practising it right along.

Well, yesterday morning it was pouring rain and we felt very blue. I tried to cheer everybody up by assuring them that it would certainly clear up at sunset—a theory that was rather laughed at by the other scholars, most of whom, with the exception of Charlie Mackenzie—who also *would* be hopeful—had resigned themselves to the collapse of the whole enterprise.

There was no school in the afternoon on account of a funeral, so Mollie came up to stay with me until we saw how the weather turned out. At four it *had* stopped raining, though it was very foggy, so we went over to her place.

It *did* clear up at sunset, as I had so faithfully believed it would. We went up to the hall early. There were only a few there when we arrived and all was confusion and excitement—men going and coming, singing out orders, arranging seats, and running hither and thither. At last all was ready—the choir and organ in place, George Simpson in the chair, and the hall well filled.

Jamie Simpson opened the programme with a march. Then came a recitation, then a song, then Mollie's recitation. She got through with it all right and could then settle herself down to enjoy the concert but I could only sit

---

1. A recital piece by Mary Anderson appearing in many anthologies such as the *Royal Reader* Series used in PEI schools since 1876.

there in nervous suspense. At last my turn came. George Simpson looked down at me and said,

"The next is a recitation by Miss Maud Montgomery."

Feeling myself grow cold all over, I rose. Clemmie Macneill, who sat behind me remarked to Emma Tobin in a sneering whisper "There she goes!" I *did* go, but how I got out and up to the platform I don't know and will never be able to tell. And how I trembled! My voice seemed to be something coming through my lips that did not belong to me at all. And I had the most curious sensation of being an enormous size—as if I filled the hall! But I got through at last and Miss Gordon whispered to me as I sat down "You did *very* well!"

I enjoyed the rest of the programme splendidly and felt sorry when it was concluded. Of course we then had to listen to several prosy speeches by "the old chaps" and finally they gave us a vote of thanks and let us go.

Mollie and I at once started up the hill. Nate was standing by his gate as we passed. He opened and shut it with an ostentatious bang for the benefit of stragglers but he *stayed outside*. Soon he came sneaking up and said,

"Will you try me again tonight, girls?"

We *did* try him and I may say that the experiment was successful. We had a scrumptious walk home. I expect Clemmie will take a conniption when she hears of this second "escapade."

Tuesday, Nov. 26, 1889

There is going to be a big ruction in school to-morrow. Clemmie Macneill and Annie Stewart have been fighting for weeks and it has been getting worse and worse. Mamie Simpson and Clara Mckenzie are in it too—on Annie's side of course, while Nellie naturally sides with Clemmie. Well, to-night Clemmie and Nellie went to Miss Gordon with a dismal tale of how the girls were treating them. I am mixed up in the affair since Annie intends to call on me as a witness because I was unlucky enough to be present one day when she and Clemmie were having a wordy scrap and heard all that Clemmie said—and Annie, too, for the matter of that, for Annie can take her own part in any affair that comes to a question of *tongue*. Now, I know too well what Clemmie Macneill is and she is especially keyed up just now. If she thinks I give evidence in Annie's favour she is quite liable to blaze out about *our* quarrel and Nate will be dragged into it and the mischief to pay all round. Clemmie got mad at me because Nate and I are such good friends, that is just the plain truth of it. If it comes out, as it probably will—for

Miss G. has a genius for ferreting—that this is why Miss Clem and I fell out—well, I would feel too awful for anything.

Wednesday, Nov. 27, 1889

The court[1] held its first sitting to-day. Miss Gordon was as cross as X all day with everyone. When school was over we knew by her expression what was coming. It came. As Nellie was not there the proceedings could not be thorough. Annie, of course, called upon me to prove the truth of a part of her defence and I had to admit that I heard Clemmie say certain things. Miss Gordon wrote all the evidence down—Miss Gordon has rather terrifying ways by times—and the trial was adjourned until Nellie should be there. What is to come I wonder.

Monday, December 2, 1889

I'm perfectly savage to-night!!!

All the parties concerned in the "grand row" were in school to-day. I had begun to hope that Miss G. intended to let the matter blow over without further investigation; but evidently she is not one who will turn her back after putting her hand to the plough.

So when school was dismissed she said,

"Clemmie, Nellie, Annie, Mamie, and Clara will remain after school. Also Maud and Lucy, as their testimony is required. Amanda, do *you* know anything about this?"

Amanda said "no" and got clear. I can't for my life see how she could tell such a fib and look so innocent. She knew as much about it as I did. But she was bound not to get mixed up in the fuss and a lie or two was an ever present help in time of trouble.

Then Miss G. began. She ought to have been a criminal lawyer. She didn't extract much from me, though, for I just kept as fast a hold on my information as I could and all her cross-questioning didn't elicit much beyond some general admission of facts which everybody knew already.

Then Mamie's turn came and she began to tell how the squabble between *her* and Clemmie began—for it seems that Clemmie has a row on hand with her, too. One day, some time ago, Clemmie had remarked to Mamie,

---

1. Mock-trial with formal testimony by students organized to promote ease in public speaking.

"Isn't it absurd, the way Maud and Nate go on?"

Mamie said—or *says* she said, which is not necessarily the same thing—

"Well, I don't suppose it is anybody's business but their own."

And then Clemmie flew into Mamie and called *her* names. That dear Clemmie must be an amiable soul!

Miss Gordon pricked up her ears.

"*The way Maud and Nate act*! Why, how *do* they act?"

Clemmie gave her head a toss and said with volumes of malice in her tone,

"Well, they are always passing notes to each other in school, and walking round together at recess—and *talking!*"

Miss Gordon looked rather blank. I think she had been expecting to hear that Nate and I broke all the ten commandments all at once every day. As for me, I was too angry to speak—and a little uncomfortable as well. For of course it was true enough about the notes and the strolls and I didn't know just what view Miss Gordon might take of it in her present exasperated mood. But Nate is a favourite of hers and more over, I fancy she didn't want another investigation on her hands. So she merely said,

"I have never thought that either Maud or Nate required watching, nor do I think so now. This has no connection with the present case."

Fancy my relief! The examination of the others went on while I sat there and tried to regain my composure. Annie defended herself vigorously and I fancy Miss Gordon got her eyes opened a bit. At last she got all the evidence she could drag out of anybody and then she "summed up." Both parties got an impartial drubbing and she solemnly adjured them to cease from quarrelling and be at rest or they would be expelled from the school. Then the welcome word of dismissal was given and I hurried out and home in a red-hot rage. Wait till I tell Nate!

Tuesday, Dec. 3, 1889

What can be going to happen? Well, something sufficiently surprising *has* happened for Clemmie actually *apologized* to me to-day for saying what she did. It is the first time she has spoken to me for months. I answered coldly but politely. I cannot believe her apology was sincere—she is simply not that sort of a girl! I know her real reason. She is badly gone on Nate herself and does not wish to incur his anger.

He is furious. Last night I wrote him a stormy letter in which I poured out an indignant account of the famous interview and all my resentment regarding it. I don't believe he will ever speak to Clemmie again. As for me, I'm beginning to cool down. After all, it was all rather funny!

Monday, Dec. 23, 1889

I am all cooled down long ago. We have been having a great time in school lately, preparing for our Xmas examination, which comes off to-morrow. We have been learning songs and practising dialogues galore. Annie and Clara are still fighting with Clemmie and Nellie. It is apparently too good fun to give up. Clemmie and Nellie persist in trying to sing and they are poor singers. Annie and Clara, who *can* sing, are cranky too, and sulk if anything happens that doesn't suit them. They made a regular kick against Clemmie's singing to-night and there was a lively spat. Well, I can't sing and don't pretend to, so I'm not in this scrap, thanks be!

Nate slipped a French grammar across the isle to me to-day and in it I found a long "poem" he had made about the night of Mr. Carruther's lecture. It was awfully funny. At least, I thought so. I don't suppose Clemmie or Emma Tobin would. It all depends on the point of view.

Thursday, December 26, 1889

I went to prayer-meeting this evening. Prayer-meeting is about the only amusement we have. Mollie and I sat together and made our plans for to-morrow night. There is another lecture at the hall and I am going over to go up with her. When we got out it was very dark and Annie Jack and I started off together. There were four or five sleighs on the ground and we had to dodge through them. As we went down the bank to the road a boy came running up and collided with us. My hat fell off and we had to claw around in the snow for it, laughing until we could scarcely breathe. Then we tried to get off on the side of the road, out of the way of the sleighs and got into deep snow and Annie fell and my hat came off again and my shawl, too, and we could hardly regain our feet for laughing. One of the boys in the sleighs jumped out and careered up and down the road, acting the clown. Of course he was only in fun but I really believe Annie was scared to death for whenever he came near she would cling to me and scream. I suppose Mr. Archibald would think the noise was shocking but we couldn't help it.

Now, I suppose someone might say,

"And what was there in all this that was so exhilarating? You fell in the snow—and your hat came off—and a boor cut up capers. What was so funny in all that?"

Really, I don't know. But it seemed funny at the time and we got a good laugh out of it anyhow.

Tuesday, Dec. 31, 1889

Well, journal, this is the last day of the old year. To-night we will say farewell to '89, with all its record of joy and sorrow, pleasure and pain, and bid the New Year welcome. God grant that it may never record unfulfilled aspirations, unsatisfied longings, or ungathered flowers. Good-bye, dear old year. You have been on the whole a very happy one for me.

1890

Cavendish, P.E. Island
Jan. 8, 1890

The week-of-prayer meetings have begun. It was in our church to-night. Mollie and I sat together and had lots of fun. Nate and Charlie were sitting behind us and the way those boys carried on was really dreadful. Mollie and I nearly choked with suppressed laughter and only saved ourselves from disgrace by a "Herculaneum" effort, as the old lady said.

Monday, Jan. 20, 1890

Mollie and I have made a decidedly startling discovery about some of our little personal affairs. I am not going to write it down because it is a dead secret. We have refused to tell Nate what it is but we have just hinted at enough to fire his curiosity to the blazing point. I presume we'll have to tell him later but not till we tantalize him a wee bit.

Max is up on the table bothering me fearfully. Max is one of my cats and he is just a beauty—a gray, tiger-stripe fellow. I do love cats. I have another named Topsy[1]—a motherly old gray-and-white.

Saturday, Jan. 25, 1890

I feel cross and horrid! Yesterday I went over with Mollie from school. There was to be a lecture at the hall and Hamilton drove us up. Then we were greeted by the unwelcome intelligence that the lecturer had not come. However, they got up a debate which was fairly interesting.

But I do heartily hate that Ham Macneill.[2] He is simply odious. If he were not Mollie's brother I would not be even civil to him. But I don't want to offend her so I put up with him outwardly. He teased and tormented me to-day until I was ready to scratch his eyes out. I have just arrived home in a very disgruntled mood.

Nate and I don't have much to say to each other just now. We have had a bit of a tiff. But I guess it will soon wear off. I hope so anyhow, for I miss Nate when he is sulking.

---

1. Max and Topsy were the first of many cats named in the journals; "Topsy" recalls the slave child in *Uncle Tom's Cabin*.

2. Hamilton Macneill, brother of Amanda. Their father William C. Macneill was LMM's second cousin.

Tuesday, Feb. 4, 1890

Nate and I are good friends again. He is certainly a nice boy—clever and intellectual, and that is more than can be said of the other Cavendish boys, although they are a nice enough set of lads. I love to talk to Nate about books. There is nobody else in Cavendish who cares to talk about them.

Saturday, Feb. 8, 1890

I feel rather *blue* to-night. I am a horrid little goose, I know—but the trouble is, I can't help being a horrid little goose.

Yesterday night Mr. Archibald[1] lectured at the hall, so I went over with Mollie from school. We walked up alone. The hall was filled and the lecture was very good, but of course all those musty old Simpson speakers—oh, don't they *just* think they are *It*!—had to get up after it and say it all over again.

When we got out at last we started home and had got a good bit past the parsonage gate when Nate came running up.

"Will you tell me that secret discovery of yours tonight, girls?" he said.

I just made some saucy rejoinder, never dreaming that he would take it seriously, for I thought Nate was too well used to my little speeches to take them for more than they were worth. But I guess he was in one of his moods tonight for he simply turned on his heel and went off—mad, I suppose.

It was just too mean. But I don't care. If Nate is so huffy he can sulk all he likes! I didn't sleep much last night, though goodness knows I tried hard enough to. This morning was so stormy that I could not get home and I was vexed for several reasons, but principally because I wanted to get away by myself and have a good cry.

In the evening it cleared up a little and Ham drove me home.

Oh, dear, I feel glum. I know Nate is mad at me and I didn't mean to say anything to vex him.

Monday, February 10, 1890

I went to school this morning, still feeling cross and blue. Nate was there but not a word did he say about Friday night and appeared the same as usual.

---

1. Rev. W.P. Archibald, M.A., B.D. (1852–1918), Presbyterian minister, born in Pictou, NS, ordained and inducted in Tryon, PEI, in 1877, served in Cavendish, New Glasgow, and Rustico, 1878–96.

I think he was feeling a little ashamed of himself. But I am glad we are good friends again. It was so dreadfully lonesome the last time we quarrelled.

We have splendid fun now, coasting[1] on Pierce's hill. The boys bring their sleds and it is so exciting. Nate always takes Mollie and me.

Monday, Feb. 17, 1890

In school to-day I got a note from Nate, smuggled over in his Latin grammar, that is going to be a nuisance. I must make a long explanation why.

One of our school superstitions is that if you count nine stars for nine continuous nights the first boy you shake hands with afterwards is to be your future husband. It is very hard to get the nine continuous nights— Mollie and I began about the first of November but we've never got them yet although if it keeps fine I really will get mine out to-night. But Nate got his out long ago. Mollie and I tried to coax him to tell us who he shook hands with. We thought it was Zella Clark, a great, gawky thing who lives at Bay View. Nate wouldn't tell then but he agreed with me that if I, when I got mine out, would tell him with whom I shook hands, he would tell me.

But I soon came to see that if I waited until I got mine out I might wait a long while and still be no wiser. So I began to tease Nate again. And just then Mollie and I made that "discovery" of ours.

So I told Nate that if he would tell me *right away* the name of his Fair Unknown, I would tell him the mysterious secret, besides keeping to my agreement of telling him with whom I shook hands if I ever got my stars out.

Nate squirmed a good deal and wouldn't come to heel for a long time. At last, however, he agreed, but only on condition that I was *to answer, fair and square, without any evasion, any one* question he might ask me. In return, I might ask *him* any one question I pleased and he would pledge himself to answer it.

I hesitated at first, but curiosity got the better of my prudence and finally I agreed for I was wild to know what his mysterious question was. So I wrote down my information last Friday and in return received his letter. When I read that it was *I* with whom he had shaken hands I nearly had a fit for I had never suspected *that*. But I forgot surprise and everything else when I saw that fatal question. "Angels and ministers of grace defend us."[2]

It was:—"*Which of your boy friends do you like best?*"

---

1. Sliding down a snowy slope on a sled.
2. Shakespeare's *Hamlet*, I.iv.

Horrors! I had never dreamed of this! *What* was I to do! Of course, I liked Nate best—nothing very extraordinary in that. He is very nice and we have always been chummy. But owning up to it in plain English is quite another thing. Besides, he may think the admission means a great deal more than it really does.

In my perplexity a brilliant idea struck me—at least I thought it was a brilliant idea then. Why not ask him the *same question* in regard to his girl friends? I *was* sure he wouldn't want to answer such a question and rather than do so would let me off and consent to let the whole thing drop. So I wrote him my decision and the next day—Saturday—when he came for the mail, I gave him my letter. He went off to read it and came back looking as foolish as a flat-fish. As I had hoped, he at once proposed to let the whole thing drop.

So I was quite at ease until this morning, when another "awful revelation came," in the shape of a letter from Nate in which he said he had *reconsidered his decision.* He would answer *my* question and I must answer *his*.

I was fairly in for it. And I thought savagely that it served me right for being fool enough to agree to answer a question I was ignorant of. I tried to escape but in vain—Nate held me to my bargain. If I had been certain that he would say he liked *me* best—I wouldn't have minded so much but I was very far from certain. In fact, I suspected Mollie would be the chosen one, because she has always been as good as gold to him, whereas I have teased his life half out.

At last I agreed to fulfil my bargain but only on condition that he would let me see his note *first.* I could see Nate didn't like the idea and I suppose he suspected my little game but he finally agreed.

So here I am in rather a plight. I've taken a sheet of paper and written this highly graceful statement.

"*You* have a little more brains than the other Cavendish boys and I like brains—so I suppose I like *you* best—though I don't see why I should, after the trick you have played on me."

If Nate likes *me* best—I'll give him that and he may take all the comfort he can get out of it. If he doesn't I'll tear it up and write Jack's name—true or not true! "Desperate diseases require desperate remedies."

Besides, it *will* be true. If Nate says he likes anybody else best I'll hate him!

Tuesday, Feb. 18, 1890

I am sure I shall never forget this date! I went to school this morning in an unutterable state of mind. Nate gave me his note during the forenoon—and he looked uncommonly foolish. After the reading lesson I asked permission to go out and ran down to my favorite old spot under a big maple tree in the school woods. I always go there to read Nate's letters or else to a dear little sprucy corner down the road.

The first thing I saw was my own name! And the next—well, I don't know what I felt like, for hadn't that absurd boy gone and written down that he not only *liked* me best—but loved me!

I felt like a perfect idiot when I went back to the school and I have no doubt I looked like one. I never so much as glanced at Nate but plunged into fractions as if my whole soul was wrapped up in them.

At noon I passed my French grammar over to Nate, with *my* confession in it and hurried off home. He seemed in high spirits all the afternoon but I was as frigid as a glacier.

I *am* sorry, when all is said and done, that this has happened. I feel that it is going to spoil our friendship. Besides, I don't care a bit for Nate *that* way—I really don't. I only just like him splendidly as a chum. I don't mean to take any further notice of his nonsense.

And yet I admit I *do* feel a queer, foolish triumphant little feeling about it. I've often wondered if anyone would ever care for *me*—*that* way—and now someone really does.

Here is a copy of Nate's letter—my first love-letter and so worthy of being enshrined in this journal

Well, Polly, it must be done. I at first intended to write quite a lengthy epistle, setting forth my poor opinion of myself, my very inferior *personal* endowments, my happiness, or rather ecstasy if your note proved favorable to my wishes etc. etc. etc. But I have altered my plan of arrangement and resolved to give you *hard, dry, plain* facts, for they may possibly appear as such to you, but they are nevertheless as true as gospel. Here goes:—Of all my feminine friends the one whom I most admire—no, I'm growing reckless—the one whom I *love* (if the authorities allow that word to come under the school boy's vocabulary) is L. M. Montgomery, the girl I shook hands with, the girl after my own heart.

Yes, Polly, it is true. I always liked you better than any other girl and it has kept on increasing till it has obtained "prodigious" proportions. Oh, *wouldn't* I like to see you reading this. But I must conclude or you will say it is very lengthy after all. Remember I am waiting for you to fulfil your part of the transaction with ever-increasing impatience.

from

Nate.

P.S. I suppose you'll say I'm very sentimental. Well, perhaps, *rather*. However, it's not much difference. I was just laughing over the tenacity with which we cling to our diverse manner of spelling Polly (Pollie). I'm going to cling to my manner *ad finem*, because it's right. I expect you'll prove stubborn, too.

N. J. L.

Wednesday, Feb. 19, 1890

After school I went up to take my music lesson. I go twice a week to Mrs. Spurr.[1] Past Mollie's gate I was alone with Nate. I felt rather frightened and silly but thank goodness he didn't say a word about our letters of yesterday. He gave me a letter however, just before we turned in at his gate. I read it after I came home, sitting curled up before the fire in the sitting room. There was a lot of nonsense in it. I don't know whether I liked it or not. In some ways I did—and in others I didn't.

We are all busy in school these days writing essays for the *Montreal Witness*[2] school competition. There was one last year. I was the only one from this school who tried. I wrote up the story of Cape Leforce and got honorable mention. This year Nate and Asher are trying, too. They are both writing about the famous "Yankee Storm."[3] I am writing about the wreck of the Marcopolo.[4] The Marcopolo was a Norwegian ship which came ashore here about seven years ago. I remember it well and all the excitement of that summer.

I am not afraid of Asher but Nate will run me close. He is a good writer. I read his essay to-day and I am afraid it is better than mine. But I thought it a trifle too florid in style.

Tuesday, Feb. 25, 1890

I've been laughing ever since last time. Yesterday evening I went down to Pensie's to go for a long-planned visit to Oliver Bernard's.[5] Lettie Buntain,[6] a cousin of Pensie's, was also there. When we were at tea the door opened and in walked Lily Bernard herself. When she heard of our intentions she

---

1. The Baptist minister's wife; Nate Lockhart was her son by an earlier marriage.

2. The *Montreal Witness and Canadian Homestead* (1845–1938), an evangelical, pro-Temperance, anti-Catholic weekly journal.

3. An October 1851 storm destroyed more than 70 American schooners near Cavendish.

4. Fastest sailing vessel of her time, wrecked July 25, 1883.

5. Oliver Bernard (1864–1943), husband of Penzie's sister Leila (Lily) (1863–1943).

6. Penzie's mother was a Buntain.

Pensie

was very sorry but said we'd better go to Minnie's[1] that night and go down to her place on Wednesday night. So after tea Alec hitched up the pung sleigh[2] and we all piled in. We were a merry party—and a noisy one! When we reached Minnie's we all rushed into the house to be greeted by the unsatisfactory intelligence that Ren and Minnie were away. Where they had gone we could not find out for the little French boy[3] who was the sole presiding genius, was either too stupid or too sulky to answer our questions. "He didn't know" and that was all we could get out of him. So we got into our pung again and left. At the road we stopped to discuss the question "Where shall we go?"—for Alec had fully made up his mind to go *somewhere*. At last we decided to go to Quil Rollings.[4] We had such fun all the way down. When we arrived in the Rollings yard Alec whooped wildly and Bertha R. appeared. Alec asked her if Quil was home and when she said "no" we all shrieked with laughter and Alec explained that we were travelling around trying to find somebody at home. However, we stayed, and soon after Quil came home and we had a very jolly evening. I stayed all night with Pensie and she and Letty and I all slept together in that dear little spare room off the parlor. I am to go down again tomorrow night to go to Minnie's.

Thursday, Feb. 27, 1890

Last night we went to Minnie's. We found the house full of company— Mr. & Mrs. Wallace Toombs,[5] Maud, Herbert and Hammond Toombs, Mr. Rogerson,[6] the Rustico school-teacher, Miss Gordon, and Nina and Stanton Macneill.[7] We had a glorious time. We played all kinds of games and laughed until the house echoed. After lunch we all went out to the kitchen. Joe, the French boy, played a tune on his jewsharp[8] and we danced

---

1. Minnie (1867–1933), second-oldest sister of Penzie, married to Lorenzo Toombs.

2. Term from Algonquin *tom-pung*: a big box on runners as in *Anne of Green Gables*, chapter 19.

3. Descendants of the original French settlers of the Island often served as hired hands in LMM's time.

4. Acquilla Rollings (1868–1935) lived in North Rustico, the nearest village east of Cavendish.

5. Minnie's brother-in-law.

6. Rogerson (1871–1925), a young teacher who would reappear in LMM's circle six years later (see note, September 30, 1895).

7. Children of George and Eliza Macneill, living two farms east of Penzie's family.

8. Simple small musical folk instrument: a metal tongue inside a lyre-shaped frame held to the mouth to make a twanging sound. No connection to Jewish traditions.

an eight-hand reel.[1] It was my first attempt at dancing and I danced with Stanton Macneill. I stayed all night with Pensie again. Oh, I've had such a good time this week! It must be awfully nice to live in a house where there are lots of people.

My mother died when I was a baby. I have always lived with Grandpa and Grandma Macneill. Father is away out west in Prince Albert, Saskatchewan. He is married again. I have never seen my stepmother or my two-and-a-half-year old sister, Kate. I have always had a good home here but sometimes it is very lonesome. Grandpa and Grandma always seem so averse to my going anywhere or having my friends here.

Saturday, March 4, 1890

I'm so tired, and I ache all over. The school has never been cleaned since last winter and since the pipe[2] was taken down it has been disgracefully dirty. The trustees wouldn't bestir themselves to have it cleaned so a lot of us girls agreed to do it ourselves if the boys would help. So Nate, Jack, Chesley,[3] Clemmie, Nellie, Maggie and I met there this morning. As it was pouring rain we couldn't light a fire outside and had to heat water over the stove—a slow job but only one of our difficulties. The boys brought water in a cask from the brook and while it was heating we took down the blinds and maps and cleaned out the inside of the desks. When the water got hot we wiped off the blinds with damp cloths but the maps were too greasy for that so we just laid them on the floor and scrubbed them with soap and water. Then we scrubbed the desks, windows, doors, and wainscotting. After that came the floor. *It* ought to be spelled in capitals. A shovel would have been the best thing to tackle it with. But in the end we got it done. Nothing more remained but the stove which we wanted to blacken before leaving. But there was a big fire on so John got a bucket of water to put it out. He opened the door and poured in nearly the whole bucketful "at one fell swoop," and oh, such a cloud of boiling water, ashes, steam and soot burst out in Jack's face. He gave an unearthly whoop and fell over backward, spilling what water was left in the bucket all over himself, while the awful swell of the gas was what somebody has called "deafening." I thought Jack was killed but when he picked himself up with a real live "cuss word" I concluded he wasn't. But his face was all spattered with soot and he did look so funny.

---

1. Traditional Scottish country dance for four couples.

2. In spring the stove pipe was taken down; in winter, running to a hole in the roof, it contributed some heat to the school.

3. Chesley Clark (1877–1968). The Clark family lived across from the Baptist parsonage. A photo of Chesley and other schoolmates mentioned in this entry appears in below, on p. 30.

We all rushed to open the windows, while Jack nothing daunted, got another bucket and went at the fire again. This time he took the precaution of lifting the damper off the top and pouring the water in there. Poof! Up flew another cloud right to the ceiling which it spattered all over with drops of water and soot. The fire seemed to burn all the brighter so we decided to leave it alone and clean the stove some other day. We wiped up the wet floor and departed. When we told the folks about the fire they were horrified and said it was a perfect marvel the stove didn't explode and kill us all. But I shall *never* forget the look of Jack!

Wednesday, April 9, 1890

Dear me, this is dreadful. Since I've given up writing about the weather I've grown very careless about my journal. But nothing much has happened this past month. I've just gone to school and had a good time with Mollie and Nate and Jack. We have been having exams all this week. We had English and history to-day. After school I went up for my lesson and had great fun, larking with the gang. But, after all, I believe I liked my lonely walk back best. The sky was all pale, pearly gray, with here and there a faint, blue strip, calm and clear and remote, as if belonging to some very distant land.

Thursday, April 10, 1890

"The shining curve of the sandshore"

I hadn't been to the shore this spring yet, so this evening after school I went. The shore is about two thirds of a mile from here. Away down beyond the brown fields lay the sea, blue and sparkling, dotted by crests of foam. The walk in the fresh moist spring air was lovely and when I got down to the shore and climbed out on a big rock I just held my breath with delight. The sea was an expanse of silvery gray. Afar I saw the purple slopes of New London scarfed in silvery hazes. To my left extended the shining curve of the sandshore; and on my right were rugged rocks with little coves, where the waves swished on the pebbles. I could have lingered there for hours and watched the sea with the gulls soaring over it.

Friday, April 18, 1890

This morning Pensie sent up word that she would go to the hall tonight if I would go with her. When she came it looked so like rain that we concluded not to go after all. So we went down to the school woods instead and hunted for gum.[1] Our search was not very successful and we soon came up and went into the school, where we stayed a long time looking over my scrap-book which was there. Then Pensie said she must go home and I went a piece with her. We met Stanton and Alec and Russell on their way to the hall. Nothing would do but we must turn back and go with them, so we did and a right jolly walk we had. The debate was on reciprocity[2] and was awfully dry.

Tuesday, Apr. 22, 1890

This morning Mollie and I concluded that it was really too fine to spend the whole forenoon cooped up in school so we decided to try to get out together. I got Emma Simpson to ask out and a few minutes later, when Miss Gordon had forgotten that Emma was out I asked out and got permission. Then, when Emma went in, Mollie stuck up her finger at once, and Miss G. seeing one girl just come in, forgot, as we had hoped, that I was just out, and let her go. We flew down the road and into the woods where we rambled about for a quarter of an hour and had a fine time. Miss G. was never a bit the wiser—or if she were, she didn't let on. I think she is a little "skeered" of running up against us big girls.

We had more fun to-night. Mollie, Lottie, Nate, John and I have been trying to get up a dialogue for Friday evening and we resolved to remain after school and practice it a bit. As John wasn't there we got Ches to read his part and Emma was also allowed to stay as she and Lottie were the only girls going west. But Everett, Prescott, Charlie, Asher, Russell and Austin[3] persisted in hanging around and we couldn't get rid of them. We were bound they should not hear us practising and they were bound they would. As reason and coaxing were of no avail we decided to resort to strategy. At a given signal we dialoguees rushed out and slammed to the porch door. In spite of their efforts we got it shut and locked. Then we cleared the fence and tore down through the woods, for we knew we must hide while we had the chance as they would be out of the window in a minute. We thought we were

---

1. Resin forming bubbles on trunks of spruce trees can be pulled off and chewed.

2. Reduction or abolition of import duties between Canada and the US was a burning political issue.

3. LMM's school mates and contemporaries included Emma Simpson (b. 1878), Everett Laird (b. 1873), Prescott Macneill (b. 1879), Charlie Mackenzie (1872–1938), Asher Robertson, Russell Macneill (b. 1874), and Austin Laird (b. 1877).

safe and were just beginning our dialogue when an exultant shout told us we were discovered and we saw the boys rushing down through the trees with Everett at their head. In our confusion no plan was made. Each of us flew in the handiest direction. I tore down the brook road, followed by Mollie and Emma and finally stopped before Cyrus Macneill's old house. We had fled so quickly that our pursuers had not seen us. Nate and Lottie were nowhere to be seen at first but presently Ches came tearing down the hill and soon after

"Down in the School Woods"

Nate and Lottie came gliding along under the big spruces by the brook. We scrambled over the brook—Nate in gallantly trying to help us girls over fell kerplunk in up to his knees—and climbed the fence beyond. Then we ran along Pierce Macneill's field to the back end. No one was in sight so we perched ourselves on a nice convenient longer platform where a haystack had been and for a second time began our rehearsal. Just at that very moment Charlie loomed in sight down in the hollow. He caught sight of us and dashed back into the woods, presumably to call the others. Over the fence we scrambled once more and fled to a thick copse of young spruces away across the brook. This time we really had baffled our pursuers, and we managed to practice our dialogue in a kind of way, although we were so breathless and excited we hardly knew what we were saying. Then we started back and after jumping I don't know how many brooks—or rather, jumping the brook I don't know how many times, for it does nothing but double and twist down there—we at last reached familiar haunts. All was quiet and we slipped up to the school, got our books and went home without interference. We have since found out that the boys were still prowling about the woods in pursuit of us but we had baffled them completely.

Do you know, journal mine, I may take a trip out west to see father this summer. Grandpa Montgomery[1] is talking of going and if he does he will take me. It has been talked of vaguely all winter but it is about settled now. I expect we will go in August; I feel so excited about it. It will be such a splendid trip. And then to see darling father again! I am frightened to think or say much about it for fear I will not get after all.

---

1. The Hon. Donald Montgomery (1808–93), a political power in Prince Edward Island, served in the provincial assembly (1838–73), first as a member, and after 1862 as speaker during the early debates about joining the Canadian Confederation. He was appointed to the Canadian Senate in Ottawa in 1873 when PEI joined Confederation.

Tuesday, May 6, 1890

We have been playing ball in school all the spring and such fun as we do have! A good game of ball is just glorious. It isn't baseball—don't know that it has any particular name—just "ball," that's enough. The thing itself is all right. We have some most exciting contests. Asher and Nate are the best players among the boys, while Annie Stewart and I are considered to be the best among the girls, principally, because of our ability to slant the bat in one direction and send the ball in another, thereby throwing the scouts out of their reckoning.

To-day at dinner hour, however, it was really too hot to play, so Annie, Clara and I betook ourselves to the woods. Those dear old woods down there are so pretty—all shadowy nooks, carpeted with moss, or paths with ferns and wildflowers nodding along them. We sauntered down under the trees and flung ourselves down on a mossy bank by the brook. And there, fanned by the cool breezes, we lay and gazed through half-shut-lids at the blue sky, smiling through the traceries of the spruce boughs, or explored by the eye the intersecting glades and dreamed idly of long, delicious summer days to come, when we might wander at will through those ferny depths and gather all the joys of Nature's bridal hours.

But at last we heard Maggie Clark's voice calling, "Teacher's coming, girls." So we sprang up from our mossy couches and fled towards the dusty realm of sums and books. I like school in winter but when spring comes I don't like it.

Tuesday, May 13, 1890

We had a "mayflower picnic"[1] to-day, and a splendid time. After school came out we started for the barrens. Jack and Nate were the only boys who went. The girls were Mollie, Lucy, Lottie, Maggie, Annie, Mamie, Emma and I, with Miss Gordon as mistress of ceremonies. Of course, Mollie and I paired off together and had our own private and particular fun. On the road up we had a comical adventure with Clarks' cows but finally reached Charlie Simpson's—Shady Lane Farm—where we had all been invited to tea. After tea we went over to the barrens, joined by Bessie

Miss Gordon

---

1. A social outing to gather trailing arbutus or ground laurel: listed in the Dictionary of Canadianisms as "Maritimes, obs."

and Lalie Fraser. We found all the mayflowers we wanted—such beauties, too. Then a party of us set off to hunt up an old well, which Mamie declared to exist somewhere in the woods. After much merry seeking we found it in a boggy fir hollow and had a sort of victorious war-dance around it.

Finally we all sat down under the firs on a mossy hill and made our flowers up into wreaths and bouquets. When going home time came we all formed in procession, Nate and Jack at the head, Mollie and I next, and so on, two by two, with our hats all wreathed and big bouquets in our hands. I assure you we made quite a show. We marched down to George Harker's, singing all our school songs and then we went in and had some music. After that we all went home and had lots of fun on the road.

We scholars are going to have a concert about the last of June, and we are preparing for it now, getting up songs and recitations and dialogues.

Saturday, May 31, 1890

The *Montreal Witness* came to-day and in it was the essay report for P.E. Island. As I expected, Nate's ranked higher than mine, but I came next and was third for the county. Asher wasn't mentioned at all.

Pensie came up for the mail this evening and we had a walk. The country is very beautiful now. The young leaves are such a bright, tender green, and the opening apple buds are pink and white. The grass is green and velvety, starred with hundreds of dandelions.

Saturday, June 7, 1890

Yesterday was a glorious day. At dinner time Nate and Mollie and I were larking about the school and I said to Mollie,

"I believe I'll go down to the shore to-night."

"Oh," she said, "come over and stay all night with me and we'll go to the shore together."

I agreed to this on the spot. Nate looked at us askance, as much as to say, "Why don't you ask me, too?"—but we didn't, for all his beseeching looks.

After school we went over and had our tea. We could not go directly to the shore as Mollie had some sewing to do. She didn't hurry any, until Ham came in and began to tease us, saying he had seen Nate going down to the shore. Although we entirely disclaimed any interest in Nate's designs or whereabouts, it was curious to see how quickly Mollie despatched her sewing, and how quickly we walked when we were out of sight of the house! As we went through the gate behind the barns we saw a black figure away down on the crest of a sand-hill but it disappeared like a flash, having no doubt been on the look-out for our appearance. We were sure it was Nate but when we

Sandhills, North Shore of P.E.I.

reached the shore not a sign of him could we see far and wide. We guessed he was hiding somewhere among the sand-hills, trying to play a trick on us, so we resolved to get ahead of him. Mollie went down to gather dulse, but I ran up to the hills to ferret him out. I nosed around for a time without discovering him but at last I saw him, hat in hand, sneaking along behind a hill and watching Mollie. The next minute he caught sight of me and went down among the long grasses like a shot, but I ran over and soon found him. We then rejoined Mollie and wandered merrily along the shore, gathering dulse and shells, and laughing and talking in sheer light-heartedness. It was a glorious evening. The sea was a rippling expanse of sparkling blue, the air was soft and clear, the sky full of brightness.

When we came to the rocks we sat down to rest and watch the beautiful scene before us. We talked of many things, we three, soberly but not sadly— we were all too happy for sadness. The sea changed from blue to gray and the little waves splashed at our feet. The sunset was not brilliant but there was a sort of savage, sullen, fascinating grandeur about it. The sun sank in a low bank of black cloud, leaving a wake of rosy gold, while below the cloud ran a strip of fiery crimson, flaked here and there with tiny cloudlets of gold and scarlet. When it grew dark we sauntered back and wandered homeward through the dewy gloaming fields, and past the tranquil starlit pond.

Wednesday, June 11, 1890

Mollie and I went up to a concert practice at Charlie Simpson's this evening. Nate, Annie, Clara, Mattie, Lottie and Maggie were there. We had a good time. At nine o'clock we broke up. Nate disappeared and Annie and Clara grabbed their hats with scant ceremony and tore after him. Mollie and I felt amused and hoped they wouldn't altogether exterminate the poor boy. We made our adieux and exit in a more leisurely fashion and when we got out there was not a soul to be seen. We were wondering whether Nate, Annie and Clara had followed the example of the celebrated Kilkenny cats[1] and clawed each other up, when Nate himself sprang out of the cherry copse where he had evidently taken refuge. Mollie and I smiled a wee bit but said nothing. He came home with us and as usual we had any amount of fun.

Tuesday, July 1, 1890

School closed last Friday and we had our concert last night. It was a great success. Yesterday we all met at the hall and a busy time we had, hanging the curtains, arranging the seats, writing out our programme and finally having a grand "dress rehearsal."

Eight boys in back row from left to right: Robbie McKenzie, Johnny Simpson, Charlie McKenzie, Chelsey Clark, Austen Laird, Arty Macneill, Frank Macneill, Fred Clark. Eight girls and teacher in second row: Maggie Clark, Lottie Simpson, Mattie McKenzie, Emma Simpson, Clara McKenzie, Lucy Macneill, Nellie Macneill, Annie Stewart, Miss Gordon. Children in next row: Ada McKenzie, Aileen Laird, Myrtle Laird, Edith Spurr, Kate Macneill, Lena Simpson, Bessie McKenzie, Ruby Simpson, Ellice Laird, Lisle Archibald, Helen Archibald, Ernest Macneill, Harry McKenzie, Wilbur Clark and Milton McKenzie. Children on ground: Ethel McKenzie, Laura McKenzie, Campsie Clark, Jean Laird, Jennie Archibald, Flenner Stewart, Garfield Stewart, Gordon Robertson, Ernest Spurr, Winchester Simpson.

I am really sorry it is over for we have had lots of fun getting it up. I have enjoyed it all, although, as usual, it was somewhat embittered for me by the fact that grandpa and grandma did not approve of it—why, I cannot say. It just seems that they never do approve of anything which means the

---

1.   In a traditional limerick two Irish cats fight until nothing survives but their tales.

assembling of young folks together. I suppose they would not have let me take part at all if it had not been for Miss Gordon.

When, away back in the winter, Miss Gordon began to talk of a concert for the end of the term we did not think it would ever come to anything; and even after we were really embarked in the enterprise there were times and times when it seemed as if the whole thing would fizzle out. There was seemingly no end to the quarrels and complaints and jealousies. Some *wouldn't* do their parts right and then when the good things were given to those who would, the snubbed got their backs up and declared that they would have nothing more to do with it—a resolution that generally lasted until the next day! Those who hadn't important parts were jealous of those who had; some wanted things arranged one way, some another. In short, we quarrelled over anything and everything and were miserable if we hadn't a row on hand. We were mostly employed in fighting among ourselves, but sometimes we all banded together and made common cause against poor Miss Gordon, and in this—for there is strength in numbers—we generally got what we wanted.

But somehow or other, goodness only knows how, everything smoothed itself out in the long run and the concert came to completion as if we had never had but one mind about the matter. As spring came on we began to have great fun practising. Every evening after school we would go over our recitations and dialogues. At first we liked this, but we soon got fearfully tired of it and *so* sick of the pieces. They came at last to have no more meaning for us than the alphabet.

Still we managed to get a lot of amusement out of the business. At recesses we would generally repair to the brook and discuss every pro and con with as much zeal as if the fate of nations were involved therein.

Last night we met at the hall at six, all in our best bib- and-tucker. We did not go in, however, as we all intended to march in in procession when the time came, so we all scampered into the birch woods behind the hall lest a premature eye should get a glimpse of our glories. There under the birches and maples we clustered and chattered like parrots and betrayed our whereabouts to everybody by the noise we made.

At last Miss Gordon called us and we ran up the slope, scrambled over the fence and assembled by the platform. Oh, how excited we all were—really it was delicious! Emma slipped in and played a march and we all paraded in, two by two, the smallest first, and so on up to the tallest. Nate and Jack were the last, before them Ches and Charlie, then Mollie and I, and so on, down to the tots who never *would* march right. The doors were opened and in we went proudly and took our seats on the platform, facing a goodly audience.

The first number was "An Opening Speech" by "Master John Laird." Snap rose and made his way rather sheepishly to the front. Such a time as Miss

Gordon had training Jack to give that speech and teaching him to bow properly. Jack gave the speech well and it made a hit but Miss G.'s pains with his bow were all lost for he just gave a little duck of head as if it worked on wires.

Then the programme went smoothly on with choruses and recitations until Neil Simpson's reading came on. Neil always read as if he had a hot potato in his mouth and this time was no exception—or so they said. I never noticed for I was occupied in screwing up my courage for the next number. I had to play and I had never played in public before. It was ten times worse than reciting. I was cold with fright. When my name was called I rose and stumbled blindly to the organ. The room was just reeling all about me. Somehow I got on the stool, placed my music before me and plunged into "The Swedish Wedding March."[1] I know I must have made an appalling number of mistakes but I got through at last and crept back to my seat in deep Thanksgiving.

Mollie and I sat together and of course had our fun out of it all, besides keeping the kids nerved up. The last number was a recitation by the whole school, called "The Ship On Fire."[2] We stood in two rows and each one had two verses to recite in turn. At the end of each verse we all had to shout "Ay, ay!" and some of the verses were recited by two performers like a dialogue. The last verse we all recited together. I think we had more fun practising that than anything else.

Well, it is all over and I fear we will never *all* be together again. But no matter where we roam, a tie of common friendship will always bind us in memory—a tie that can never be utterly broken. All these little festals of ours, our concerts, practices, picnics and games, tend to make the tie closer. Perchance in after years, when a lifetime has intervened between us and last night, a chance song or verse may recall the whole scene to mind and we will pause to smile or sigh over the memory of our concert.

Monday, July 14, 1890
Cavendish, P.E.I.

Early this morning Lu, Murray Macneill—Uncle Leander's son who is here for his vacation—Pres, Frank—Lu's brothers—and I went back to "Montana" to pick berries.[3] "Montana" is a big leafy stumpy waste away back of Charles

---

1. A popular recital piano piece by August Söderman (1832–76).

2. A popular recitation piece (1869) by Henry Bateman, based on an 1851 fire at sea and published in *Fret Not and Other Poems, Including Hymns with Music.* Each verse ends with the shout "Ay! Ay!"

3. Montana, Indiana, and C.P.R. were names given to particular fields or woodlots.

Macneill's farm, and we always have splendid expeditions there every summer. After we had picked our jugs full Lu and I took a walk down a lovely old lane we call the "C.P.R." It is all arched over by maples. We went to "Indiana" which is a big clearing in the heart of the spruce woods where we go to pick raspberries. The woods were beautiful. The

View from kitchen doorstep

path was bordered by ferns, pink-pinks and "ladies-lips." The last have the sweetest perfume in the world and the pink-pinks come next.

I enjoyed the day—for I do so love the woods and fields. But I would have enjoyed it much more if the boys had not been along. I like most boys and can always get along well with them; but I do *not* like either Murray or Pres or Frank and am miserable when I am in their company. There is such a mean, *petty* streak in every one of them. Frank I particularly detest.

I am sitting on the kitchen doorstep as I write. It is a lovely evening. Everything is so clear and beautiful and I feel almost sad when I reflect that soon I shall be far away from those dear hillslopes and clover fields—for it is all settled that I am to go for a trip west and will probably stay there a year. We will leave in August I expect. I am looking forward to it with great delight.

Thursday, July 17, 1890

This afternoon I went down to Pensie's and we had great fun. After tea we went for the cows. They were away in the back field of the lower farm and when we were about half way there a there a thunderstorm came up and the rain just poured down. Pen and I got under a thick tree and managed to keep tolerably dry until it began to lightning. Then we were too scared to stay under trees any longer so we sprang up and tore down the lane in a panic, tripping over roots, slipping in the mud, dashing our faces into low boughs and screaming like demented creatures at every flash.

When we got out to the main road the storm was at its worst and we were literally soaked to the skin. Albert's old barn was the nearest refuge and to that we ran. Alas, every door was locked and we were obliged to crawl up a strawstack behind the barn which was quite dry. In scrambling up it I stepped on my dress and tore the front breadth clean across! I pinned it up in quite an artistic loop and then sat down and laughed till I cried. We got home finally, cows and all, and got dried.

Saturday, July 26, 1890

Yesterday afternoon I went over to Mollie's and after tea we went to the shore. Nate had promised to meet us there but there was no sign of him when we arrived. A set of Hunter River people were having a picnic at Cawnpore, so we did not like to go there, but we went as near as we could and then sat down and had a merry little chat all by ourselves. We had sat there nearly two hours and were just concluding to go home when away upshore we saw Nate at last. Just at the same time two H.R. boys came up and asked us to go over to the picnic grounds. Just for fun we went and about half way there Nate overtook us. He seemed to be in an ill-humor over something— perhaps over the presence of the other boys. We invited him to go along with us but he complied so grumpily and was so curt that I felt annoyed and let him severely alone.

When we reached Cawnpore the boys got the piper[1] to play the bagpipes for our edification and we had some fun but soon left for home. Nate thawed out when we were alone but *I* didn't. The fact is, Nate is absurdly sentimental these days—or would be if I would allow it. I hate that sort of thing. He has just spoiled our lovely, old comradeship completely. He is *so* nice when he is sensible and *so* horrid when he isn't!

Thursday, July 31, 1890

This morning I had a book spree—reading a novel Uncle Leander brought home with him. Uncle Leander is "Rev. L.G. Macneill" who ministers to souls in St. John, N.B. The novel was "Devereux" and is by my favorite author, Bulwer Lytton.

Pensie came up in the afternoon and after tea, Lu, Pen and I took the men's tea to the shore. While we were there Uncle L. came down and got Pen and me to help him row a little trouting boat from our shore to Cawnpore. We had such a time! The boat was a villainous old tub—leaky as a basket,

---

1. Highland bagpipes, played on formal occasions.

and the water half filled her. Pen and I were complete novices in the art of rowing, so that, what with making mistakes and correcting them, we had no time to protect ourselves, and our feet and the tails of our dresses got soaked to the core. But we had great fun.

Friday, Aug. 8, 1890

This morning I went picking raspberries down in the school woods. Nate happened along and we had our last chat and said good-bye, for I expect to go to Park Corner to-morrow. I was sorry to say good-bye to Nate—who goes to Acadia College in September—but not so sorry as I would have been if he had not spoiled our friendship by falling in love with me. I've been rather stiff with him of late, just on this account, and as he resented this, our relations have been a little strained.

I feel excited about starting away to-morrow—and a little blue, too. I've never travelled any but I think I'll like *that*; but what about Prince Albert? Shall I like it? And my stepmother? I do not know. She seems nice from her letters and I mean to love her if I can, just as if she were really my mother.

Park Corner, P.E. Island
Aug. 9, 1890

Well, here I am! This morning Uncle Charles Crosby[1]—Aunt Jane's husband—came down for me. Thus brought up against the realization that I was really leaving home, I didn't feel at all exultant. I was relieved when all the farewells were over and we got away.

We had a hot, dusty drive to Park Corner. At Clifton, Uncle C.—part of whose creed is certainly to take things easy—stopped at a certain Mrs. McKay's, of whose existence I was never before aware but who is, it seems, a remote relation of mine. I was taken into the parlor and introduced to several ladies. That was just it exactly—I was introduced to *them* but *their* names were not mentioned to *me*. How I hate that way! How in the world am I to know who people are, even if they are my relatives, if I've never seen them before? It does make me feel so awkward. By dint of holding my tongue I got through our call without any bad breaks but I felt decidedly relieved when we were once more on our way, even if Uncle C. did begin

---

1. Charles Crosby (b. 1823). Married LMM's Aunt Jane Montgomery (1835–1902) in Montgomery home at Park Corner, February 1856.

an abstruse discussion on the probability of the spirits of the departed ever returning to revisit the scenes of their earthly pilgrimage and kept it up with variations until we reached Grandpa Montgomery's.

And here I am, sitting all alone in this strange bedroom, writing in my journal for comfort because I feel a bit lonely. I am all ready to hop into bed, so good-night, and as there is no one else here to do it for me, I will wish myself "pleasant dreams and sweet repose" and seek my maiden couch.

Monday, Aug. 11, 1890

This has been *such* an exciting day. It was pouring rain when we got up this morning and I felt real sick, too, so the outlook was not cheerful. I couldn't eat any breakfast, which greatly alarmed Grandpa Montgomery. He thinks if a person can't *eat* she must be dying. That is just his besetting sin. I believe if he hadn't persisted in stuffing me so yesterday I wouldn't have been sick to-day. I am sure he imagines I am hollow all the way down to my boots!

But he is the dearest old soul! Although I've lived all my life with Grandfather Macneill I haven't anything like the affection for him that I have for Grandpa Montgomery. And the latter is *such* a handsome old man—just like a grandfather out of a story. I love him. He is always so good and kind and gentle to me.

At last we got off. It wasn't a very pleasant drive for it drizzled rain all the way. Finally we reached Kensington where we were informed that a special containing Sir John[1] and Lady Macdonald—who are touring the Island—would be along in an hour; so Grandpa—who is a Senator and a great crony of Sir John's—telegraphed to Hunter River for Sir John to stop at Kensington and take us on. I assure you I was quite excited over the prospect of seeing the Premier of Canada. When the special came I followed grandpa on board and the next moment was in the presence of the great man himself. He was very genial and motioned me to a seat between himself and Lady M. where I sat demurely and scrutinized them both out of the tail of my eye.

Sir John is a spry-looking old man—not handsome but pleasant-faced. Lady M. is quite stately and imposing, with very beautiful silver hair, but not at all good looking and dressed, as I thought, very dowdily.

I never was on a train before but I enjoyed this, my first ride, very much. We reached Summerside in about thirty minutes and went to Aunt Nancy Campbell's where I was warmly welcomed by my aunt and cousins. After

---

1. Sir John A. Macdonald (1815–91), first prime minister of Canada, served as prime minister for nineteen years.

dinner I attended Sir John's reception in the Market Hall.[1] I went with a Miss Cairns[2] from Freetown. The stage and hall were beautifully decorated. An address was read to Sir John who replied to it in an interesting speech.

Later on, Miss C. and I strolled down to the wharf to see the St. Lawrence, the boat which was to take the Premier and his suite across to Pointe du Chene. In the evening we all went to the Salvation Army "Barracks." I never was in such an old rookery. The dirt was enough to terrify one had not the danger to one's bones from rotten boards, rickety steps, projecting cornices and loose plaster served as a counter irritant. I don't like the "Army" at all. I can't see any real religion in such performances.

Tuesday, Aug. 12, 1890

This morning I woke up with my heels on the pillow and my head where my heels should have been. After breakfast Uncle Dan drove us down to the wharf and we were soon on board the boat. The day was fine but cool and cloudy and the sea had by no means a glassy appearance. I was afraid I would be seasick but I wasn't and we had a fine trip over to Pointe du Chene. We got on the train and we have just started. We are flying along at a great rate and I have all I can do to take in the new sights. I "journalize" in a little notebook and will copy it into my regular journal later on.

Night, Aug. 12, 1890

Here we are in St. John. We have had a splendid trip so far. The scenery was so picturesque. The road went through high wooded hills. Here and there they would sweep around to disclose a beautiful lake or river curve, like a mirror set in an emerald frame.

We are at the Belmont House. We learned while at supper that our train would not leave until 11.20 so I came up to the waiting-room while grandpa went to get our tickets. The only other occupant was a tall, thin lady who was for a time severely silent. At last, however, we drifted into conversation and I found her to be very nice. She was "Yankee" to the core—hails from Providence, R.I., and talks with a big accent. We went out for a walk and had a very nice time. Soon after she left on the Halifax train.

---

1. On Queen's Square, designed by Isaac Smith, 1823; destroyed by fire, 1958.
2. The Cairns family still live in Lower Freetown, south-west of Charlottetown.

Wednesday, Aug. 13, 1890

We are on our way to Montreal. Last night after I finished writing I yawned away a dull hour and was very glad when at last Grandpa came in and said our train was due. We then went over to the depot where we found it was half an hour late. But I did not find the time long—there was so much to see. At last the headlight of our train flashed like a fiery red eye through the outer darkness and a few seconds later the long line of cars thundered in. We went on board and soon were flying through the night.

When the sleeping berths were made up I crawled into mine. The upper berths are not at all nice. They are so small you don't dare to move in them and if you forget once in a while and sit up *whack* goes your head against the roof.

When morning dawned we were among the wooded hills of Maine. I got up—or rather I got *down*—and I've had a splendid time so far. I love travelling. We are now passing through a rough country. There is nothing but steep, wooded hills. Now and then we pass a little clearing where a log cabin stands with a cluster of ragged children around it. The banks along the track are yellow and purple with billows of golden-rod and fireweed. The scenery about Moosehead Lake is enchanting.

Same day. Montreal

Here we are in the big St. Lawrence Hall. The views you see when crossing the St. Lawrence River on the C.P.R. suspension bridge are magnificent. We got there about 5.30. The thronged streets were brilliantly lighted by electricity. You hear as much French as English here.

Thursday, Aug. 14, 1890

This morning after breakfast I felt rather lonesome and, as grandpa was out, I formed the somewhat daring resolution of going out for a walk by myself. I was very careful not to lose my way and I enjoyed myself very much and all the more from the little spice of adventure in it. After lunch Grandpa took me for a five mile ride in a street car. Montreal is a fine city but I am sure I wouldn't like to live here.

Friday, Aug. 15, 1890

We are now whirling across Ontario. Last night after I finished writing I went down to the balcony of the Ladies' Parlor. The only other occupant was an old lady who did not seem at all companionable and I was soon making up my mind to go back to my room when she suddenly said,

"Are you staying here?"

I believe I really jumped I was so startled but I was dying for someone to talk to and I soon found myself engaged in a very animated conversation. I have seen some people who could ask a pretty decent lot of questions but I never saw anything to equal her. However, we got on very well until the time came for me to go so I bade her good-bye, probably for all time and, in *her* opinion, doubtless for all eternity, for she had discovered that I was a Presbyterian and she, being High Church, seemed to regard me as little less than a pagan and entirely outside the pale of Christianity.

We left at eight, but had to wait at the junction an hour and a half for a belated Boston express. A long freight train stopped beside us for a quarter of an hour. It was loaded with live pigs and the odor which blew in therefrom could never have been mistaken for those spicy breezes that are reputed to "blow soft o'er Ceylon's isle."[1]

I had a lower berth last night and slept like a top—though why a top should be supposed to sleep sounder than anything else I could never understand. But I don't feel at all well to-day. My head aches horribly. We are passing through a very bleak, desolate country. There is absolutely nothing to be seen but stumps—and goodness knows there is enough of them.

Seven O'Clock

We are still in the region of stumps and rocks. *Sam Slick* in "The Clockmaker"[2] says they have all the ballast out of Noah's Ark on the east coast of Nova Scotia, but if he had ever travelled over the C.P.R. he would have changed the locality to the northern wilds of Ontario. Rocks are all well enough in their way—"in moderation" as Everett Laird says of girls—but they pall on the taste finally. At some of the stations we all get out and pick blueberries which are very abundant.

I read and doze by turns. I wish I had somebody to talk to. Grandpa is rather deaf to be of much use in that respect. If only Mollie were here what fun we would have!

---

1. From "Greenland's Icy Mountains," a missionary hymn (1819) by Bishop R. Heber.
2. Character created by Thomas Chandler Haliburton in a regular column in the *Novascotian* beginning in 1835.

Saturday, Aug. 16, 1890

I have enjoyed myself immensely to-day. When I woke up this morning and pulled aside the curtains of my berth I almost imagined I was down on the shore at home. Below me lay a line of rugged brown rocks with foam-crested waves dashing against them, while far as eye could reach was an expanse of tossing water. I knew that this must be "cold Superior's rock-bound shore" and all day I have been revelling in the exquisite views which every turn reveals.

Sunday Evening, Aug. 17, 1890

This has been a dull day. We saw the last of the rocks this morning and all day we have been whirling over the prairies of Manitoba. They are beautiful but monotonous. Acres of ground are covered with sunflowers as with sheets of light. They remind me of a certain boggy field at home where buttercups abound. We reached Winnipeg at 12.30 and had to wait four hours. It was dreary for I had no one to talk to and grandpa did not leave the train. I did take a little walk by myself but there was nothing to see, as we were some-where in the outskirts. I don't admire Winnipeg. It looks as if someone had thrown a big handful of streets and houses down and forgotten to sort them out afterwards. But no doubt the centre of the city is better.

Monday, Aug. 18, 1890

This has been a most surprising, delightful, exciting day. We got to Regina at five this morning. It was cold and dim and foggy. We went to the Windsor Hotel and got rooms. Then grandpa went out, saying he would go up to the Lansdowne Hotel and see if there was a letter from father there. In a short time a knock came at my door. I opened it—there stood grandpa, smiling broadly;—

"I have brought a friend to see you," he said, stepping aside.

And there was—father![1]

I can't describe the time we had! I laughed and cried. Oh, it was so delightful to see dear father again. He hasn't changed at all, although it is five years since I saw him. Such a day as this has been! Father took us out for a drive in the afternoon. Regina itself is not a bad little place but the country

---

1. Hugh John Montgomery (1841–1900), since 1887 working in Saskatchewan as real-estate sales-man, auctioneer, and purchaser for the new trans-Canada railway.

around it is the nearest approach to a desert of anything I have ever seen. We leave to-morrow morning. There are no passenger trains running on the new branch line to P.A.,[1] yet, so we will have to go in something they call a "caboose." That sounds bad!

Prince Albert, Saskatchewan
Wed. Aug. 20, 1890

Here I am at my destination at last—in this little town on the Saskatchewan, 3,000 miles from home.

Yesterday's ride in the "caboose" was dreadful and I was almost played out when we reached Duck Lake[2] at eleven at night. We then drove a mile and a half in a "buckboard" to a Mr. Cameron's house where we spent the night. When morning came I got a good look at the country and was delighted to see that it was fair and green and fertile-looking— altogether unlike those dreary wastes around Regina.

Father had telegraphed to P.A. for a team and Mr. McTaggart,[3] his father-in-law—or rather, the

Father's house in Prince Albert

second husband of his mother- in-law—was along bright and early. I enjoyed our drive very much. The prairies are jammed with flowers. I thought the prettiest were the exquisite little bluebells, as abundant as they are beautiful.

We reached Prince Albert at four. It is quite a pretty little town—rather "straggly," built along the river bank. Father's house is a nice one on Church Street. Mamma seems quite nice and friendly and my two-year-old half sister Kate is a very pretty child. There is also a girl staying here and going to school—Edith Skelton.[4] She belongs to Battleford, and is just my age. I have met so many strangers that I feel bewildered—and very tired.

1. Prince Albert, home of LMM's father, step-mother, and step-sister, a village of 1,090 people in 1890: now Saskatchewan's third largest city. See Gary Abrams, *Prince Albert: The First Century, 1866–1966* (1960).

2. A village 14 miles (22 km) south-west of Prince Albert; central point in the Riel Rebellion seven years earlier.

3. Government land agent, originally from Cannington, Ontario, married to the mother of LMM's step-mother.

4. Hired as a household helper in Battleford, a village 109 miles (176 km) southwest of Prince Albert, where LMM had been working prior to Prince Albert.

Saturday, Aug. 23, 1890

I am desperately homesick! I have fought it off as long as I could but to-day I succumbed and had a fierce cry all to myself. I'd give anything to see dear old Cavendish for half an hour. Oh, for a glimpse of the old hills and woods and shore! There, the very thought of them makes me cry!

Father and his second wife

I am to go to the High School[1] here. It opens Monday week. I don't know how I shall like it. I suppose it will be very different from Cavendish School. But I mean to study hard and do P.E. Island all the credit I can.

It is lovely to be with father again, though. He is *such* a darling. His eyes just *shine* with love when he looks at me. I never saw anyone look at me with such eyes before.

But, to speak plainly I am afraid I am *not* going to like his wife.[2] I came here prepared to love her warmly and look upon her as a real mother, but I fear it will prove impossible. I have been here only three days and already my eyes have been opened by several little things. For instance this morning at breakfast she did not pour any tea for me. Of course I knew this was just an oversight and waited for a minute or two after the others had begun eating before asking for it, as grandpa was speaking and I did not want to interrupt, but before I could speak she turned to me and said, in the most cutting and insulting tone of voice I ever heard and with the *blackest* look, "What are *you* waiting for, Maud?"

I suppose she must have imagined that I was expecting something to be on the table that was not on it. But what a way to speak on mere suspicion! I shall *never* forget that tone and the look that accompanied it! I answered quietly, "My tea, please" and she looked silly enough, poured out the tea, slammed it down before me with such force that the tea spilled out of the cup in the saucer and hardly spoke a word to anyone the rest of the meal.

She also informed father yesterday that she wanted him to stop calling me "Maudie," as it was entirely too childish. I believe it is the affection

---

1.   The building, opened in 1885, having burned down in spring 1890, classes met in temporarily in the Town Hall.

2.   Mary Ann McRae (1863–1910), born in ON.

implied in the diminutive of which she disapproves. In my short sojourn here I have already seen several displays of temper and sulkiness on her part towards father which were utterly unprovoked. She seems to have a dreadful disposition—sulky, jealous, underhanded, and *mean*. Why, she never goes out of the house without locking the pantry door—for fear, I suppose that Edith or I would help ourselves to a bite to eat in her absence. I *know* I am not going to be happy here. I have been as nice and respectful to her as I could be but already I find myself disliking and fearing her, and that is not a pleasant prospect.

I am sitting here alone at my bedroom window. In the next house a lot of children live and it is *so* funny to hear them when they are out playing. They quarrel pretty often—they are at it now and one lad is howling at the top of his voice while another is angrily and repeatedly demanding, "Where is my hat?" A third is flinging biting taunts at the "baby" for crying, and a fourth, who seems to be a neighbour's boy, has beaten a retreat with his hands in his pockets and a very lordly air.

My only comfort here is Edie. She is such a lovely girl. We room together and have any amount of fun.

Tuesday, Aug. 26, 1890

I had a letter from Lucy to-day and it was very welcome. It was full of home news. I read it over half a dozen times and then had a good homesick cry after which I felt much better.

This afternoon Edie and I, together with Jennie and Will McTaggart—mamma's half sister and brother—went hazelnutting up on the hills and had lots of fun. P.A. is built on several natural "terraces" along the river bank, with "bluffs," as the hills are called, behind it, sloping back to wide, rolling prairies dotted with groves of willow and poplar and countless tiny blue lakelets. Across the river are great pine forests and the views upstream are very beautiful.

Edie and I had a confidential talk this evening over various things. I found out that she does not like mamma at all, either; and she told me several things that made me feel very sorry for poor father. He himself told me that he finds it hard to get along with his wife and asked me to put up with some things for his sake. I notice that she picks and nags at him unceasingly and on some days he cannot make the simplest, most harmless remark but she snubs him for it. For example—at dinner time to-day father and I were talking about Aunt Emily and Uncle John Montgomery. Father said he did not think Aunt Emily cared a great deal for Uncle John when she married him.

"Oh, I suppose you think she wanted you," sneered Mrs. Montgomery, in her most insulting tone.

It seems to put her in a rage to hear father talking to me of any of his old friends and haunts. She will go around for days at a time without speaking a word to anyone when she gets into one of her tantrums. I could bear the way she treats me but I *cannot* bear the way she uses father. He is so good and kind to her as he is to everybody, and there isn't a shadow of justification for the way she behaves—unless the fact that he is not rich is a justification. She seems to resent that most bitterly.

Monday, Sept. 1, 1890

This cold, wet morning Edie and I scrambled out of bed at dawn and dressed ourselves for school. Annie McTaggart called for us. She is a young half-sister of mamma's and I do not care much for her so far. Away we went, myself trying to look as if I liked it. The High School is not far away but it is in a very bleak place and when we went in things didn't look very cheerful. The room looked as if hadn't been swept or dusted since the year one. There were only nine pupils there—we three girls and six boys. The teacher, Mr. *Mustard*[1]—what a funny name!—seems fairly nice and I think I shall get along all right, when I get the hang of the studies. The text-books and methods are all new to me and I find them rather bewildering. I am going to study for a teacher's certificate.

Tuesday, Sept. 2, 1890

It rained cats and dogs all day. Edie had to stay home to do the washing, so I ploughed off to school alone through the mud, with tears running down my nose when I was going through vacant lots where nobody could see me. I felt so homesick for dear old Cavendish school with all my chums and our jolly goings-on. But when school went in we got a good fire on and things began to be cheerful. I was the only girl there to-day but I didn't mind that, and we had a real nice time over our lessons.

---

1. John Mustard (1868–1950), once a schoolmate of Mary Ann McRae in Ontario, had graduated from University of Toronto, B.A., in 1889.

Wednesday, Sept. 3, 1890

Company came last night—Mrs. McKenzie of Toronto and her two daughters. Her husband, William Mckenzie[1] is my step mother's uncle, and is a railroad king and millionaire I understand.

I like school here now pretty well. When the room is warm and tidied up a bit it is rather cosy. We actually have an open fire place in it. There are eight boys going now and I must say they are a rather queer assortment. Arthur Jardine[2] and Willard Goodfellow[3] seem quite nice. Frank Robertson and Willy MacBeth are not half bad either. But Tom Clark,[4] Joe McDonald,[5] Douglas Maveety[6] and Henry Oram[7] are detestable. They are "nitchie"[8]— which means that they have Indian blood in them—and are as homely as stump fences, especially poor Douglas, who looks as if he had ten times too many teeth for his mouth.

Thursday, Sept. 4, 1890

This evening I went over to Mr. McTaggart's. Annie McTaggart,[9] and Mary and Mabel and Gertie McKenzie,[10] wanted to go down to the station to present a bouquet to some visiting potentate's wife. So we got it made up and started. Rod McKenzie and John McTaggart were down at the station, so we had no one to escort us. It was very dark and the girls were too frightened to

---

1. William Mckenzie (1849–1923), president of the Canadian Northern Railway, had brought his family from Toronto for ceremonies marking the opening of passenger service from Regina.
2. Age thirteen, born in ON, third son of Dr. Robert Jardine, M.A., D.D., who resigned from St. Paul's Presbyterian Church in 1890 in a dispute over salary.
3. Age twelve, born in ON in 1878, came to Prince Albert with his Scots–Irish parents and five siblings; later became a carpenter.
4. Perhaps son of Lawrence Clark, prominent in 1880.
5. Born 1878, son of a Cree butcher; became a teamster.
6. Born 1878, son of J.D. Maveety, publisher of the Prince Albert *Times.*
7. Aged thirteen, son of a hotel-keeper; after serving in WWI, became a bartender.
8. From an Algonquian word applied in a derogatory way to children with Aboriginal blood. French and Scottish fur-traders and Hudson's Bay factors in early days had taken "country wives"; children of a French father were called Métis, those of a Scot were called breeds (half-breeds). LMM's only story based on her Prince Albert experience, "Tannis of the Flats" (1902), centres on a young Métis woman.
9. John McTaggart's daughter, finishing high school before beginning work as teacher at Lindsay School, 1891.
10. With their father attending the opening of the branch railway.

go around by the road, so we took a roundabout way that led through a thick growth of young poplars. I really never expected to get out with my eyes in my head. When we got to the private car where we had expected to find Mrs. Holt,[1] no one was there, so we had to start back, this time going up the track and skipping from tie to tie. Gertie and I were together and once we both fell into a drain. At last by good luck we came to the very car where John and Rod were and they brought us home. We all went to Mr. McTaggart's where we danced until eleven. But I can't say I really enjoyed myself. I can't seem to feel at home with this crowd—they are not "my style" that is all—except Gertie whom I really like.

This evening I wrote a long letter to Pensie. How I'd love to see her—and go to the "back fields" for the cows with her! We always had such fun when we went together for the cows. But oh, those sunny woodlands and fields are three thousand long weary miles of prairie and mountain, forest and stream away.

Tuesday, Sept. 9, 1890

Oh, I *am* tired and sleepy! But I must prop my eyelids open long enough to write in my journal—sure, and isn't it the only comfort I've got!

Last night we had a party here in honor of the McKenzies. I had to answer the door and show the guests upstairs—something I didn't like doing for they were all strangers to me and I felt awkward enough. After everybody had come Gertie McKenzie and I fooled around together but found it all dreadfully dull. We were only school girls, so weren't dancing, and there was nothing else to do. The party broke up at one and I tumbled into bed, too tired to move.

Edie and I are up here in "Southview," as we have named our room. "Mephistopheles," our black kitten with the goblin-green eyes, is sleeping on the bed. He is a great pet with us.

Friday, Sept. 19, 1890

We had quite an exciting time in school to-day. This afternoon Mr. Mustard had a cranky fit on—he takes them occasionally although between times he never makes any attempt to secure order—and nearly snapped our heads off if we spoke a word, so Edie and I resorted to the old device of writing on our slates. We were thus carrying on quite an animated conversation about our own personal affairs, when I became aware that that little sneak of a Bertie

---

1. Herbert Holt (1856–1941) Montreal-based contractor, had worked with McKenzie and others to complete the trans-continental Canadian Pacific Railway.

Jardine, who sits behind us, was looking over my shoulder and reading all I wrote. So, just to "give him a run for his money" I began to write rather caustic comments on all the boys present, fully aware as I did so that Master Bertie was copying everything I wrote down on a piece of paper. I didn't say a word about him or his brother, however, so that he had no excuse for what he did at recess. He showed the other boys the paper with all my comments and they were furious and went to Mr. Mustard. I explained the whole affair and Mr. M. took my part and gave Bertie a good drubbing. So after awhile they all cooled down. Bertie J. is a meddling little sneak, anyhow, and nobody can bear him. Arthur is so different—such a nice gentlemanly little chap.

The country around town is very beautiful now for every tree is purest yellow. The view from the schoolroom window is just lovely. You can see away up the blue river between its golden banks. But oh, I'd rather look out into an old spruce wood with ferns growing in its glades and a sea-wind purring in the treetops.

However, it can't be denied that school here is rather good fun, although very different from old Cavendish school days. There are a lot of rooms in the building—it was formerly a hotel—and they are all utilized for various purposes. The one above ours is a public ballroom and on the occasion of a ball our room is used as a ladies' dressing room. On the next morning we generally find numerous hairpins, feathers, flowers etc. strewn over the floor, and sometimes a hand mirror or two. On the other side of a big dusty, cobwebby hall is the Town Council Room and above it is the Free Mason's Room.[1] In the back of the building are the patrol quarters, where two or three mounted policemen are stationed to patrol the town. When they arrest a drunken man they bring him in there, haling[2] him through the hall and locking him up in one of the row of small dark cells, which runs directly back to our room.

Mr. Mustard has a pretty hot temper and as several of the boys have a fair share of "nitchie" in them, we have lively times occasionally. When Mr. Mustard starts in to thrash anyone he locks the door and uses a murderous-looking raw-hide whip as long as himself.

Our amusements are very limited. At recess we girls wander around the dusty old place or sit out on the verandah and watch the boys playing football. Or perhaps we idly watch the passers-by—Indians for the most part—"braves" with their dirty blankets over their shoulders or chattering dark-eyed squaws with their glossy blue-black hair and probably a small-faced papoose strapped to the back.

---

1. Secret society connected with anti-Catholic sentiment. LMM's father belonged to the Kinistino Masonic lodge, named for the local Saulteaux tribe.

2. "Haling" means to draw forcibly.

As for our studies I am not satisfied at all. Mr. Mustard is not a good teacher and the work seems to drift along without any "go" or life in it.

Saturday, Sept. 27, 1890

After dinner to-day father drove out to a Mr. Rennie's[1] in the country and took Edie and me along with him. We enjoyed it so much. It is so delightful to go anywhere with father. He is such good company.

The country is magnificent now—one great, golden sea sheathed in purple mist. When we got out to the place we found the folks all away in the harvest field and the house locked up. Father went out to where they were and Edie and I prowled around to amuse ourselves. We first discovered the dearest little well down in a hollow under a big willow—such a romantic little spot. It made me think of the "Well of St. Keyne"[2] in Southey's humorous ballad. We hunted up a dipper and got a good drink. Then we wandered down into a charming wilderness of golden poplars with an undergrowth of leafless rose-bushes that were gay with roseberries.[3] We scrambled around, eating lots of nice, acid fruit they call the "high-bush" cranberry,[4] and had a lovely time. I could have stayed for hours and hated to leave but we had a lovely ride home.

Friday, Oct. 3, 1890

Well, the Bible assures us that we shall never have another deluge and it is very consoling that it does, for otherwise I fear me we should have had uneasy minds to-day. It has simply poured down since daylight and tonight I was really terrified. The water seemed to descend in sheets, while vivid bolts of lightning went hurtling through the darkness and thunder crashed incessantly overhead.

School was quite brilliant to-day. When Mr. M. was hearing the Junior Latin we all somehow got going laughing—I'm sure I don't know what at. The very imp of laughter seemed to take possession of us and it was impossible to stop. We saw a joke in everything and even Mr. Mustard seemed to catch the infection.

---

1. Thomas Rennie, pioneer farmer, helped build St. Catherine's Church in 1874.
2. Robert Southey's humorous ballad on the battle of the sexes (1798), based on a Cornish legend.
3. No dictionary definition. Perhaps viburnum berries, or the berries of a Guelder rose bush.
4. A marsh viburnum, not related to the low-growing cranberry.

Monday, Oct. 6, 1890

School was very dull to-day but we had some excitement in the afternoon. At dinner hour Douglas Maveety had killed, or aided in killing, a *skunk* over at the public school, and when school went in after dinner the smell was dreadful. There we all sat, with our noses buried in our hankies, while poor D. sat dejectedly in one corner, as much avoided and shunned as if he had been a leper or a smallpox patient. At last Mr. Mustard sent him home to change his clothes but the odor pervaded the place for the rest of the day.

I am feeling lonely and dejected to-night, for father is away and I miss him so. He is all that makes life livable here at all for me. Otherwise it would be intolerable. Mrs. Montgomery—I *cannot* call her anything else, except before others for father's sake—has, I think, the most dreadful disposition ever put into the heart of a woman. She is sulky, jealous, utterly unreasonable. She just makes father's life miserable, continually carping, complaining, and fault-finding. But there is no use in writing anything more about her. Besides, I am constantly afraid she will sometime find and read this journal, although I keep it locked up. She reads all my letters and everything else she can find in my room when I am out. I suspected that very soon after I came here and I laid traps for her which proved it to me. I did not, however, let her know that I found it out for I am determined I will not make a fuss, for father's sake. He has enough to bear as it is.

Saturday, Oct. 18, 1890

I am in the blues to-night and with good reason. Edie is going home to Battleford on Monday's train and oh, dear me, whatever will I do? I have grown so fond of her that it just seems to me like parting from a dear friend whom I have known all my life. I shall be so wretchedly lonely when she is gone. No one to talk or joke or plan or laugh with! Oh, I am too miserable to write of it anymore.

Monday, Oct. 20, 1890

Edie went this morning and I felt dreadfully. It has been a dismal day. I am up here in Southview now and I feel so lonely. I missed Edie bad enough all day but it is tenfold worse now because this was always the time when we had the most fun, when we got up here away from Mrs. Montgomery's eye. She hated my intimacy with Edie and would have put a stop to it if she could. If Edie and I laughed together over some little innocent, mutual joke she seemed to take it as a personal insult. She even descended low enough to try to make my friend a spy upon me, too, but Edie was too loyal to me for that.

When I came to P.A. Mrs. M. did not approve of my wearing my hair up. She said I was too young for it. I admit I was, but her reason for disapproving of it was that she was afraid an apparently grown-up step-daughter would make *her* seem older. I was willing to please her and I have always worn it down since I came. But last Saturday morning I was dressing in a big hurry and, hunt high or low, I couldn't find a hair-ribbon. So at last I twisted it up in a knot behind, poked a handy hair-pin or two through it and thought no more about it. I was not out of the house all day, so didn't suppose it mattered. I never thought about Mrs. M. in connection with it. She was in a vile temper all day, but that is too common to excite wonder and I never dreamed of connecting it with my hair. But that night Edie came up to our room where I was studying, and said, "Why did you put your hair up to-day, Maud?" "I couldn't find a hair-ribbon," I answered indifferently. "Oh, I'm so glad you said that," said Edie. "Why," I asked in amazement. "Because," said Edie, "Mrs. Montgomery *told me to ask you if you put it up to annoy her.* Now, when she asks me what you said I can tell her the truth."

I think it showed her own disposition when she attributes such motives to other people. It must be the sort of thing she would do herself. And then to stoop to ask such a thing of a girl in Edie's position—household help. It has made me feel absolute contempt for her.

To-day I got a letter from home with some pressed flowers in it—red poppies and purple pansies. It just seemed as if they *spoke* to me and whispered a loving message of a far-off land where blue skies are bending over maple-crimsoned hills and spruce glens are still green and dim in their balsamic recesses.

Tuesday, Nov. 11, 1890

When I came home at noon to-day I found four letters awaiting me, from Lu, Mollie, Pensie—and Nate. I felt a little dubious as to what might be in his letter but it was all right. There was a little sentimental nonsense in it but not much and the rest was in a pleasant, friendly strain. I can heartily respond to *that* and I have written him a long letter full of fun. He is at Acadia College, Wolfville, and stands high in his classes. I think he is likely to do well for he is very clever.

Wednesday, Nov. 12, 1890

This is the anniversary of "that famous date." Dear me, how much has happened since this night last year! How far severed now are the three who walked down the road together from Cavendish Hall then! Mollie still in Cavendish, Nate in Nova Scotia, and I away out here. Don't I wish I could see Mollie to-night! Since Edie has gone home I have no chum in P.A. I see a good deal of Annie McTaggart but I really cannot bear her, though of course I get on quite civilly with her.

The Sunday School children here are to have a concert for Xmas. Mary McKenzie is at the head of it. I am to recite and take part in a tableau.

Sunday, Nov. 16, 1890

A Mr. McLeod[1] preached for us this morning. I don't think I ever in my life heard a minister I liked so much. He was a benevolent looking old Scotchman and although he could not be called eloquent there was such a touching *earnestness* about all he said and every word held so much. His address went straight to the heart and made one want to be better and live better just because goodness was so beautiful.

To-night I have been writing a composition on Evangeline.[2] Nice Sunday evening's work. Not quite a logical outcome of Mr. MacLeod's sermon. But we have to hand them in tomorrow and as I have no Longfellow I had to wait until Annie had finished hers and could lend me the book.

Wednesday, Nov. 19, 1890

To-night I went to a concert in St. Alban's[3] church and I never enjoyed such a treat in my life before. The chief features of the entertainment were eight recitations by Miss Agnes Knox, a Toronto elocutionist.[4] It was a pleasure to look at her as well as listen for she is a very beautiful woman and looked like a queen in her dress of black velvet, with an exquisite bouquet fastened at her shoulder.

---

1. Probably Samuel McLeod, leading businessman, filling the pulpit in the absence of an incumbent.
2. Narrative poem (1847) about the harassment of French pioneers in Nova Scotia by American poet Henry Wadsworth Longfellow (1807–82).
3. Original Anglican church, preceding St. Alban's Cathedral built in 1905.
4. A travelling one-woman show by Agnes Knox Black from St. Mary's, Ontario, wife of a noted editor of Shakespeare's plays.

Monday, Dec. 1, 1890

Oh, oh, winter is upon us at last. No making a mistake about *that*. It was *sixty degrees below zero* to-day. And yet there are people who will tell you that this climate is no colder than down east! Of course, we don't really *feel* the cold so much. I was a funny-looking object going to school to-day. I had on a big buffalo coat—the *real* buffalo[1]—with its collar turned up around my head, so that nothing of me was visible but nose and legs—all the rest was fur. But I didn't care a cent for appearances. What I was after was to keep from freezing to death!

Mr. Mustard has been in the doleful dumps for a week and you can't get a word out of him. He takes these spells frequently. He says he doesn't know what is the matter with him. Well, neither do I, but I *do* know that he is abominably cranky.

Thursday, Dec. 4, 1890

This evening papa was out and Mrs. M. was upstairs, so I was alone. Presently a knock came at the door and when I opened it there stood Mr. Mustard himself. He comes now and then to call on Mrs. M. as they were old High Schoolmates in Ontario. So I showed him into the room and skipped upstairs to inform her. But she was in bed or pretended to be—I think she had rolled in, clothes and all, when she heard his voice—so I went reluctantly down to make her excuses, hoping with all my heart he would go away when informed that she could not see him. But such an idea evidently did not enter into his head so there I had to sit the whole evening and entertain him. And he is *such* a bore! He stayed until I thought he would never go. When the door finally shut behind him I gave a tremendous sigh of relief.

Friday, Dec. 5, 1890

We have lots of fun in school these days. A new boy is going now—Willie Pritchard. He has red hair, green eyes and a crooked mouth! *That* doesn't sound attractive and he certainly isn't handsome—but he's splendid. I have lots of fun with him.

To-day we were all a little hilarious and poor Mr. Mustard lost his patience, kept a lot of us in after four, and gave us a sum in compound interest, a yard

---

1. Buffalo robes had become so popular in the 1870s that over-hunting contributed to the disappearance of the prairie herds, and later the production of artificial robes.

long, to work. The rest of them did it, or tried to, but I was just bound I *wouldn't*. If he had kept me there until midnight I wouldn't have made a figure. But he couldn't exactly rawhide a girl, so he had to let me go with the rest. Annie and I hurried home and went to a concert practice at the church. Willie P. was also there and we had lots of fun. I was introduced to his sister Laura.[1] She seems like a lovely girl. She and I and Willie and Annie are going to have a dialogue called "Trapped." I don't care for it—it's such a mushy kind of thing but Mary McK. has settled on it so I suppose we must go ahead with it.

Willie P.

Sunday, Dec. 7, 1890

Well, this has really been the proudest day of my life! I *feel* at least three inches taller than I did yesterday. About three weeks ago I wrote a poem on the legend of Cape Leforce and sent it down home to the Charlottetown *Patriot*.[2] I did

Cape Leforce

not dare hope it would be printed, so I never squeaked a word about it to anyone. To-day when I came down, ready for Sunday School father came in with last night's mail and among it a *Patriot*. I seized it with a beating heart and trembling fingers and opened it. I grew dizzy—the letters danced before my eyes and I felt a curious sensation of choking—for there in one of the columns was my poem! I was just too delighted to speak. Father was *so* pleased and I am so glad and elated and happy. I can't find words to express my feelings.

Mrs. Montgomery looks as if she considered the whole thing a personal insult to *her* and has never mentioned the poem at all.

---

1. Laura Pritchard (1876–1932), daughter of a farmer and sister of Willard, became a life-long friend; LMM dedicated *Anne's House of Dreams* to her in 1917.

2. Founded 1859; paper delivered three weeks after LMM sent the story away.

Monday, Dec. 8, 1890

Was at practice to-night and went through our dialogue but Laura and Willie and I dislike it so much that we are trying to have "The Census Taker" instead. But Annie is cranky—because she would have "too little to say in it"—and Mary seems awfully offended because we don't like the dialogue *she* selected. So I don't know what it will be yet.

Wednesday, Dec. 10, 1890

Annie came down off her high horse to-day and we agreed to have the *Census Taker* and meet at Mr. McTaggart's at seven to-night to practice it. School dragged along as usual until evening. When Senior Cesaer came on we all got rather unruly. We laughed and whispered too much and Mr. Mustard lost his patience completely and threatened to keep us all in if we didn't keep quiet. We weren't any quieter than before so he did keep us in—Annie, Willie P. and me, who had been the worst offenders. In a few minutes a man came along in red-hot haste for Willie P. to go up to the M.P. barracks to identify a steer, so he got off, leaving Annie and me to our fate. Meanwhile, although we had to sit in separate seats we kept talking to each other. Mr. Mustard gravely announced that we would have to be silent for a certain length of time before we could get out. This statement he repeated every four or five minutes but we thought we could stand it as long as he could and kept on talking. When we couldn't think of anything to say we whispered verses of poetry which served the purpose just as well. Mr. Mustard lit a wax candle and took to writing at a terrific rate. He looked as solemn as an owl but he *had* to grin once in a while when one of us said something funny in a pigs' whisper. Then I'd whisper, also according to piggy, "He's relenting, Annie." He *didn't* relent however. I found a scrap of candle in my desk, lit it, and began reading but by his order had to put out the one and consequently stop the other. But Annie and I still kept on talking, for we were bound we wouldn't give in.

"Leave hope behind all ye who enter here,"[1] I groaned at last. Mr. Mustard had to smile and then he rose.

"Well," he said, "I see it is of no use to keep you any longer. You can go."

We did not stand upon[2] the order of our going but went at once. We hurried home, got our teas, and went up the hill to practise. Our dialogue went

---

1. Dante's *Inferno*, Canto IIII, 7.

2. Shakespeare's *Macbeth* II.iii.

on swimmingly. For me it had many old memories—for we had it at home last summer at our school concert, Mollie, Ches, Annie Stewart, Nate and I. We stayed at Mr. McTaggart's till nine and then Laura and Willie and I came home together. We had lots of fun, too. (Snakes). They are both so nice—they are "my style" and I am right at home with them. We are kindred spirits.

Thursday, Dec. 11, 1890

When school came out we all went direct to Mr. Pritchard's to practice our dialogue. Then I came home to find that father and Mrs. M. were going out for the evening. This scared me, for Mr. Mustard had said something in school to-day about calling this evening. I didn't care then, but *now* if he came when they were out *I* would have to entertain him and I didn't pine for *that*. So, when they went, I blew out all the downstair lights, came up to Southview, pulled down both blinds, pinned a heavy shawl over the window to keep out any ray of light and then I resolved if he came not to answer his knock but just let him think there was no one at home. He hasn't come so far—at least, I haven't heard any knock—so I hope he won't. I don't want to see *him* but I would welcome almost anybody else for I'm awfully lonesome. I've been very lonely and homesick of late. Oh, for one glimpse of Cavendish! Of course I know it is winter down there now, just as here, but in thinking of it I always remember it just as I left it in the prime of summer with buttercups and asters blooming by the brooks, ferns blowing spicily in the woods, lazy sunshine sleeping on the hills, with the beautiful sea beyond, blue and bright and far-reaching. There is no spot on earth more lovely.

Friday, Dec. 12, 1890

We had lots of fun in school to-day. We moved into the room across the hall, as it is larger. Our old one was too small and too cold, as it was only heated by a grate. We have a stove in the other one. As we could not take our seats in to-day we all sat in chairs around the big table and it was jolly.

Was at practice tonight and had such fun with Willy P. and Willy McBeath. The latter is a real nice little chap now that I come to know him. In fact, I have come to the conclusion that most of my school fellows here are a pretty good sort after all, even if they are a mite "nitchie" and I am on friendly terms with them all, except that sneak of a Bertie Jardine. I never speak to him.

Sunday, Dec. 14, 1890

Went to S.S. and unexpectedly found myself transformed from a pupil into a teacher. Kate McGregor was not there, so I was asked to take her class. I did so with a great deal of inward "sinking awayness." My class was of little girls and not one of them knew a single thing about the lesson, not even its name, but they had a fearful knack of asking awkward and irrelevant questions. It all seemed like a chapter out of a "Pansy" book—but I did not feel at all like a "Pansy"[1] heroine!

Wednesday, Dec. 24, 1890

Cold enough to freeze your marrow—40 below zero. I've been more than busy to-day, however, for this was our concert night.

When father came in last night and woke me up to give me a letter I was too sleepy to care much about it and so didn't read it until this morning. When I woke up I looked at it and in the dim light could not see the writing very plainly but something in its bold outlines reminded me of Nate's and I thought it was from him. So I jumped out of bed and pulled up the blind. Then I saw it wasn't Nate's writing and whose it was I didn't know; so I very sensibly concluded to open it and see. It turned out to be from Asher Robertson, the very last person in the world from whom I would have expected a letter. But I was pleased to hear from him for I always liked him. The letter was Asher all over—very commonplace but friendly and nice.

Our concert came off tonight and we had a pretty good audience in spite of the cold. Everything "behind the scenes" was turmoil and confusion for our "dressing room" was only about four feet square and everybody piled their wraps in it. Such a mess as we had! We performers *couldn't* find our things and were all the time hunting and puffing, for it was awfully warm in that corner and so jammed I don't know how we ever managed at all. But we continued to keep the confusion pretty well out of sight. One of our tableaux fell through altogether and other things were just pulled through by the skin of their teeth. I got on all right with my recitation "The Child Martyr" and our dialogue was a big success. Our tableau "The Five Foolish Virgins" was also very pretty. We were all dressed in white with shawls on our heads and empty lamps in our hands.

---

1.   Mrs. G.R. Elder published a series of sanctimonious books about child life from 1876 on.

Laura P. and I were down to see the train come in last night and had great fun. She is a lovely girl. Willy was there and walked home with me, and Andrew Agnew came home with Laura. Willy is *awfully* nice—the nicest boy I ever met.

Monday, Dec. 29, 1890

Somebody has been trying to play a joke on me I guess! When father brought up the mail yesterday there was a parcel for me and as it was addressed to "Miss Montgomery, *Town*," I knew it must be from somebody in P.A. When I opened it I found a nice little memorandum book and a cute pencil, also a slip of paper with the name of William McBeath[1] on it.

Now, you wouldn't imagine that Willy McBeath ever sent it. I know Willy P. sent it for a joke and I am going to talk to him about it. Willy McBeath is, or tries to be, a regular little lady-killer, and always deluges us girls at school and practices with candy. I get my share of it and Willy P. sees fit to tease me about him. So I know that he is at the bottom of this but he has not succeeded in hoaxing me for all that. I suppose he thought it would be great fun if I wrote a note to Willy M. thanking him for a present he never sent. No, no, Master Willy P. Try someone else.

Wednesday, Dec. 31, 1890

This is the last day of the old year. As I look back over the past year—the most eventful one in my life so far—I cannot help feeling sad. What a year it has been—so full of change and joy and grief! But there has been a lot of pleasure mixed up with it too. Altogether, I don't grumble at the old year. All I ask of the new is that it will take me back home.

---

1. Aged thirteen, living with his Scottish-born parents; later worked as a machinist.

1891

Monday, Jan. 5, 1891

We are in the council-room for good now and have our desks moved in. Two new girls are going—Martha and Aggie Thompson[1]—both nice girls but not especially "my kind." I sit with Martha.

Mind you, Willy P. has declared himself innocent of that joke. I was very cool to him all day and coming home he asked me what was the matter. I flared out, of course, but he stoutly declared he hadn't a thing to do with it, so I got left there.

I am afraid it really was Willy M. that sent the book, for Willy P. says Willy M. told him he sent a book to a girl for a Christmas present. *I* feel kind of cheap over the way I went for Willy P. about it. However, I don't think he bears me any grudge. We are just the best of friends. He always walks home from school with me and carries my books.

Wednesday, Jan. 7, 1891

Mr. Mustard has been dreadfully cranky for a week and to-day his ill-humour reached a climax. He quarrelled with Annie this morning and she wouldn't go to school this afternoon. I came in for my share of it, too, as he kept me in at dinner-time to lecture me on my "haughty manner of speaking" and my use of "slang"—to which last, however, I am *not* notably addicted, Mustard to the contrary notwithstanding. But he affects to be a great purist in regard to English undefiled. As for my "haughtiness"—alas and alack! So much for what I had flattered myself was a dignified reserve!

I might have taken the reproof amiably enough from some men, but *not* from him, for I have no respect for him. I froze up and was as chilly as an iceberg to him all the afternoon, while taking particular care to keep all the rules. I can tell you he found me "haughty" with a vengeance!

Thursday, Jan. 8, 1891

Annie McT. declares she won't go to school to Mustard again and is going out to teach in the Lindsay district. I didn't thaw out towards Mustard at all and he kept me in again to "explain," saying that his action had been prompted by his "sincere friendship" for me. I do not want his "friendship" and I listened in stony silence, for I was angry clear through. I did not say *one* word

---

1. Two women born in England, aged thirty-two and forty-two. Agnes later married John Bradshaw, a controversial politician. Chester Thompson had been Prince Albert's first blacksmith.

and *that* seemed to discomfit him more than anything else. When we came out Willy P. was waiting patiently in the cold hall and as he took my books and helped me on with my coat he got some very black looks from Mr. M. I confided my grievances to him as we went home over the cold snows, and I got enough sympathy to soothe my ruffled feelings.

This evening I went down with Laura to see the train come in. Oh, I forgot to say that last night I got another parcel from that horrid little Willy McBeath enclosing an illustrated booklet. He didn't sign his name this time but wrote "From a Friend in the Junior Class." I shall just have to snub that kid!

Monday, Jan. 26, 1891

I seem to have budded into a regular S.S. teacher now, as for the last two Sundays I have had to take Annie's class of boys and from present indications I fancy I shall have to keep them. Such little imps as they are too, full to the lips with mischief. But I like them for all that. I'd far rather have a class of boys than one of girls.

To-day in school I still kept up my reserve towards Mr. M., never speaking to him unless spoken to, and then most freezingly polite. But alas for my dignity! This evening when I went to answer the door, who should stand there but he himself, smiling and bowing most amiably. Of course, I had to be civil and then, as father was away at a council meeting[1] and Mrs. M. took excellent care not to come down stairs I had to sit there the whole evening to entertain him. And that is no enviable occupation for he is a fearful poke. Whatever did he want to come here again to-night for, when he was here only Friday?

There was a heavy white frost to-night and this morning the town looked beautiful. All the trees were dreams of mist, looking as if a breath would demolish them, and across the river the forest looked like fairyland.

By the way I believe it was not Willy McB who sent that last booklet, after all, but—worse and worse—Frank Robertson. Willy P. has found out all about it. He is a regular detective.

Tuesday, Feb. 1, 1891

To-day was a son and heir born unto the house of Montgomery. The baby is a pretty little fellow and father is pleased as Punch over having a boy. I'm glad it is a boy, too, somehow. I always like boy babies better than girls.

---

1. LMM's father had won a seat on town council; he became chairman of the Board of Works. Council erected a new town hall in 1891.

Friday, Feb. 13, 1891

School is really quite lively nowadays. We have great times in it over the elections. Father is going to run on the Liberal ticket[1] and as Willy P. is a rabid *Tory* we have interesting debates. He and I have adopted a cipher alphabet. He is constantly writing notes to me and sometimes they go astray and fall into the hands of the other boys who show no mercy. So Will suggested we employ a cipher and we are going to use the one Nate and I used to use. It comes in very useful. Poor "Snip" and "Snap." How I'd like to see them again—perhaps meet them on the dear old school playground when the trees cast long shadows, and the golden light fell across the old spruces that rustled and crooned so softly!

Monday, Feb. 23, 1891

Mr. Mustard was furious with me to-day because he caught me exchanging notes with Will. What *does* make him act so? The note which riled him so proved to be an invitation to go with Will and Laura to a toboggan slide up at the barracks[2] tonight. At about seven this evening Laura came over and soon after Will drove up with a dandy turn-out. As we were too early we went for a drive away out into the country. When we got back the fun was just beginning. The chute[3] had arches all over it at regular intervals hung with Chinese lanterns and it looked like fairyland. As I had never been on a toboggan before I was very nervous and hung back for some time. But finally Laura and I summoned up enough spunk to go. All I was conscious of was an arrow's speed, a whirl of fine snow in our faces, a dazzle of colored lights overhead, two or three awful "dips," and then a long level spin. It was splendid, and after that we went often. Spills were numerous and lots of funny things occurred. Once my hat blew off going down and fell right on the slide and how it escaped being crushed flat by the next toboggan I don't know. Will rescued it from the scrimmage and we went off merrily again. Another time Laura, Katie Fulcher and I went down with two of the soldiers. It was a very narrow toboggan and I knew the minute we started that we were "in for it." Down we shot until we reached the first "dip." There was an awful bounce and over we went in one grand spill. I was dragged for several yards

---

1. The 1891 election was called on Free Trade; Montgomery ran as a Liberal in spite of his father being a leading Conservative.
2. Prince Albert was the district centre for the North West Mounted Police.
3. A wooden structure for tobogganing, packed with snow and ice for speed.

with my face in the snow and really thought I'd be smothered. But on the whole it was a jolly evening.

Friday, Feb. 27, 1891

Last night there was a reception in the manse for our new minister, Mr. Rochester[1] and his wife. We had quite a concert, singing and playing etc. and I recited "A Backwoods Wedding."[2]

Presbyterian Manse P.A.

Mr. Mustard had one of his "bad days" to-day and as a result there was not much fun going. Rather an amusing kink of the "Lady-Killer's" came to light to-day. The L.K. is Willy McBeath. "Generosity" is another of his nicknames. Willy P. and I call him that, but he is known to the rest as "Minty." Last night no one, strictly speaking, "came home" with me, but Rod McTaggart[3] and I happened to be together as far as our gate. However, Willy P. said to "Minty"—just to tease him, I presume, for he certainly knew the truth—"I heard you went home with Miss Montgomery last night."

"Well, and what if I did?" demanded Minty.

"Oh, that's as good as an admission, isn't it?" retorted Willie P.

"I guess so," said Minty.

Poor kid! If he could have heard Willie P. and me laughing over it!

Talking of nicknames they do have some original "nicks"[4] in that school. Tommy Clark is called "Sorghum"[5] and Willy McKay "Brigham."[6] It doesn't matter much what Tom is called for he has too much of the "nitchie" in him for any earthly use.

---

1. Dr. Jardine was replaced by Rev. W.M. Rochester, D.D., from Burnstown, ON, educated at McGill University, who came to St. Paul's, Prince Albert, from Erskine Presbyterian in Montreal; he left to go to Cowan Presbyterian in Toronto and eventually became editor of the *Presbyterian Record* in Toronto.

2. A skit perhaps based on a story by Susan Hartley, *Ballou's Magazine* (1889). Skits for children's performance, like this one and "Lady Killers" were commonly passed from one community to another.

3. Son of John McTaggart, the government land agent.

4. "Nitchie" meaning "Métis."

5. A dark grain crop.

6. Implies being of the Church of God.

Saturday, March 7, 1891

Father has lost his election[1] I am sorry to say. But I never expected anything else. This is a confirmed Tory riding—and so Gov't money has been spent in showers. I am glad it is over for this past month has been nothing but excitement and worry. I have not been in school for a week and am going to start again now, as we have got a servant girl—Fannie McLauchlin, a "breed" girl. I had to give up my dear little "Southview" to her and sleep in the spare room. It is too bad. I just loved Southview. It was my haven of rest where I could fly with all my troubles.

Monday, Mar. 9, 1891

Went to school to-day and found things pretty much the same. Mr. Mustard was terribly cross and had a sickening hand-to-hand fight with Frank Robertson. If Will P. and I ventured to say a word to each other he pounced on us, though everyone else seemed at liberty to talk as they pleased. This evening I went over to see Laura. She is a lovely girl and we are devoted chums. She and I were alone in the earlier part of the evening but later on Will came in and of course his advent didn't exactly depress us any.

Tuesday, Mar. 10, 1891
Prince Albert

Fannie has skipped out—left us unceremoniously in the lurch, giving as a reason that Mrs. M. was "too cross and particular"—which is too true to be funny. So there is no more school for me until we get another girl.

The Temperance Concert[2] came off tonight. I recited "The Christening,"[3] was encored, and gave "The Other Side." I had a fine time all round.

---

1. Prince Albert was notorious for rowdy election days: Wilfrid Laurier (who ran in this riding in 1896) cited "rough and tumble politics" there.
2. The Canadian Temperance League, incorporated 1890, fought a vigorous campaign for the prohibition of alcohol in the west.
3. A comic piece by E.J. Corbet: Uncle Silas, horrified to hear the baby's chosen name, shouts "Jehoshaphat"—and the minister conforms.

Friday, Mar. 20, 1891
Prince Albert

This evening as I was sitting, swinging Baby Bruce in his hammock Laura popped in to ask if I would go for a drive with her and Will. I didn't need to be coaxed and soon we were speeding down the street with the bells jingling a merry chorus. Oh, such a jolly time as we had! We went away up the river for miles, then back and away down to Goschen. It was a glorious night— bright moonlight, with brilliant stars shining in the dark blue sky and a rare splendor in the air, clear, crisp, exhilarating. A merry trio we were, laughing, talking, joking and star-hunting, the last named being especially amusing.

I had a letter from Nate to-day—very jolly and interesting. He enclosed a small photo of himself—a very good one. He seems to be doing finely at college.

Saturday, Mar. 28, 1891

To-night I felt horribly ill with a cold and intended to go to bed right after tea—or rather right after I had finished the dishes. But alas, by that time Mr. Mustard arrived and stayed till eleven. I thought he would *never* go and I was so dull and sleepy I could hardly sit up straight in my chair.

I have never been in school since the first week in March and have come to the conclusion that I am not to get any more. Mrs. M. is not trying to get a girl, I can plainly see that, and I have to stay home and do the work. She does nothing but attend to her children. I do really think it is too bad. I came out here in the hope of getting to a good school and this is the result. I do not say a word, however, because it would make father feel so bad. I would put up with anything to save him trouble.

Monday, Mar. 30, 1891
Prince Albert

Got an invitation to Mary McKenzie's wedding to-night. She is to be married to Mr. Stovel[1] on April 8. "Such is life," as Asher Robertson used to say every time he heard of Stewart Simpson going home with Mamie.

I am here in my room, sitting up in bed scribbling in my journal, as I used to do down home. Dear old Cavendish! I can just imagine how it looks at

---

1. Richard Stovel, a twenty-seven-year-old dental surgeon, born in MB, who married Mary McKenzie, half-sister of Mrs. McTaggart.

this moment. Let us take a peep on it. It is nine o'clock here, so down home it is about eleven. All is dark and quiet. Let us suppose ourselves standing on Laird's Hill. Through the gloom we can distinguish the outline of many an old familiar spot. There, clothing the slope of the opposite hill, are the school woods, dark and still, with the sombre spruces whispering eerily. Set back in its nook we can see the old white school. There, on the other hill, is home almost hidden in maples, birches and poplars, with the orchards sweeping away to the right and the big barns beyond. Far, far out, past the white lowlands, a dark line tells us where the sea is moaning on its rocky shore, and away to the west, stretch field after field, grove after grove. All is wrapped in silence, save for the sigh of the night breeze, the dull surge-roar of the gulf, the bark of some predatory fox back in the woods, and the gush of snow streams as they trickle down the icy hills. Above the stars are shining cold and clear in the dark sky. Slowly the vision fades—fades—fades, until it is lost in the darkness and we find ourselves here.

Monday, Apr. 6, 1891
Prince Albert

This evening Laura came over and we had a jolly talk which was interrupted by the advent of Mustard at nine o'clock. I don't know how it came about but we got up to our ears in theology and began to debate about the doctrine of predestination.[1] I denied it; Mustard upheld it. Laura sat on the fence and shot arrows impartially at both sides. We had an argument worthy of the name, for theology is one of the few things Mr. Mustard can really talk well on. In the end we both agreed to retain our own convictions on the subject. As for me, a million Mustards could never make me believe that God ordains any of his creatures to eternal torture for "his own good will and pleasure."

Thursday, Apr. 9, 1891

That detestable Mustard came again to-night and stayed until 11.30. To be able to keep up a conversation with him one ought to be posted on every subject from Adam down, to be blessed with a large supply of patience in order to listen to all the stale anecdotes he never fails to rehash at every call, and, in brief, to assume interest in *everything*. Let me just see! I will recount the subjects I have scratched over this evening for morsels of conversation:

---

1. Calvinist belief that man's destiny is pre-determined by a God, wrathful at human sin.

Mary's wedding—which, by the way, came off yesterday—weddings in general—rather risky topic, say you?—card-playing and dancing—M. is down upon them of course—education, civil-engineering, Montreal, autographs and auto-hunters, school days, various personal likes and dislikes, ancestry, nomenclature—Mustard thinks *his* name "was assumed for political reasons"!!!—genealogy, various events about town—no, *not* gossip. M. never indulges in anything so interesting!—school-teaching, letter writing, another whack at predestination and—but oh, if that wasn't all it ought to be! My poor brain is in a state of collapse. I must go to bed straight off and get my "beauty sleep" and if Mr. Mustard calls again for a fortnight I will even fall upon him and rend him limb from limb!!!!

Monday, Apr. 13, 1891

Well, it is nearly 12 o'clock and I am just boiling over with rage. *Mr. Mustard was here again* to-night. That is the fatal secret! He stayed till 11.30, too. *What* possesses the man? I can't, of course, pretend to be ignorant that it is I whom he comes to see but surely he doesn't mean anything by it. I certainly hope not, anyhow. But pshaw! He'd surely never dream of getting foolish over a chit of sixteen, especially since I've led him such a life of it.

Monday, Apr. 20, 1891

This is the night Mr. Mustard generally comes—I suppose because father is always away at Council meeting. I did my best to escape him. First, I thought I would run over to Kennedy's and see Laura. (Pritchards have moved out to their farm now but Laura, who goes to the convent school,[1] is staying until vacation with her aunt, Mrs. Kennedy, who lives right next door to us.) But I couldn't get away. So then I ran over and got Laura to come over with me and help me out. We tormented poor Mustard terribly to-night—it *is* such fun to tease him—he gets so confused and sheepish. Laura had to go at nine but father was home by then and he stayed in the room and read, for which I was very thankful. I *hate* to be alone with Mustard!

I must admit that his attentions are becoming rather serious. All the town is talking about them. I am teased to distraction about him and all sorts of jokes on his *name* are fired off at me. Even father can't ask me to pass him the *mustard* at the table without a grin! It makes me simply furious!

---

1. St. Anne's convent, opened 1884.

Thursday, Apr. 23, 1891
Prince Albert

This evening Laura and I went for a walk in the delicious spring twilight. These western twilights are remarkably beautiful. We went up to the cricket grounds where Will was playing and watched the game for awhile. Then we came back and walked up Church St. as far as McColl's. Just by Judge McGuire's[1] house we met Willy who had a huge parcel of vanilla creams for us. We strolled around for an hour and had a delightful time. It was bright moonlight and the little town was sheathed in misty silver light, dreamy and lustrous.

It is so delightful to have Laura living right next door. She and I are always having delightful chats in the back yard.

Monday, Apr. 27, 1891

Anticipating Mr. Mustard's arrival to-night I got Laura over. You may be sure we led him a pretty dance of it. Father and Mrs. M. were both out so we tormented him to our heart's content. In the course of the evening I found a chance to put the clock on half an hour, so M. left at what he fondly believed to be 10.30, whereas it was only 10.

I am going to get home all right this summer. I have been very hopeless of it for some time but it is all settled now. I shall be sorry to leave father and Laura and Will and a few other friends, but that will certainly be all my regret. It will be so wonderful to escape from the atmosphere of suspicion and petty malice and persecution which Mrs. Montgomery seems to exhale wherever she is. Sometimes I feel as if I were literally smothering in it. I work my fingers to the bone for her and her children and I am not even civilly treated for it. I do all the work of this house, except the washing, which she gets in a squaw to do. She herself is never happy unless she is gadding out somewhere. However, I don't complain of *this* last, for the only hours I *live* in this house are when she is out of it. I *love* it when father and I are alone together for a meal. We can be as jolly and chummy as we like then, with no one to cast black looks and sneers at us.

This evening at sunset Mr. and Mrs. McTaggart called and took Katie and me for a drive in the phaeton.[2] We had just a lovely time. We drove away down to Goschen in the soft, sweet twilight with the pale hues of sunset lingering in the west and reflected in the broad river.

---

1. A long-lasting jurist, still powerful in 1913.
2. A sporty style of horse-drawn carriage with large wheels and minimal body, designed for speed.

Friday, May 7, 1891
Prince Albert

This afternoon father took Katie and me for a drive of three miles out into the country and it was charming. The day was perfect and the prairies are very beautiful now. An unlimited expanse of gentle slopes and velvet meadows, dotted with groves of poplar and clumps of willow, clear and distinct near by but in the distance mingling to a seeming forest, clothed over the outlines of the distant hills in hazy purple mists. Here are level grassy reaches sweet with dainty bluebells; there, ranges of picturesque bluffs which curve around to enclose a tiny blue lake in its encircling of yellow grasses like a sapphire set in gold.

Saturday, May 8, 1891

This evening Laura ran in to invite me over, as two of her schoolmates, Lula and Maggie Taylor, were at Mrs. Kennedy's. We had fine fun. Will dropped in at nine and we all went down to meet the train and had no end of a good time. We always get a bit of a ride on her when she is shunting.

The station, P.A.

In a letter from Pensie to-night she said that Will Spear had been killed by a falling tree in B.C. He was an English boy who stayed at Darnley Clark's a winter long ago and went to school. He was a dark, nice-looking boy, much given to teasing the girls, especially Mollie and me, who sat in front of him. Poor Will, he is the first of my schoolmates to go. It has begun I suppose—the first bead on the string has slipped off and one by one, sooner or later, all the rest must follow. Sitting alone in the twilight this evening before Laura came, swinging Bruce in his hammock, I fell to thinking of my early schoolmates and among others of Maud Woodside who was my seat-mate and devoted chum when I first began to go to school before Mollie went. We used to have lots of fun together. Maud W. was a nice little girl and we were two small, happy, thoughtless mites with a world of our own behind that old brown desk at school, shared also by Minie Kesley, another of my early mates. Maud and I sat together for only one summer. Then we formed new combinations. Mollie began to go to school. It was always thought a great thing among the older scholars to have a new pupil sit with them. Pensie and Emma Stuart had corralled Mollie and kept her for two days. I was sitting alone in the seat just ahead. I offered Pensie and Emma four big sweet apples if they would let Amanda sit with me. We had almost the only orchard in C. at that time and I was a power in school because of this. Apples would purchase almost anything, from "chews" of gum up to "new girls." They bought me Mollie. Pensie and Emma took the apples and Mollie was transferred chattel-wise from their seat to mine. We were never again separated from that day until we left school last summer. Mollie and I sat together through thick and thin, through evil report and good report. It was not a bad bargain for four apples!!!

Wednesday, May 13, 1891
Prince Albert

After tea I went over to see Laura. Will was there, too, so we all went over to their town house to feed a cat he has there, and then we sauntered down the street to Goodfellow's. Will went in there to invest for our benefit and Laura and I went down to the river to pick up pebbles. The evening was lovely and the river perfectly exquisite. Presently Will rejoined us, loaded with candies, and we sauntered down the Goschen sidewalk as far as Strachan's photo gallery. While Will and I were looking at the photos Laura ran down to the river to get a drink and during her absence Will asked me to give him my photo when I should have some taken and I agreed on the prin-

ciple of a fair exchange. Then Laura came back and we walked home slowly and got to Kennedy's at 8. We sat down on their steps until 10, and had just a jolly time, laughing, talking, and telling stories, while the air grew duskier and sweeter and the eastern sky was lurid with a prairie fire and the frogs chorused faintly in the distance. Will stole my

River Street, P.A.

little gold ring and put it on his finger. He wouldn't give it back but then I didn't coax *very* hard.

Thursday, May 14, 1891

I'm fearfully tired to-night and have a pair of skinned heels into the bargain. Alexina McGregor[1] and I were out all the evening selling tickets for our church concert to-morrow night. We tramped everywhere, did pretty well, and had some fun, too. But it's a *mean-feeling* business.

Alexina

I am trying to realize that I am actually going home this summer. There are two or three things to which I look forward with special delight. One is going to the shore again. Oh, how I long for the sea! I feel lost sometimes without it and its never ceasing murmur. And then I want to go berry-picking back to "Montana." How glorious it used to be—starting out at sunrise with our cups and pails and our lunch of ham and cake, to tramp through fresh dewy fields where the buttercups danced and nodded in every passing breeze, up over the hills to the woods, through that long woodland lane beneath the arches of beech and maple, with the banks of moss on either side, covered with clumps of ferns and spangled with pigeon-flowers and June-bells, on through the fields beyond and past the maple woods until "Montana" was reached, and we began picking, wandering around in the maple paths, sprawling among the ferns and vines, catching the breezes in the glades, startling the birds and rabbits, and having a glorious time.

Father

This morning at breakfast father was relating to me some of the incidents of his life in Boston. I really know so little of father's life—and it has been a life full of incident and adventure too. First, on the farm at Park Corner where he was brought up, then a young sea-captain, cruising to England, the West Indies and South America, then a merchant at Clifton—where I was born—then a clerk in Boston, then a Government clerk in Battleford and P.A. He has had all sorts of adventures, especially in the Indian rebellion here in 1885[2] when he was a volunteer. It has not been a very successful life. Father is a poor man to-day. Yet he is one of those

---

1. Alexena McGregor (b. 1871), daughter of Prince Albert pioneers from Aberdeen; her father Duncan was a contractor. In 1933 LMM dedicated *A Tangled Web* to her and her husband, Fred Wright, whom she married in 1897. In 1931 LMM gave his name to "Diana's" husband in *Anne of Avonlea*.

2. Prince Albert militia played a part in quashing the Riel Rebellion. In 1885 a party of ninety-five North West Mounted Police and volunteers marched to Duck Lake; twelve were killed and eleven wounded.

men who are loved by everyone. And I—I love him with all my heart—better than anyone else in the whole world—dear, darling father!

May 25, 1891
Prince Albert

Have had a lovely time to-day. It is the Queen's Birthday—or rather the birthday itself was yesterday and was celebrated to-day. We, with several other families, were all invited to spend the day out at Mr. McArthur's ranch. It was a tip-top day, cool, clear and—for a wonder—calm. We left at 9.30 this morning. It is about 12 miles out to the farm, over a very pretty trail. We all got lost on the road and were some time finding our way again but that only added to the fun. We got there about twelve. After we were rested Lottie Stewart and I went for a walk. She is fearfully quiet and slow however. There was a rough bridge built over the dried bed of a lake and beyond it was a beautiful prairie, miles long, dotted with white-stemmed poplars. After dinner Mr. Stovel made some bats and we all went over to the lake and had a game of baseball. It was glorious. Mr. S. and I were on the same side and we just made things hum. We won the game, too.

We left for home at seven and I came home in Mayor Johnson's[1] rig and drove the team all the way. When I told father this when I got home Mrs. M. remarked in her amiable fashion, "It is a wonder Mrs. Johnson would feel safe if *you* were driving."

I suspect that Mrs. Johnson, having a better temper, has also better nerves than Mrs. Montgomery.

Sunday, May 31, 1891

Had a letter from Nate last night. His year at the Academy will soon be up. It closes on June 4 and he expects to be in C. by the 10th. Wish I could be there too. I've no idea just when I'll be going as I have to wait until Parliament adjourns.[2] I'm going down to Ottawa to go home with Grandpa Montgomery.

I sent down to the *Patriot* to-day a little poem called "June."[3] I remember so well the time I composed it—two years ago one lovely June day when I

---

1. Mayor for one year only.

2. When Sir John A. Macdonald suffered a stroke, the date of adjournment became problematic. Macdonald died June 6, 1891.

3. Ten four-line stanzas, published June 17 in the *Patriot*. LMM's early publications are reproduced in F.W.P. Bolger, *The Years Before "Anne"*.

was sitting on the banks of the brook under the maple tree up by the hill spring, while the sky was blue and the air sweet.

Was in to see Mrs. Kennedy this evening. She is such a dear little woman. Lolla was out. Will is away to Battleford now on a business trip and we miss him dreadfully.

I've moved back into dear old Southview again and I'm so glad.

Saturday, June 6, 1891

Will is back and looks fine after his trip. I saw him to-day for a few minutes before he went out home. This evening Mr. Mustard came shuffling along at nine and stayed till eleven. I wished the cats had him. He was quite confidential and said he was going down east to go to college. He then asked me what profession I thought he'd better follow! I felt like snickering but managed to keep a straight face and said very gravely,

"Oh, Mr. Mustard, I couldn't advise, not knowing what you are best fitted for. Follow your own inclination if you wish to succeed."

And then Mr. M. sheepishly informed me that he was thinking of going to Knox College[1] and meant to be a minister. I don't know how I kept from laughing right out in his face. Mustard a minister!! Oh Lordy—how it will sound—Rev. Mr. Mustard. I pity the poor woman whose fate it will be to write "Mrs." before such a combination. I have a dim suspicion that Mr. M. intends asking *me* to accept that honor but I may be mistaken. I think I see him in a pulpit! Well, I suppose as far as looks go he'll do well enough; he isn't bad looking, being tall and fair, with blue eyes and a golden moustache which he cultivates very carefully. But if he couldn't find something more interesting to say than he does in *our* conversations he'd be anything but a brilliant preacher.

Now, I must go and look up my Bible class lesson. We have Bible class in the manse now every Sunday afternoon after S.S. and it is very interesting.

I am writing an article on Saskatchewan for *The Times* here,[2] and have it nearly done. I've given a description of the prairies and scenery and the characteristics of the Indians and will finish up with a flowery peroration on the possibilities of the country as a whole.

---

1. Presbyterian theological college in University of Toronto.
2. "A Western Eden," published June 17 in the *Prince Albert Times*, gives an enthusiastic description of the Prairies, the Saskatchewan River, and the Aboriginal peoples who were facing extinction.

Tuesday, June 16, 1891
Prince Albert, Sask.

I was invited to spend the evening at the Kennedy's and of course we had a scrumptious time. Andrew Agnew, Mr. Sinclair, and Willie were there and we had such fun making a table rap.[1] Willie asked me to go with him to the convent school closing to-morrow night and I agreed. Mrs. K. got us lunch and we all sat around the table and told ghost stories until I vow when I got home I sneaked upstairs in mortal terror and stood with my back to the wall all the time I was undressing so I couldn't fancy there was anything behind me!

Wednesday, June 17, 1891

I had a perfectly scrumptious time this evening. Will and I went to the convent at 6.30. It is in such a pretty place. All the girls were dressed in white and looked so nice. Their paintings, drawings, fancy work etc. were on exhibition and were lovely, as were also the decorations. Will and I got a good seat and I enjoyed the performance immensely. Laura won the gold medal for drawing and it was a beauty. I was as proud as if I had won it myself. After the programme we had ice-cream and lemonade.

St. Anne's Convent, P.A.

Thursday, June 18, 1891
Prince Albert

Mr. Mustard was here this evening and was as limp as usual. He is going back to Ontario in three weeks time. He asked me to go with him to an ice-cream social to-morrow night at the manse, but as I have to stay home with the kiddies I had a good excuse for declining. I had been feeling a little

---

1. Playful experiment with psychic phenomena: a group places fingertips on a table and wills it to move.

disappointed because I was not going to go but I would rather stay home and look after a whole orphan asylum than go anywhere with him. He also asked me to correspond with him and I consented rather stiffly because I didn't know how to refuse. Anyhow, I can drop it gradually.

My article is out in *The Times* and is making quite a bit of sensation.

> T'is pleasant sure to see one's name in print;
> A book's a book although there's nothing in it.[1]

Laura has gone out to the farm now and I simply feel lost without her.

Monday, June 22, 1891

This evening was lovely—too lovely, indeed, since it put a wretched idea into Mustard's pate. I was busy washing the tea dishes when he came shuffling along to ask "if I would mind"—he always prefaces his requests with this graceful please—"going out for a walk?" I *did* mind very much indeed, but I couldn't think of any valid excuse on the spur of the moment, so I consented rather grimly and told him to call at 7.30. I also felt properly scared. He is going away in a fortnight's time and I was terrified lest he were looking for an opportunity to say something I didn't want to hear.

We started at 7.30 and I managed to tow him through the back streets and away up the river trail where I thought I'd run no risk of meeting acquaintances. But it's always the case that you are sure to meet the very people you most want to avoid and in the most unlikely places. And so of course we met Mr. and Mrs. McTaggart and Min Wheeler—a girl who is visiting them—square in the teeth. Just imagine my feelings. I hope they didn't show too plainly in my face. Such a grimace as Min made at me as the carriage passed! Won't I catch it when I see her!

I talked on nervously, uttering I don't know what silly nonsense, so as not to give M. any chance of saying anything embarrassing. I'm firmly convinced that that was just his aim and object for he was silent and pre-occupied all the time and acted as if he were trying to screw his courage up to some sticking point or other; and once he picked some wild roses and sheepishly—oh, he is *so* sheepish *always*—asked if I would wear them! I took the roses—but I didn't wear them! Instead I picked them deliberately to pieces and scattered them over the trail as we walked along. I didn't give him the ghost of a chance but hurried back as soon as I decently could. On the way back he said,

---

1. From Lord Byron's *English Bards and Scotch Reviewers* (1809), satiric poem on the effect of reviewers' scorn on author's pride.

"Oh, say, *would you mind* going out for a drive some evening soon?"

I nearly took a fit. Cooped up in a buggy with Mustard where I couldn't get away from him! *No*, thank you! So I told him I would be too busy to go driving *any* evening. He must have thought me a most hard-working mortal!

When we got back he came in and sat for two hours! *What* possesses the man! He *must* think something of me when he is so persistent and yet how *can* he? Why, I've never been half decent to him. I've snubbed him times without number! I've made fun of him to his very face and he knows it—and yet he comes and comes! Thank goodness, he's going soon!

Friday, June 26, 1891
Prince Albert

After dinner I took a jug and went away out to the east flats to pick berries. I was away two hours and had such a lovely time. It was clear and cool and I was all alone among the sweet grasses and leaves, with the birds singing in the poplars. At such time the charm of this north land comes home to me and I felt that I could have loved it and been contented here if Mrs. Montgomery had been a different woman.

Mustard did another of his queer things to-day. He called in the afternoon and asked for me. I squirmed darkly into the parlor and he gave me my set of book-keeping books he had brought from the high school. Then, as he rose to go, he asked me if I'd be in to-night. As I was expecting to go up to Mrs. McTaggart's I said "no."

"To-morrow night then?" he insisted.

As I had unfortunately no engagement on hand I had to say yes.

"May I come and see you?" he asked.

Now, considering the fact that he has been coming here two and three times a week all winter, to see me—or papa?—without troubling himself about the formality of asking if he might, this question struck me as unique.

"If you wish to, Mr. Mustard," I said ungraciously. He turned a shade or two redder and showed himself out. *I* felt like a perfect fool. Oh, I'm mortally afraid he's going to say something yet.

Sunday, June 28, 1891
Prince Albert

Last night it simply poured and I was comfortably sure that Mustard would never venture out in such a deluge. But come he did—"to see me." I suppose he "saw" me, for I sat in front of him for two mortal hours, and talked or tried to talk. But that blessed pater of mine was home and sat reading in the room all the evening, so Mustard couldn't say anything if he wanted to. I was *so* thankful. If I can *only* head him off until he gets away! I don't care what he says by letter—I can manage *that* but I shall die if he says anything by word of mouth. There is something about the man which makes me feel so self-conscious and positively *ashamed.*

In the *Patriot* to-day was a list of those who had passed the exam for Second Class license and Jack Laird's name was in it. I suppose he will be teaching now. How *funny* to think of "Snap" being a teacher!

Tuesday, June 30, 1891

To-night Annie McTaggart had a school concert out at Lindsay where she has been teaching ever since her quarrel with Mustard. Mary Stovel and I had promised to assist her, so we drove out this morning. The prairies are just one blush with wild roses now and we had a charming drive. We had dinner at Mr. Millar's, where Annie boards, and then drove down to the log schoolhouse. It was in a state of glorious confusion, with loads of poplar boughs, wild roses, and orange lilies heaped about. And the children— *such* faces, *such* costumes! But some of them were pretty and they sang wonderfully well. We set to work to decorate. Annie had got the lend of an organ—the only one in Lindsay—and we banked it up with poplar boughs and those lovely orange lilies. We wreathed windows and blackboard with poplar and piled up lilies and roses and wild peas wherever we could. When all was swept and garnished that school looked quite gorgeous. It was four by this time, so we went back to Mr. Millar's, had our teas and donned our war-paint, which we had brought out with us in a valise. Then we went to the school. Mr. Stovel came out and was chairman. Quite a number of our town friends were also out but the rest of the audience were the queerest assortment I've ever seen. After it was all over—about nine— Mr. McNiven, one of the trustees, got up to make a speech and upon my word I laughed until I was nearly sick. He was so drunk that he could hardly stand—but *that* was not what I was laughing at—and he spoke for *a whole hour.* He would begin,

"Gentlemen, chairman, gentlemen and ladies"—he would repeat this four or five times, with variations—such as "lairmen and chadies"—and then he'd say, referring to Annie's pluck in taking a hard school like Lindsay, "that darling little *lion,* Miss McTaggart, with the courage and the abilities of a *tager.*" When he referred to the concert words failed him. "I regret my unability to express my thoughts on *this grand subject*. It's in this poor human critter"—patting himself with both hands on the breast—"but he can't get it out."

They finally induced him to stop and we started for home. Mr. Stovel came with us and we sang comic songs all the way. It was a cold night with a white fog and the mirages were wonderful. At times you seemed to be driving down to an ice-covered bay. Then it would change to a sunset lake dotted with islands. We got home at 3 o'clock after a very amusing but fatiguing jaunt.

Wednesday, July 1, 1891

The first thing on to-day's programme was going this forenoon to see the laying of the cornerstone of the new Presbyterian church.[1] When I came home from it I found Mrs. Montgomery indulging in a fit of hysterical crying and raking father down for something he had done or left undone—I couldn't make out which—during the progress of the ceremonies. What that woman needs is a good spanking.

After dinner I went to see the Dominion Day[2] sports. Laura and I were together as usual. The athletic sports were fine and the horse races were splendid. Will rode a horse and won easily. He did look so cute on horseback with his little jockey cap on. Laura asked father if I could go out and stay a few days with her next week and to my great delight he consented. I had been afraid he would not, for of course Mrs. M. will make a fuss about doing her own work while I am away.

Ten O'Clock

I feel like shrieking. It would be a great relief but it might make too much of a sensation in the neighborhood, so I'll have to exercise some self restraint.

Mustard actually *mustered*—oh, forgive the pun. It just *made itself*—up enough courage to put his fate to the test this evening. He did it about as awkwardly as possible but he did it.

Now, I've been expecting it for some time and I thought I'd be awfully confused and nervous, but I wasn't—not a bit. Instead, I wanted to laugh all the time. Well, perhaps *that* was a phase of nervousness because there really

---

1. The first Presbyterian church, built in 1872, was torn down in 1891.
2. July first celebration of confederation of four provinces in 1867.

wasn't anything at all funny about it. In fact, the only truly descriptive word I know of to apply to the whole interview is *sickening*.

There was an excursion[1] down the river to-night and father and Mrs. M. went on it, so Mr. Mustard and I were left alone in the twilight—a very dangerous time. I was sitting in a corner of the sofa, rocking my snoozing and unconscious baby brother, and Mr. M. was sitting opposite me on a rocker. He talked very jerkily for some time and then ensued a period of uncomfortable silence. I had what Laura calls "a creepy, crawly presentiment," that something was just on the point of happening. He looked out of the window while I glared at a piece of yellow yarn on the carpet—I shall remember the shape and location of that yarn as long as I live—and wished myself a thousand miles away.

Finally Mr. Mustard turned with a very ghastly sort of smile and stammered out painfully,

"Do you think, Miss Montgomery, that our friendship will ever develop into *anything else?*"

And his look and tone plainly revealed what he meant by "anything else." Well, I had to say something, so I said,

"I don't see what else it *can* develop into, Mr. Mustard."

I said it very well and composedly, too. I had expected to be flustered—but I wasn't. It all depends on the person, I suppose. Now, when Will says anything significant to me I color up and look foolish and lose my voice instanter. But I wasn't troubled with any such symptoms in poor M's case.

"It's just as *you* think," he said slowly.

Just at this point the gate banged and Mrs. McTaggart's hearty old face appeared in the doorway, little dreaming, good woman, what she was so unwittingly interrupting. On finding that Mrs. Montgomery was out she went away again and another *awful* silence ensued. I stared steadily at the aforesaid piece of yarn and held my tongue for I was determined not to speak until he did, if I sat there for a thousand years. At last he stammered out that he "hoped I wasn't offended—he did not wish any misunderstanding—"

This was my chance so I dashed in nobly and blurted out,

"Certainly not, Mr. Mustard. And I shall always be your friend but nothing more."

Then—silence! Oh, dear, it was really dreadful. And there were actually tears in his eyes. But *I* didn't cry or feel like crying. He has brought it all on himself, for any sane man might have taken the hint that I had no use for him long ago. I just wanted to laugh but at last the situation got so unbearable that I explained,

---

1.   Hudson's Bay Company had established steamboats on the Saskatchewan River in 1872.

"I'm very sorry that this has happened, Mr. Mustard. I hope you won't feel hardly to me because of it"—Here I floundered helplessly again and he broke in with an assurance that he would not and that, I am glad to say, ended it. He stayed a little while longer and carried on a jerky conversation on several subjects. I continued to feel like a fool, and I suppose it is likely Mr. M. felt like one too. Anyway, he soon went away. And I am devoutly thankful that the dreaded ordeal is over.

Sunday, July 5, 1891
Laurel Hill Farm

This has been a most delightful day. I was to come out here to-day. Willy came in to Bible Class and said he would call for me after it was over. Shortly after I got home Mustard also called to say good-bye, as he leaves tomorrow. Really, I was never so heartily glad to see the last of anyone in my life before.

Soon after Will came and we set off. I was glad to get out of the house for Mrs. Montgomery was in a white fury over my going at all. Will and I had a lovely drive and got here at six. Mr. Pritchard's house is in such a pretty place. Lolla

Laura Pritchard

and I had such an enthusiastic meeting. Mr. Agnew[1] and Mr. Gunn—a pair of Laura's admirers—were also here. We had such fun. After tea Willy and I and Laura and Mr. A.—poor Gunn wasn't in it—went for a long, delightful ramble thru' the green fields just starred with all kinds of flowers. Then we came back and sat at the front door until dark. Presently another gentleman came along— a Mr. Weir who is likewise all broke up on Laura—and we adjourned to the parlor to finish up our Sunday evening with some hymns. I sat down on one corner of the sofa and Will sat down on the other—a very proper arrangement to be sure. But there must have been something queer about that sofa because the space between us gradually narrowed in the most mysterious manner until it wasn't there at all! I'm sure *I* never moved. There I just sat in my corner!

Laura sat on the organ stool and Mr. A. hung over her, bending down very close at times—to turn the music of course! They sang *for* the rest of us and *to* each other. Willy and I had such fun watching them and intercepting

---

1. Andrew Agnew, son of T.J. Agnew whose ox-cart line preceded the railway as main means of transport into Prince Albert. Andrew worked in his brother's store; he later married Laura Pritchard.

numberless kiss-and-let-me-die-love looks. We snickered to ourselves under cover of the music—but didn't spend *all* our time watching Laura and Andrew. I daresay if anybody had been watching *us* they wouldn't have found it bad fun either—but of that deponent sayeth nothing.[1]

Finally the gentlemen took their departure and Laura and I came upstairs where we are now, all ready for bed. But we don't expect to do a great deal of sleeping tonight. We are just going to *talk*.

To-night on the sofa I got Will to give me back my ring but I promised to give it to him for "keeps" tomorrow. He also asked me to give him a lock of my hair and although I pretended to refuse I *may* change my mind.

It's all rather funny, isn't it? I wonder if this will ever come to anything. No, of course it won't. We will just be good friends. I *like* Will better than any boy I ever met but I *know* I don't love him—he just seems like a brother or a jolly good comrade to me.

Monday, July 6, 1891
Laurel Hill Farm
Prince Albert

Oh, if Laura and I weren't sleepy this morning! We talked most of the night. This morning we spent picking strawberries. After dinner we began casting about for the best way to have some fun this afternoon. Laura proposed a drive over to Mr. Keyworth's, so we asked Mr. P. for a horse. The teams were all in use and the only free horse was a mare who rejoiced in the aristocratic name of "Courtney"—why, deponent knoweth not.[2] They had just bought "Courtney"[3] and her reputation was considered doubtful, but we coaxed and at last got permission to drive her. Will went out to harness her and Laura and I waltzed upstairs to put on our war-paint. It looked like rain and you never saw such a flutter as we were in for fear our nicely curled bangs would be all straight before we got to Keyworth's!!!!

At last we were ready and went down jubilantly. Laura was taking her medal along to show it and as she had no pocket she got me to put it in mine for safety. Then we got into the buggy. I didn't particularly like "Courtney's" style. She kept casting queerish looks back at us out of the corners of her eyes. However, we got gaily in, myself with a big umbrella held at an angle of 45 degrees, and Laura took the reins somewhat gingerly. We pranced out of the

---

1. Manor Keyworth's, named for a town near Nottingham, England.

2. A common mock-legal quotation, from Walter Scott's *Redgauntlet* (1824).

3. Perhaps named for Courtney Lake, 31 miles (50 km) from Prince Albert.

gate saying that we "hoped we'd have some nice little adventures on our road." Now, I'm firmly persuaded that "Courtney" heard this and being, as Will says, a "well-meaning little beast on the whole," decided to gratify our wishes; and the only trouble was that she overrated our capacity for enjoyment!

When we cleared the gate the first thing we encountered was a hill and "Courtney" tore down it at a fearful rate. This scared us and Laura set her teeth and took a big grip of the reins for the next hill. It was fearfully steep and "Courtney" began to act queer. She was jumping from side to side and humping up her back. I remarked that I thought "Courtney" was in good spirits. No sooner had I said this than "Courtney," having got through the preliminaries, began in good earnest. She stopped in the middle of the hill, planted her forefeet firmly in a you-don't-get-me-to-move-till-I'm-through sort of way and tried apparently to stand on her head. In plain English—"Courtney" kicked! At the first kick the cross-bar was shattered and I put down my umbrella. At the second, her white heels came into such close proximity to my face that I thought it was high time to get a move on. Both Laura and I were *slightly* excited. I *think* we screamed—at least, I have a dim remembrance of hearing a noise *somewhere*. Laura called for "papa." So did I. Then, as "papa" did not come Laura climbed down at the third kick. I stood up, and as "Courtney" gave a farewell kick by way of good measure, I sailed serenely over the wheels and landed right end up just as "Courtney" bolted. Laura ran up to me, clutched me by the arm and whispered tragically, "Maud, *is the medal safe?*"

I said I thought it was!

We sauntered over to the pasture where "Courtney" had rejoined her companions, and Will and Mr. P., who had come tearing frantically down the hill, took her in charge. Laura and I came back to the house in a subdued mood. We had had our "adventure" and our bangs were in good condition still! After tea we went over to call on the Smiths[1]—a family just out from Scotland. On our way back through the lovely fields and clear fresh air Laura saw a horse tied to the fence. But on discovery that the rider thereof was *not* Andrew A. she at once lost interest in it and, seating herself on the grass, gave herself up to maiden meditation. Will came over to meet us and he and I also sat down and pelted each other with daisies and bluebells until we wearied of such an intellectual amusement. Then the rider of the horse—Billy Lovel by name[2]—came over and Laura got on his nag and off they coolly went, leaving Will and me to walk home by ourselves—which didn't worry us any!

---

1. Robert Smith, a newcomer from Scotland in 1891, became deputy registrar of lands and titles in 1921.
2. Billy Lovel had travelled in 1885 to Little Trout Lake to gather food for the community, becoming the founder of the fishing industry in northern Saskatchewan.

Tuesday, July 7, 1891

Laura and I didn't talk *quite* as late last night but our eyes rebelled this morning. We wrote a "ten-year" letter to each other in the forenoon and spent the afternoon picking berries with Will. It is so delightful here—just like home. And it is so strange and lovely to feel that I can move around and talk without feeling myself constantly under the espionage of a hostile and malevolent eye, ever on the alert for anything that can be twisted and interpreted to my disadvantage.

Wednesday, July 8, 1891

Here I am back in town again—worse luck! How I hated to come back! Last night after milking we got ready. When we saw Will harnessing up "Courtney" we protested, but he said he could manage her all right. Lolla and I were very skeptical however and said we would walk a piece first and see how she behaved before we got in. We started and so did he—and just on the hill "Courtney" began her performance. Will whipped her soundly but it only made her worse and she kicked and reared and plunged until we were terrified Will would be killed or hurt. Then the old beast flung herself right down in the shafts and Mr. P. had to take her in hand. *He* settled her—drove her round and round and thrashed her until she was as meek as Moses. Then we climbed gingerly in, Laura and I all ready to jump out again at the least alarm. But "Courtney" had learned her lesson and we got into town O.K. Then we went down to see the train come in and had a lovely time. Andrew A. appeared and of course annexed Laura, while Will and I came home together.

I am here alone in my room now and I feel horribly lonely. I believe I'll go to bed and have a good cry. But on second thoughts I'll do nothing of the sort. Crying always makes one feel wretched the next morning and puffs one's eyes all up. So I'll fight it off as long as I can.

Tuesday, July 21, 1891
Prince Albert

I've been sick, off and on, ever since writing last, with some kind of intermittent fever. I've really had a miserable time and have swallowed enough horrible medicine to kill or cure anyone. The truth of the matter is I've been working like a slave for the past eight months and I've just gone beyond my strength. I've had to do all the work of this house, except the washing, and help tend the baby, besides, while Mrs. Montgomery parades the streets or visits with her relatives.

I spent a couple of days after my worst attack up on the hill with the McTaggarts. Mrs. McTaggart is such a dear old soul. Her daughter does not resemble her in *any* respect. I had a good rest and a lovely time while up there. One morning I was a little amused. Mrs. McTaggart, out in the kitchen, told her youngest son Willy,[1] a bright lad of twelve, that he must go down town and stay for the day at our place, since father had to be away. "I just won't," said Willy. "I hate going down there—Mary is so cross."

"Hold your tongue and don't talk so," said his mother. But I noticed she didn't say that "Mary" *wasn't* cross. It would seem that her young half-brothers have pretty much the same opinion of Mrs. Mary Ann Montgomery as I have.

I'm better now and beginning to enjoy life again after a fashion. I was in to see Mrs. Kennedy[2] tonight. Mrs. and Miss Gunn[3] were there and Willy also dropped in—he seems to have contracted a chronic habit of "dropping in" places where I am! We went down to the station, but finding that the train was two hours late we didn't wait for it.

Friday, July 24, 1891

I was out to the Methodist S.S. picnic at Maiden Lake to-day and had a scrumptious time. We all went out in trams.[4] Mrs. McLeod,[5] Mr. & Mrs. Rochester, Mrs. Coombs and I were in the same tram and we had a very jolly drive. It is four miles out, over such a beautiful trail, and Maiden Lake is a perfectly lovely spot—a long sloping hill dotted with white-stemmed poplars, and at the foot a big blue lake. At first I prowled around with Aggie and Martha Thompson, although out of the corner of my eye I saw quite plainly that Will P. was shadowing us.

"Oh," you said—didn't you?—"*now* I begin to see why you had a good time." Don't be impertinent, you journal, you!

---

1. Willy McTaggart. Son of John McTaggart.

2. Alex and William Kennedy had owned lots on the Saskatchewan River since 1878.

3. Several men named "Gunn" appear in records of Saskatchewan at this time. LMM is probably referring to George Gunn, a divinity student from Emmanuel College, Toronto, who was a suitor of Laura Pritchard.

4. The electric railway ran four miles from Prince Albert to Maiden Lake, a park 4 miles (6 km) south of Prince Albert.

5. Sam McLeod ran a small lumber business. He had bid for the right to provide electricity in 1890.

After wandering around for some time Miss T. and I sat down under a tree and were chatting away when a shadow fell over us and looking up I saw Will. He coolly sat down beside me. Miss T. evidently concluded that there was a huge crowd just then and left us alone. Will and I went for ice-cream, heard a recitation given by a school-teacher—a capital one it was, too—and then Will suggested a walk. So off we went, followed by several encouraging remarks from his chums. We had a delightful walk of over a mile. The prairies were just abloom with asters, bluebells and daisies. Will picked a bunch of daisies and sweet clover and remarking that their language was "innocence and beauty" he pinned it on my dress. He also produced a parcel of delicious candies and I nibbled at them as we walked.

When we got back we had tea. A lot of our chums were at the same table—Holdenby[1] and Stevie and Miss Cassie[2] and the McGregor girls—and we had no end of fun, especially over some Scotch shortbread[3] that was nearly all dough and sandwiches minus any filling. I'm sure I hope the builders thereof weren't about or they must have writhed at our remarks.

After tea we had some jolly swings and then Will and I wandered away to a big poplar down by the lake. I cut my initials on the bark and he cut his right under and then we conjointly cut the date over them.

When going home time came I had to hustle off to catch the last tram. It was so full I had to wedge down on the floor with half a dozen others as tight as a sardine, and so had a very uncomfortable ride back to town. But then, I had the loveliest time at the picnic.

"Just because Willy walked with you," you remarked scornfully—didn't you?—"and said pretty things to you and generally made a fool of himself, over you"!!!!

Well, and what if that was why?

Friday, July 31, 1891

Picnics are all the "go" now. The Bible-class one came off to-day and was rather slow until the wind-up came. We all met at the manse in the morning. There were 17 in our tram going out and we had a very jolly time. When we got out to the place we had dinner but after that things dragged dolefully. We did try a game of baseball but it was too hot. We had some fun at tea, though

---

1. Alonzo Holenby (Haldenby). A twenty-three-year-old harness-maker born in Ontario of English-Irish parents.

2. Margaret Jean Cassie, aged twenty-one, daughter of a land officer, married Haldenby in 1892, and continued to live in Prince Albert.

3. Traditionally rich biscuits made with butter and brown sugar.

Charlie Newitt[1] and Alexina and I sat together. Newitt is an Englishman and the oddest thing that ever happened. He talks so funnily and acts so absurdly that he is as good as a play.

We left for home at 8. I sat between Laura and Will. Newitt was on the other side of Laura and he kept things stirred up. We had a most hilarious drive. About a mile from Goschen[2] a thunderstorm came up and there was a skirmish for cloaks and umbrellas. I muffled myself in mine and Will held my umbrella over us—quite *low*—and then, as it was getting dark and everyone else was likewise lost under umbrellas I leaned back, cuddled up against him and we had a nice little talk. Among other things, we were talking of writing each other a "ten year letter." I said dreamily, "Dear me, ten years is a long time. I wonder where we'll be when we read them."

"Perhaps we'll be reading them *together*," he whispered.

I didn't say anything, only laughed rather awkwardly. It gave me a pleasant little thrill—but still, I can't quite see *that*.

Laura came home with me to stay all night. She is here now and we are just going to have a good-night's talk.

Saturday, Aug. 1, 1891

We had it—I rather guess! We *talked* and *talked* and *talked*. I never met a girl I could confide in as I can in Laura. I can tell her *everything*—the thoughts of my very inmost soul—and she is the same with me. We are twin spirits in every way. We talked until 2.30. Fancy!

Once we had a glum fit on and were squeezing each other and lamenting our approaching separation.

"Do you know," whispered Laura, "I believe Willy will just break his heart when you go away. Look here, I never say anything but I know this—he just worships the ground you tread on."

I laughed and said "nonsense." But I smiled a wee bit to myself in the darkness. It's nice to be—liked!

Sunday, Aug. 2, 1891

Had such fun in Sunday School to-day. My class is right up by the bookcase and as Will is librarian he sits there, too, and we have lots of fun on the sly.

---

1. A twenty-eight-year-old Englishman, working as a clerk. During the Riel Rebellion he had been wounded and taken prisoner, but saved by an Aboriginal person from death.

2. A community at the east end of Prince Albert named for the Hudson's Bay governor in the 1880s.

I took my "ten year letter" with me and he brought his and we exchanged. That absurd boy had directed his to "Mrs.—-." Said he didn't know what my name would be when I opened it!

Monday, Aug. 10, 1891

A horrible day, this—dull, cold, gloomy and windy—a day that for all the world seems astray from November, with a chill wind that moaned around the damp eaves and shook the shivering trees until every leaf hung limp and beaten.

We are going to have a great bat on Wednesday week—a congregational picnic to Duck Lake.

Wednesday, Aug. 12, 1891

This forenoon a rat-tat-tat came at the kitchen door and when I opened it there stood my darling Lolla herself. She said she and Mrs. Kennedy intend going blueberrying over the river to-morrow and want me to go too.

Thursday, Aug. 13, 1891

There is no use in talking—such another day I never did spend in my life and—although it was good fun on the whole—I'm quite certain I never want to spend such another again. My feet feel—oh, now they *do* feel! And every bone in my body is letting me know it is there!

This morning I was up at five and flew over, according to agreement, to waken the Kennedy's who were all sleeping soundly. My pounding on the door soon dispelled their dreams and I came home and got my breakfast. My costume, when ready for a start, was certainly striking. I had on an old cotton skirt that barely reached below my knees, an old blue jersey, and a straw hat in the last stages of decrepitude. But as over all I wore my long gray mackintosh I wouldn't have looked so awfully terrificable if it hadn't have been for the hat.

We set off carrying enough cans and buckets for an army. We started for Goshen as it is down there the squaws cross and we hoped to get some of them to row us over. Our plans were rather hazy and when we did get down we had a terrific time trying to get across. A dozen times at least we raced along that river bank through the thick shrubs dripping with dew until we were wet to the skin. There was no sign of any boat or squaw and though we shrieked "watoo" and "minnecossa" to the breeds in the tepee across the river until we were hoarse it was all in vain. At last we found a squaw's "dug-out" on the shore and Mrs. K. and Laura declared they could paddle it over themselves but I refused to go on the grounds that I hadn't made my will before leaving home. I was wet to the ears, mud to the knees and tired all over, so I sat down on the bank in a disconsolate heap while Mrs. K. and Laura held a council of war. It resulted in Laura's going up to a Mr. Macdonald's house near by to see if she could get a man to paddle us over. She came back without that desirable biped, however, and with her came Bella Macdonald who declared that she could paddle us over as well as any man. After much hesitation Mrs. K. and Laura decided to risk it and the three of them got into the dug-out. I told them I'd meet them in the happy land later on, as I didn't intend to drown myself just now, and they pushed off. About five yards from the shore a panic seized them all. Mrs. K. stood up and jumped clear out of the boat. Fortunately the water was only up to her knees, and she dragged the dug-out back to shore. The rest of us laughed frantically and Mrs. K. stood on a stone and wrung the water out of her skirt.

At this juncture a man came rowing down the river and took us across!

Once landed on the opposite shore we took the road to the Indian camp. It was a pretty walk and the breath of that pine wilderness was delicious. But we were getting awfully tired. It was three miles to the camp, when we inquired of a breed the way to the berry barrens. Then we set off again with renewed faith and courage. We trudged two more weary miles until we came to where the breed had told us we would find berries. Alas for the breeds! They are truly "the fathers of lies." The berries were few and far between, and although we extracted a lot of fun out of our search fun didn't fill our gaping buckets.

At last we gave up in disgust and scrambled down the steep banks of the Little Red River to see if we could find any raspberries in default of our blueberries. What a wilderness it was! Steep banks covered with mighty, heaven-sweeping pines, weird with age; below, a thick undergrowth of poplar through which we forced our way to a most romantic little spot. In a little hollow stood a rude, deserted lumberman's hut. On all sides rose the wooded banks. We were tired out, so we sat down at the root of a huge old pine stump and ate our lunch as well as the mosquitoes would let us. A picturesque spot it was—that wild, yet beautiful wilderness, where nature ran riot in untrained luxuriance. If ever I write a novel I must put that scene in.

After lunch we resumed our hunt for blueberries but found none, and at last, wearied out, we resolved to start for home. Our feet were so sore that we had to take off our shoes and walk our five miles barefoot. When we reached the river bank we had no end of a time coaxing the squaws to take us over. They didn't want to and at one time I really feared we'd have to stay there all night. In the end they relented and took us over. We had to make three trips of it—Laura first, I next, and Mrs. K. last. When we were all safely landed at Goshen we gave a huge sigh of relief and trudged home. No more over the river excursions for me if you please!

Sunday, Aug. 16, 1891
Prince Albert

I have felt quite mixed up to-day—sad and glad in about equal proportions. When father came downstairs this morning he kissed me and said, with a tremble in his voice,

"I had a letter from father last night and I expect you'll have to start on Monday or Thursday week."

I felt dreadfully over the thought of leaving father and just ran upstairs and cried. But then, to go back to dear old Cavendish—I just *had* to feel glad over that. And to escape from Mrs. Montgomery's ceaseless petty tyranny and underhand persecution—what a relief that will be!

I went to church this morning and after dinner went to S.S. Will, as usual, was at his post. When I told him I was going away next week he looked dreadfully glum all the rest of the service. Well, I felt glum, too.

We have had it pretty well understood that we were to correspond but he has never asked me to in just so many words. So when *he* said,

"You'll write us from Ottawa, won't you?"

I said demurely, "Who's us?"

He laughed and said, "Well, write to *me* then. How will that do?"

"It's much less ambiguous," I answered and of course I said I would.

After Bible Class Annie McTaggart came over with me to tea, as father had gone down to Colleston for Mrs. M. and the children who have been there for several days. After tea it came up a fearful thunderstorm and it is pouring rain now. Annie and I are going to church but it doesn't look as if there would be too many there.

Monday, Aug. 17, 1891
Prince Albert

Last night Annie and I went to church. When we came out it had stopped raining and Annie McT., Willy P, Rod McTaggart, and Frank Robertson[1]

---

1. A sixteen-year-old boy, living with his widowed father and six siblings.

came over. Will was on horseback so he tied his nag at the front gate. We all went into the parlor and had no end of fun. At about ten the boys decided to go home and as the folks had not returned I went up with Annie. We got ready, "doused the glim,"[1] and rustled out to the gate.

"Why, Will," I exclaimed in dismay, "your horse is gone!"

It was only too true. Perhaps the nag wished to teach his master a lesson on Sabbath observance. Perhaps some of the boys around had seen him tied there and let him loose for a joke. Anyhow, he was gone, there was no doubt of that, leaving his bridle behind him on the fence. And there that poor boy would have to walk three miles out home in that awful mud!

We started up the hill, Will patiently carrying his bridle. We had a serious time. The grass was sopping and the mud was simply terrible. However, we got up at last. Will said good-night and took the road to Laurel Hill farm while we sneaked into the house in a pretty plight of mud and wet. George Baker and Min Wheeler[2] were in the parlor and when we appeared suddenly at the door there were the two geese sitting on the sofa with their arms around each other. I began to laugh.

"Oh, you two spoons," I said; but I got no further for Min exclaimed,

"Oh, *you* needn't talk. We just saw *someone* go past!"

And George said loftily, "*I* am not so bad off to see my girl that I'd walk three miles on a night like this and carry the bridle."

That silenced *me*! I didn't try to be funny any more but decamped upstairs to bed.

Wednesday, Aug. 19, 1891

Our much-talked-of excursion has been and come and gone. Everybody and his sister were there. We went on the train to Duck Lake. Laura, Andrew A., Mr. Gunn and I were together going up and the ride was nice. But it blew a perfect hurricane all day and I never put in a duller time. Will and I took a walk to see the Lake. We had some fun but we both felt rather glum over the fact that this was our last picnic together—for a long time, anyway.

I am to leave next Thursday. Eddie Jardine[3] is going down to Toronto to go to school and we will be together that far. I am going by the Lakes. They say it is much prettier than the other route.

---

1. Naval slang: put out the light.
2. A courting couple related to the McTaggarts. George was perhaps also related to T.E. Baker, a builder and contractor living on River Street.
3. The older son of the Anglican minister had been born in India.

I was down to the Stovels' this evening and had fine fun. Mary was very nice—which is not always the case with her at all. She is very squiffy sometimes. Newitt was there and we had lots of fun making a table rap.

Sunday, Aug. 23, 1891

My last Sunday on the banks of the Saskatchewan is nearly over. I attended service this morning. After dinner I went to S.S. Poor Will was there but there wasn't much fun in him. I felt so badly when bidding my poor little class good-bye. Will is going to take it after I am gone and I hope he'll succeed with it.

Then we went, to Bible Class where we have spent so many happy hours in Mr. Rochester's pleasant room. When we stood up to sing the last hymn— it was "God be With You Till we meet again"—my eyes filled with tears as I realized that it was really *the last time*.

Tuesday, Aug. 25, 1891
Prince Albert

This evening Alexina came up to ask me to go for a drive. We had a perfectly lovely time. Mr. Stovel came in to-night and gave me the "Sketch Book"[1] and "Emerson's Essays"[2] for a parting gift. It was very kind of him and I was very much pleased.

Wednesday, Aug. 26, 1891

It has come at last—my last day in P.A. And a weary, fatiguing, heart-breaking day it has been. In the morning I packed up and spent the day making good-bye calls.[3] After tea Mrs. Davies and Miss Patterson[4] called to bid me good-bye, and after they had gone Mrs. Pritchard came. I was so sorry to part with her—she has been so kind to me. Laura and Willy were at Mrs. Kennedy's[5] and Laura soon came over. Father and Mrs. M. went out and Laura and I washed up the tea-dishes together. We then went into the

---

1. Washington Irving's essays (1819–20) covered his travels to Britain and retold American folk tales such as "The Legend of Sleepy Hollow."

2. Transcendental meditations on self-reliance and nature, published in 1841.

3. Prince Albert friends, coming from far-flung places, included Miss Davis, aged thirty, born in England.

4. Miss Paterson, aged twenty-two, born in QC.

5. Mrs. Kennedy, aged thirty-three, born in MB.

garden where we each picked a bouquet of mignonette, petunias and sweet peas and exchanged them for farewell keepsakes. Will came along as we lingered at the gate in the red glow of the sunset and we all chatted very sadly. Previously, Laura had told me that Will had been in a fine worry all day for fear he wouldn't be able to get in to bid me good-bye—Mr. P. being away—and that he had written a letter to send to me in case he couldn't.

Presently Mr. and Mrs. Rochester[1] came over and we all went in. Mr. R. gave me a letter to his people in Ottawa, bade me good-bye and went off with father to a lecture. Katie Fulcher[2] and Lottie Stewart[3] also dropped in and then came Fred Porter[4] and Miss Wheeler. We were quite a roomful and were very merry but the fun all seemed a little bit strained—to me, anyhow, and Will didn't look as if he were enjoying himself extremely.

Presently the girls went and then Laura tackled Porter—who couldn't seem to see that he wasn't exactly wanted—while Will and I had a confidential chat in the corner. Will produced the letter, explained how it came to be written, and said I might as well have it anyway. After awhile it did dawn on Freddie's brain that four was a tremendous crowd just then, so he made his adieux and left. Then we three had the room to ourselves. Laura amused herself at the piano and was discreetly deaf and blind to all that went on in the corner behind her.

About ten we all went over to Mrs. Kennedy's. Laura was going to stay in to see me off but Will had to go out. He and I walked back in silence. At the steps we paused. Above us the stars were shining tranquilly in the clear August sky. About us was the soft, dewy dusk. Down the slope glimmered the lights of the town. It all looked dream-like and I felt as if I were in a dream.

"Well," he said, holding out his hand—and his voice wasn't *very* steady—"good-bye. I hope you will have a very happy time—and don't forget us."

"I'll never forget you, you may be sure," I said, as we shook hands. "Good-bye."

"Bi-bi," said he. Our hands fell apart and he was gone. I felt so badly I couldn't cry—I just felt stupid. I went up to my room and read his letter. He said in it that he loved me and always would. I curled up on my bed after I had read it and had a good cry. I felt so lonesome and horrid. If I hadn't known that Will had left town I believe I'd have run out after him.

I am very glad I came to P.A. although once I did not think I could ever say so. I have been a whole year with dear father, I have made a few good

---

1. Rev. William, aged twenty-seven, born in QC, and Minnie, aged twenty-three, born in the US.

2. Katie Fulcher, aged seventeen, born in MB.

3. Lottie Stewart, aged sixteen, born in QC.

4. Fred Porter, aged twenty-three, born in NS.

true friends whose friendship has enriched my life and I have had a very pleasant social time this summer. I will have had two fine trips and seen a good deal of Canada. Yes, indeed, I shall always be glad that I came to P.A. and I shall look back to it kindly in the years to come. I wonder if I shall ever come back to it. Perhaps I shall, if Will—but no, somehow, in spite of all, I can't think *that*—at least, not yet.

And this is the last night I shall sleep in Southview. Poor little room! How bare and desolate it seems now with all my things gone!

Thursday, Aug. 27, 1891

It's all over—the dreadful parting and all—and here I am flying along the rails to Regina and feeling fearfully lost and lonely. This morning we were all up early. After breakfast we heard the train whistle and I went slowly upstairs, put on my hat and cloak and bade farewell to little Southview. Mrs. M. did not go to the station so I said good-bye to her at the house. I could not pretend that I felt sorry for she has used me very badly indeed and I shall never be able to think of her with anything but aversion.

On our way to the station we overtook Alexina. It was a sad walk and I could hardly keep back the tears. When we got down to the station there was quite a crowd to see me off—Mr. Stovel, all the McTaggarts, Mrs. Kennedy, Laura, and the Jardines. We stood around and talked until "all aboard" was shouted.

I'm going to skip the next ten minutes. I shall not forget them if I live to be a hundred. At last they were over and the train pulled slowly out in the fresh morning sunshine. One by one my dear P.A. friends vanished and as Laura's face passed out of sight I realized that I was really off and "homeward bound."

I rushed to my seat in an agony of tears and cried for the first three miles. Then I sat up, wiped away my tears, and determined to grin! Eddie Jardine was in the seat before me; all the rest in the car were strangers. To-day has not been very interesting. Eddie is no company; he doesn't seem to know he has a tongue; and I don't think he has any ideas either. We don't get to Regina until nine and it is now seven. It is growing dark and the country is as flat as a pancake and as featureless. I feel forty different ways at once—and I do wish I could see father and Laura and Will!!

Friday, Aug. 28, 1891

Heigh-ho for Winnipeg. Thither are we tending. We reached Regina at 9.30 last evening. We had scarcely alighted when we were met by Mr. Weir—Laura's

Scotch admirer—who is in Regina now. We found that the eastern train did not leave until 11.30 so Mr. Weir proposed a stroll around town. As we—I speak in the plural but I really don't know what Eddie thought about it. He evidently believes that silence is golden—didn't relish the idea of waiting in a dreary depot for two hours we assented and sat off. I enjoyed the walk after a fashion although my boot hurt my heel dreadfully and I was very tired. Finally we went to Mr. Weir's boarding house and sat down in the parlor. I was more than amused to hear the solicitude with which Mr. Weir inquired for "Miss Pritchard." Won't I tease Laura about it when I write! Dear Laura! I wish that she and Willie were with me in place of that unsociable E.J.—and I actually believe that Willie himself would do even if Laura wasn't here!

When our train came in we hurried down and got on board. The car was jammed with people. At first we could not even get a place to sit down but at last a gentleman gave me his seat and I crowded down and tried to read a prosy Scotch magazine Mr. Weir had given me, he being evidently under the delusion that it might help to wile away the time. I've felt seedy all day, having slept but little all night, but it has been fairly pleasant. There are lots of stations and it is a good deal of amusement to pass them. We will reach Winnipeg about four.

6.20 P.M.

It is just about half an hour since we left Winnipeg. We got there at five and John McTaggart met us. We went for a short walk with him but as it was blowing a hurricane and beginning to rain there was not much pleasure in it. It is raining now and is generally dismal.

Saturday, Aug. 29, 1891
Somewhere In The Woods

It is raining and foggy. We expect to be in Fort William at one o'clock and have to wait there over night for the boat—I am making faces over this. We are in a rough country—all woods; but oh, it does my heart good to see the spruces again!

9 o'clock P.M.

Have been through a lot of fuss and worry. When we got to Fort William and disembarked I felt dreadfully at sea. Eddie is no earthly good in an emergency evidently. A gentleman on board, whose name is Porter and who belongs to the Island, advised us to go to the *Avenue Hotel*, as it is considered the best—or rather, the *least worst*! So we came here. If it *is* the best I am glad we did not strike the worst!

As the place is crowded I had to be satisfied with a wretched little room right at the head of the stairs. It is about as big as a closet and utterly destitute of conveniences—except a cracked basin and pitcher. There wasn't even a match wherewith to light a smoky lamp to curl my demoralized "bangs." However, it was Hobson's choice[1] for I couldn't camp in the street. After a poor dinner I went to this charming apartment and tried to fight off the blues. It was pouring rain outside but anything was preferable to that dreary room, so I put on my coat and cap and sallied out. For about an hour I rambled around and in spite of the rain I rather enjoyed it. Fort William is a pretty place. The mountain scenery around it is very beautiful and there are some nice houses. But it is all as yet pretty rough; the streets are full of charred unsightly stumps among which promenade numerous pigs!

After tea I went out again, for that room got on my nerves. How lonely I felt! Last Saturday night I was in Prince Albert with Laura and Will, and now here I was, a thousand miles away, prowling alone about the streets of Fort William. If only Will and Laura had been with me what a jolly time we could have had! Then the rain and grime and discomfort could only have been a joke for us.

Sunday, Aug. 30, 1891
One O'Clock
Fort William, Ontario

This is a perfectly lovely day—couldn't be finer. This morning after breakfast I concluded to go to church so, after inquiring my way to a Presbyterian church I sallied out. As it was not yet church time, however, I prowled around a bit to see the sunny side of Fort William. In my ramblings I fell in with Eddie J. and we walked about a mile down the railroad track to get a good look at "the mountain." When we stopped it didn't seem to be any nearer than before—the distances in regard to these mountains are very deceptive. When we got back to the church we heard singing and thought we were late. I was quite taken aback to find only about a dozen people in the building. I slipped into a back pew where I looked around and wondered if that were all the Presbyterians Fort William could scare up. But I soon found it was

---

1. No choice at all: from an anecdote in *The Spectator* (1712), about a liveryman named Hobson who made each customer take the horse nearest the door or get no horse at all.

not a regular service. We had strayed into some sort of a Bible class and it was decidedly dull. After it was over we hurried back to the hotel and got our dinner. We are just ready to leave and I am thankful for this hotel is the dirtiest and most uncomfortable place I ever was in.

Sunday Evening
Ten O'Clock

Have been having a lovely time. We came to the boat at one. It is the "Manitoba" and she is a dandy. The promenade deck is the favorite resort. The sunset on the lake this evening was superb. I am writing this in the saloon under the brilliant electric light, while a hum of conversation rises from the groups around me. I am very sleepy. This hasn't seemed like Sunday at all. I wonder how poor Will got on teaching my class to-day.

Monday, Aug. 31, 1891

A glorious day—fresh breezes, blue skies, blue waters. I have enjoyed every minute of it, haunting the promenade deck, reading and writing at intervals. At noon we got to the "Soo"[1] and went through the "locks" of the canal, a very interesting experience. We were there until 3 o'clock. The American side of the "Soo" is very pretty but I must admit the Canadian side is very scrubby-looking. When we got out of the locks we passed down the St. Mary River. The scenery was exquisite. Then we emerged into Lake Huron.

Tuesday, Sept. 1, 1891
3 O'Clock P.M.

Am on my way to Toronto. This morning we were in the Georgian bay and at noon we sighted Owen Sound—the jumping-off place. The train was waiting for us and off we went at a dizzy rate. The country is lovely. Ontario is a beautiful place.

Evening 11 O'Clock

We reached Toronto at 4 and as I had 5 hours to stay there I decided to go and see the McKenzies'. Eddie's cousin met him and we took a street car and drove three miles up Sherbourne St. to Mr. McKenzie's house. I was delighted

---

1. Colloquial name for the Ontario city of Sault Ste Marie; "Sault" is pronounced "soo" in English.

with Toronto. It is a beautiful city. When we got to my destination I got off, bade Eddie good-bye—not at all regretfully—and ran up the steps. To my disappointment I found that Mr. and Mrs. McKenzie, Gertie and Mabel were out in the country. However, the governess and a Miss Campbell who was there were exceedingly kind and so were the children. I had a lovely time. Later on Rod McK came in. He is very nice and I spent a delightful evening. At 8.30 Rod drove me to the depot and put me on board the train. I am to be in Ottawa in the morning but I have to change cars at Smith's Falls during the night.

Wednesday, Sept. 2, 1891

Arrived in Ottawa at 5 this morning. Not a trace could I see of Grandpa Montgomery so I took a street car and went to the Windsor Hotel where I knew he was staying. Here I found that he had gone down to meet me. He soon came back in a great flurry, bless his dear old heart, but calmed down when he saw me safe and sound. When he had to go to the senate I went out to do a bit of shopping. Ottawa is nice but not nearly so nice as Toronto. When Grandpa came back he said he had met a Mr. and Mrs. Hooper[1] of Ch'Town who were going to leave for home tomorrow and he thought I had better go down with them, as he cannot go for some time yet.

After dinner Grandpa took me all through the Parliament buildings. They are magnificent. I sat down for a minute in the Governor General's chair and felt at least two inches taller after that, of course! The library is fine. Wouldn't I like to ransack it!

Then we attended a session of the Senate. The Senate Chamber is beautiful. We met the Hoopers there and we all went up to the gallery of the House of Commons[2] and heard Sir Richard Cartwright speak on the Census. Then Grandpa showed us all around Parliament Square. It is beautiful and we saw the Chaudiere Falls in the distance.

Thursday, Sept. 3, 1891

Yesterday evening Mr. and Mrs. Hooper called on their way to the House of Commons and I went, too. We heard a debate on the census—very dry. I

---

1. Perhaps related to the Hoopers of Charlottetown who had Cavendish connections.
2. Parliament building in Ottawa, the Canadian capital city.

simply got sleepy. This morning Mrs. Hooper and I walked out to the Rifle Ranges. It was fearfully hot.

Mr. Rochester's father and brother called on me to-day. Very nice people.

Ten O'Clock
Montreal

We left Ottawa this afternoon and here we are at the St. Lawrence Hall. We came by the Intercolonial. I am simply tired out and am going straight to bed.

Friday, Sept. 4, 1891

We left Montreal early this morning. It was very wet and dismal. We passed through the Victoria Bridge—the longest iron tubular bridge in the world. All day we have travelled through Quebec. The scenery didn't amount to much. At noon we reached Point Levis, opposite the city of Quebec. I saw the famous plains of Abraham and the Montmorency Falls. Mrs. Hooper is very nice but the same can't be said of her lord and master. I don't like him at all. It is dark now and we are somewhere near Miramichi. This time to-morrow night I shall be in dear old P.E.I. Isn't that good to think about?

Saturday, Sept. 5, 1891
3 O'Clock P.M. Northumberland Strait

A beautiful day—and here I am in sight of the Island! We will be there in another hour and meanwhile I am feasting my eyes on its distant green hills. This morning we got into Moncton at 5 after a very miserable, cold, sleepless night. We had to stay in Moncton till ten, so went to the Brunswick Hotel. At 10 we left and at one we reached Pointe du Chene, where we took the boat. It has been very rough but I have not been at all seasick. I kept an eager look-out for land and the minute I saw it I flew like the wind to get a good look at the "ould sod."

Eleven O'Clock
Park Corner, P.E. Island

Here I am!!! We got to Summerside at four this afternoon. It *did* seem a rather chilly home-coming for there was not a face in all the crowd that I knew. Never mind—it was home and that was enough. Still, I *was* tired and lonely; and I had to wait two dreary hours in the station for the train. I got to Kensington about sunset, trudged up to the Commercial House and hired a team to take me to Park Corner.

How I did enjoy that drive! It was all so lovely—the beautiful sunset, the rich harvest scenery, and the aroma of the firs along the road. I just gazed my eyes out. And when we came in sight of the sea I could not speak for emotion. I listened to its hollow roar in unspeakable delight. It was quite dark when we drove up to the Senator's door. The first face I saw was Lucy Pickering's and then Uncle Jim and Uncle Cuthbert came running up. They hardly knew me at first—they thought I had changed so much. After tea I hastened over to Uncle John Campbell's. Aunt Annie and Uncle John were sitting in the kitchen and they actually did not know me until I told them who I was. *Such* a time as we had! The girls were in bed but they got up and came tearing down. Clara and Stella[1] have both grown so tall I wouldn't have known them either. I am going to stay here all night.

Tuesday, Sept. 8, 1891
Cavendish, P.E.I.

I am at home—actually at home in dear old C. and it is jolly. Uncle Crosby brought me down this afternoon. It was such a delightful drive. When we got to Stanley I began to feel pretty well excited and my excitement increased all the rest of the way as I gazed my eyes out on all the familiar spots until Uncle Crosby must have thought he had a crazy girl on his hands.

When we got here, I sprang down, tore in, hugged everybody, and ran through every room in the house. Then I ran over to Uncle John's. All the children have grown especially Kate.

At dusk Lu[2] and I set out for a walk. We went to the school first, then to Uncle Jimmy's and the manse. Then we ran down to Robertson's to see Miss Gordon but found her away. On our way back whom should we meet but Pensie and hadn't we a time!

---

1. Clara (1877–1932) and Stella (1879–1955), two of the Campbell cousins of Park Corner, daughters of LMM's Aunt Annie (her mother's sister) and Uncle John Campbell. Frederica (1883–1919), their youngest sister, is not mentioned in this entry, nor is their brother George (1881–1918).

2. Lucy Macneill (1877–1974), daughter of LMM's Uncle John in the farm next to LMM's.

Wednesday, Sept. 9, 1891

After dinner to-day Lu and I went to the shore and along to the old "Hole in the Wall."[1] There was quite a surf on and it was so lovely to see the big waves rushing up into the old cave and flinging showers of foam to the very top of the cliff. To-morrow is dear Mollie's birthday and I am going over as I am dying to see her.

Hole in the wall

Friday, Sept. 11, 1891

Yesterday afternoon I set off. I went to the school first and saw all the girls. The old school is unchanged. There were the old desks where Mollie and I and Nate and Jack sat—how long ago was it? It seems *ages*. There were the initials cut into the porch, there was the old nail I used to hang my hat on—we girls all had our own particular "nail" and woe betide a trespasser—there written above it by Nate my nickname in our old cipher "Ἰδλλυη"; there on the walls the scribbled names of dozens of flirting couples, and then the old hacked door. What memories haunt that poor old school!

When I got over to Mollie's I found, much to my disappointment, that she and her mother had gone to Rustico and would not be back until evening. As Lillie was home however I waited for them and at 8 they came. Mollie and I had a most enthusiastic meeting. I stayed all night and we talked until nearly morning. Bessie Fraser is away in Nova Scotia and Jack and Nate are both off to college again.

Saturday, Sept. 12, 1891

Mollie came over this afternoon and we had a high old time. After tea we put on our hats, linked our arms, and sallied forth in old time fashion, down the lane, under the birches, until we reached the school, wrapped in drowsy September sunshine. We pushed up a window and climbed in. How deserted the poor old school looked with its rows of empty seats! We finally climbed out again and found our way down the path to the brook. We loitered around familiar spots for awhile and talked over old times. We finally pulled up in "Pierce's Woods," where we sat down to rest and fell

---

1. Sandstone formation on the Gulf shore.

"The lane under the birches"

into a reverie. I gazed dreamily down the vistas. The yellow sunshine fell lazily athwart the tall gray spruces and the gossamers glimmered like threads of silver among the trees. The crickets were chirping and all the air was full of music. How jolly it would have been to have seen Jack or Nate come whistling through the woods as they were wont to do of yore. At last, recalling ourselves to realities, we sauntered home, with a lonely sort of feeling, as if we somehow belonged to those past days and had no business in the present at all.

Sunday, Sept. 13, 1891
Cavendish, P.E. Island

Went to Sunday School this afternoon and saw dozens of old friends. It was so nice to float up to Bible-class and settle down in one corner with a happy sigh to think that no restless class of mischievous boys awaited my efforts on their behalf. I smiled as I thought of them. After all, they had a warm spot in my heart. I do wonder how Will gets on with them. He has his hands full I'll be bound.

After Bible class Mollie and I went down to the post seat. We always did get full of mischief in that seat. Mollie had her S.S. paper with her. I opened it and there, in big letters at the head of one of the stories was the name "Snip." We had a chummy laugh and then read the story together. At some of the sentences we almost choked—they seemed so pat. I haven't laughed so much since the day of "the cabbage chicken."

Monday, Sept. 14, 1891
Cavendish, P.E.I.

This afternoon Miss Gordon sent up a note saying that she and the girls were going to the shore after school and hoped I would join them. So I packed a lunch basket and went down to the school at four. It seemed quite like old times to walk into the school with a basket on my arm but the illusion vanished when I opened the door and missed so many familiar faces. When school came out Lu, Clara, Emma, Lottie, Nellie and I set merrily off down the Big Lane. We prowled around, collecting specimens of seaweeds until the boats came in and then Geo. R. took us all out for a sail. We had a lovely time and quite a programme. The girls sang and I recited and then we had lunch. We sailed four miles and back and then finished it up by singing "Good-bye, ladies," as the boat grated on the pebbles. We jumped ashore and discovered that it was quite dark, so we gathered up our specimens and beat a hasty retreat across the fields homeward.

Saturday, Sept. 19, 1891

After dinner Lu and I drove ourselves down to see Minnie Toombs. We had tea there and a very nice time. Ren is as comical as ever. Minnie has a baby— positively the ugliest baby I ever saw in my life, but of course I didn't tell *her* that. After tea we drove down to see Lily, stayed there till 6.30 and then drove home through the cool dusk under a sky aflame with an autumn sunset—deep-red fire and pallid gold.

Sunday, Sept. 20, 1891

Went to church to-day and saw a lot more old acquaintances, including the famous Clemmie, who actually flung her arms about me and kissed and hugged me until I almost gasped for breath. Clemmie can "put on" when she likes. I suppose that is uncharitable. But I cannot easily forget all that girl has done and said against me in times past.

But, speaking of kissing, I must tell you of my meeting yesterday with old Mrs. John Wyand. It was too funny for any use. She came for the mail and I went out to see her. I held out my hand for a cordial handshake with the poor old soul but lo, she opened her capacious arms and gave me an embrace and kiss that almost overwhelmed me. Then, backing up to sit down on her chair, she mistook the place and sat plump down on the floor instead! You should just have seen her!

Tuesday, Sept. 22, 1891

Had a letter from Will to-day and I consider the event to be worth recording. It was a long letter and very interesting. I was so glad to hear from him. He seems pretty *lonesome*!

Saturday, Sept. 26, 1891

Pensie came up this afternoon. After tea we went out for a walk for it was just a perfect evening. We went down to the school woods and meandered about there until we came out at the "old Cyrus place."[1] Then we went up to the school and got in at one of the windows. We had no end of fun but when we wanted to leave we discovered a lot of kids playing croquet in the field and the only window that would open was in their full view. There seemed nothing to do but sit down and possess our souls in patience until they would go away. But after waiting until we were tired we concluded to try a window on the other side. It was nailed down but we managed to force it up and scrambled out. Our next difficulty was to climb the tremendous structure Pierce Macneill calls a fence. Once over that we ran down through the woods, visited the springs and sauntered home by way of Pierce's field.

There is a maple tree behind our barn that delights me to look at. All the other trees are quite green yet but it has turned early. I think it is dying and its death is a glorious funeral pyre. From top to bottom it is one royal glow of color—blood-crimson above, fire-flame below.

Monday, Oct. 4, 1891
Cavendish, P.E.I.

This morning I drove grandpa to the station, as he was going to town to attend an Exhibition. Just as I left Hunter River for home it began to rain and was soon a very dirty day. The rain simply poured down—but I rather enjoyed it. I must have some duck in my composition for I always love to be out in a rainstorm. At tea-time Aunt Emily and Uncle John Montgomery arrived, likewise on their way to the Exhibition.

Friday, Oct. 8, 1891

It is a very weary little mortal who is trying to scribble in this old journal to-night. I have got to the Exhibition[2] and got home again—"which is the better fate the gods alone know." Lu and grandma and I drove ourselves in yesterday morning. When we got to Milton it began to rain and from

---

1. Cyrus Macneill (1829–1893), a contemporary of LMM's grandfather; son of James Macneill and Sarah Dockendorffer.

2. Annual fall fair at Charlottetown.

there into town it simply poured. We got to Uncle Chester's[1] about 9.30. It rained all day and naturally the effect was rather depressing. After dinner we drove out to the Exhibition grounds and hadn't too bad a time in spite of the weather. Lu and I stayed all night at Louisa McLeod's.[2] Her two nieces, Marian and Edith, are very nice girls. We had a fine time and no end of fun. To-day we spent shopping, started for home early and had a very cold drive.

Thursday, Oct. 13, 1891

After dinner to-day I set out for a ramble. The school woods are lovely now and I explored the old brook all over. Then I went away up to the Trouting Pool and through Lover's Lane.[3] The maples and birches that met overhead were pale yellow and green and the field beyond was encircled by little, fairy-like yellow birches. Somehow, all these things appeal to me more keenly this autumn than they ever did before. I enjoyed myself every minute of the time.

I spent the evening at Uncle John's playing parchesi.[4] Ella and Lem MacLeod—Lu's cousins from French River—were down and we had a very jolly evening.

Birches above the trouting pool

Friday, October 16, 1891

This morning Ella, Lem, Lu, and I went down to the shore. We went to the Hole in the Wall and back, and then along to Cawnpore[5] and up the sand hills. We had a jolly time but just as we got back to Cawnpore it began to rain and we had to hurry home at the rate of no-man's-business.

---

1. Youngest son of LMM's grandparents, born in 1856.

2. Louisa McLeod (1840–1924), an unmarried lady in Charlottetown, sister of Henry Collingwood MacLeod, a prominent Charlottetown banker (born in New London, and later General Manager of the Bank of Nova Scotia). Her nieces were a little younger than LMM and Lu: Edith, aged thirteen and Marian, aged twelve.

3. First mention of LMM's favourite walk, from the school house toward the home of David and Margaret Macneill.

4. From the Hindu *parchesi*: a board game similar to backgammon.

5. Section of the seashore named in memory of the siege of Cawnpore in India, 1857.

Sunday, Oct. 18, 1891
Cavendish, P.E. Island

After dinner to-day I went for another long ramble through the school woods and Lover's Lane. It is so lovely there. I had a charming time all through except for a scare I got with one of David Macneill's[1] cows, and having to skulk about the woods for nearly an hour while the Baptists were going through the lane to Sunday School in at their church. I do love rambling all alone by myself through the woods.

Monday, Oct. 19, 1891

After dinner Lu and I took all the apples we could carry and betook ourselves

Tree up which we scrambled

back to Lover's Lane. We had no end of fun, especially in scrambling up a big beech-tree after what we innocently took to be beech-nuts but which turned out to be only seed-cones of some kind. We went away out around David Macneill's back field to the Baptist church and home by the road.

I had a letter from Mr. Mustard to-day. It was as dry and poky as himself.

Thursday, Oct. 22, 1891

I finished writing a sketch of my trip home to-day and sent it to the *Patriot*. I have been working at it for a good while. I wrote it because Grandpa wanted me to.

This afternoon Lu and I set off for Sam Wyand's field, with a basket of apples. The "Intercolonial" is beautiful now and we found loads of delicious gum along it. When we got through we had some excitement dodging Laird's cows and climbing the breakneck fences that abound back there. We broke a longer on every fence we climbed to-day and sometimes more than one. The lane to the field is as pretty as ever and as is the dear old field as it lay bathed in amber sunshine, amid its crimson maple trees. We loitered around it for awhile and then went on. In the next field were Wyand's cows and as they

1.   David Macneill (b.1836), the elderly cousin whose home inspired Green Gables. His life dates appear in records of Cavendish cemetery, though not found in genealogical lists.

had an unfriendly look we had to make a wide detour through thick woods and over *awful* fences to avoid them. I don't know how it is that we have got to be such cowards over strange cows. We never used to be so. Finally we reached the fence below "Montana." It is one of old Mrs. John Wyand's construction so you may be sure we destroyed some of its symmetry in getting over it. Then we went up the path but when we reached the top—oh, horrors! There right before us were two cows and they *looked* simply savage. In a panic we turned and flew down that path headlong. We struck against the worst panel in the lot and over it went with a crash! We ran until we got to the corner. Such idiots! To go any further was out of the question for nothing could induce us to face those cows again. So we took to exploring all the fields around and had no end of fun in spite of the fences. Then we went back to Sam Wyand's field, sat down under the maples and demolished the rest of our apples. We had no end of a time getting home, in deadly fear of cows, and smashed some more fences of course.

Miss Gordon is going to get up another school concert for Xmas and wants all her old pupils to help in it also.

Tuesday, Nov. 3, 1891
Cavendish, P.E.I.

When the mail came to-day I got an invitation to a wedding—Uncle Cuthbert[1] Montgomery's, no less. He is to be married tomorrow night to Miss Mary McLeod. I have never met her. They say she is a very nice girl. It is high time Uncle Cuthbert was married. He is not overly young now.

Saturday, Nov. 7, 1891

Grandpa drove me up to Park Corner Wednesday morning. Just by Stanley we met a young man in a buggy who looked very intently at us as he passed but we took no account of the circumstances then. We got to Aunt Annie's in due time and after dinner I went over to the Senator's. Aunt Maggie Sutherland and Aunt Mary McIntyre were there, "baking and brewing and boiling and stewing." And now I discovered that the young man we had met was my cousin, James McIntyre on his way to Cavendish to bring me up. When he got back we had a hearty laugh over our hit—or missing. He is quite nice and nice-looking. When we went to Long River he drove me over.

---

1. Youngest child of Senator Montgomery, and youngest brother of Hugh John. LMM used his name as the surname of Marilla and Mathew in *AGG*.

It was a glorious evening and we had no end of fun. There was a white frost and a beautiful young moon "with the old one on her arm."

Grandpa Montgomery's house

The bride was dressed in white muslin with a tulle veil. Uncle Jim was best man and her sister, Miss Lizzie McLeod, was bridesmaid. In a few minutes Uncle Cuthbert had crossed his Rubicon[1] and I had a new aunt.

I must say the rest of the evening was frightfully dull. We just sat in a row around the parlor and stared at each other like simpletons. Nobody seemed to be acquainted with anybody else. I was very glad when it was all over. But Jim and I had another merry drive home through the keen starlit night.

Thursday was a glorious day. After dinner James and I started for a drive. We had no particular goal in view save to have a good time so we drove everywhere—in to Long River and then through to Clifton and down to Stanley by way of Campbelton. Then we drove back to Clifton, turned up a new road and followed it until we came to what we took for a branch road, so James told me to turn up it—I was driving "Plato" the lazy old gray horse. Such oceans of fun as we had over that horse! We went on and on and were so engrossed in an argument we were having that we never noticed where we were going until we suddenly discovered that our supposed road had developed into a perilously narrow and danger-strewn lane, leading to goodness knew where. This woke us up with a vengeance but turning was impossible so we had to keep on, and luckily we came out into a ploughed field where we were able to turn and then we went back down that lane at a fearful rate of speed. We went directly home then and got there after dark when half the guests had arrived. I dashed up the back stairs, gained my little room over the hall, and dressed against time. We had a fine time all the evening with games and the party did not break up until two. James brought me home yesterday and went into town to-day.

I have been reading my various printed articles over to-night. I wonder if I shall ever be able to do anything with my pen. Dr. Stovel assured me that I

---

1. Saying derived from the history of an Italian river that was the point of no return for Caesar in 49 BCE.

would but that was only a guess. If I could only manage to get a little more education! But that seems impossible. I wish I could peep into my future for a moment—and yet no! What if it were gloomy?

Monday, Nov. 16, 1891
Cavendish

This evening I went down to the school as we are beginning our practice for the concert. Dear me, it seemed at once so strange and yet so natural to be in that school again. But there were so many familiar faces missing—Charlie, Asher, John, Everett, Mollie, Ella, Mamie and Nate. Their seats were filled by a lot of "kids" who knew and cared nothing about those old days. We got underway with recitations and dialogues and made a fair start. Nellie is as cranky as ever.

Thursday, Nov. 19, 1891

This afternoon I went to see Mrs. Spurr and had a very nice time. She showed me Nate's class picture. He is not at all well taken. Still it is like him.

This evening after sunset I had a delicious ramble through the fields up to the spring grove. It was a heavenly evening. The sky was a most exquisite blending of creamy yellow, rose pink, heliotrope and silvery blue, with big stars blinking in and out. All was still, save for the low murmur of the brook and the rattle of a cart going down the hill road between the rows of slender spruces

The spring grove

that stood out in rich, dark beauty, like cloudy lace, against the bright sky. It was nature's vesper hour.

After dark to-night I set to work to study. I can't quite give up the hope that I may get to college yet and meanwhile I don't want to forget all I've learned. So I have mapped out a course of studies for the winter. To-night I began with English history, Physical Geography, Latin, geometry and English literature.

Thursday, Dec. 3, 1891

Spent this afternoon at Mollie's and had a fine time. We came over to prayer-meeting and sat with Pensie. Of course it was dreadful but Pen and I got to laughing at several things and stop we could not. We shook with smothered mirth the whole time. Fortunately we were away in the back seat so we escaped notice.

I had a letter from Mr. Mustard to-day. It was a frightfully dry epistle. He also sent me a Knox College magazine—very exciting literature!

Friday, Dec. 4, 1891

Everett Laird came down to the school to practice this evening. He is the "teacher" in our dialogue "The Country School." He is the same old Everett with his dry, funny remarks, and we had lots of fun. I was up to Literary to-night. There was a programme. I recited and played a couple of pieces—much to the rage of Deacon Arthur Simpson who hates me almost as much as he hates music. He hates music because he was born that way; and he hates me because I belong to a family who have never given any indication of thinking Deacon Arthur the most wonderful man in the world. The Deacon is known to irreverent young Cavendish as "Pa" and his pallid, malicious wife as "Ma" because of their habit of addressing each other thus upon all occasions. I think Arthur Simpson is the one and only man in the world I hate with an undiluted hatred. I hate him so much that it is nice and stimulating. And it is such fun to do things—perfectly innocent things which other people like, such as playing on the Hall organ etc.—which infuriate him!

Saturday, Dec. 19, 1891
Cavendish, P.E.I.

Really, it's a wonder I'm alive to tell the tale! In fact, I'm not quite sure I *am* alive—I'm so tired and stiff and generally petered out. We all met at the hall this morning to get it ready for our concert which is to come off Monday night. Lu and I went up early to find Ches and a good fire awaiting us. Most of the others soon arrived and we fell to work in good earnest. We first put up a big fir motto "Welcome" in the centre of the wall, high up, and decorated it with pink and white tissue roses. Then we put up another motto, "We Delight In Our School" and just as we were struggling with it along came Austin and Everett—and guess who else! Why, Jack himself—"Snap" in the flesh, home for his Xmas holidays from Prince of Wales. You may be sure we had an enthusiastic meeting. Jack is the same old sixpence. He is tall and slim and very nice-looking.

After we got the curtain hung we had a "dress rehearsal," and then finished with the decorations. On one side of the "Division" charter[1] we hung a Union Jack[2] and on the other a scarlet banner with a Latin motto "*Non scholae sed vitae discimus,*"[3] on it, ornamented with ferns and moss rosebuds. Then we put a triple arch of fir sprays over the banners and charter. Ches and I built this and were all puffed up with earthly pride over our success. Then everybody went home except Annie, Mamie, Everett, Ches and I. We cleaned things up, arranged the seats and swept the floor, raising a most tremendous dust in the process. Will Stewart came along about 8 with a buggy and drove us all home. We had a lively drive.

Tuesday, Dec. 22, 1891

Our wonderful concert is over and everyone, up to latest accounts, has survived. Yesterday was growly; it spit snow all day but cleared up beautifully at night. We had stacks of fun behind the curtain, peering out at the arrivals or prinking before the glass in our improvised dressing room. There was a good audience and the programme went off slickly. There wasn't a hitch or breakdown from beginning to end. Our dialogue brought down the house. I am glad it is so well over but I am sorry it is past. I shall feel quite lost having no pleasant practices to go to. We've had so much fun at them.

This evening I have been reading Washington Irving's "Sketch Book." He is delightful—his style is so easy and graceful. "Rip Van Winkle" is charming.

Thursday, Dec. 31, 1891

The old year did not slip away in a green twilight and a pinky-yellow sunset. Instead, it is going out in a wild, white bluster and blow. It doesn't seem possible that another year has gone. Taken all around, it has been a very happy year for me.

I am cosily tucked up in bed now, sitting up to write this. It is a wild night out—one of the nights when the storm spirit hustles over the bare frozen meadows and black hollows and the wind moans around the house like a lost soul and the snow drives sharply against the shaking panes—and people like to cuddle down and count their mercies.

---

1. Banner of the Temperance movement.
2. The British flag was the flag of Canada until 1965.
3. Latin motto: "We learn not for school but for life."

1892

Saturday, Jan. 9, 1892
Cavendish, P.E.I.

This afternoon was especially lovely—so mild and sunny. So Lu and I went on a gum-picking expedition. We first visited "the Intercolonial" and under its trailing arches drank in the resinous breath of the firs. Then we rambled along the wet edges of the woods, across Robertson's and Laird's farms. The sky was blue and scarfed with silken vapors. Around us lay moist, golden fields sleeping in the sunshine and sloping from where we stood in a gentle decline down to where the sea lay soft and hazy and blue. At last we brought up back of Charles Macneill's and thought it high time to speed homewards—which we did, having discovered what has long been a constant source of speculation—the location of Laird's cranberry swamp.

Tuesday, Jan. 10, 1892

I went to church this morning like a dutiful Presbyterian, and spent the afternoon and evening reading Emerson's Essays. To be interested in Emerson you must get right into the groove of his thought and keep steadily in it. Then you can enjoy him. There can be no skipping or culling if you want to get at his meaning. I admire and appreciate Emerson, although I do not always understand him—I suppose I am too young. His style is clear, precise, and cold, with all its beauty. I think his ideals are rather impracticable in this sort of a world. He doesn't seem to take "human nature" sufficiently into account.

What a difference there is between Emerson and Irving. Yet each is a fine writer in his own way. Emerson had the greater *intellect*, Irving the greater *heart*—"which is the better the gods alone know." But for my own part I go in for the *heart*. I like the jolly, *lovable* folks ten times better than the clever, brainy folks who are not lovable—and *livable*.

Friday. Afternoon. Feb. 13, 1892

Grandma went up to Park Corner last Tuesday and I've been head cook and chief bottle washer every since—not the most enviable position in the world where a man like grandfather is concerned. Nothing I do pleases him when grandma is away.

Last night was stormy and Lu came over with me from prayer-meeting to stay all night. We went to bed and were just dropping off to sleep when suddenly the kitchen door opened and a minute after I heard Uncle John asking if we were in bed. Grandpa called out "yes" and then Uncle J. said "There's two young McIntyres[1] from town stuck out here in a snow bank."

Lu and I sprang up, dressed and hastened out to get on a fire. I did not mind that in the least, but grandpa acted so crankily and disagreeably that I felt dreadfully bad. He is always so unjust and insulting when any of my friends come to the house and this time he was worse than I have ever seen him before.

Uncle John brought them in all covered with snow and it turned out that it was James McIntyre and some Mr. Mytton from town on their way to Uncle John's with a "trial" organ.[2] They had got upset in a snowdrift behind our barn. I was glad to see James, or would have been if I could have made him welcome. Mytton was a case! He was a thin little Englishman, dressed as if for a party in light summer clothes and patent leather shoes and he was half frozen.

We got them down to the fire and thawed them out. Grandpa had not got up at all and—although it was not just easy for me to arrange for them and show them to their room etc.—I was very thankful for this, for I knew he would only have made a show of himself if he had.

Finally, Lu and I got back to bed. We decided that we must get up at six in the morning to get breakfast for them and be on hand if they should wander down too early and fall into the clutches of grandfather. So we two geese determined to stay awake all night for fear that if we went to sleep we wouldn't wake early enough. Now *wasn't* that a brilliant idea! We lay and laughed for about two hours over Mytton—who had had a spasm of tooth-ache when he came in and who would have had a spasm of another kind if he had known all the fun we were making of him with the laudable purpose of keeping ourselves awake. Then, do our best, we began to get alarmingly sleepy, so we sat up, lit a candle and played parchesi until we were too cold to play anymore. Then we put out the light and fell to talking again. We extracted a good deal more fun out of Mytton and fought off our drowsi-ness heroically. I never knew I was asleep until I was conscious that it was broad daylight and that Lu was bending over me saying, "It's half past seven." Perhaps I didn't jump!

But fortunately the boys were not up. When they came down I had breakfast ready for them and although Grandpa was very surly to them he

---

1. First cousins, six children of Aunt Mary Montgomery McIntyre: Jim, Harry, Lewis, Cuthbert, Bertie, Laura.

2. A pump organ, sold on trial door-to-door for home entertainment. Pump or reed organs were developed in the 1870s and reached the height of popularity in the 1890s.

at least refrained from insulting them openly, as I had dreaded he would do. After breakfast he simply turned them out, for he told them to go on up to Stewart's[1] and they might sell their organ there. So they went and under the circumstances I was heartily relieved to see them go, for I felt bitterly mortified.

Nine O'Clock P.M.

Mollie came over this afternoon and we have had a jolly time. We are in bed just at present and Mollie is making herself useful as well as ornamental by holding my ink bottle for me as I write.

Tuesday, Feb. 16, 1892
Park Corner, P.E.I.

Here I am, a somewhat weary mortal. I have come up to give Clara, George and Stella a quarter's[2] music lessons. I rather guess we are going to have some fun. I am too dead tired to write anymore.

Uncle John Campbell's house

Thursday, Feb. 18, 1892

A delicious day and a delicious evening, mild and calm and creamy. I spent the afternoon at the Senator's, visiting Aunt Mary Cuthbert.[3] She is very nice and I like her very much. At tea-time James McIntyre and Mytton came along. Poor little Mytton. He isn't a bad sort, although everyone, myself included, seems disposed to poke fun at him. He is really quite intelligent.

There was a heavy white frost last night and the woods were dreams of fairy beauty this morning.

---

1. Alexander and Margaret Stewart and their family lived beyond the Baptist parsonage in one of the oldest farm homes in Cavendish.
2. Three months as music teacher to the Campbell cousins.
3. Mary McLeod (b. 1856), wife of LMM's uncle Cuthbert Montgomery.

Monday, Feb. 22, 1892
Park Corner

I'm really half dead from laughing. Clara and I talked most of the night last night. When the girls came home from school to-day we began to make and eat pancakes and we laughed until the pancakes nearly choked us. My head is splitting from the racket. It is all very foolish I suppose but it is delightful foolishness.

This New London[1] is really a dreadful place for gossip and "fights." "Eye hath not seen, nor ear heard, neither hath it entered into the heart of man to conceive" what the New Londoners, and especially the natives of that section of it known as French River, can do when they get started. Most of them seem to spend half their time deliberately inventing pure, unmixed fiction and the other half

Clara Campbell

in diligently circulating the same for Gospel truth. Every day I am treated to some harrowing account of a quarrel or a feud. Even Aunt and Uncle indulge entirely too much in gossip. I have vowed a deep and solemn vow that during my stay in Park Corner my conversation will be yea, yea, and nay, nay, only.

Saturday, Feb. 27, 1892

Although it was freezing cold to-night Cade, Stell and I went to the Literary Society in French River Hall.[2] Quite a crowd was there. Capt. Geo. McLeod came up to me and we had quite a talk. He asked me for a recitation for their programme and then paid me some compliments on my writings—"told me to be sure and keep on." Ta-ta, Capt. George, that is just what I mean to do.

Then we drifted into an interesting discussion about books, especially "Robert Elsmere"[3] which is setting the literary world by the ears just now. As I have not read it Capt. George got it out of the library for me.

---

1. In LMM's day, New London was the name for the area 8 miles (14 km) west of Cavendish, containing Park Corner, French River, Clifton, and other towns.

2. A village lying northwest of the New London Bay.

3. Bestselling novel of 1888 by Mrs. Humphrey Ward preaching social Christianity and downplaying miraculous elements.

Cade and I sat together. Edwin Simpson[1] sat right across from us. He is attending school here and although we've never been introduced I've seen him several times and heard a good deal of him. He is very nice-looking and has fine eyes.

Midway in the programme was a "social intermission," in which everybody talked. Lem McLeod[2] came over to me and we had a nice little chat. Also Edwin S. came up and spoke to me. I had a nice time all round.

Sunday, Feb. 28, 1892

This has been a very lazy Sunday. It was too cold to go to church, so after breakfast Cade[3] and I betook ourselves upstairs and went to bed again, where we talked and napped till dinner time. We got up then, helped devour a roast goose, went back to bed and slept till tea-time.

We are going to have a grand racket[4] next Saturday, roads and weather permitting. Aunt Emily[5] has invited us all, and also Ed Simpson, Irving Howatt, Jean Howatt,[6] Mort Howatt and Jack Sims to go up for a visit. We have had a great time arranging everything but I think all the details are settled now—if only Jack's mare's leg gets well in time.

Stella and I slept together last night and such fun as we had. We laughed until after midnight.

Friday, Mar. 4, 1892
Park Corner, P.E.I.

Here's a mess! A huge thaw is on and the bottom has fallen out of the roads. Cade is sick with a cold and Ed S. also, so rumour runs. Bother the luck! I'm cross and snappy and disappointed.

---

1. A second cousin from Belmont who had been a teacher in Bideford and was now at school in Park Corner, preparing for college.

2. Lemuel McLeod (1875–1937) came from a large French River family, including Theophilus, Beatrice, and Evaline.

3. Nickname of Clara Campbell (1877–1932), eldest of the four cousins.

4. Island slang: a sociable time.

5. Aunt Emily (1856–1927), younger sister of LMM's mother, married to John Montgomery of Malpeque.

6. Irving and Jean Howatt, Jack Sims, and others mentioned in the 1892 entries appear in a photograph "Park Corner Scholars, 1892," below, p. 119. Jack Sims (1872–1945) was in LMM's class at Prince of Wales College.

Monday, Mar. 7, 1892

Neither Cade nor I slept ten consecutive minutes Friday night. At five George and Stella rushed in, woke us, then went down to light the fire. Clara and I were just beginning to pry our eyes open when Stella again appeared and exclaimed tragically, "Our joy is all over! It is pouring rain!"

Well, we were a pretty blue lot. Then we rushed to the other extreme— laughed, danced, made all the queer speeches we could think of, sang comic songs, and parodied "We won't go home till the morning" in the following striking fashion

> It's pouring rain in the morning,
> It's pouring rain in the morning,
> It's pouring rain in the morning
> And we'll stay home to-day.

Meanwhile, it *was* pouring rain, and it didn't "clear up at sunrise" either, as we had fondly hoped. Clara tried to make the porridge but she had no salt and she let it burn, so at last she gave it up and went to playing parchesi with George, while Stella and I tried to make some toast and burned that also.

After breakfast Stell and I resolved to make the best of the business and have some fun at home. So we pitched into the work and had it all done by ten. Then Clara and I set to work to overseam[1] a couple of blankets. Getting hungry in the process, we put some slices of pork ham and a couple of eggs in the oven to bake for a snack. When it was cooked Cade took it out and set it on top of the oven to cool a bit. Suddenly George burst into shouting, "Girls, Ed Simpson's coming."

We rushed into the room and looked down the lane. Sure enough, he was. We made a wild dash up the stairs, dragging our blankets behind us, and screaming out "Hide the pork—hide the pork," to Aunt Annie! In the bedroom we collected our wits and sent Stell down to explore. She came back and reported Ed anxious to go, as he couldn't go next Saturday. There was confusion in the house of Campbell for a spell, but at last we decided to go and posted George off on horseback to tell the Howatts. Jack Sims was too far away to get word to, so we regretfully concluded we'd have to go without him. When Howatts came we got dinner for all hands. Clara and I, being too excited to eat in regular fashion, got away in the pantry and stayed our stomachs with our cold pork and eggs.

Then we started—Stella and Irv, Clara and George and Mort, Jeannine and Ed and I. It had stopped raining and we were a merry procession although

---

1. Making a French seam when joining narrow widths of woven wool cloth, so that no raw edges appear.

the roads were something fearful. We had some trouble in finding the right road to the ice but we got over all right and after innumerable twists we came in sight of Uncle John Montgomery's barns. Then our troubles began! There were half a dozen cross-lot roads[1] and, as luck would have it, we choose the wrong one. It turned out to be merely a wood-road and presently we found ourselves in a wilderness of stumps. We all turned around and Irv's and our sleighs got out all right, but George's runner caught on a stump, broke in two, and the whole bottom fell out of the sleigh. Such a smash-up you never saw!

The boys unharnessed the mare, Mort got on her back, Clara got in with Irv and Stell, Geo. crawled in on the bottom of our sleigh, and off we started again. At a little house inhabited by a family of Murphys[2] we stopped to inquire about the road. A red-headed woman and an alarming number of children rushed out to inform us and at last we got right again. Next thing we came to a fence gap where the snow was deep and soft. George made the front too heavy, down went the sleigh and snap went something. I thought it was our runner too and promptly relieved my feelings by a scream; but it proved to be only a broken trace. We all scrambled out in the slush, Ed replaced his trace with one of George's and off we went once more. This time we did manage to make harbor at Uncle John's, although we were all nearly engulfed going through a huge pond of water in Uncle Edward Montgomery's field.

Back view of Uncle John Montgomery's house at Princetown

We had a jolly enough time at Uncle John's to atone for all our tribulations. We spent the afternoon and evening playing games of all sorts and Uncle J.—who is the most comical soul alive—kept us all in roars of laughter. At eleven we went to bed. Cade and I slept in the room above the kitchen and when we went upstairs Uncle John came too and get rid of him we couldn't. He just carried on, and we laughed until the tears ran down our faces. At last, however, he took himself off to torment the boys and we went to bed.

Sunday was fine although the roads were still bad, and we went to church. Getting back, we had a spluxious[3] turkey dinner then sat around the table till three o'clock, while Uncle J. kept us laughing straight on. At

---

1. Across adjacent lots or fields, as a short-cut.
2. A Park Corner farm family, settled there since 1798; in LMM's childhood Mrs. Murphy had worked for her grandmother Montgomery.
3. A neologism: splendid and luxurious? No dictionary definition.

last we regretfully decided that we must leave, so home we came. We had a most merry ride and lost our road only about half a dozen times. We got home at dark, pretty nearly tired to death, and have been all day getting over our racket.

I am invited to a wedding next Wednesday night. Uncle Jim Montgomery is to be married to Mrs. Eliza Johnson of Clifton.[1]

Thursday, Mar. 10, 1892
Park Corner, P.E.I.

I feel so sleepy I don't know whether I can write connectedly or not. Yesterday it poured rain but after dinner I went over to the Senator's. James McIntyre was out and drove me over to Clifton. Quite a long procession of us went and such roads I never was on before. We went by the ice, although it was very bad, and passed over some pretty risky places. Just below Clifton we were brought to a dead stop by open water ahead. So we had to turn and go all the way back to Anderson's, where we took the road again and it was wilder than ever. But we got over at last and had a very pleasant evening. Addie Johnson was bridesmaid and James McIntyre was best man.

At eleven we all started for Park Corner and came around by the Long River road. I shall never forget that awful drive as long as I live. The night was pitchy dark and our horse did nothing but rear and plunge and balk in the slush and soft snow, falling down now and then by way of variation. I got deathly sick from sheer nervous terror and was almost demoralized by the time we got to the Senator's. However, after I had recovered, I had a fine time. We had tea and played games for several hours. As the Clifton people could not go back before daylight there were not enough beds in the house to go around so Jim McIntyre, Jim Crosby, Lewis McIntyre, Russell Crosby, Will Sutherland,[2] Louise Crosby[3] (all cousins of mine), Addie Johnson and I said we'd sit up the rest of the night in the parlor. We sat around the fire, told ghost stories galore, and kept up a racket of jest and laughter all night. When morning dawned we were a pretty seedy-looking lot. I nearly fell asleep at the breakfast table and I actually did at prayers. After breakfast I came straight over home and went to bed—never woke up until 4 o'clock and then felt as if I wanted to sleep half a dozen weeks longer. However, a wild frolic with Clara this evening has pretty well wakened me up.

1. Village south of Park Corner. This was LMM's birthplace and is now part of New London.
2. First cousins Will, John, and others: children of Aunt Margaret Montgomery Sutherland.
3. First cousins Jim, Russell, and Louise: children of Aunt Jane Montgomery Crosby.

Saturday, Mar. 12, 1892
Park Corner, P.E.I.

I was over to the Senator's to-day. My new Aunt Eliza was very nice to me. But there doesn't seem to be over much cordiality between the two brides. Uncle Cuthbert is going to build on his own farm next spring. I am sorry—I should like to see Aunt Mary mistress in the old place. She would fill the position much better than Aunt Eliza, unless Dame Rumour belies the latter.

This evening the girls and I went down to our pet dissipation, "Literary."[1] They had a debate on that venerable conundrum. "Which was the greater general, Napoleon or Wellington!" Wellington carried the day and then we adjourned. When Clara and I got out Lem McLeod asked us if he and Jack Sems might drive us home. They had a nice comfy pung so we scrambled in, along with Jim Crosby who invited himself, and had a merry drive of it.

Wednesday, Mar. 16, 1892

A glorious day this—mild and sunny; moreover, it has been one of those rare ones when everything goes exactly right and life seems bright and serene. This morning I took a walk through the woods down to the spring—the loveliest spot. Oh, it was all so beautiful! The calm, fresh loveliness of the woods seemed to enter into my very spirit with voiceless harmony—the harmony of clear blue skies, mossy trees and gleaming snow. All the little fears and chafings shrank into nothing and vanished. Standing there beneath that endless blue dome, deep with the breathing of universal space, I felt as if all the worlds had a claim on my love—as if there were nothing of good I could not assimilate—no noble thought I could not re-echo. I put my arm around a lichened old spruce and laid my cheek against its rough side—it seemed like an old friend.

Aet. 17 [L.M. Montgomery, age 17][2]

---

1. Like Cavendish, New London's long-established society presented debates and lectures by visiting authorities.

2. "From Latin *Aetatis*, meaning "of age.""

Saturday, Mar. 26, 1892

Uncle Cuthbert, Aunt Mary and I went down to Cavendish this morning and had a lovely drive. We came back this evening and stopped off at the hall for Literary. We had quite a nice little programme and Ed Simpson walked home with me. Such a time as we had! The girls and George and the Hiltzes[1] and Jim Crosby and Lucy Pickering[2] kept behind us all the way and tormented our lives out. I'm sure Ed must have been secretly furious. We talked about books etc. all the way home and pretended to ignore the racket behind. I don't know whether I like Ed or not. He is clever and can talk about everything, but he *is* awfully conceited—and worse still, *Simpsony*. To anyone who knows the Simpsons a definition of that quality is unnecessary; and to anyone who doesn't it is impossible.

Sunday, Mar. 27, 1892

Irving Howatt came up this morning to take us girls down to preaching at the English church.[3] Just as we were starting George kicked up a fuss because he wanted to go and take a rig and had no one to go with him. To appease him I went with him, though I felt more like spanking the young cub.

Coming home from church, just as we passed Cameron's house at French River, George exclaimed "There's Amanda Macneill." I jumped up just in time to see her wave her hand to me from the window. We brought Jean and Annie Howatt home to dinner and had lots of fun through the afternoon. In the evening Irv took Clara and me to Long River preaching. Mollie was there and we had a long confab and I heard all the Cavendish news.

Saturday, Apr. 9, 1892
Park Corner

We had a hooking[4] here to-day and Jean and Annie Howatt, Edie Pillman, Hannah, Beatrice and Eveline MacLeod, Blanch and Mrs. Donald, Sue Stewart, Mamie Cameron and Josie Hiltz were here. We had such fun. In the evening we all went down to Literary and the walking was simply dreadful. The first

---

1. Josephine Hiltz (1878–1939) was one of the children in Park Corner school photo.
2. Lucy B.M. Pickering, born 1874 and thus an exact contemporary of LMM; daughter of William Pickering, who was born in New London but moved west to the Bideford area.
3. Anglican (Episcopalian) church in the bride's village.
4. A women's party or "bee," where friends get together to create rugs by cutting very narrow strips of cotton or wool from worn-out clothing and then hooking the strips to a burlap backing, following a pattern drawn onto the backing.

Second grade in Park Corner School. Back row: Mr. McIntyre, Clara Campbell, Louise Crosby, Addie McLeod, Jack Sims, Edwin Simpson, Bessie Cameron, Stanley Bernard, Josie Hiltz, Lem McLeod, Irving Howatt. Middle Row: Mamie Cameron, Stella Campbell, Hannah McLeod, Nettie Palmer, unknown, Beatrice McLeod, Unknown, Edie Pillman. Front row: George Campbell, Mel Donald, Unknown, Ev McLeod, Annie Howatt, Kate Bernard, Jean Howatt.

thing at Literary was a big "row" between Captain George and Albert Simpson over some constitutional clause. They squabbled until nearly nine and we didn't get out till ten. It was pitch dark and the mud was awful. Stell and I were standing by the steps when Lem came slyly up. I made some original remark about the mud and he made some brilliant comment on the rain; then he managed to get up enough spunk to ask if he might see me home and we slipped away. We came home a different way from the others and had lots of fun. Lem is a rather nice, jolly boy but there's nothing much in him.

Friday, April 27, 1892
Park Corner

I have been having a very jolly time of late but at present I am laid up with a bad cold. I won't be able to go to Literary tomorrow night and I am more than vexed, for by all accounts there is going to be a lively "row." The French River people have tasted blood and fur will certainly fly.

Mr. McIntyre, the teacher here, was telling me to-night a good thing that an old shoemaker named Hamilton once said. Somebody told him that, according to newspaper reports, the devil's footprints had been seen in Missouri! "It's a lie!" exclaimed old Hamilton. "To my personal knowledge the devil hasn't been out of French River for the last 24 years!"

Excellent! His Satanic Majesty is getting in his fine work down there just now.

Monday, May 2, 1892

We are daily expecting Theophilus MacLeod up here to spend his vacation. This MacLeod is quite a "famosity" round here. He was a music teacher here for some time, and seems to have considerable mastery, not only in music but in the noble art of setting people by the ears. His "disciples" as they call themselves—Howatts, MacLeods and Uncle John's in especial—are ready to swear *by* him, and his enemies—the Bernards, Simpsons etc.—are ready to swear *at* him. I have met him once or twice but can't say I liked him at all. There seemed to me to be something very peculiar about the man. But they absolutely worship him here. Certainly he's not a commonplace individual, whatever else he is.

The girls and I had a fine game of ball to-night. I thought back vividly to my mind the dear old C. schooldays and the glorious games of ball we used to have.

Thursday, May 5, 1892

After dinner Stell and I took a pail and went back to the marsh to gather cowslips[1] for greens. We didn't get any cowslips—it seems to be too early for them—but we did have a perfectly glorious time. It is a lovely place—a boggy soil green with the greenest of marshy hillocks, with a silvery brook meandering through it, and spruces all a trail with gray-green mosses, their roots overgrown with all sorts of woodland lovelinesses—tiny ferns and June-bell[2] vines and golden moss. We explored it for hours.

Friday, May 6, 1892

There was preaching in the French River Hall to-night and we all went. When we came out Lem and Ed were both standing before the steps. I would gladly have sneaked away from them both if possible but Ed was too quick for me and asked if he might see me home before I could slip past the corner of the hall. We had a pleasant enough walk home and talked of everything talkable, I believe. The night was as cold as Greenland and the northern lights[3] were as bright as the moon.

---

1. A low-growing spring wildflower, usually yellow; related to the primula (primrose).
2. Perhaps lily of the valley. A localism, not in dictionary.
3. Aurora borealis, a curtain of light in the northern sky.

Saturday, May 7, 1892

Literary to-night and everybody and his brother were there. First and foremost the powers that be had another lively skirmish which occupied so much time that the programme was cut severely short. Meanwhile, I was wondering how I could escape from Lem and Ed—for it makes so much gossip when there are two of them trying to rival each other in that fashion, and besides I am sick and tired of being teased about them. So I made up my mind to rush right out the moment Literary adjourned and get away up the road before the boys could get out. Accordingly, I made a dive for the door—but so did everyone else apparently and I found myself packed in a crowded, squirming mess below the stove. I pushed frantically on, flattering myself that I was far ahead of the boys, when I discovered Lem right behind me and Ed right beside me. I was as mad as a wasp. I made another wild effort to get through the crowd and as a result got jammed in between the two of them! But at last we got to that blessed door. I clutched Clara's arm, bolted headlong down the steps, and gained the road in safety. But I hadn't got my breath before Lem had caught up with us, he gasped out a request to see me home and whisked me off before I could answer yea or nay. Since it had to be one of them I was glad it was Lem. Ed is much cleverer but somehow I never feel at ease in his company. Lem and I had lots of fun coming home, although the crowd of factory boys[1] on the road kept up a terrific racket just behind us.

Saturday, May 14, 1892
Park Corner, P.E.I.

After tea Cade and I went back to the swamps for cowslips. We got a pailful and we deserved to, for we had a wild time, scrambling and crawling and jumping over roots and bogs. But we had such fun and it is such a lovely place.

Wednesday, May 18, 1892

O-o-o-o!!! "From Greenland's icy mountain."[2] I'm positive the north pole can't be very far off. But after all, never mind, as long as we don't freeze to death.

---

1. Workers at Sawyer's lobster cannery at the mouth of the French River.
2. Mission hymn by Bishop Heber (1819).

Summer will come again,
Roses will bloom again,
Friends will all meet again,
By and by.[1]

Will they, I wonder!

To-day Cade and I, having nothing better to do, set to work and invented nicknames more or less appropriate for all the boys of our acquaintance. Lem is "The Elm Tree," from his initials; Ed is "The Dancing Master"—because nothing else could be so little like him—Jack Sims is "Jessie," also from his initials, Stanley Bernard is "The Saint" from the first two letters of his name, Irv Howatt is "The Quaker," from a certain broad-brimmed black hat he wears—Howe Pillman is "The Doctor," Stewart Cameron is "Shakespeare," Archie Pickering is "The Monkey" and George is "Butter and Eggs"—because of his fondness for those articles. The fun of this is that we can drive the others wild with curiosity talking about these mysterious folks.

The wonderful Theophilus MacLeod arrived to-day and is being bowed down to and worshipped by his satellites—among whom I am *not*. I do not like the man—but he is a mystery.

Saturday, May 21, 1892

Went to Literary to-night and had such fun. When Literary went in they had another big fight. It was simply disgraceful the way they went on and I never was so sick of anything in my life. After they stopped wrangling there was a lengthy programme of three and then they "adjourned," as they call the rush and scramble that always ensues after that announcement. Lem walked home with me and we had a very jolly walk. When we got here I asked him in and he came. MacLeod and all the rest were sitting in the kitchen when we entered and I have no doubt we were a precious silly-looking couple. However, nothing was said and we all sat down and fell to discussing that abominable Literary squabble in all its pros and cons. Then Aunt Annie spread us one of her suppers and we ate and drank—whether to the glory of God I know not—and neither does Theophilus MacLeod.

---

1. From "A Song of Farewell," by Dora Greenwell (1821–82), which appeared in many school anthologies

Sunday, May 22, 1892
Park Corner, P.E.I.

The first thing I heard when I came down stairs this morning was that Lem had stolen Uncle John's boots, left a grubbing fork under the stove and spilled a package of hayseed all over the pantry! That is a sample of what I have had to endure all day.

I expect to go home next week and I am real sorry. I know I will be horribly lonesome. I have had such a lovely time since I came here and I'll miss the girls and all our jolly rackets so much.

It is one of the most heavenly evenings imaginable. I am writing here on the front doorstep drinking in the fresh beauty of the young earth. The sky is

The "front door." Park Corner.

blue, blue, blue, with long veils of filmy vapor scarfing it; the birches are a misty green against the darker spruces, the grass is like velvet, the robins are fluting vespers, and the frogs are singing sweet and sad down in the pond. Dear old world you are very lovely and I love you. I am glad to be alive in you.

Wednesday, June 1, 1892

Stella and I had the greatest fun to-day hunting in the orchard for four-leaved clovers.[1] We agreed whoever found the first was to receive a present from the other. We crawled and re-crawled over that orchard and were just going to give up in despair when I found one—the dearest little one you ever saw. Then we hunted another hour for a five and Stell found one.

The orchard at Park Corner

Saturday, June 6, 1892

Literary night again. On our way down we met Lem bowling along in a buggy behind a dashing gray horse. He took us in and we went for a drive and had great fun. Literary was very quiet to-night and Lem and I had a splendid moonlight drive afterwards.

---

1.   Legendary bringers of good luck: about one in 10,000 clovers develop four-leaved forms.

Tuesday, June 7, 1892

I feel rather disgruntled to-night. We went to prayer meeting at French River to-night and as I'm going home to-morrow I wanted to have a nice little racket to finish up with. Ella Johnson of Long River and her cousin Dan McKay were there and when we came out they came up and offered to drive me home. I didn't want to go because I could see Lem waiting out on the moonlit road, but I had no excuse for not going. Or rather, to refuse to go and then to walk home with Lem would have seemed too silly. So I assented reluctantly for very shame's sake. Lem waited till the very last and I'm sure he would be vexed when he saw me drive away with Ella and Dan. I'm not a bit "struck" on Lem and I don't care about this on that account; but we have been good friends and have had lots of fun together this spring, and I wanted to have a farewell walk to-night and say good-bye decently by way of a pleasant wind-up; but it's all spoiled now.

Monday, June 20, 1892
Cavendish, P.E.I.

I've been home ever since the 8th. I was dreadfully lonesome at first but I am getting over it now and beginning to enjoy myself again. I went to prayer meeting to-night—Mr. Archibald is holding revival meetings now—and as Pensie and I were too early we went for a walk to the school where we crawled in at a window and enjoyed a good long chat about various matters. Miny Robertson passed and we called her in too. We saw a crowd of boys coming up the hill and had to lie low till they passed for we didn't want them to see us. Then, afraid we would be too late we rushed to the window, flung it up, and Miny and I sprang out. "Hold the sash," cried Pen—but she let go and jumped before we could catch it. It came down with a fearful bang and a piece split clear out of one of the panes; besides, nearly all the putty fell off. If the trustees get on our trail they'll make us repent in sack cloth and ashes.

Friday, June 21, 1892

Who should pop in for the mail to-day but—Nate? I ran out to see him, feeling silly—but I didn't let him see I felt so. He hasn't changed a bit except that he has grown a lot taller. He doesn't expect to be home long. Jack Laird is also home from town. It's such fun to see the boys again and have a good chat over old times.

Wednesday, June 22, 1892

I took a prowl away back to Montana this morning, to see if there was going to be any strawberries. I had a lovely walk.

Went to prayer-meeting this evening, met Pen, and we again went down to the school. We didn't go in but leaned against the north-east window for some time, talking about a lot of little matters dear to our hearts. Presently we heard a buggy coming up the hill and as we didn't want to be seen we pushed up the window to get in and hide. And then—well, I just didn't know whether I stood on my heels or my head, for there in the corner stood Miss Gordon!!! All the nonsense Pen and I had talked flashed back in naked horror over my mind. She must have heard every word we said. But I think she felt as foolish as we did at being caught. Whatever could she have been there for, all alone—and it was as dark as anything! We talked lamely to her for a few minutes to hide our confusion, and then went, gasping at each other up the road, laughing and lamenting by turns, and thanking our stars that among all the things we *had* said, we had *not* said anything about her and Geo. R. Macneill, who is going with her. I suppose we *would* have come to them sooner or later, if it hadn't have been for that providential buggy coming up the hill.

I wish Junius Simpson *would* clear his throat out before he begins to pray. Perhaps one could make out a word once in a while then, and anyhow he'd get through quicker.

Jack Laird came home with me and we had a jolly chat. College has smartened Jack up a good bit and he is very nice, although there is not a great deal in him.

Wednesday, June 29, 1892
Cavendish, P.E.I.

I spent this afternoon at Pensie's. The Baptist missionary concert came off to-night and Alec took Pensie and me in. The church was crowded but of course the concert wasn't wildly exciting. Missionary concerts are not apt to be I suppose. I passed most of the time looking out of the open window beside me and watching the play of shadows under the spruce trees. What a mysterious tree the spruce is! It always seems to be brooding over some secrets of the past—always

Under the trees by Baptist Church

wrapped in solitary majesty, a hermit among trees. The evening breeze blew past the window and the drooping branches swayed slowly, lingeringly, sadly to its breath. Whenever I watch the spruces, especially in the dim twilight, they have a strange influence over me. All the happy memories of old days come back to me, all the vague, sweet hopes and illusions of childhood seem real to me once more.

Thursday, June 30, 1892

Miss Gordon was here this evening to say good-bye. She is going to Oregon. Oh, how sorry I am to part with her! I have lost a true friend—the only one in Cavendish who sympathized with me in my ambitions and efforts. I shall miss her dreadfully and I feel too blue to write anything more about anything.

Friday, July 1, 1892

After tea tonight Lu and I went back to Montana and had a lovely walk. There are lots of berries. We had got our jugs nearly full when a heavy shower came up. We raced for the "C.P.R." and tore frantically down it under the wet branches but by the time we reached the end we were as wet as we could be. We had to wade through five dripping hayfields on our way home, so you can imagine what a state we were in. It has cleared up now and is a perfect evening with a blue sky and a pale little ghost of a moon, a fresh breeze, and golden brown sunshine on the green hillsides.

Sunday, July 17, 1892

Murray is here for his vacation and yesterday he and Lu and I drove over to New London. I had a scrumptious time. Grandpa Montgomery was telling me that he had met Lieutenant-Governor Schultz[1] of the Territories in Ottawa and that he had read my article on Saskatchewan and admired it very much, and he told grandpa to ask me for my photo and anything I might have written since! Quite a compliment for little me, isn't it?

In the evening we all went down to Literary. The meeting didn't amount to much but I had lots of fun foregathering with old friends. When we went out Lem appeared. I shook hands and said "How do you do?" *very* demurely. He walked home with me and we had lots of fun. When we turned in at Uncle

---

1.   (Sir) John Christian Schultz had been a prisoner of the Métis during the Red River Rebellion.

Johns' gate we saw a dark figure wriggling up the bank under the trees and few feet further on we were brought to a stand by a stout rope stretched across the road. Evidently George and Jim Gains, the hired boy, had been at their old tricks. There was no breaking this, as we had broken a cord once before but Lem was equal to the occasion. "Don't move," he whispered. "Wait a minute." Before I guessed what he meant to do he had cut the rope with a stroke of his pocket knife and we passed on as if it were all in the day's work.

We came home this evening.

Friday, July 22, 1892
Cavendish, P.E.I.

After sunset this evening Murray, Lu and I started off for a walk with no particular object in view save to have a good time anyway that might turn up. I do not go looking for good times with Murray by choice, for he has a tendency to rather spoil good times, unless he is the centre of them, with everybody else revolving around him, like obedient and adoring little Satellites. I am not one of his satellites and consequently I am no favorite of his. Lu is, because she flatters him to the top of his head—and then ridicules him behind his back. He eats up the flattery and is happily ignorant of the ridicule.

We went in along the road. It was a lovely twilight, cool and breezy, with tones of blue and amber, green and gold, threading its dusk.

We went as far as the Baptist church and then came back. On the hill a sulky[1] passed us with Don McKay and Jack Laird on it. Jack is teaching school at North Rustico now. At the foot of the hill Jack sprang off and joined us. We all stood there about half an hour and laughed and chatted—at least Jack and Lu and I did, while Murray glowered in silence. To Murray, it was a deadly insult that any girls, even one he disliked, should take any notice of another boy when HE was around. Finally Jack and I came home by the road, while Lu and Murray went across the fields. It was very jolly to be walking up that old road with Jack again. We talked over all our old rackets and school jokes, and had a fine time.

Saturday, July 30, 1892

Little twilight "rackets" are the order of the day now. Mollie came over for the mail at dusk and we took a walk in along the road. On our way back

---

1. A two-wheeled carriage with a single seat.

Jack pounced out on us from among the trees, as suddenly as his namesake in a box and came along with us. We both went home with Mollie and had fine fun. Then Jack and I came back in the moonlight and Jack began to simmer; but the more sentimental *he* got the more saucy and independent I got. When he said he "loved" me I laughed at him so much that he got sulky and sulked for ten minutes. Then, seeing that *that* didn't worry me any he got friendly and sensible again. Jack doesn't "love" me any more than I love him. It was just the moonlight.

Monday, Aug. 1, 1892

I had to turn out early this morning and help take in a load of hay. I rather enjoyed it though. The air was so fresh and cool and everything looked so lovely in the early morning. Cavendish is so pretty now. The rich, ripe beauty of August is as fair as the first blush of dawning summer. The hayfields are golden-brown, the grainfields are a pale, creamy green, and the woods are dark and deep-tinted.

Wellington and David Nelson
and their sister

Who do you think came after dinner? Why, Well and Dave Nelson![1] You may be sure I was glad to see them. Well has changed very much and has grown stout but not tall. Dave has changed less in the face but has shot up into a slim, leggy fellow. We had no end of fun revisiting the scenes of our early life together and recalling the events, comic and tragic, of our lang-syne playdays.

Scene of our playhouse

Wellington and David Nelson were two orphan boys who boarded here and went to school, when I was seven to ten. Well was just my age, Dave a year younger. We used to have splendid times together.

The first summer they were here we built a little playhouse in the spruce wood, north of our front orchard and

---

1. Wellington and David Nelson, like the fictional characters Bev and Felix in *The Story Girl* (1911), came from Toronto to live briefly in PEI.

we kept it up as long as they stayed here. The house was in a little circle of young spruces. Those poor little trees—how hacked and barked and nail-holed they were! We built our "house" by driving stakes into the ground between the trees and lacing spruce boughs in and out. I remember having frequently excited Well's admiration by my knack of filling up obstreperous holes in our verdant castle. One summer Well proudly manufactured a door for our house. I shall never forget that door and our huge pride in it. It was a very rickety affair—three rough, irregular boards nailed uncertainly across two others and hung to a long suffering birch tree by means of ragged leather hinges cut out of old boots. The tree is there yet and so are the bits of leather, all over-grown with lichen. But alas, that beautiful door, as precious in our eyes as the Gate Beautiful of the temple was to the Jews of old, is not in exist-ence. I suppose some vandal hand finally chopped it up for kindling woods.

Then we had a little garden, our pride and delight, albeit it rewarded all our labor very meagrely. We planted "live-forevers" around all the beds, and they grew as only live-forevers *can* grow. For that matter, they are growing there yet. They were almost the only things that did grow. Our carrots and parsnips,our lettuce and beets, our phlox and sweet peas either failed to come up at all, or dragged a pallid, spindling existence to an ignoble end, in spite of all our patient digging, manuring, weeding and watering—or per-haps because of it, for I fear we were more zealous than wise. But we worked persistently and took our consolation out of a few hardy sunflowers which, sown in an uncared for spot, throve better than all our petted darlings and lighted up the spruce wood with their cheery golden lamps. I remember we were in great tribulation because our beans persisted in coming up with their skins over their heads. We promptly picked them off, generally with disastrous consequences to the beans.

Occasionally we had picnics there—gala festivals those. One in particu-lar I remember. While we were eating a shower of rain came up. The thick bough roof overhead kept us dry, but a few big drops splashed down on our banquet board—a board literally as well as figuratively, for our tables and seats were the work of our unskilled hands. We laughed so much that we could hardly eat. We had a little plate with three cakes on it—one apiece—and Dave, in trying to grab more than his share, upset his cup of milk over everything. Then we had one of those heaven-blessed gales of laughter that come only to children.

A few feet from our mansion were two diminutive spruces and, having one day found in the woods two pieces of rotten rope we tied them together and rigged up a swing on the aforesaid spruces. We had a good deal of fun out of it, too, until its calamitous end. One evening Well and I were both swinging on it when it suddenly broke and we fell in a heap on mother earth.

One summer grandpa put us up a real swing in the bush behind the well and "high old times" we had there. One summer Dave broke his leg while home for vacation at his grandfather Mutch's in South Rustico and was away a whole month during which Well and I ran things to suit ourselves. Out by the swing, was an old green boat, called "Daisy Dean," turned upside down. On, and under, this boat we played a game of "housekeeping" in which Well was my "mistress" and I was his "servant"—a rather curious arrangement but one which worked exceedingly well. I did all the work (?) while he looked on, gave orders, and now and then condescended to help. One day, when I had just finished covering the floor of our "parlor"—i.e. the space under the boat, with a beautiful fresh, green carpet of newly gathered "chicken weed," I said to Well, remembering that the labourer is worthy of his hire,

"Now, when I work so hard for you you ought to praise me a little. Just say, as if you were talking to a visitor, 'I have such a good servant. She does everything I tell her and does it well.'"

Wellington, without moving an eyelash, immediately addressed an imaginary visitor.

"I have such a bad servant. She can't do anything right and she won't obey my orders."

I had a fortunate sense of humor, even then, so I sat down, with my hands full of "chicken wood" and laughed until I cried.

When Dave came back we returned to our playhouse and service on the "Daisy Dean" was forgotten. I remember we ruthlessly hacked all the tender boughs off all the young spruces we could find for our "walls" until grandfather grew so angry with us that he very nearly put a summary stop to our building operations altogether.

One summer we decided to make two new garden beds, as our old one was too full of birch roots to be easily worked. So we made them and carried baskets of manure to them for a whole day and then dragged home loads of pebbles from the shore for borders. Doubtless some of those pebbles are there yet for Dave, under the impression that there was no use in doing things by halves, dug a hole and buried a lot of them in the middle of a bed—to make a firm foundation for an ornamental pile of them on top, as he explained.

When they came here the boys, although brought up in a nominally Christian family, were veritable little heathen, knowing almost nothing about God or a future state. Their sole knowledge of the supernatural was a firm and rooted belief in ghosts—a belief that no amount of reason or ridicule could ever shake out of them. I used to argue with them over it with the depressing result that I became infected myself. Not that I really believed in "ghosts" pure and simple. But I was inclined to agree with "*Hamlet*" that there might be more things in heaven and earth than were commonly dreamed of—in the philosophy of the Cavendish authorities anyhow.

There is a pretty spruce grove below our orchard which to this day bears the name of "the Haunted Wood" bestowed upon it by us. We considered all the places around too commonplace so we "invented" this for our own amusement (?). None of us really believed at first that the wood *was* "haunted," or that the mysterious "white things" which we pretended to see flitting through it at various dismal hours were aught but the creations of our own fancy. But our minds were weak and our imaginations strong; we soon came to believe implicitly in our own myths and none of us would have gone near that grove after sunset on pain of death. Death! What was death compared to the unearthly possibility of falling into the clutches of a "white thing."

Apart from this I had small sympathy with the boys' legends. One evening when, as usual, we were perched on the back porch steps in the mellow summer dusk, Well undertook to convince me and told me blood-curdling stories galore, until my hair fairly stood on end and I would not have been surprised had a whole army of "white things" suddenly swooped on me from around the corner.

One tale was that his grandmother, having gone out one evening to milk the cows, saw his grandfather, as she supposed, come out of the house, drive the cows into the yard, and then go down the road. The "creep" of this story consisted in the fact that she went straight way into the house and found him lying on the sofa where she had left him, never having left the house at all. Next day something happened to the poor old gentleman—I forget what, but doubtless it was some suitable punishment for sending his "wraith" out to drive cows!

Another story was that James R. Smith—a dissipated youth of the vicinity—was going home one night from some unhallowed orgy and was pursued by "a lamb of fire," with his head cut off and hanging by a strip of skin or flame. For weeks afterwards I could not go anywhere after dark without walking with my head over my shoulder, watching apprehensively for that fiery apparition.

Well's *chef-d'oeuvre*, however, was a tale of one, Joe Ralph, a Frenchman. The said Joe and a

The front apple orchard

crony were playing cards one evening in the woods when a huge black man, higher than the trees, came striding along, seized the cards and the stump on which they were laid and disappeared in a whirlwind! These and many other similar narratives did not serve to dispel my ghostly doubts, though I pooh-poohed them in daylight.

One night Dave solemnly affirmed that he had seen "a white thing," come out of the pig-house window and fly off into the woods. Another time he

joined Well and me in the front apple orchard at dusk, with his eyes nearly starting out of his head and whispered that he had heard a bell ringing in the then deserted house. To be sure, the marvellous edge was soon taken off this by the discovery that the noise was simply a newly-cleaned clock striking the hour, which it had never done before in our recollection.

The "x" is just above the spot on the dyke where we saw the "ghost."

But one night we got a real ghost scare—the "real" qualifying "scare," not "ghost." One evening in the lemon-hued twilight we three were down in the hayfield below the house, engaged in chasing each other around the fragrant coils of new-cut hay. A white calf came racing down from the barnyard, frisked through the field and then made a bee-line for the lower pastures. We returned to our game. The evening was clear and cool, the west was tinted in rose-pink and creamy yellow, and our gay voices and laughter echoed far over the fragrant, dewy fields. Suddenly I happened to glance up in the direction of the front orchard dyke. A chill began galloping up and down my spine—for there under the juniper tree was really "a white thing," shapelessly white in the gathering gloom. We all stopped and stared, as if turned to stone.

"It's Mag Laird," whispered Dave in a terrified tone. Mag Laird was, I may remark, a harmless lunatic who wandered begging over the country and was the bugbear of children in general and Dave in particular. As poor Mag's usual apparel was dirty, cast off garments of other people it did not seem to me likely that this white visitant were she. Well and I would have been glad to think that it was, for Mag was at least human—while this—!

"Nonsense!" I said, desperately striving to be practical. "It must be the calf."

Well agreed with me with suspicious alacrity.

But that shapeless, grovelling thing did not look in the least like a calf. Besides, we knew that the calf had gone to the lower pasture.

Suddenly Well exclaimed in terror, "It's coming here!"

I gave one agonized glance. Yes, it was creeping down over the dyke as no calf ever did or could creep. With a simultaneous shriek we started for the house, Dave gasping at every step. "It's Mag Laird" while all that Well and I could realize was that it was "a white thing" after us at last.

We reached the house and tore into grandma's bedroom where we had left her sewing. She was not there. As with one impulse we swung around and stampeded for Uncle John's. I could barely keep up with the boys and kept gasping out "Oh, boys wait for me," and "Oh, boys, hurry, hurry," in contradictory alternation. We arrived at Uncle John's, trembling in every limb, white and terror-stricken. We gasped out our awful tale—and were laughed at of course. But no persuasion could induce us to go back, so the servants—Charlotte "Pullying" and Peter Butter set off to explore—the former carrying a bag of oats and the latter armed with a pitch-fork—while Tillie Macneill who was visiting there, suggested that we had seen an owl. An owl! We never had much opinion of Tillie's intelligence after that!

Charlotte and Peter came back and announced that nothing was to be seen. This did not surprise us. Of course, "a white thing" would vanish when it had fulfilled it mission of scaring three wicked children out of their senses. But home we would not go until Grandfather came over in a rage and marched us home in disgrace.

And what do you think it all was?

It seemed that a white table cloth had been bleaching on the grass under the juniper tree and just at dusk, grandmother, knitting in hand, went out to get it. She flung the cloth over her shoulder and then the ball fell down and rolled over the dyke. She knelt down and was reaching over to pick it up when she was arrested by our sudden stampede and shrieks of terror. Before she could move or call out we had disappeared.

So collapsed our last "ghost" and spectral terror languished after that for we were laughed at for many a day.

One year we had a craze for playing ball—Dave and I against Well. This arrangement was not so unequal as it may seem, for Well was quite a match for the two of us. We agreed that we must give "straight balls" and "flies" for two strikes, so that no scouting would be required. The third ball might be "a sweeper" and we had to run after our own missed balls.

Besides, we invented numberless plays which afforded us great amusement. Our favorite was "Grasshopper." At least, it got corrupted to that after a time. At first it bore the dignified title of "The Great Shielded Locust of Papua." In a children's paper which we took was a sketch and picture of this locust. It was a hideous thing, and, falling in love with its grotesqueness, we christened our newborn play after it. It was not at all complex. One of us, counted out by lot, crept into a corner and, governed by certain rules, pounced out on the others as soon as they came within reach, dragged one unfortunate victim into the "den," and "et" him, often making such a noise— for the one being eaten did not submit to his fate stoically—as brought the wrath of our elders on our unlucky heads. When the victim was devoured "body and bones," he underwent a resurrection and became the "grasshopper" in turn. Another play, true to our instincts, we named "Ghost In The Garden." We had a sort of head-dress for this which consisted of one handkerchief folded triangularly and bound around our foreheads, letting the flap hang down over our eyes, and another, knotted into a dunce cap, on our heads. We had a specially invented name for this but I forget what it was.

Summer was our glorious time but in winter we had fun, too; of sliding we had plenty and in school coasting was the order of the day. One coasting incident I shall certainly never forget. The boys and I were spending a Saturday afternoon at Charles Macneill's and were coasting behind the barn with Pensie and Russell. Pen and I had a sled to ourselves—one with a wooden "tongue" which was turned back at a sharp angle over our heads during the coast. Well and Russell had started on a coast, but their sled stuck midway down the track and Dave ran down to start them again. Then he stood squarely in the middle with his back to us, just as Pen pushed me off. I screamed to Dave to get out of the way but I was up to him before the words were fairly out of my mouth. The sled caught him squarely between his legs and he flew back over the tongue, as if shot from a catapult, in a bewildering whirl of arms and legs. It all passed in a second of time and Dave fell in a heap on the snow behind while I spun helplessly on down the course. As soon as I could stop I ran back to Dave, who was dazedly picking himself up. I was certain his neck must be broken but he wasn't even hurt. He said he thought a tornado had struck him and I don't wonder at it.

Every summer we devoted our playtime to our "house" and gardened and swung and picnicked and had "no end of fun." When dandelions were in bloom we would make chains of their supple milky stems to decorate our house. In the purple dusk of a fragrant summer evening we would go out into the front orchard, and, lying at ease in the delightful tangle of musk and caraway and "dandies" we would pull the yellow stars to make the "curls" and "chains" that were so plump and brave while fresh and so withered and unsightly when they dried.

One spring we were fired with a desire to change our location and planned to remove to a spot locally known as the "little bushes." Armed with axe and ladder we set out for our Eldorado, but just as we were ready to begin operations grandpa came along and, taking in our scheme at a glance, sternly ordered us to return to our old site and not hack up anymore of his young trees. We thought this very hard indeed and marched off in high dudgeon to grumble and sulk an hour or so before we reconciled ourselves to the old spot. It was really by far the better place of the two, and we recognized this fact after we had worked off our ill-humor in a good bough-cutting expedition. Indeed, who *could* keep angry amid the sweet-smelling, resinous boughs of those dear old tangled groves? Not we at anyrate. All our troubles dissolved in the breath of the firs and the birch breezes swept away our bitterest resentment.

One spring we had a bow and arrow made and an immense deal of fun we had out of it, albeit we did not shed much blood. We were always planning to "kill crows or something," but the black croakers of the tree-tops did not grow noticeably less. One almost victim that arrow had, however. We were "housecleaning" one day, and I, for lack of a better place, put the arrow in my mouth to hold while I "sorted out" a shelf. Well, who was lifting a box, turned suddenly around and the top of the box struck against the end of the arrow, driving the point into the roof of my mouth—or so I thought. I screamed. Well dropped the box and stared at me with a pallid face. I think we expected to see the arrow sticking out of the top of my head. Luckily the wooden point was very dull and no harm was done beyond skinning the roof of my mouth.

Another time we made a pair of stilts. We bit the dust to an alarming degree in our efforts to learn the art of walking on them, but at last we succeeded and could go stalking around, a yard or two higher than ordinary mortals, performing wonderful feats of dexterity with that pride that goes before a fall until some incautious step hurled us ignobly down.

Stilts were the rage for weeks. We had always some pet fad on hand. When one thing grew stale another took its place. At one time our rage was for hop-poles—or "hopples" as we called them—long slim pickets as high as our heads, with which we would "hop" about. This lasted until Uncle John, vexed with our devotion in to what he regarded as a silly sport, made away with my hopple. Uncle John, I may remark, was not then, anymore than now, noted for his consideration of other people's rights or feelings, especially if the said other people were smaller or weaker than himself. My "hopple" was a particularly nice one and it took the heart out of me to lose it. I refused to be comforted with another and the craze died out.

We were always wild about gum-picking. All creatures of nature as we were, nothing seemed more delightful than to roam at will through fresh spruce groves, scrambling through thick copses of young trees which always repaid us for sundry rents and scratches by "blobs" of yellow gum, of the sweet, nutty flavour we prized so highly. Shrewd connoisseurs were we! We knew at a glance what quality a "find" of gum was and we knew the best of all was the clear yellow, like drop of sunlight on the lichened boughs, that turned a creamy pink when chewed. There was always a good deal of friendly rivalry in our gumming expeditions and the lucky finder of an unusually large "blob" was quite a hero to our simple minds. We had our favorite trees—trees that were abundant and never-failing. The woods behind the pig-house, the "little bushes," and—in the days before the ghosts—a thick copse of saplings in the Haunted Wood were our chief hunting-grounds. One winter we had a "gum-saving" craze. Every bit of gum was jealously saved, rolled into a shining ball about the size of a pea and consigned to a box. Our ambition was to be the possessor of the largest number of balls. The honour fluctuated between Well and me; Dave fell far behind owing to his propensity for chewing his gum up as soon as he had got any saved. I remember I had 103 balls once.

It was the same winter that Well and I took to "writing stories out of our own heads." Wonderful productions indeed! Only one is now extant—a particularly brilliant effort of Well's which I thought worthy of preserving. As the copy is now sadly worn and defaced I will transfer the thrilling tale to this journal to ensure its safe-keeping:—

The Battle of the Partridge-Eggs

Once upon a time there lived about half a mile from a forest a farmer and his wife and his sons and daughters and a grand-daughter. The farmer and his wife loved this little girl very much but she caused them great trouble by running away into the woods and they often spent half-days in looking for her. One day, she wandered further into the forest than usual and she began to be hungry. Then night closed in. She asked a fox where she could get something to eat. The fox told her he knew where there was a partridge's nest and a blue-jay's nest, full of eggs. So he led her to the nests and she took five eggs out of each. When the birds came home they missed the eggs and flew into a rage. The blue-jay put on his top-coat and was going to the partridge for law when he met the partridge coming to him. They lit up a fire and commenced signing their deeds when they heard a tremendous howl close behind them. They jumped up, put out the fire, and were immediately attacked by five great wolves.

The next day the little girl was rambling through the woods when they saw her and took her prisoner. After she confessed having stolen the eggs they told her to raise an army. They would have to fight over the nests of eggs and whoever won would have the eggs. So the partridge raised a great army of all kinds of birds except robins and the little girl got all the robins and foxes and bees and wasps. And best of all the little girl had a gun and plenty of ammunition. The leader of her army was a wolf. The result of the battle was that all the birds were killed except the partridge and blue-jay and they were taken prisoners and starved.

The little girl was then taken prisoner by a witch and cast into a dungeon full of snakes where she died from their bites and afterwards people who went through the woods were taken prisoner by her ghost and cast into the same dungeon where they died. About a year after the woods turned into a gold castle and one morning everything had vanished except a piece of a tree.

Isn't that a literary gem? Really, considering his age—only nine—it wasn't too bad, although some parts are deliciously absurd, especially that about the unfortunate heroine having "a gun and plenty of ammunition" and the birds' encounter with the wolves. As for the tragic conclusion, it must have been the outcome of Well's perusal of Grimm's fairy tales.

Of my story, written the same evening, I remember nothing save that it was about "a peasant girl" named "Nelly" who herded sheep and was accused by her master of stealing them.

Another winter our "fad" was "making" money. Our *modus operandi* was to place a cent or other coin—the bigger the more valuable—under a sheet of white paper and then rub the blunt end of a lead pencil over the spot. The result was a clear black reproduction of the coin on the paper. This was carefully "trimmed out" and consigned to a box with hundreds of others. It was really amazing how the craze possessed us and it lasted months with eager, absorbing interest. But the end came as ends always will and one day our riches went up in smoke—I emptied them into the cook stove. The next winter our craze was picture collecting and then nothing was safe from our rapacious paws. We had several boxes filled with pictures of all sorts, from farm implements to lion hunts. They went the way of our "cash" in course of time. Well, at least our fads were harmless and we got a great deal of fun out of them while they lasted.

Since I was nine I had kept a childish diary—long ago committed to the flames—in which all my small transactions were faithfully recorded every day. I was always in a state of chronic terror lest someone—the boys in particular—should see it. I generally kept it on a little secret shelf under the sitting room sofa. One winter Well began to keep a diary also and in his turn would never let me see it although of course I was devoured with curiosity. At last, in an evil hour, I chanced to discover where he hid it—between the end of the kitchen cupboard and the wall—and one night after the boys had gone to bed I went and read them—half a dozen little yellow notebooks! If you imagine that I was at rest then you are much mistaken. Satisfied curiosity counted for nothing at all and for weeks my conscience pointed the finger of scorn at me. Nine years cannot draw a very fine distinction between an honorable and a dishonorable action. Nevertheless, I was haunted unceasingly by the galling conviction that I had done something *mean*. What worse could befall me? For in our code the epithet of "mean" was to as what "nith-ing" was to the Saxons of old. To call a boy "a mean coward" was to offer him a deadly insult. Judge then what I suffered when I *felt* "mean" in my inmost soul. That is one of the little mistakes of my childhood which I would gladly blot out if I could and yet it was one that taught me a valuable lesson. Never since have I read anything not intended for my eyes.

I was a week older than Well. Dave was a year younger. The brothers were totally dissimilar in looks. Dave was fair, with mild blue eyes and a pouting mouth. Well was a dark handsome lad with laughing eyes and a merry face. Both boys were very hot-tempered and many a fight they had. Well was bright at his books but Dave was a born mechanic, never hap-pier than when tinkering away with the scraps of old iron and wood in our "table drawer." Dave always got the worst of their fights for he generally lost his wits entirely. His temper was the quicker of the two and he used to get so red in the face that Well and I—I always sided with Well in right or wrong—nicknamed him "The Rooster." The application of this never failed to bring on a fight between the two boys; yet they were affectionate little fellows and would be hugging each other ten minutes after a grapple with teeth and nails. A fight was a positive enjoyment to them. Grandpa usually put a stop to this kind of pleasure when he was round. But one winter or autumn evening Grace Macneill got married. Aunt Annie and Aunt Emily came down to go and grandmother went with them. Aunt Annie left Clara, then a girl about six with me and grandpa stayed home to look after us all. He told the boys that they could fight the whole evening, if they wanted to. They took him at his word. From eight to ten the kitchen resounded with howls, yells, and thumps, as they rolled in clinch around the floor. Clara and I stayed in the bedroom off the sitting room and played calmly there, safe from the racket and din out in the kitchen. At ten o'clock grandpa sent everybody to bed. Well and Dave were black and blue for a week but they had had the time of their lives. I'm sure they wished Grace Macneill could have got married nightly.

In the long winter evenings we would play "dominoes," "keep your tem-per," "tit-tat-x" and other age-old games. The boys were always very kind to me and many happy hours we had together. But one day the boys went away suddenly for good and all—so suddenly and unexpectedly that there was little time for good-byes or grief. I was sorry and lonely too, for I had few other companions. But youth forgets speedily.

They went away this evening. Well talks of going out west.

Tuesday, Aug. 9, 1892
Cavendish, P.E.I.

I feel happier and more contented to-day than I have felt for a long time. It was decided to-day that I am to go to school here again and study for Prince of Wales[1] and a teacher's license. I am delighted. I have always longed for this. I realize that I must do something for myself and this seems the only thing possible but grandpa and grandma have always been so bitterly against it that I was getting discouraged. They have given in at last however and I am to begin school when it opens next Monday. A Miss West[2] is the teacher. I mean to study very hard for I *must* get some more education.

Saturday, Aug. 13, 1892

I generally have some little racket on Saturday evenings and I had a jolly one to-night. Pen came up for the mail and we set off for a walk. We went down to the school and found Sarah Jack just finishing cleaning it. She gave us the keys to take to Uncle John's and then Pen and I went along to the church. Presently William George and Neil Simpson[3] came along on a buckboard and invited us to go for a drive. We perched on behind with Ches Clark and rattled off. Such fun as we had! I laughed until I was tired; and so reckless was W.G.'s driving that we were spattered from toe to crown with mud.

Monday, Aug. 15, 1892

I went to school this morning and it seemed so natural to be there again. And yet I missed the "old crowd" so much. There are not many of them left. I got in a lot of work and had a good time. It was delicious to sit in my old seat and look through the window away down into the old spruce woods, with their shadows and sunlight and whispering. At recess I took a ramble through them by myself. They are deserted now. None of the small fry ever think of playing there. When the "old crowd" and I were small we fairly lived in the woods. Dear me, the summer is nearly gone. The asters and golden-rod are blooming and the twilights are pink and chilly.

---

1. College located in Charlottetown that was established in 1860, and offered post-matriculation training in teaching, business, and farming.
2. Izzie West, appointed in 1892, left after a few months owing to illness.
3. William George (1869–1920) and Neil (1876–1940), Bayview brothers, sons of William and Helen Simpson.

Saturday, August 27, 1892

I am so busy these days, every moment seems to be occupied.

It is just a year to-day since I left Prince Albert. It has been a very happy year. This night last year at this very time I was in Regina station. Now I am in my quiet little room with its simple furniture and muslin-draped window, and the poplars swishing outside.

I had a walk to the shore this morning. Everything speaks of the autumn now. The sea roars hollowly day and night, the fields are bare and sere, bordered by strips of deep-dyed golden-rod, asters, and life-everlasting; and the ponds are blue—blue—not the steely blue of winter, or the pale azure of summer, but a clear, steadfast serene blue, as if the water were past all the moods and tenses of passion and had settled down to tranquillity.

Saturday, Sept. 24, 1892

Mollie was here at dusk for the mail and as usual I went a piece with her. So interesting was our chat and so lovely the night, with a big new moon burning out under the purple-black clouds in the southwest that I was beguiled into going nearly to her gate. As I was coming back Alec Macneill appeared and walked home with me.

Thursday, Sept. 29, 1892

I spent last night with Mollie. We were up to Darnley Clark's[1] for the evening and had a very nice time. When I got up this morning I sauntered out to see what the family was doing. They were churning[2] and Ham was at it. I offered to "take a spell" and for about fifteen minutes I churned happily away beneath the soft blue skies with the morning sunshine streaming over the dewy fields and sparkling on the pond, seen bluely between the trees, while in their old-fashioned garden big red dahlias were flaming out gallantly. But alas! When I stopped churning, Ham, rather anxious to show off, I suppose, made a vigorous dash at the churn. Snap! went something and in a trice all was confusion.

For my own part, in the first few minutes, of dazed surprise, I was tempted to think that what ever had happened must be a matter of life and death,

---

1. Father of one of two Clark families with large farms at the western edge of Cavendish.
2. The end process of creating butter from cream.

judging from the half-frenzied behaviour of the entire family. I really cannot describe the consternation that ensued. It was dreadful and yet so ludicrous. I huddled in a corner of the porch, feeling guiltily that they probably held me responsible for it all and yet harassed by an awful desire to burst into a peal of laughter. Poor Mrs. Macneill kept wringing her hands and exclaiming tragically "I know not what to do—I know not what to do," while Lillie and Amanda berated poor Ham as if he had broken all the ten commandments. Finally however, Mrs. Macneill, finding that groaning and wringing of hands would not make the butter come, left off and proceeded more sensibly to rake about in the cream with a long-handled spoon. After all the commotion the damage proved slight and was easily rectified. Ham was sent off in disgrace and I finished the churning, taking care not to break anything more.

Miss West is ill with lung trouble and has to give up the school. A double pity, for her and us,—for we were just getting well down to work and everything will be disarranged by a change of teachers. Miss West was a fairly good teacher, though she was none of the *personality* possessed by Miss Gordon.

Friday, Oct. 21, 1892

When school came out a few drops of rain spit viciously down in my face, but I obstinately refused to believe it was going to rain, because it was the night of the "Jubilee Concert" and I had built a very airy air castle over it. Rain it did, however, in spite of my disbelief. Everyone said it was going to be a wild night but I had made up my mind that I was going to the hall and go I meant to if everything turned blue. So I went over to Uncle John's and found out they were going up in the cart. We bundled up in shawls, crept into the cart; and started off through a night of Egyptian darkness. Well, we *had* a dandy ride! "The rain descended and the floods came and the winds blew."[1] I gave up trying to hold up my umbrella, put a shawl over my head and resolved to grin and bear it. We finally got there and found that we were not the only lunatics in Cavendish, after all. There were about twenty more out and we were a forlorn crowd. We sat in rows and thought over our sins. Then we "adjourned." That is, we went out, crawled helter-skelter into our cart, and jolted home. And yet, for the life of me, I couldn't help laughing. Everything was so funny and so horrid; and my dress—but that was something too harrowing to be contemplated. I said all the amusing things I could think of under the circumstances but the rest didn't seem too enthused over

---

1. "And the rain descended, and the floods came, and the . . . winds blew, and beat upon that house; and it fell not: for it was founded upon a rock." Matthew 7:25.

them. When I reached home I vowed a solemn vow to have a little sense in future—if possible.

Friday, Nov. 4, 1892
Cavendish, P.E.I.

'Tis such a day as this—cold, raw, surly, that brings to us a sharp, sudden realization that frosty nights and snowy days are coming on apace. *Where*

*A corner of the pond at Park Corner,
seen from the bridge*

has the summer gone? It doesn't seem a week since I went over the bridge at Park Corner and, noting how the birches were hanging out green banners over the blue pond, felt with a delicious thrill that summer was here once more.

Pen, Lu and I went up to Literary to-night. We began to laugh when we started and when we got back we were still at it. When we got to the hall there wasn't a soul there except Ches, lighting a fire, so we sallied forth again and went for an exploration up Wm. Simpson's cow-

lane. When we got back to the hall we got into a seat with a chosen few and how we all laughed! Funny things kept happening right along. As it was a "Scott night" I recited a selection from *The Lady of the Lake*.[1] Jack Laird walked home with me and we'd lots of fun.

Monday, Nov. 21, 1892

Miss West left a week ago and to-day our new teacher, Miss Selena Robinson,[2] came. It is to be hoped that in this case at least, appearances *are* deceptive, or I much fear me that Cavendish

*A photo of Miss Robinson
(taken seventeen years later)*

---

1. Epic poem (1810) by Walter Scott portraying an innocent, isolated girl courted by a disguised king and a Highland chieftain; contains sensitive descriptions of Trossach scenery.

2. A gift from this teacher, Selena Robinson (1868–1953), is centred on the first page of LMM's Blue Scrapbook, reproduced in Elizabeth Epperly's *Imagining Anne: the Island Scrapbooks of L.M. Montgomery* (1908).

educational institution will *not* go forward this winter by leaps and bounds. She is a short, dumpy little person, with brown eyes, excessively red cheeks, and a very expressionless face.

I am going to take up Greek. I expect it will be tough, especially the verb. I have heard a few things about the Greek verb.

Friday, Dec. 2, 1892

I haven't got as far along as the verb yet, consequently I am still enjoying life. Lu and I went up to Literary to-night and called for Miss Robinson, who is boarding at Pierce Macneill's. We had quite a jolly walk up, despite the mud and mist. Coming home Jack was with us and we had lots of fun.

Sunday, Dec. 4, 1892
Cavendish, P.E.I.

This afternoon I went for a ramble in the school woods. Had a lovely walk. The old brook has degenerated sadly of late years, but the recent rains have

filled it to overflowing so that it has grown young again and is a wild, headlong thing tearing madly along, often losing itself, and after meandering recklessly among the bogs finds its way back, not a whit subdued, boiling up in whirlpools here and there, and tumbling heedlessly over mimic precipices. Dear old brook! Many a fair dream have I spun over your dancing silver in

Down in the school woods

days gone by, when the mosses and ferns grew on your banks and blue summer skies mirrored themselves in your pebbly shallows.

Thursday, Dec. 10, 1892

Went to a magic lantern[1] show in the hall to-night and had a fine time. Miss R. and I were the only girls coming east. She is quite a jolly girl when

---

1. An image projector, throwing pictures onto a screen by inserting slides into a box, illuminated originally by limelight.

you get to know her—though she certainly isn't much of a teacher—and we had quite a gay time. Jack Laird and Elton Robertson[1] drove us home.

Thursday, Dec. 29, 1892

Last Monday Miss R. came up to tea and stayed all night. She is real jolly. We talked until nearly morning and had such fun.

To-night I went to prayer-meeting. After prayer-meeting they had choir practice and, as we didn't want to stay for it, Pen and Lu and I went out. Ab French, Alec Macneill, and Don McKay came too. We all piled into a big pung sleigh and drove down to Pen's, where we went and stayed for nearly an hour.

Saturday, Dec. 31, 1892
Cavendish, P.E.I.

This is the last of the old year. '92 dies to-night—a glorious death, for the white earth floats in aerial silver of frost and moonshine and the sky is powdered with thousands of stars to watch its deathbed. I am sorry to see it go for it has been a very happy year for me. Will '93 be as good, I wonder. What does it hold for me in its upsealed days and months?

---

1. The Robertsons' farm lay across the road from Uncle John Macneill's.

1893

Thursday, Jan. 12, 1893

So far the new year hasn't been dangerously exciting. Had a jolly letter from Will to-day. I wish I could see him and just chatter nonsense for an hour or so.

Ches and I are clubbing together to send for books. I am going to get "Scottish Chiefs," "Valentine Vox" and "Midshipman Easy."[1] How I do love books! Not merely to read once but over and over again. I enjoy the tenth reading of a book as much as the first. Books are a delightful world in themselves. Their characters seem as real to me as my friends of actual life.

We have lots of fun in school these days. Austin Laird and Ches Clark are going and we keep things stirred up.

Wednesday, Jan. 25, 1893

Had a glorious lark to-day. Grandpa went up to Park Corner and I went too. It was a fine day; a white frost had converted the birch groves into forests of fairy beauty and the spruces into stately silver palms. When we got to the P.C. school I jumped out and ran in. When the master came to the door I asked for the girls and Clara and Stell and Fred[2] came bouncing out and all grabbed me at once. They went right home with us and how our tongues did go! And *how* we laughed! After dinner Cade and I got away in her room, shut the door, and "talked it out." There was so much to ask and tell. We had to leave for home at seven but I'll live on this day for weeks.

Thursday, Jan. 26, 1893
Cavendish, P.E.I.

Went to prayer-meeting this evening and Pen, Lu, Miss R. and I sat together. When practice began we didn't like to get right up and start out, so we tried various ways of amusing ourselves and succeeded pretty well. But at last, as there seemed no prospect of practice coming to an end, we slipped out. Lu, Pen, and I got into Alec's pung, along with Russell and Ab. We

---

1. Jane Porter's long-popular romance *Scottish Chiefs* (1810), based on the life of William Wallace; *Valentine Vex the Ventriloquist* (1840), a British adventure novel by Henry Cockton; *Mr. Midshipman Easy* (1836), a story of sea-life by Captain Frederick Marryat (who also wrote boys' books, including *The Young Settlers in Canada*).

2. Frederica Campbell (1883–1919), youngest daughter of LMM's Aunt Annie (Macneill) and Uncle John Campbell of Park Corner. Though years younger, she later became LMM's dearest friend.

drove up to Uncle John's gate, then turned and went back. We thought we'd get past the church before the rest came out but it was just our luck to meet them there in a heap. I suppose Mr. Archibald would be more than horrified, especially as we were making a considerable racket before we saw them.

My jonquil and narcissus bulbs are out now. They are lovely. The narcissus has frosty white flowers with golden hearts, and the jonquil is a star of purest gold, with a golden trumpet in the centre. It whispers of summer tide when blue skies shall dip down over far green hills and on the brooklands a thousand dancing blossoms mimic its pale gold.

Monday, Feb. 13, 1893

This morning grandpa and grandma went to town, leaving at six. Left alone I lounged around waiting for daylight. Darkness hovered over the hills, and silence, unbroken save by some stray wind from far sea caves, sat on its shrouded throne. But along the sky from north to south crept a pale, phantom brightness, like the ghost of light arising from its nightly grave. The thrill of re-awakening life ran through the pulses of nature. The air seemed to tremble in the struggle between life and death—the old, old struggle in which, as ever, life was victor, and beneath its conquering kisses rosy blushes streamed across the pallid cheek of morn. The stars, those silent sentinels at the gates of darkness, fled from their posts as the vanguard of light rushed up the silver steeps; and from the eastern glow, like a mighty king from his royal couch, arose the sun.

To descend from the sublime to the ridiculous almost as abruptly as is done in real life, morning came and I went about my work in a philosophic spirit. One cannot dream forever under the fresh born glories of the dawn—cows must be milked, pigs fed, floors swept up.

At dinner time Ches and Austin came up. We talked enough nonsense to last a lifetime with care and economy.

Thursday, Feb. 15, 1893
Cavendish, P.E.I.

The funniest thing happened in school to-day. Lu had slipped over to my seat to discuss a scheme and I was whispering behind a book. Jim Wyand was up in his class and the last word in my sentence was "Jim"—referring to quite another Jim. Just as I got to it Austin Laird leaned across the aisle and gave me a vicious punch in the side. As a result I involuntarily screamed out "Jim" at the top of my voice. The sensation produced was enormous and poor Jim Wyand looked flabbergasted, as well he might.

Went to prayer meeting this evening. Don took Lu and Pen driving and Alec walked home with me. When I got home I found a thumb and finger frozen white and stiff.

Friday, Feb. 17, 1893

Made Austin awfully mad in school to-day writing a piece of poetry about him called "The Boy With the Auburn Hair." He dared me to do it, so he needn't have got his fur up so about it.

Lu and I have invented a lot of nicknames for our friends and foes. Russell is "The Mud Hen," Alec is "Midshipman Easy," Ab is "The Black Knight," Elton is "Green Cheese," Jim is "The Cabbage Chicken," Jack is "Mamma's Pet," Austin is "Cavendish Carrots," Neil is "The Swamp Angel," Ches is "Chow-Chow" and Don is "Rats."

Thursday, Feb. 23, 1893

School was very dull to-day for Ches wasn't there. Austin was, but no fun was to be had out of him, for it is a sad and sorrowful fact that nowadays Austin and I "never speak as we pass by." He has not yet forgiven me for burlesquing him in that unlucky rhyme and persists in treating me with what he doubtless imagines to be lofty disdain.

The mailman didn't get along, and tonight being prayer meeting night, our evil genius had to brew up a storm and prevent it. Too bad, when prayer meeting is the only "social function" we poor "kids" have!

Friday, March 3, 1893

When I was washing the tea dishes tonight whom should I see coming up to the door but Clara Campbell. I tore out and grabbed her and we laughed and joked and flew about wildly. Lem and Ella had brought her down and they were at Uncle John's.

In the evening we all went up to the hall in a big wood sleigh, but the Literary was a fizzle tonight. However, we had our own fun so the expedition was a success. I suppose Cade and I will now proceed to talk all night.

Saturday, Mar. 4, 1893

We did!

This evening we were all invited to Mollies, so we went, again in the trusty wood sleigh. We got over uncertain whether we were alive or dead as Lem had taken us through the many pitches[1] at break-neck speed. We had a rather dull time at Mollies. Old William C.[2] is such a wet blanket and none of the family have any gift of entertaining in a social way. We left at 10.30 and when we got to the gate Lem turned the horse west and said we'd have a drive before going home. Bounce through the pitches we went until just by Stewart's gate the other girls slipped off the sleigh and took to their heels. Lem and I, thus deserted, consoled ourselves by remembering that two were company and drove on as far as the forge before we turned back. We did not overtake the others until we got down to David Macneill's gate. We whizzed past them at a furious rate of speed in our imposing chariot but at once turned and went back for them. Do you think they'd get in? Not they! So we went off in disdain and didn't stop till we got to the church where we had a long wait of it, for they sneaked up across Pierce's field and the first thing Lem and I knew they were going up our lane. We flew after them and, making too short a turn at the gate, banged into the post with tremendous force. The post suffered more than anything else, I fancy, for there was a hole knocked in it as big as a quart. However, "all's well that ends well" and so did our racket.

Wednesday, Mar. 8, 1893

I took a ramble through the school woods this lovely day, plunging around in the soft snow and renewing the freshness of life. The brook was purling softly past its snowy banks and the lacy boughs of the spruces waved softly athwart the clear blue skies.

Sunday, Mar. 12, 1893

Selena was here to dinner today and in the evening we went to church. Selena was coming back with me to stay all night so after service we elbowed our way out to find ourselves in a perfect pandemonium. It was pitch dark, the yard was full of a hustling jostling crowd, the mud was to our ankles, and wildly

---

1. Potholes in the dirt road.
2. Amanda's father, W.C. Macneill, second cousin of grandfather Alexander Macneill.

rearing horses were apparently on all sides. As soon as it was safe we started. Elton Robertson overtook us and we went for a drive with him, having some very funny adventures.

Wednesday, Mar. 15, 1893

Austin is very anxious to make up now, but I never take any notice of him. His dignity will not let him address me directly but he talks *to* others and *at* me. I am apparently deaf, however.

I went to the Missionary Sewing Circle this afternoon. They are making quilts for the Indians so I chipped in to do my mite for the poor heathen. Mollie was there and she and I sat together and sewed a long pleasant chat into our gay seams.

Thursday, April 4, 1893

School was going on as usual this morning when three smart youths walked in. One was Judson Clark, the others we did not know, but found out later that they were Everett Macneill and a Mr. Lucas, P.W.C. students who are visiting at John C. Clark's in the Easter holidays.

Selena called out the history class and got Judson to "hear" it. He kept up a running fire of would-be funny comments the whole time and we were in a state of continuous "giggledom"—not that his witticisms were at all brilliant but simply because we were dying to laugh anyhow and were glad of an opportunity to work off our dangerous tendency. Then came geometry and I nearly took a fit while trying to prove two props in the third book and work out a couple of exercises. Whenever I went to draw a line Macneill or Lucas would make a dive to steady the debilitated old blackboard or hand me a book or compass or chalk until I got hopelessly rattled.

Austin ventured to speak to me today. We met in the porch and he said "good morning." But I simply ignored him. I will never speak to him again, the cad!

Friday, April 7, 1893

Was at Literary to-night and we had quite a nice programme. When we started home Selena and I were ahead, Lu and Mollie just behind, and a crowd of boys all about. Just at Mr. Spurr's gate somebody came up to me and coolly drew my hand through his arm without so much as a by-your-leave.

I thought it was Alec but on looking up was disgusted to find that it was Mac Macneill.[1] I pulled my hand away and said coldly,

"I'm not going to leave Miss R., thank you."

But Mac seems to be incapable of taking a hint no matter how broad. He mumbled something and then stepped back to Will Stewart who thereupon came up and took Miss R. This left me no resource but to cast in my lot with Mac and walk along fairly choking with vexation. Mac is the biggest muff in Cavendish or out of it.

Tuesday, April 11, 1893

This evening Selena and I ploughed up through the mud to Darnley Clark's to practice a dialogue for the Literary concert. Herbert Simpson, William George Simpson and Ches are also in it. Ches and Herb drove us home and we had a merry time. Goodness, how we *did* laugh!

Thursday, April 20, 1893
Cavendish, P.E. Island

We had another practice at Darnley's this evening. Our dialogue is coming on swimmingly and we had lots of fun. Ches and W.G. drove us home in a pung sleigh. We drove in as far as the church and then back to our gate where we stopped and talked nonsense for nearly an hour. Selena came up and stayed all night with us.

Sunday, April 23, 1893

Selena and I walked into Baptist preaching this morning and nearly got drowned. But we had heaps of fun. Not just the thing to go to church for, say you? Well, we didn't go hunting for it—it just came along and we took it. Austin was there, arrayed in a brand-new salt-and-pepper suit, with a fawn hat into the bargain. Sure, and didn't our hearts go pitty-pat!

The Baptist Church

---

1. Perhaps Arty Macneill, who had been a younger schoolmate at Cavendish school.

Tuesday, April 25, 1893
Cavendish, P.E.I.

I had a really fearful time with Austin to-day. He has been trying several ways of making up recently but I've never taken the least notice. This afternoon he kept making remarks to Jim who was sitting between him and me on the back seat. Poor A. would say in his solemn way,

"Jim, I don't know how you can resist the temptation to sit over closer to that girl"—here he would give Jim a fierce shove in my direction—"I'm sure I couldn't if I were in your place. 'Watch and pray lest ye enter into temptation'—that is what *I* have to do. 'The spirit is willing but the flesh is weak'"[1]— and so on, until in spite of my efforts to appear deaf I *had* to laugh. This seemed to encourage Austin—he evidently thought I was relenting at last. So he got Jim to exchange places with him and then he slid right over to my desk.

"Look, Jim," he said, "This is for old acquaintance sake. This little girl and I are old friends."

But I got up and marched to another seat. Austin need not suppose for a minute that I'm going to make up in that fashion. He got mad over a joke and said very nasty things; and if he isn't man enough to apologize for it he can just go. Ches was in this evening and told me that Austin had told him a long yarn to the effect that he and I had made up and were better friends than ever and that we had signed a written contract never to quarrel again!!! Did you *ever*! Well, Austin may romance all he likes. *I* shall stick to facts.

Monday, May 1, 1893

I've been on quite a jamboree[2] since I last wrote. Saturday was a lovely day and after dinner Uncle John and grandpa took Aunt Ann Maria[3] and me over the harbor in a boat. We had a perfect sail over and landed by the light-house. The men went back and we walked up the harbor road. Aunt A. went to Captain George's[4] and I to Uncle John C.'s.[5] I was dead tired when I got there after such a long walk but the fun we had in the evening soon revived me. Clara and I talked for all hours after we went to bed and of course were

---

1. Misquoting Bible verses from Mark 14:38 and Matthew 26:41.

2. A boisterous celebration.

3. Wife of Uncle John next door.

4. "Captain" George MacKenzie (1817–98) was a shipbuilder in New London. "Captain George" could also refer to Capt. George MacLeod (1843–1905) and Capt. George MacLeod (1836–1906).

5. John Campbell, husband of LMM's mother's sister Annie.

desperately sleepy Sunday morning but had to get up early, as we intended walking through to preaching at Long River. We set off about nine and after wading bogs and crossing ploughed fields and climbing a few dozen fences and scrambling through a mile of brush we got to Long River church and sank wearily into our pew. I was so dead tired that I actually fell sound asleep while the Rev. John M. was praying. I still could hear the words he was saying, however, and I dreamed that Uncle John C. was having family worship in the kitchen and that Albert Stewart was singing those words to a psalm tune! I woke up in time to save my face, however, and by the time church was out I felt tolerably spry again. Lydia Clark and Ella MacLeod came down with us and we got home about two, hurried over our dinner and then walked to Sunday school at French River.

In the evening Lem, Will Paynter, and Stan Bernard came up and we had a nice time. This morning Uncle John C. drove us down to the harbor and Colin McKenzie and Captain George rowed us across the channel. Pres[1] was waiting for us in a cart and we had a jolty six mile drive home, arriving at 10.30. After dinner I went to school and got the worst "give-away" on myself I ever had in my life. Don't know how in the world I ever came to make such a break. I was just going through our gate. They were playing ball and Neil Simpson was scouting on the road. "Come and play ball, Maud," he said.

Now, I was at that moment mentally composing a note to accompany a recitation I had promised to send a certain youth over at French River. So I said absently,

"Oh, I can't. I'm too dead tired, *Lem*."

Then I made matters worse by exclaiming in dire dismay,

"Er—er—*Neil*, I mean."

Neil takes a good deal of time to get anything through his thinkers so I was well across the road before he said,

"You must have 'Lem' on your mind."

As for me, I was completely posed. I couldn't think of one solitary thing to say so beat a hasty retreat. Wasn't it awful?

The weather keeps miserably dull and cold. Will summer *ever* come? Truly, "hope deferred maketh the heart sick."[2] That old Hebrew Poet-King, who lived among his oriental gardens so many centuries ago, did manage several times to get off some remarkable pat assertions. Well, no doubt human nature was human nature even in that far-off time and beneath the purple and fine linen of Eastern sovereignty; and all the trappings of royalty could not ward off the pangs of disappointment.

---

1. LMM's first cousin Prescott (1879–1910), son of Uncle John Macneill and brother of Lu.

2. Proverbs 13:12.

Wednesday, May 10, 1893
Cavendish, P.E.I.

Summer arrived sometime last night—to-day was as fair a day as poet ever dreamed of or painter ever put on canvas. The breeze was of June softness, the grass is like velvet and,

> The little birds sang as if it were
> The one day of summer in all the year.[1]

View from my window   My window

I have just been sitting here at my window indulging in day-dreams. The view from here is such a pretty one and it is also dear to me for all the sweet old memories associated with almost every feature—brooks, woods, fields. O you birds, singing out there, my spirit rises on the wings of your melodies and floats free of earth, far into those blue infinities of sunlit azure.

Selena and I spent noon-hour to-day down by the brook, that ran by us, a dimpling, sun-flecked stream, and sang its "old sweet song" to the listening spruces. This evening after tea she and I went to the shore. It was exquisite down there—the sea was a pale silvery blue breaking into foamy ripples like overlapping sheets of silver on the sandshore, or gently purring at the base of the rocks.

Tuesday, May 16, 1893
Cavendish, P.E.I.

This evening Selena came up for the mail and I went as far as the church with her. We went into the graveyard just as the Baptists were beginning to

---

1. From James Russell Lowell's "The Vision of Sir Launfall" (1848). Quoted in *AGG*, chapter 2.

go past to prayer-meeting. Charlie McKenzie came along and we walked down the hill together and had a good deal of fun, although both Selena and I really detest poor C.

Wednesday, May 24, 1893

To-day was hot and windy. Selena and I went for a walk through Lover's Lane. The trees are quite green now, and blue and white violets, and golden "dandies" are in season. It is delightful to sit at my window and watch how green everything is, how blue the sky and sea, and how gracefully the rich shadows fall along the moist edges of the woods.

Lover's Lane

Saturday, June 3, 1893

This evening Lu and I went down to Pen's on an errand and Pen came back with us for a walk. At the church we met William George Simpson and we all stopped for half an hour and talked sheer, delightful nonsense. Then, as it was getting dark, Pen made Lu and me go back with her, and W.G. evidently thought we all needed looking after for he came too. We went right home with Pen. On the way back W.G. informed me that *Nate* was expected home to-morrow night; and though I had known it before I said, with quite an imitation of surprise in my voice, "Is he really?"

"Yes," said W.G. "I expect he'll be a great fellow now."

"Oh, yes," I said indifferently, "I suppose he will," and wished desperately that W.G. would find some other topic of conversation.

"Perhaps he has some powerful attraction in Cavendish," was W.G.'s next brilliant effort.

I hadn't expected *this* and was badly disconcerted.

"Oh, well," I said lamely, "you seem to know all his"—then I stopped, realizing that *that* wasn't just the thing to say and furious with myself that I couldn't think of anything else. As I couldn't I didn't, but straightway began to talk of some other subject and left W.G. to infer what he liked. There certainly ought to be another branch added to our common school curriculum called "First aid to the injured," teaching people what to say under such circumstances.

Sunday, June 4, 1893

Selena and I went in to B. preaching to-day. Nate was there, sitting up in the corner of the choir pew. He looked over my way a good deal— and so did other people, to see how I was taking it. When church came out I hurried away at once for I didn't care about speaking to him under all the eyes of the "Jesuits." He looks just as usual and hasn't changed a bit.

Interior of Baptist Church

Thursday, June 8, 1893
Cavendish, P.E.I.

I had a letter from Mr. Mustard to-day. It was a very incomprehensible epistle. He seems to be tired of life—or the life he is living—and says he is thinking seriously of "retiring and becoming a sort of college recluse and celibate"—and so wants *my* advice to "steer him past the rocks of his delusion if delusion it is."

Fancy giddy *me* advising an embryo Presbyterian minister what to do!!! Poor Mustard, I can't think it would be a great loss to the world if he did "retire" from it. But I shan't say so. Instead, I'll preach away just so-so and give him heaps of good advice, if that is what he wants.

Ten O'clock P.M. Same day

I suppose I ought to be in bed—but people aren't always where they ought to be and I don't feel sleepy. Went to prayer-meeting to-night and all "our crowd" was there, including Alec, Elton and Don. When meeting came out I had a drive with Alec. It was a lovely night, calm and cool, with no dew, a faint lemon-light in the air, pale rose-tints in the north west, and a few lazy stars blinking out and in. I enjoyed my drive immensely.

Friday, June 9, 1893
Eight O'Clock in the morning

It's such a beautiful day and such a beautiful world that I must "bubble over" to someone and you, old journal, are the only one I dare bubble over to. Oh, the world is so lovely now. It is the very prime of glorious springtide. The apple orchards are a pinky blush, the cherry trees are wreaths of perfumed snow; and in the mornings the fresh moist air is dizzily sweet with their delicious odors and resinous breaths of fir. The fields are like breadths of green velvet and birches and maples swing heavy curtains of green leaves. Oh, it's a dear beautiful world!

Friday, June 16, 1893

After tea this evening Selena and I went for a walk as far in as Chester Wyand's new house and then came back to the school where we sat down on the steps to rest. While we were there Jack and Austin came up the hill. Austin, as soon as he spied us, made a frantic dash into the woods, but Jack came over and sprawled himself down on the platform at our feet. We sat there and talked until the mosquitoes got so troublesome that we decided to go inside. Selena pushed up the only unnailed window, put a stick under it and climbed in. As she did so, her foot knocked out the stick. Down came the window with a crash and split went three panes clear across, a piece falling right out of one. Half choking with laughter I tore around to the back, where Jack was trying a window, and got him to come to the rescue. We all got in finally and settled down in a seat for a long jolly talk. We had lots of fun until it began to grow dark, when we scrambled out and went our several ways.

Monday, June 19, 1893

There is to be a week of special meetings and they began to-night but I did not intend to go to this one, as I had some extra studying to do. All the rest went and as I was hungry I was broiling some ham for myself when in popped Selena, bent on carrying me off to the meeting. Argument being of no avail, I left her to finish broiling the meat and was ready by the time it was cooked. I whisked it off upstairs to make sure of it and when I got home I devoured it. Very good it tasted, too, although Howard Simpson's invocations to the "Holy *Spilit*" had rather taken the edge off my appetite!

Saturday, June 24, 1893

This has been quite a gay week, so much religious dissipation going on. The "gayety" came after the meeting when a nice little drive was the order of the night.

To-night Pen, Lu, Selena and I were out for a walk at sunset. We met Ches Clark and Will Stewart driving. Lu and Selena went with Will, Pen and I with Ches. We went east and had a lovely drive and no end of fun. Coming back we dropped Pensie at her place and then Ches and I had another very pleasant drive by ourselves.

Friday, June 30, 1893
Two O'Clock P.M.

I'm off in another hour to town to put my fate to the test. Oh, I wish the entrance exams[1] were over! I've studied very hard all the year. But Selena, though a jolly girl and good friend, isn't any kind of a teacher. I might just as well have stayed home this past year and studied, for all the good going to school every day did me. So I don't know how I'll come out and I'm much afraid of some things.

I went to school this morning. It was the last day and I felt sorry. Of course it was nothing to what it would have been if it were the "old crowd" I was parting with but still I felt many a twinge of regret at leaving the old school forever. When we were dismissed at noon I bade good-bye to every old corner but I wouldn't let even one weeny teeny tear come to my eye, because Austin was looking at me! Pres is to drive Selena and me to the station and we leave shortly.

Saturday, July 1, 1893
Charlottetown,[2] P.E.I.
10.30 P.M.

Here I am, a stranger in a strange land. We got in about 8.30 and I came up to Selena's as I am to be her guest during the exams. After tea we went out for a walk and had a very enjoyable time. To-day being Dominion Day we all went out to the Park after dinner. It is a pretty place but I found the

---

1. The faculty of Prince of Wales College (PWC) set their own entrance examinations to augment the provincial matriculation exams.

2. Capital of Prince Edward Island, founded 1750; its population in 1893 was 11,000.

afternoon very dull, having nothing to do but sit on a bench and watch a crowd of people I didn't know. This evening Selena and I went over the ferry to Southport and had an enjoyable little trip.

Sunday, July 2, 1893

This morning we went to St. Paul's (Episcopal) church, as Selena is an Episcopalian.[1] I found the service very interesting but the seats were extremely uncomfortable—narrow box seats whose back took one— or took me, anyhow—just across the neck. After dinner we took a walk to the cemetery but the heat and dust rendered it anything but pleasant. This evening we went to St. Peter's Church—the "highest" of the "high"—Roman Catholic in all but name. I felt devoutly thankful that I was a Presbyterian. If I went to that church a year I'd have nervous prostration—that is, if they always go through all the kididoes[2] they went through to-night.

Old St. Paul's

Monday, July 3, 1893
Charlottetown, P.E.I.

After a shopping excursion this morning I sat down to study—for tomorrow is the beginning of sorrows and English and history lead off. I revised Goldsmith[3] and half the English history before noon and finished it in the afternoon. After tea I revised Canadian History until dark. I am tired to death and filled with the bluest of blue forbodings!

Tuesday, July 4, 1893

I am still alive but so tired I don't know if it is worth while!

---

1. An American term: *Anglican* or *Church of England* would be more commonly used in Canada. Elsewhere LMM refers to the "English" church.

2. Slang: mischievous tricks.

3. The play *She Stoops to Conquer* (1773) and the novel *The Vicar of Wakefield* (1762) by Oliver Goldsmith (1728–74) were both commonly part of the matriculation curriculum.

This morning Selena and I went down to the college. The crowd of candidates was huge. Austin was there, too, smiling expansively—but *I* didn't smile—at least not at him. It was 10.30 before we got to work. I found myself in Professor Caven's[1] room, with about 60 others, not one of whom I knew. The French professor, Arsenault,[2] had charge of our room. When he put the English paper on my desk I trembled like a leaf; but when I had glanced wildly over it I knew I could do *it* all right. I finished it in an hour and a half and feel sure I did pretty well. To be sure, I was frightfully provoked to discover, after I had come home, that I had simply overlooked the second division of the second question entirely—so maddening when I could have answered it in full.

In the afternoon we had history and a hard paper it was but I think I did fairly well in it. I was awfully tired when I came back, but there was no rest for the wicked, for to-morrow we have Agriculture, Geography, French and arithmetic. I plunged into the latter for I'm desperately anxious about it, as it is one of the vital subjects. I worked the problems till I was dizzy. I can do well enough in arithmetic when I know I have plenty of time and that nothing very important depends on the result. But otherwise I lose my wits and do silly things.

Wednesday, July 5, 1893

The arithmetic paper was terrible—it fairly made my hair stand on end. I don't know whether I made a pass in it or not. The problems were "catchy." They seemed to be deliberately designed to trip candidates up, instead of to discover what their grasp of the subject was. As for the other three subjects I think I got along all right. Tomorrow is the last day for which glory be! It is also the worst, for we have Latin, Geometry and Algebra. I dread the geometry but am not afraid of the others. I am dreadfully tired but must go and revise the Latin.

Thursday, July 6, 1893

I'm free! Hallelujah!

---

1. John Caven (1826–1914), educated at Edinburgh and Rome, taught English and school management at PWC. Professor Rennie in *Anne of Avonlea* (chapter IV) seems to be modelled on Professor Caven.

2. Joseph-Octave Arsenault (1866–1918) supervised practice teaching; in 1893 he became principal of the Model School, founded that year.

When the papers were passed around this morning I quaked from my toes to my crown. But they were all easy; even the geometry wasn't half bad. Reviewing all the papers I think I'll get through all right if the arithmetic doesn't knock me out. I shiver when I think of it.

Monday, July 10, 1893
Cavendish, P.E.I.

I came home Friday. To-day Lu and I decided to go back to Montana and see if we could get any berries. So we started bravely off, plus the usual outfit of cups, jugs, and lunch baskets and had a pleasant walk back, subtracting mosquitoes and fences from the sum total of pleasure. Presently we were in Montana—but the berries were *not*. In vain we scoured all the old reliable spots and scrambled through brush and briar and over fences. We got only about half a jugful apiece and came home thoroughly disgusted.

Tuesday, JULY 18, 1893

The date is worthy of capitals for I am truly—as Selena prophesied in her last letter I would be— the happiest girl in Cavendish. The pass list came out to-day and I am fifth in a list of 264 candidates. If I had not made that silly mistake in the English paper and another one equally silly in the arithmetic I would likely have led, or nearly, as the highest was only 21 marks more. But I am well content. The relief from the suspense of the past ten days is enormous. I had worried much over that arithmetic paper that I had begun to believe I had surely failed.

Poor Austin did not pass. Selena has gone to teach in Flat River.

To-night I went to the shore. It was a glorious evening. The sea was gleaming blue, the

A rock on C. shore

western sky a poem of rose and gold, emerald and azure. The sea's blue changed to silver gray, with the boats gliding over its shimmering glory, homeward bound. When our boat came in I came home through the purple dusk, with lurid bolts of lightning hurtling over the dark clouds on the south-east horizon.

Thursday, July 20, 1893

Went to prayer-meeting to-night. I have not been there since before I went to town, for I don't want to drive around with Alec Macneill any longer and I have hoped he would take the hint. He wasn't there and I had a jolly drive after it with Ches.

Saturday, July 29, 1893

Lu and I spent this afternoon with Pensie and had a jolly time. Just as we started home it began to rain and Alec declared he would drive us home. To refuse under the circumstances would have been absurd but I did not accept very gushingly. Alec hitched up his dandy horse, "Doctor"—he always has splendid nags, I'll say *that* for him—and the rain held up for a little. We started, and I'm bound to admit had a rather nice time, and went up west as far as Mr. C.'s gate, when the rain began again, so we turned back and drove to Uncle John's where we let Lu off. Of course I supposed we'd go home then too, especially as it was now pouring cats and dogs, but Alec had other views. He drove clear up to Stewarts and then walked that horse every inch of the way back. He gave me several hints about my cool behavior recently but I took no notice of them.

Wednesday, Aug. 3, 1893

Yesterday word came that Grandpa Montgomery was dead. It was no surprise for he has been very ill for a long time. I feel so badly. He was such a dear, lovable old man and I have loved him dearly. He was always very, very kind to me and I shall miss him very much when I go to Park Corner.

To-day Grandpa Macneill took me up to the funeral. It was a very large one and Rev. J. M. MacLeod preached a beautiful sermon. Poor grandfather was sadly changed. The dear old face was wasted but had a singularly peaceful look.

We came home this evening and I feel very tired. Uncle Leander is here now for a visit.

Wednesday, Aug. 16, 1893
Cavendish, P.E.I.

This evening we had a rehearsal at the church for a missionary concert we have been practising for tomorrow night. There was quite a crowd of us there and we went through the whole performance.

Thursday, Aug. 17, 1893

Well, I suppose there has been a concert in some corner of the world to-night—perhaps even a missionary concert—but it certainly was not in Cavendish. It rained all day and wound up with a terrific gale at night. Murray and I—he is here for his vacation—fussed all day getting ready the letters of a motto Mrs. Archibald had asked us to make, but needless to say there was no rush about putting it up.

Dear me, where has the summer flown to? Here it is the middle of August and P.W. College opens in two weeks. It seems only yesterday that Selena and I lay on the brook's banks and saw in its dancing waters the reflection of spring's first smile. Verily, time is brief. Once, long-ago, when I was a pale-faced, big-eyed tot, I could not see from one end of the summer to the other. It stretched before me as an unending season. Now it is as a space which one steps across in a moment.

Monday, Aug. 21, 1893

This afternoon I took a walk back through dear old Lover's Lane. Surely, it is the prettiest spot in the world. Apart from its beauty I have a strange love for it. In those divine woodland solitudes one can hear the voice of one's own soul—the voice of nature—the voice of God. I wish I might go there every day of my life— I always feel better after a stroll under those green arches where nature reveals herself in all her beauty.

Lover's Lane

Tuesday, Aug. 22, 1893

Went to the church this evening for another missionary practice. Mollie and I got together and had lots of fun. We were sitting by one of the windows when Alec and Will Stewart stepped outside and asked us to go driving. As our recitations were over we slipped out; it was a lovely moonlit night and we had a fine time.

Saturday, Aug. 26, 1893
Cavendish, P.E.I.

Our concert *did* come off at last on Thursday evening and was quite a success for that sort of thing. Last night I went to a magic lantern show in the hall. It was fine. Also who should be there but Lem and Ella McLeod. Lem drove me home after it and we had a lovely drive. Lem is going to the Business College[1] in town this winter and Jack Sims and Irv Howatt are to be at P.W.C. so I'll not be entirely among strangers.

Friday, Sept. 2, 1893

I was collecting my traps together to-day for emigration—a rather dismal task for I simply hate the thought of leaving Cavendish. We had prayer meeting to-night instead of last night. Don McKay took me driving afterwards and the way that wild mare of his flew over the road made me dizzy. It was moonlight and we had lots of fun.

So ends the long list of jolly drives for me. Many a pleasant time I've had this past year on prayer meeting night. It is over for me though not for others. Prayer meetings will go on, the girls will hurry down the dark roads when it is out, go driving with the boys, sit in the back seats, and laugh at the Simpsons. But I'll be far away, among strange new faces and ways of life. It makes me blue to think of it.

Monday, Sept. 4, 1893
Charlottetown, P.E. Island.

At four this morning I was roused from a most interesting dream that some girl in Melbourne, Australia, had written me a letter in which she wanted to

---

1. Located on the second floor of the Brown block on Richmond Street, Charlottetown.

know if she couldn't "send me one of those delightful little auburn-haired *sheep*." I think Austin must have been haunting my pillow.

Grandma drove me into town. We reached here about nine and came to a Mrs. Alexander MacMillan's,[1] she having been mentioned to us as wanting boarders. I am to board here but I don't know whether I shall like it or not. Mrs. M. is a widow, living quite near the college on a very ugly block on Hillsboro Street. She has a daughter Mary, about my age, a son, Jim, about 20, and another, Dan, of 12. Miss Florrie Murchison, a pronounced "strawberry blonde," is the only other boarder here. I felt pretty lonely when grandma went home but I guess I shall get on all right.

Tuesday, Sept. 5, 1893

Well, the first day is over and I have got off with rather more than my life although I feel dreadfully tired. At nine this morning I went to college. At ten Dr. Anderson[2] called all the girls[3] in and registered us one by one. That over, I went out and had a chat with Irv Howatt whom I met in the hall. Then I went out and sat down under the trees of the campus with some of the college girls and had a good deal of fun, although we were ravenously hungry. We had to "grin and bear it," however, as we do not get out until two. When the boys had all been enrolled

Old P.W.C.

we girls were called in to Professor Caven's room where the sheep were divided from the goats—that is to say, all of us who were going in for "First Class"[4] were "sorted out" from those who were to take second class work. The latter were let off at once but we poor F.C.s were kept there until nearly

---

1. McAlpine's City Directory in 1888 lists "Barbara McMillan, boarding house, 24 Hillsborough"—a house near the harbourfront, about five blocks from Prince of Wales College.

2. Alexander Anderson (1836–1925), a gold medalist from the University of Edinburgh who emigrated to Canada in 1862, became PWC and Normal School principal in 1868. Awarded an LL.D. by McGill University in 1888, he was revered by many later students including Sir Andrew Macphail and LMM.

3. PWC became co-educational in 1879; LMM's class in 1893 consisted of seventy-seven women and ninety-nine men. Annual fees for the year were ten dollars for Charlottetown residents, five dollars for country students.

4. First Class students normally attended for two years, adding Greek and Trigonometry to advanced studies in basic courses: English, history, geography, arithmetic, French, chemistry, agriculture, school management, school laws, teaching, and music. Second Class students took the basic courses plus algebra, geometry, physics, Latin, and scientific temperance. Third Class students attended only from August to December.

three before Dr. Anderson came in to interview us. We have to take an extra arithmetic exam next week before being allowed to skip the first year's work and meanwhile we begin First Class work tomorrow by 20 lines of Virgil. Also we have to be there at 8 every morning to take Agriculture.

Wednesday, Sept. 6, 1893
Charlottetown, P.E. Island.

The first thing this morning was Agriculture in Prof. Harcourt's[1] room over at the Normal. Then we went to Dr. A.'s room for roll call, then upstairs to Prof. Shaw's[2] room for mathematics, then down to Prof. Caven's room for French. Then we had a 15 min. recess. First-class English[3] came next and then third-year English which I am taking as a substitute for Trigonometry.

The First Class girls seem rather stiff. I find the second-class girls more approachable—perhaps because they are strangers like myself.

Sunday, Sept. 10, 1893

After dinner to-day I went down to Aunt Mary McIntyre's—she is a sister of father's and lives in town. Aunt Elizabeth was there too, from Boston, on a visit. I had a lovely time.

Monday, Sept. 11, 1893

I love going to college. It is simply delightful. To be sure, I don't believe I will ever get acquainted with the First Class girls. They seem to be an "unacquaintable" lot, with the exception of Annie Moore who is not quite so stand-offish—perhaps because she, too, is a newcomer. I only sit with her in Mathematics though. In Dr. A.'s room I sit with a Miss Huestis, who has no

---

1. George Harcourt (b. 1863), a graduate of the Ontario Agricultural College who taught LMM agriculture and chemistry, retired in 1894 and returned to Ontario. He eventually became, among other distinctions, Deputy Minister of Agriculture in Alberta.

2. Herbert Shaw (of Brackley Point), having graduated B.Sc., McGill University, had been appointed in September to teach mathematics and drawing.

3. The heavy curriculum included Shakespeare's *The Merchant of Venice*, Scott's *Lay of the Last Minstrel*, Addison's "Sir Roger de Coverley," Tennyson's "Guinevere," Pope's "Essay on Criticism," and Meiklejohn's *English Literature of the 18th and 19th Centuries*, in addition to the Second Class list—*Paradise Lost*, Book I, and Macaulay's "Essay on Milton"—and the Third Class readings: *Macbeth*, Scott's *Lady of the Lake*, selections from Addison's *Spectator* essays, and Macaulay's *Lays of Ancient Rome*.

more animation than a statue, and in Prof. Caven's room with Clara Lawson who is fearfully quiet and slow.

I am all alone in my room now. I am not homesick—I have never been a bit homesick since I came to town—but I *am* rather lonesome to-night and would like very well to see some of my Cavendish friends—girls preferably but boys would *do*—and have a good jolly chat.

Monday, Sept. 18, 1893

We had our extra Arithmetic exam last week and this morning after prayers Dr. A. came in with a folded paper in his hand. My heart began to thump violently, for the exam had been very hard and I was badly frightened that I had not made a pass—which would mean dropping back to Second-Class work. Dr. A. opened the fatal document with awful deliberation and began to read with as much composure as if a score of half-stilled hearts were not awaiting their owner's names in order to beat again. "There was silence deep as death," as one by one the names were called and at last mine *did* come. I made only 68—but that was 19 marks higher than I had feared. What a huge relief it was!

Wednesday, Sept. 27, 1893
Ch'town, P.E. Island.

This was one of the "Exhibition"[1] days and grandpa was in. After dinner I went down to see if Selena had arrived, as she was expected home for her vacation. She herself opened the door and how we laughed and hugged each other and then had a glorious talk! At seven this evening she came up and we went out for a walk. The streets were thronged and very soon we met Ches Clark. Such fun as we had! We also met Jack Laird and had a chat with him.

Thursday, Sept. 28, 1893

Selena and I went out to the Exhibition grounds this afternoon but as it poured rain the whole time we did not enjoy ourselves frantically. The rain also spoiled our project for going out to a concert this evening.

---

1. Established in 1879, the Charlottetown Exhibition had moved to grounds outside the city in 1890, but Queen Square, three blocks from the College, still hosted horse and cattle parades and Scottish dancing at Exhibition time.

I had quite an exciting letter to-day. Soon after I came to town I wrote a little poem called "The Violet's Spell" and sent it to *The Ladies' World*[1] of New York. And it has really been accepted! They offer me two subscriptions in payment. It is a start and I mean to keep on. Oh, I wonder if I shall ever be able to do anything worth while in the way of writing. It is my dearest ambition.

Tuesday, Oct. 3, 1893

This evening Nell R. and I started for the social in Zion Church[2]—I attend Zion church, by the way. We picked up seven other college girls on the way, so that we were quite an imposing procession when we finally reached there. We had a splendid time at the social but it was spoiled for me by the fact that Wallace Ellis,[3] a second class booby, whom I despise walked home with me.

Everything is in unholy confusion here at present for Mrs. MacMillan is moving to another house down on Fitzroy Street.[4] The new house is a double tenement and the rooms are just boxes. Besides, it is quite a long way from college. I don't care very much for boarding with these folks, anyhow, but I must just put up with it.

Friday, Oct. 6, 1893

We are settled down at last in a very *un*settled condition. My room is a back one on the third floor. At present, in the terrible jumble of things belonging to Mrs. M. which are piled into it, it is a work of art to navigate around with anything like safety to myself or the surrounding articles.

---

1. This respected magazine, founded in New York in 1886 and selling at fifty cents a year, published LMM's poem in July 1894: seven rhymed stanzas depict a violet, trampled in a city street, but bringing memories of the woodlands.

2. The stylish downtown Presbyterian church with its upholstered pews and instrumental music was erected in 1860 on Grafton Street, when a group of families seceded from the Old Kirk of St. James, the Free Kirk, and the Athenaeum. The incumbent, Rev. David Sutherland (not related to LMM's Sutherland cousins), died in 1899.

3. Student from Suffolk, PEI, who won a second class teacher's license in 1896.

4. 187 Fitzroy is one block north of the Kent Street College buildings.

Sunday, Oct. 8, 1893

In the park

I went to Zion church this morning. After dinner I went with a couple of college girls to the Park.[1] It was a divine day—one of those delicious days which October gives us occasionally. The Park is such a pretty place. The beautiful Hillsboro bay stretched out before us in sparkling blue, with the sloping shores in the distance scarfed in faint amethyst vapors. The beeches are golden brown and the air under them was full of delicious fragrance. We sat on a bench beneath their overshadowing glory or wandered idly around, drinking in deep draughts of the wine—like air. It was so lovely to be with nature again, away from the dusty city street.

Dear me, I hope we'll soon get "sorted out." Imagine trying to live, move, and have your being in the midst of trunks, boxes, piles of furniture etc. of which it might be truthfully said, "no place for anything and nothing in its place."

Friday, Oct. 13, 1893
Ch'town, P.E. Island.

This evening I went with Nell, Lucetta, Mary and Ida to a social in "The Kirk," as St. James Presbyterian church is always called. The college students were out in great force and we had quite a nice time. Wallace Ellis was there and was determined to join us and we were equally determined he should not and we dodged him until I was breathless from laughter. Finally he gave up in despair and took his stand by the door, ready, I suppose, to pounce on me when I went out. So I made the girls promise they'd go right to my door with me and as soon as we got

St. James' Church (Presbyterian)

---

1. Victoria Park, forty acres of parkland on the harbourfront of Hillsborough Bay at the west end of Charlottetown; a central feature is the viceregal mansion Fanningbank, built in 1834.

out I made a frantic dive between Mary and Ida and there I stuck like a burr the whole way home. Soon as we got to the door I whisked in like a shot and reached my own sanctum sanctorum in safety.

I am to have a room-mate henceforth—Bertie Bell of Hope River who is coming in to learn the dressmaking. I am not overjoyed at the prospect as she is a stranger to me. However, she looks quiet and harmless. She and Mary MacMillan are very chummy—which is a pretty sure sign that she and I will *not* be. I cannot bear Mary McMillan. She is precisely the style of girl I detest—pert, shallow, ignorant, with a furious temper.

Tuesday, Oct. 17, 1893

I'm really too furious to say my prayers, so must calm myself by "writing it out" before I go to bed. After tea this evening I was down in the sitting room studying my Greek when the door-bell rang. Mrs. MacMillan answered it and I heard a voice asking for me—the voice of that *unutterable*—Wallace Ellis. I gazed wildly around for some loophole of escape but none presented itself and I heard her showing him into the parlor. I was meditating retreating out of the back door and hiding in the yard, leaving Mrs. M. to explain my disappearance as best she might, when she sailed in, beaming significantly. I took her by the shoulders and said with awful impressiveness,

"Mrs. MacMillan if that *creature* ever *dares* to call on me again, remember that I'm not in. *Remember!*"

And, leaving the solemnity of that final "Remember" to sink deep into her soul, I went in to the parlor. *Such* an evening! I tried to be decently civil while all the while I was wishing him in Jericho. He is a fearful bore. He stayed until 9.30, thereby demoralizing my whole evening's work and exasperating me to my present pitch of fury. The horrid pig!!!

Thursday, Oct. 19, 1893

After Greek this morning, as the boys were passing out—they always take precedence of us in Dr. A.'s classes because the blessed man says they take less time to get out than the girls do—Irv Howatt stopped at my seat long enough to whisper that Lem was in town. So when I went out for a walk this evening I was not surprised to meet him and Stewart Simpson on the street. I stopped to speak and Stewart S. evidently thought there was too much of a crowd just then for he whisked himself out of the way while Lem and I had a walk and chat together.

Sunday, Oct. 22, 1893

At dinner to-day Mrs. MacMillan proposed to Bertie Bell and me that we go over to Southport on the ferry boat for an outing, so we went. We got our tickets and Mrs. M. marched us down a dock and on board a ferry. I had been over to Southport in the summer with Selena and I was sure we were

on the wrong boat but I couldn't convince Mrs. M. of this because the old tub—I mean the boat not Mrs. M.—had "Southport" painted on her. So we started and in about ten minutes Mrs. M. and Bertie came around to my views, with, gratifying completeness. There was no doubt that we were on the wrong boat—the one that went to Rocky Point![1] Here was a pickle! They would certainly have to take us there, since they couldn't very well dump us off in mid-harbor but suppose we didn't get back in time to keep our several engagements for the evening! Or, worse still, suppose we couldn't get back that night at all! We were busy supposing all sorts of complications when the captain came around and relieved our minds by accepting our tickets, plus an extra cent all round, and stating that they left for home at five. We got over at 2.30 and while Mrs. M. went to call on some friends Bertie and I, on the strength of some rather vague directions, set off across the fields to hunt up the remains of the old French fort. We went down lanes and across scrubby commons, along steep cliffs and over sandy bogs, and finally climbed a fearfully steep hill. There was the fort—no great sight for so much trouble—just a square grass-grown mound, surrounded by a deep ditch. The view from it is, however, very beautiful.

We had a lovely sail home. I went to tea at Mrs. Young's,[2] had a rather dull time and attended the Big Brick Methodist[3] with her. The music was fine—they have the best choir in town. Lem was there and we strolled about until nine, as is the custom in this goodly town. Upper Prince is the favourite promenade and a very pretty street.

---

1. The old French Fort Lajoie, on Rocky Point at the mouth of Charlottetown harbour; Professor Caven had written a popular poem about this historic site.

2. Letitia Young, widow of Judge Charles Young, lived in Fairholme, the elegant house built in 1838 at the corner of Prince Street and Fitzroy.

3. The handsome Wesleyan church built in 1863 on Prince Street had been satirized in Charlottetown papers as "The First Disorderist Church . . . where the preacher shouts, and the ladies exhibit their loud and extravagant fashions."

Thursday, Oct. 26, 1893
Ch'town, P.E.I.

In School-Management class to-day Professor Caven read out the names of all those appointed to give an object lesson to the Normal kids next week and I was quite startled to hear mine as I had not expected it so soon. I am to go on Tuesday. I intend to take the Prince Albert Indians for my subject. I feel fearfully nervous. I wouldn't mind it so much if Prof. Caven didn't have to go with us and criticize our performances before the School Management class next day.

I had a letter from Mr. Mustard to-day. He is back at Knox again and is more utterly utter than ever. Poor mortal—he seems to have an uncomfortable sort of temperament—always torturing himself and others on the rack of self-analysis.

Tuesday, Oct. 31, 1893

This has been quite an exciting day. This morning in Latin Composition Class everything was going smoothly and we were drinking in the rules about the relative when Dr. A. suddenly paused in his harangue, looked out of the window and said "How do you do?" to some invisible person below. "Is Miss Montgomery in your room?" called out the invisible person, and I recognized grandfather's voice. Dr. A. motioned me to go and I raced up the aisle, scuttled over the bare space and slid out of the door, conscious that I was being as closely scrutinized by some 60 pairs of eyes as if the reason for my summons might be read in the appearance of my back. I found grandfather and grandmother outside. We put in a busy morning shopping and at 12 I went back to the college, as I had to be there at one to teach. I followed Prof. Caven quakingly over and saw a roomful of children, from ten to twelve. I advanced to the front, announced my subject and plunged headlong in. Then I warmed up, forgot to be nervous and got on swimmingly. The subject was new, so it took the children's fancy and they kept good order. At the close when I questioned them about the lesson I had given, they shouted out the answers with gratifying promptness and vigor. I am very thankful that the ordeal is over. Prof. Caven gave me quite a puff in class about it.

Thursday, Nov. 9, 1893

There is never anything new to write in you, journal. Five days of the week I go round and round in a pleasant, monotonous circle. Then on Saturdays and Sundays I fly off at a little tangent. Look at that! From working at geometry exercises for two mortal hours my head has got so full of the terms that they pop out at all times.

I'm half homesick to-night. Never mind, Christmas and Christmas holidays are not far off. Blessed thought—even if between now and that happy time loom up the woes of examinations and the cares of this world.

Saturday, Nov. 11, 1893
Ch'town, P.E.I.

Lem was down to-night as *usual* and we discussed many subjects and talked nonsense about most of them. Once Lem said he was going out west[1] when he got through Business College and I said I thought he'd be a goose if he did.

"Why, wouldn't you go with me?" he said.

"No, indeed, I wouldn't," I remarked decidedly. "I've had enough of the west, thank you."

I meant it, too. I haven't the least intention of going anywhere with Lem McLeod. He's a nice, jolly lad, but if I see him for an hour once a week for a newsy chat that is quite enough for me.

Tuesday, Nov. 14, 1893

Studied hard all the evening—too hard for I got tired and discouraged.

I sat with Ida Scott in Virgil[2] to-day. She is a very nice girl. In fact, I have concluded that most of the first-class girls are nice, although it was so hard to get acquainted with them. Virgil is always a quiet class. It is hard and requires constant attention. Not a whisper is heard, for Dr. A. has the knack of keeping perfect order with no apparent trouble. Virgil over, we go upstairs for mathematics. Annie Moore[3] and I sit together in this class. After mathematics we go downstairs again for Roman History. This is one of the most interesting classes we have. Dr. A. gives us a lecture on each chapter.

---

1. Population of PEI, which in 1891 had been 109,000, was now rapidly declining because of migration to the Prairies.

2. *Aeneid,* the epic poem by Virgil (70–19 BCE) on the travels of Aeneas: a text in Latin class.

3. Pictured on p. 188, this top PWC student later moved to Western Canada.

We have it only once a week. I wish it came every day. Then comes recess. Formerly we all went outside to eat our lunch and watch the boys play football, but it is too cold for that now and so we hang around the radiator in groups and discuss college matters. After recess comes English literature. The last hour to-day was French in which I sat with Annie again. We got to saying funny things *sotto voce*, and I laughed till I cried. Catch us doing that in Dr. A.'s room! But Prof. Caven is very indulgent to me—I seem to be his "pet" this year. He always has a "pet" in each class—and wouldn't say a word to me unless I did something very terrible. Our French class is nice. We are translating "Iphigenia"[1] and find it very interesting. About dusk this evening Mary Campbell and Ida McEachern called. They are two jolly girls and we had lots of fun.

Saturday, Nov. 18, 1893

As usual on Saturday nights I am writing at a time very near the hour when churchyards are supposed to yawn. *I* am yawning, anyhow, and feel awfully sleepy. I spent this afternoon at Aunt Mary's and had a lovely time. This evening Ida M., Mary C. and I went for a walk. Lem came down later on and we had a pleasant chat. But there is so little in Lem. He's very shallow, and can talk of nothing but gossip. I like a bit of gossip, myself, as a spice, but I tire of it as a steady diet. Lem knows and cares nothing about books and scoffs at my literary ambitions. "What is the good of that sort of thing?" he says. And of course, if a person can't see the "good" for himself, you can't explain it to him.

Tuesday, Nov. 21, 1893
Ch'town, P.E. Island

Bitter cold! There were oh's and ah's and shivers in the P.W.C. corridors to-day. The good doctor hinted that the evil day of exams is at hand. I shall have to bestir myself and study double hereafter.

I had a delightful letter from Laura to-day. It was so full of fun it made me feel young again.

James McIntyre is home now and looks well.

---

1.   The tragic story (1674) of Agamemnon's daughter dramatized by Jean Racine (1639–99).

Sunday, Nov. 26, 1893

I was busy writing letters this afternoon when James McIntyre came up for me. He said John and Will Sutherland were also to be there. So I went and we had a lovely time—as we always have. After tea we went to church. Will and Lewis went to the Kirk but John, James, Bertie and I turned our faces, like good pilgrims, Zionward. After service John and I went back to Aunt Mary's and stayed there until nearly eleven. Then we came home, my little self between my two tall cousins holding me so tightly that if anyone had met us they might have thought I had "a jag on"[1] and was being convoyed home in an alamagorious condition.

Monday, Nov. 27, 1893

O—o—o—o! "From Greenland's icy mountains"![2] It has been awfully cold to-day. In consequence of last night's late hours I overslept myself this morning and great was my consternation on hopping out of bed to find it twenty minutes past seven. Well, exactly forty minutes from that I was in my seat at agriculture class, so imagine how I wiggled!

Mary Campbell and her brother Norman[3] are coming here to board. She came to-night. We are to room together in the big front room. I am very glad she is here for she is so jolly.

Friday, Dec. 1, 1893

Norman C. came to-day. He is a lively chap and excellent company. The exam time-table is out and Latin Composition leads off on Tuesday.

The boys have a college debating club and meet every Friday evening. As a rule they will not let the girls in but they invited us to go to-night, so we all did. The debate was on "Free-trade vs Protection" and was very good and also quite funny.

This evening Hedley Buntain[4] came down and asked me to go to the opera with him to see the play "Jessie of Lucknow."[5] He is a second cousin

---

1. Slang: drunk.
2. A missionary hymn (1819) by Bishop R. Heber.
3. Cousins of LMM from Darlington.
4. A connection of Penzie's mother, who was a Buntain.
5. *Jessie Brown or the Relief of Lucknow*, a three-act play about a siege in India, 1857, by Dion Boucicault (1820–90).

of mine and is living in town. We went and it was lovely. I enjoyed every minute of the time.

Saturday, Dec. 2, 1893

I'm "going to the dogs" completely I fear. Here are exams coming on apace and I've never opened a book to-day! Bertie McIntyre and I were invited up to tea at Mrs. Sutherland's. We had a pretty nice time, and loads of fun when John and Will came home. They board there, Mrs. Sutherland being their aunt. I am getting really acquainted with my two tall cousins now and fine nice fellows they are. At 7.30 Bertie and I started home and escorted by Jack's six feet of young manhood. At Judge Young's corner we met Hedley Buntain looking for me to go to the opera again—so we went. The play was "Arrah-na-pogue"[1] and was even better than last night. I laughed and cried and enjoyed it enormously.

Monday, Dec. 4, 1893

Mary and I overslept until 8 this morning and so missed our Agriculture. We were furious, for we've never missed a class before. It wouldn't have hurt old Mrs. McMillan to have called us but that would have been too obliging.

I "crammed" Latin Composition this evening until nearly ten. Then Mary and Norman and I got out in the hall and had a wildly hilarious time—laughed until we ached. We are a merry trio and can always find something to laugh at in all our tribulations.

Tuesday, Dec. 5, 1893

We had our Latin Composition Exam to-day and it was dreadfully hard. I began to revise Chemistry to-night, for we have the exam Thursday and I'm very much befogged in it, owing to not having had the first year's work. But just as I got well started John and Will S. came in and stayed till nine. That meant no more chemistry of course but it meant lots of fun.

---

1. This old-fashioned Irish melodrama (1865) by Dion Boucicault was still on stage at the Abbey Theatre, Dublin, in 2011. The playbill from this performance appears in LMM's Blue Scrapbook, reproduced in Elizabeth Epperly's *Imagining Anne* (2008).

There is some Mr. McDonald here to-night—an acquaintance of Mother Mac's. He is a tall and lank old fellow with a considerable "jag" on, and they have put him to sleep in the spare bedroom. I'm really frightened to go to sleep with such a creature in the house. Mrs. McMillan might exercise charity in some other fashion, I think—for instance, in giving us a decent meal now and then. She keeps a wretched table—and worse than that the food isn't even *clean*. Why, Mary found a piece of *soap* in her slice of bread last night at supper.

Wednesday, Dec. 6, 1893

I hardly know whether our recent adventures belong to yesterday or to-day but I think they might piece in with both, since the racket began before twelve and lasted after it. Mary and I went to bed before eleven. She was soon sound asleep and I was nearly so when suddenly I saw a light—the door opened softly and a tall gaunt form appeared on the threshold! Stricken dumb with terror I simply stared at this apparition with dilated eyes and couldn't utter a sound but began to dig frantically into Mary with my elbow.

Then he spoke. I have since come to the conclusion that what he really said was, "Will you come and unlock the door?" but at the time I took it to be, "Did you hear me knock at the door?" and I gasped out "No" plump and plain.

"O—o—o—h," he said softly and was apparently about to close the door when Mary came awake and gave a howl that might have wakened the dead. We jumped up in a panic, lit a lamp, and bolted into Florrie's room. She and Mary M. were scared, too, and when we heard him coming upstairs again we held the door. He called out several times for Mary M. to "come and unfasten the door" but she, thinking he meant the bedroom door, wouldn't stir, so he lumbered downstairs again. Then Mary C. and I went in and wakened Norman, who had slept calmly through it all. He and I then went downstairs to see what the disturber of the peace wanted. He said he wanted to go to the boat for fear he would miss it—it was only twelve then and the boat was due to leave at seven! So we let him out, re-locked the door and came up again. Mary and I, between excitement, fright, and cold hardly closed an eye the rest of the night and I felt like "something made in Germany"[1] all day.

---

1. The reputation for flimsiness reflected the phenomenal rise in the 1890s of cheap imports from Germany.

Saturday, Dec. 9, 1893

This evening, Mary C., Mary M., Nell D., and I went up to the Post Office and as we were too early for the mail we went for a walk around the square. Presently along popped Hedley Buntain, as primp and prim as you please—he always looks as if he'd just been starched and ironed. I didn't want his company at all but talked amiably to him until we reached the Post Office. Lem was there, as usual, and as soon as I got my letters, we went out together, leaving Hedley to Mary M.'s tender mercies. He came down with

POST OFFICE, CHARLOTTETOWN

her and into the parlor where Lem and I were sitting. I felt rather uncomfortable; but Hedley seemed very much taken aback to find Lem there and presently took himself off. Lem was sulky, too, evidently suspecting something fishy. But *that* didn't worry me much. Lem must find out, if he doesn't know it now, that he is really of no more account to me than Hedley if it comes to that.

Sunday, Dec. 10, 1893

I wasn't in church this evening so at 8 Mary M. and I went out for a walk. Just by Crabbe's Corner[1] Hedley Buntain came along in a sleigh and asked me to go for a drive. I went but I was really bored to death. I never can find anything to say to Hedley. When we got home he said he was coming down some evening to take me for another drive. I said "Thank you" very coldly, so probably he'll take the hint. He is engaged to another girl so has no business to come poking around here. Besides, I don't like him.

Monday, Dec. 11, 1893

I *do* hate geometry. I'm such a dunce at it—and I simply cannot apply myself to it in class. I'm sure to drift off into daydreams under Shaw's very eyes, until suddenly something rouses me from my reverie just in time to catch

---

1. Eight miles (13 km) northwest of downtown Charlottetown, but no longer on the map of PEI.

the fag-end of some very important explanation which I ought not to have missed. And so it goes.

We got back our Latin Composition papers to-day and I got an unwholesome surprise. I knew I had not done very well in the exam but I certainly expected 60 or 70. Well, I made exactly 44! Isn't that *awful?* I never made such a low mark in my life, even in geometry. I can't understand it, although Dr. A. is a merciless "marker down."

We finished with horticulture to-day and have the exam on Thursday. I must try to wipe out my Latin compo. disgrace. I studied until 9 this evening and then fooled about with Mary. We have had no end of fun since she came. It is just jolly to have someone to be crazy with.

Wednesday, Dec. 13, 1893

Freezingly cold. We had our algebra exam to-day and it was hard but I dare to think I didn't do too badly. I felt awfully tired all the rest of the day and was nearly frozen coming home. It wasn't much better when I got here for I never saw such a cold house. The wind seems to blow through it like paper; besides, Mrs. M. is *very very very* economical in regard to coal. We are *never* warm except when we are in bed and not always then unless we pile every stitch of clothes we own on the bed and sometimes even the mats from the floor!

I was busy cramming agriculture to-night when Jack S. and James M. called. They stayed about an hour and we had such fun. Before they came I had been feeling blue and worried and as if agriculture would press me down all my life but their visit cheered me right up. They are two such nice boys.

Sunday, Dec. 17, 1893
Ch'town, P.E. Island

I "crammed" agriculture and geometry all day yesterday, until I felt as if I were full of some awful mixture. James M. came up for me this afternoon and I went down with him and had a lovely time. Jack S. was there and in the evening we all went to Zion. After service James and Jack came down with me, we got Mary C. and we all decamped to Aunt Mary's again and stayed till ten.

Oh, just think of those two awful exams tomorrow! I wish I were dead or that it were tomorrow night.

Monday, Dec. 18, 1893

Well, one of my wishes has come true—it is "tomorrow night," and I am *not* dead although I am so tired it seems hardly worth while to be alive. Mary and I arose at 6 this morning and got into our togs with dismal forebodings, "cramming" agriculture for dear life at odd moments as we dressed. I curled my bangs with the book propped up against the mirror.

But the agriculture paper wasn't too bad at all. At 12 came geometry. The paper couldn't have been any harder than I expected it to be so it wasn't the shock it would have been if I had looked for anything easy. It was *Beastly*. I know I made a shocking mess of it. But it's over, thank goodness.

Tuesday, Dec. 19, 1893

I begin faintly to discern clear water ahead where no examination breakers loom. I was all tired out when I got home to-day for our Greek exam began at 9.30 and lasted until 2. The doc has a heart of stone where exams are concerned. I did the most of it and perhaps I made a good paper—and perhaps it was bad enough to make the ghost of Homer rise from his grave.

Thursday, Dec. 21, 1893
Ch'town, P.E.I.

Had an immense time in college to-day. Owing to the Trigonometry exam, we had no Latin class, so we girls got into Caven's room and had an hilarious hour. We got back our chemistry and horticultural papers to-day. I made 67 in chemistry which was fair, considering how badly I was handicapped in it, and 92 in Horticulture which is respectable.

Friday, Dec. 22, 1893
Cavendish, P.E.I.

Here I am in dear old Cavendish again and a good place it is after the wear and tear of much "examining." Our English exam began at 11 to-day and was a snap. Shaw also gave us back our geometry papers. I had been sure I had not passed but I just made it out by 52. When I got home I found that grandpa was in for me. John S. came down before I left and brought me a sweetly pretty Xmas card. We left at 2.00 and it was fearfully cold. For awhile I enjoyed the drive but soon began to suffer keenly from the cold. At last we got to the "Halfway House" and I went in and got thoroughly thawed out. Then we set off again and I could once more enjoy the cold pure beauty of the landscape. The sun set, throwing long rose-lights over the snowy hills. A pale, chilly moon looked out from behind a fringe of purple clouds in the east. The west was a pinkish yellow shading up into crushed raspberry and from that into ethereal blue, while thin veils of cloud floated across and caught the tints of that shining arch. The snow crackled and snapped under the runners. The sky faded out but the strip of yellow along the west got brighter and fierier, as if all the stray gleams of light were concentrating in one spot, and the long running curves of the distant hills stood out against it in dark distinctness and bare birches hung their slender boughs against the gold with the very perfection of grace.

Wednesday, Dec. 27, 1893

Have been having a very pleasant time but not dangerously exciting. Have been resting and reading in a "Boy's Own"[1] all sorts of enthralling tales about wonderful heroes who seem blessed with a miraculous faculty for getting into scrapes from which they are usually delivered by an earthquake or volcanic explosion which blows them high and dry out of their troubles, lands them in a fortune, and closes the story with proper *eclat*.

Thursday, Dec. 28, 1893

To-day has seemed like a page from last winter. Mollie came over to spend the afternoon. We had a delightful cosy time, playing parchesi, eating candy, and chatting over old times when we went to school together, wore short dresses, stiffly starched white aprons, and long braided "tails" of hair. In the evening Lu came over and we started for prayer meeting. The walking was vile but at the foot of the orchard we found Alec and Ab.[2] waiting for us in a pung. Pensie was also waiting for us at the stove and we all went to our old seat and had some quiet fun. After meeting I went for a drive with Don McKay. He had a dosy befurred sleigh and a dandy gee-gee.[3] We had a jolly

---

1. Published in the UK from 1855 to 1890, *Boy's Own Magazine* once the most influential boys' magazine with work by Conan Doyle, Jules Verne, etc., was being replaced in popularity by *Boy's Own Paper* (1879–1967).

2. Ab is Albert Macneill, oldest brother of Penzie, Alex, Russell, and others.

3. *Slang*: a good horse.

drive in along the Cavendish road under the dark spruces, with the snow-powdered trees standing up on either hand in white, silent ranks and the silvery bells sending tinkles of melody through the still woods.

Sunday, Dec. 31, 1893

It snowed all day by spells. Went to church in the evening. Lu, Pen, and I marched up to the very top seat of the church and "sot" in a pew under the very eyes of all the prim "plaster saints." When we came out I went for a drive with Alec but as it was snowing quite thickly it was not a very gay one.

Interior of old church

1894

Tuesday, Jan. 2, 1894
Cavendish, P.E.I.

The Manse

Lu and I were invited to spend the evening at the manse. Stuart, Mabel, Blanch and Birdie Simpson[1] were also there. Of course we had a very dull, prosy evening—for Mr. Archibald does not approve of games, it seems—and came home as soon as we decently could. Stuart drove us all home and after letting Lu out he drove to the end of the pumphouse to turn, mis-calculated the distance and went over the edge of a big drift. The sleigh promptly upset and we girls were completely emptied out against the house, with three buffaloes[2] and a pile of straw on top of us. With much laughter we disentangled ourselves, gathered up our buffaloes, and scrambled in again.

Friday, Jan. 5, 1894

Alec

Have been dissipating mildly ever since my last entry. This afternoon I spent at Mollie's and in the evening went up to Literary. Alec and I had a drive after the meeting and a wild one it was, for "Doctor" was all fire and simply flew and the pitches were *diabolical*. We went through them *lickety-split* and it was just *bounce, bounce, bounce* right along. I hardly dared open my mouth for fear of biting my tongue off. We had no end of funny adventures.

Saturday, Jan. 6, 1894

I had a letter from Miss West to-day, saying that there is to be a concert in Winsloe Hall next Monday night and that she wants me to go down to her uncle's, where she lives, next Monday and recite for them. It is to be a basket

---

1. LMM's contemporaries in Bayview among her Simpson cousins included Stuart (1876–1949), who became the general practitioner for the Cavendish-Stanley district; Mabel (1880–1953), who moved to Massachusetts; Blanch (1878–1973), who afterwards lived in Charlottetown; and Birdie (1880–1937), who moved to Saskatchewan.

2. Blankets made of buffalo skin were in common use for winter sleigh rides.

social[1] also. Guess I'll go. It will be a jamboree to wind up the holidays with. College opens Tuesday.

Sunday, Jan. 7, 1894

This morning Pensie came over with me from church and after dinner Alec came along in a pung sleigh and took us and Lu over to New Glasgow preaching. There was no end to the slews and pitches but that only added to the fun. We laughed from the time we left until we got home again—except in church, of course. We *are* the jolliest little crowd in the world.

Tuesday, Jan. 9, 1894
Ch'town, P.E.I.

Here I am back at "the old stand"[2]—and I can't say I think it has improved much in my absence! We left home yesterday morning at 4.30. It was quite dark and not a bit cold and I enjoyed the drive very much. We reached Mr. Holman's at 8 and I stayed there while grandpa went on to town. Mr. and Mrs. Holman seemed nice and Miss West was there—also her brother Fred West, B.A.[3] who is quite a famosity in a not altogether desirable way. The Methodist choir from town was coming out to give the music and were to have a goose supper at Mr. Holman's. I found I was expected to give two recitations and take part in a dialogue from Shakespeare with Fred West. Just imagine how silly I felt over the latter performance! I had never seen the selection before but I studied it up through the day and finally concluded I could do it as well as West could—if that was anything to boast of. They fixed up a basket for me also. It was bitterly cold at night but all the folks came out and after supper we drove to the hall which was packed full. I gave my recitations which were well received and West and I had our "dialogue." *It* didn't take at all enormously. I fancy Winsloe audiences don't altogether appreciate Shakespeare especially when interpreted by "Freddy." The sale of baskets was very amusing. Mine went highest at four dollars. Fred West bought it, which didn't please me at all—I don't like him. We didn't get to bed til 2 o'clock and I was so tired that not even the awful coldness of the room could keep me awake. West drove a lot of us into town after breakfast and it was bitterly cold. Things are much as usual here. Mary and Norman and I had a joyful reunion.

---

1. Young women packed fancy food into decorated baskets for basket socials; an auction decided which man would buy each basket and claim its creator as a supper partner.

2. Irish slang: home again, a common name given to pubs in Ireland and the US

3. Frederick West (brother of the Miss West who taught briefly at Cavendish), a graduate of Dalhousie University, had resigned in September from the faculty of PWC.

Wednesday, Jan. 10, 1894

First class Students at P.W.C. 1893–94. 1. My cousin, Will Sutherland. 2. Annie Moore. 3. Myself. 4. Fannie Wise. 5. Mabel Fielding. 6. Alberta Huestis. 7. Dave Shaw.

Still bitterly cold. Mary and I almost froze while dressing this morning. As Agriculture is done we do not have to go until 9 this term—fortunately. As soon as I got to college I was surrounded by my chums and it was so nice to be back again.

Prof. Caven gave us back our English papers to-day. Dave Shaw and I led, tied at 98 marks.

We have a new boarder now—Alec McDonald, a harmless little nobody. Bertie Bell has gone and is boarding elsewhere. Of course, she had some plausible excuse but I believe the truth was she was frozen out.

Jim McIntyre called this evening and we had a jolly chat. When he left it was such a delightful moonlight night that he insisted I go for a walk round the square with him and we had a delightful stroll.

Public Buildings, Queen Square Gardens, Charlottetown

Thursday, Jan. 25, 1894
Ch'town, P.E.I.

We are going to lose Norman. His home school at Darlington is vacant and he is going home to take it. I am sorry. Norman is such a jolly fellow.

As it was wet to-day Mary, who is just recovering from an attack of grippe,[1] did not go out and I went to college alone and lonesomely, I did not feel very spry and as the day wore on I felt less so. Latin Composition was uninteresting, School Management a bore, Greek a positive martyrdom and French a purgatory. Greek Composition was the last straw. When I got home I knew I was getting ready to be sick but I said nothing and tried to study as usual after dinner. However, I soon gave *that* up. My head is aching and ditto my bones. I'm going to bed.

Friday, Jan. 26, 1894

I've been in bed ever since. My throat is still very sore but I feel better otherwise. I *hate* being sick!!

Sunday, Jan. 28, 1894

I am on the convalescent list now. Jack S. and Lem came down to see me this afternoon and we had a very jolly time.

Friday, Feb. 2, 1894

We finished Virgil to-day and there was a vigorous clapping. We have the exam in it on Monday and I wish the unseasonable thing were over. After dinner to-day Mary and I went back to the college to attend the Mock Trial which the Boy's Debating Club[2] is getting up. It was very amusing. James Stevenson, Albert Saunders, and Tom James were the attorneys for the defence and looked very legal in their black gowns. Frank Dougherty is the prisoner and is accused of murder. The Crown Staff were James Macneill, Howard Leslie and Dave Shaw. Will Sutherland is Chief Justice and Norman Hunter and Ed McFadyen are the other two judges. Chesley Schurman is Clerk of the Crown and swore in the jury and witnesses on a well-worn textbook—"so help you, Julius Cesaer."

---

1. Influenza.
2. LMM's classmates named here came from various parts of the Island and eventually did well in their exams: James Stevenson of New Glasgow (valedictorian, and honour diploma), Albert Saunders of Summerside (First Class), Frank Dougherty of Charlottetown (teacher's certificate), James Macneill (went on to a McGill M.D.), Howard Leslie of Souris (First Class teacher's licence), Dave Shaw of Cove Head (top marks for teacher's certificate), Ed McFadden of Tignish (First Class), Chesley Schurman of Summerside (honour diploma).

Monday, Feb. 5, 1894
Ch'town, P.E.I.

We got back our agriculture papers to-day. Prof. Harcourt has been away, hence the delay. I led with 81. Then we had our Virgil exam and it was one after the doctor's own heart. We were at it for four hours and I felt like a "demoralized dishrag" when it was over. Still, if any man but Dr. A. were going to correct the papers I'd say I must have done pretty well.

Dr. Anderson

Friday, Feb. 9, 1894

Fate has a spite at me I verily believe. I've been laid up with the cold again for two days. However, I was bound to go to the Mock Trial to-day and go I did. But it was rather a farce and two of the boys got into a quarrel and Dr. A. had to be called in to settle it; so I expect the trial will be put under his ban.

Tuesday, Feb. 13, 1894

"Oh, mi dere diry," as saith the famous "Bad Boy,"[1] this is awful! Mary and I were almost frozen last night and this morning the ice on our jug was two inches thick. It was very cold in college also, especially in the Normal where I simply felt my nose turning blue. When we got out we hurried home and after another dinner of "ditto"—as Mary and I call the lean boiled mutton which has formed our constant mid-day repast for the last three weeks—I sat down to those unfailing studies. But about three who should appear but Selena who is in town on a visit. We had a delightful confab.[2]

Thursday, Feb. 15, 1894

It is really worth while to record that *we didn't* have "ditto" for dinner to-day. Instead, some fried potatoes and antique bacon. Mrs. MacMillan really keeps a wretched table. We are half starved most of the time.

---

1. *A Bad Boy's Diary: By Little Georgie*, a comic novel (1880) by American author Metta Victoria Fuller Victor, attributed to Walter T. Gray, was the first of a very popular series. An earlier "bad boy" had appeared in T.B. Aldrich's *The Story of a Bad Boy*, a bestseller of 1869.

2. Slang: confabulation, a chat.

The college boys have started a college paper and to-day Tal MacMillan[1]—no relation of *our* MacMillans—asked me to write something for it. I have built a "pome" and will send it in.

Jim McIntyre was up this afternoon to bid me good-bye. He was going on the night train and I have just heard it blow, so he is off. I am awfully sorry and will miss him muchly.

Fannie Wise and I had no end of fun in the Byron class to-day. We have finished "Childe Harold"[2] and I suppose the next thing will be an exam in it, although old Prof. Caven, bless his heart, hates giving them, I really believe, as much as we hate taking them.

Tal MacMillan

Thursday, Mar. 1, 1894

Certainly March has made its debut in the character of the meekest and mildest of lambs. To-day was a spring poem. To be sure, the streets were far from perfect, but that is only the beginning of the end.

The "College Record"[3] was out to-day. It is quite cute and well edited. My "pome" came in for a good deal of notice and even Prof. Caven himself told me, pulling his long gray beard the while, that it was "excellent." At least, he said "There was some excellent poetry in the *Record*," and as mine was the only verse in it I appropriated the compliment!

Eleven O'clock

More excitement. At ten Mary and I began to prepare for bed. Mary was in bed and I in very scanty array, was braiding my hair, when suddenly the stillness was broken by the harsh, metallic "Bim-bome" of the fire bell. We both shrieked excitedly and sprang to the door, as Mary MacMillan rushed

---

1. Talmage MacMillan of New Haven graduated with 88 percent and an honor diploma.

2. *Childe Harold's Pilgrimage* (1812–18), a romantic poem by Lord Byron, remained a favorite of LMM; her copy, heavily underlined, is now in the University of Guelph archives.

3. Hedley McKinnon of Charlottetown edited the school paper during this college year. LMM's contributions included "The Usual Way" (a spoof on schoolgirl studying—interrupted by gossip, candy, and talk of new hats and boys) and "Extracts from the Diary of a Second Class Mouse" (PWC as seen from a mouse's perspective). In the following year Edwin Simpson, Norman Campbell, and Cyrus Macmillan edited the *Record*.

in "Girls, the fire bell! Let's go!" she exclaimed. "Of course," I gasped as fran-tically. "Hurry, Mary, hurry."

We all lost our heads. Mary C. made a wild dash for stockings and clothes, I flung on my skirt and waist—jammed on my overboots—on the wrong feet of course and then had to yank them off again. Mary M. kept calling out incoherent remarks from her own room and we could hear Dan and Mother MacMillan in high altercation below. We finally got dressed and downstairs we all rushed. Mrs. Mac tried to stop us but we swept her aside like a straw. And we went and tore up three blocks to the corner of Queen and Grafton where we found it was only a false alarm after all. There was no fire, so we turned ourselves flatly about and came home. When we got back Mary C. and I sat down in our room and laughed wildly for half an hour. We are going to make another effort for bed now but I fear we won't sleep much.

Sunday, Mar. 4, 1894
Ch'town, P.E.I.

Mary and I went to Zion as usual this evening and Lem walked home with us. Then Mary went in while Lem and I went for a walk around Queen Square and Victoria Row. When we got back he went home and I went in to find the two Marys in the parlor. It was too fine a night to stay in so we went for another walk. Mary C. and I would have preferred Mary M. to be a minus quantity but as she was decidedly a "plus" we had to make the best of it. We started up Prince St. and at the brilliantly lighted crossing at the entrance to Upper Prince came full upon a crowd of college boys and also Jack S. We bowed to Jack, who of course lifted his hat—and then equally, of course every hat in the crowd of twenty or thirty boys flew up—it was more than comical. We laughed about it all the way up the street until we reached a place where several enterprising cats were giving an open air concert. I'm sure a Wagnerian opera wouldn't be a patch on it. We had no end of fun over those cats and the unbelievable noise they were making.

Monday, Mar. 5, 1894

Awaking this morning from a dream of being serenaded by a cat with John Sutherland's face I girded up my loins and betook myself to P.W.C., got through classes respectably, and then came home and fell to studying. Presently Will Sutherland called and we had a jolly chat. He brought back our albums which he had to write in. Mary and I then asked Alec to write in them and after we had finished studying we went downstairs to see the result. We managed by a great effort to keep our faces straight while we read them but when we were safe in our room again we went into such paroxysms of laughter that it's a perfect marvel someone didn't ring the fire bell—especially as our window was open and our cachinnations[1] might have been heard a block off! Poor Alec! I hope he will sleep in "pease" and that our howls above him haven't disturbed his "peaseful" slumbers. Really, his autographs were too funny for anything!

Thursday, Mar. 8, 1894
Ch'town, P.E.I.

In college and had a gay racket during chemistry hour. We had previously voted to get up a "peanut party" and all of us subscribed two cents each. At School Management hour the First Class girls, who do not take it, sneaked off uptown and got four pounds of peanuts. After recess we all went over feeling pretty mutinous. We got the peanuts distributed, cracked, ate them and threw the shells at one another. The air was thick with flying shells and beans, while

Prof. Harcourt

a big carrot and a red herring also passed and repassed. Harcourt was furious but powerless. He took down—or pretended to—a lot of names and I expect we'll hear something more of it yet: but they can't kill us and Dr. A., who dislikes Harcourt, never pays much attention to the latter's complaints. Harcourt is no good whatever as a teacher and is not respected in his classes at all.

Saturday, Mar. 10, 1894

The peanut affair blew over harmlessly. To-day has been a tough day. This morning our landlady took a most unusual cleanly spell and overhauled the sitting room and kitchen from floor to ceiling. Mary C. and I could find no rest for the soles of our feet or any other part of our anatomy, and it was too cold to stay in our room. I studied most of the afternoon and by tea time life didn't seem worth living. I meditated thoughtfully at the tea table.

---

1. Loud, convulsive laughter.

Lem would come but there was no fire in the hall and the parlor, which is heated—or supposed to be—from the hall would be icy cold. I was too sick to talk and the room would make me more so. The fruit of all this rumination was a resolve to go to bed at once. I gave Mary C. instructions as to the disposal of Lem and then went off to my flea-box.[1] But poor Mary C. when she had sent Lem off with a dismal tale of my sore throat etc. came up and was much disgusted to find the poor invalid sitting up in bed revising *Childe Harold* for the exam on Monday!

Tuesday, March 13, 1894

Lem came down for a farewell call tonight as his term at the B.C. is ended and he is going home tomorrow. Mary C. was in with us until nine and we had oceans of fun and teased poor Lem unmercifully. After she went I kept it up, for I was in mortal terror lest he should become sentimental. He *did* come perilously near it once or twice, on perceiving which I would immediately utter some wild speech and so side-track him. We hadn't an affecting parting at all for I was frosty in the extreme. Still, I was sorry to see him go and I shall miss him a good deal. But we are not exactly boy and girl now and our harmless little affair is beginning to assume a shade of seriousness that does not please me at all, so it is best that he is going.

I am invited out to Mary's home in Darlington for the Easter holidays. We are to have two weeks and won't we make Rome howl![2]

Saturday, Mar. 17, 1894

I am just a wee bit homesick tonight for Cavendish and some of my dear haunts there. I feel as if I would like to go back on a blue summer day to "Sam Wyand's field," fling myself down on the thick ferns under the maples and lie there for hours, with the blue sky peering through the trees, the robins whistling to each other in distant woods, the June-bells empurpling the moss under the spruces with patches of perfumed color and a faraway cow-bell tinkling drowsily through the air.

---

1. Commonly slang for a cheap boarding house. Here it means "bed." Not in dictionary of Canadianisms.

2. Western slang phrase used by Mark Twain among others, comparable to "paint the town red."

Sunday, March 18, 1894

Mary and I went to church this morning. As usual I tucked myself away in the corner of Aunt Mary's pew where I could take a sly squint every now and then at Mary and Ida out of the tail of my eye. After Sunday School we went for a short walk up Prince St. After tea Mary and I shut ourselves in the parlor and had a nice little jollification all to ourselves. We sat down by the window and tried to see which could say the funniest things about various folks of our acquaintance and howled with laughter between speeches. Mary is such a mimic and can "take off" anyone, especially Dame MacMillan, to the life.

In the evening we again went to church and I coaxed Mary to sit with me but repented having done so, for she kept me in a state of perpetual giggle-dom right under the nose of the Rev. David himself. We came home and are now up in our sky-roost, with one of our spells of talking and laughing on.

Monday, March 19, 1894
Ch'town, P.E.I.

Mary

Went to college and got through alive. Have been studying ever since I came home and feel "dead tired" now. For a wonder Mary and I have the room to ourselves to-night, everyone else being out. It is deliciously quiet—a welcome change from the usual noise which always makes it so difficult for us to study. We are both busy writing but I suppose when we go upstairs we will get going on that everlasting topic—the virtues of Jack Sutherland—and talk ourselves dumb on it. Mary and I *do* have jolly times in spite of all our tribulations—there is no disputing that. What a blessing for me that she came here! *What* would I have done this winter if I had been here alone?

Tuesday, Mar. 20, 1894

Last night we went to sleep to the tune of "Rockabye-baby" for it was blowing a hurricane and this crazy old house was waving to and fro. But we slept serenely on and awoke this morning to see all the snow gone and everything clean and hard-frozen. Mary and I started for college just as the huge funeral procession of a government official was passing up the street. I had a big load of books under my arm and was gazing at the procession when a terrific gust of wind came tearing up the street and whisked off my sailor hat before

I could wink. I had to chase it up that slippery street with my hair and skirts blowing madly. That provoking hat would slide along and stop until I caught up. Then, just as I stooped to clutch it off it would sail again! I gave up in despair finally and was just turning back when it got jammed up in a little ditch and I pounced on it.

We had such fun in college to-day, especially in advanced English. That is the nicest class in college. There are only a few in it and we have such nice sociable times. Fannie Wise and I sit together in it

Reggie

and have no end of fun with each other and with Reggie Stewart and Hedley McKinnon, two cute little "Academics."

Thursday, Mar. 22, 1894
Ch'town, P.E.I.

Mary got a letter from home to-day saying that Norman was coming in after us and we were more than provoked, for we wanted the fun of going out on the train, especially the spice of romance in starting off at nine o'clock at night.

School Management hour was particularly awful to-day. It is a farce at the best of times but to-day it was worse than usual. The boys kept firing rotten apples about the whole time and I am sure the noise could have been heard a block off.

After dinner Mary and I went down to the sta-

Hedley

tion to see some of the girls off. Quite a number of collegians were going on the train and nearly all the rest were there to see them off. Then Mary and I came back and ate caramels and chocolates in our room until we set our teeth jumping. At tea time, while we were making a feeble pretence of eating—for our indulgence in the flesh-pots of Egypt[1] had completely ruined our appetites—Norman appeared. It is now about 8 and we are waiting for him to call for us. I expect we will freeze stiff going out to-night. One good thing is that we have been well used to it already this winter.

---

1. Luxurious living regretted by the wandering Children of Israel. From Exodus 16:3.

Friday, Mar. 23, 1894
Darlington,[1] *P.E. Island.*

Here are Mary and I, at a table in the habitation of Donald E. Campbell, Esq., both busy scribbling. Last night when I stopped writing we were waiting for Norman. We *had* to wait, too. A whole hour passed before the missing lad appeared and when he did another half hour passed, getting the horse, etc., so that it was 9.30 when we were finally packed in and set off on our 12 mile drive in the frosty silver moonshine. We had the jolliest drive. The night was glorious, the roads fine, and we all three congenial spirits. We finally arrived at Darlington at 12.30 and got off to bed as soon as possible.

There is a large family here. Besides Mary and Norman there are Sarah, Annie, Louisa, Maggie, Flora, Lottie and Archie.

After dinner to-day Mary and I visited Norman's school. There were about eleven pupils there, all small and rather stupid looking. Mary and I fooled around, rummaging in Norman's desk, writing our names in the register, and hearing some classes. We had a little excitement when the stove suddenly collapsed on the floor. Luckily there was not much fire in it and Norman and his squad soon righted it but we were smoked out.

Sunday, Mar. 25, 1894

I am "dead" tired and sleepy. This morning Mary, Annie, and a friend of theirs, Janie Brown, and I all went over to Brookfield church. It is two miles there and as it is a lovely day we had a fine drive. But the Brookfieldians are an odd-looking lot and the church is a very old tumble-down affair. The Rev. Mr. McKenzie preached. He is a good speaker but it was a missionary sermon and I'm tired of them—I've heard so many lately.

After church Mary went to her grandfathers and the rest of us came home. After dinner Sarah, Norman and I drove to preaching at Hunter River. We were abominably late and had to go in when the minister was well underway with his sermon—another missionary effort, by the way. I think I must be destined for a cannibal lunch. Just at dusk Mary and Joe McPherson—who is her uncle but very little older than herself—arrived and whisked us off for another drive over to Wiltshire.[2] I never had such fun. We laughed until we were actually stiff. I shall certainly collapse if I don't get to bed at once.

---

1. Village 13 miles (21 km) west of Charlottetown.
2. The nearest village about 3 miles (5 km) north of Darlington.

Monday, Mar. 26, 1894

After tea tonight Norman hitched up a nag and he and Mary and Louisa and I went for a drive away down to the "Bluefield School," wherever that locality may be. We laughed, told ghost stories and witch stories, ate dates, and sang hymns and songs until if any of the natives were out I imagine they could think we had just escaped from Falconwood.[1]

Tuesday, Mar. 27, 1894

Mary and I got up this morning feeling pretty stiff after our last night's junketing.[2] After breakfast we tried to study but did not make much progress. We are having too good a time but I fear we shall pay up for our indulgence with many a sleepless hour when the exams come on.

Wednesday, Mar. 28, 1894

Mary, Annie, Louisa, Norman and I went to prayer meeting at Brookfield tonight. It was just a perfect evening and we hugely enjoyed our drive. We sat near the front; an old patriarch got up and began to pray in Gaelic[3] and at the same time a cat began to yowl weirdly outside and I had the time of my life to keep from laughing. One was about as intelligible to me as the other. You can't imagine how funny it sounded.

Friday, Mar. 30, 1894
Darlington, P.E.I.

Yesterday afternoon James Edward Brown came over from Hunter River.[4] They wanted me to recite at a concert there. So Mary and I went over with him and had a splendid drive. The concert was in the church and Mary and I stayed all night at Mr. Brown's and came home this evening.

---

1. "Insane asylum" at Charlottetown.
2. Slang: going on a pleasure trip.
3. Ancient language of the Scots, still in common use among older generations in rural districts of PEI.
4. Mr. Brown was inviting the girls to perform in a village one mile southwest of North Rustico—not far from Cavendish.

Saturday, Mar. 31, 1894
The Old Stand,
Ch'town, P.E.I.

Blessed is the promise which assures us that there is a rest for the weary, for now if ever I need its consolation. This morning there was heard in Darlington the announcement that the sluggards must arise and return to their forgotten books. Norman drove us in and we arrived here at two, to find things quite the same except that Dan is out in the country, for which all good angels be praised. He and Mary M. fight without cessation when he is home.

Mrs. Donald Farquharson[1] called on me to-day and I am invited there to tea tomorrow evening.

Sunday, April 1, 1894

Glorious "All Fools"[2] has come once more. No fools were made in "our house." I suppose Mrs. MacMillan would say it is because there were plenty of us all ready made. In the afternoon I went to Mrs. Farquharson's. They have a lovely place on Upper Prince St. and I had a very nice time.

April 2, 1894

In Cicero class this morning Dr. A. appeared with a handful of papers and was greeted with a vigorous clapping, for these were our long unheard from Virgil papers. I made 82 and Dr. A. added that it was a good paper. Words of commendation from the doctor are like angel's visits and hence are muchly appreciated. Prof. Caven also gave us back our Byron papers. John Riley[3] led with 97 and I followed with 96. I ought to have had 98 but Caven took two marks off for the

Dr. Anderson

---

1. Donald Farquharson (1834–1903), member of the legislative assembly between 1878 and 1898, became premier of PEI, 1898–1901.

2. April first, traditional day for playing tricks, making fools out of friends.

3. John F. Reilly of Summerside appears second in the PWC honor diploma list.

expression "humble pie" which he said was "slang." Mean old thing! Besides, I do not agree with him that it is slang. It is an old proverb or rather old colloquial metaphor.

Mary and I intend to stay up until eleven to-night and study. This is our new programme as we want to get used to staying up late against the fatal day of exams.

Wednesday, April 4, 1894

At recess to-day we First Class girls, being ripe for mischief, went to work and changed all the books in Caven's room. We had just finished our performance and began to look innocent when the bell rang and the boys trooped in. Of course the scene of confusion we had counted upon took place. Everybody was tearing frantically around searching for books while Caven, fairly foaming with rage, stood upon the platform and shouted orders until he was black in the face, but all to no effect. It was a good half hour before we got settled down to work and even then there were ripples of disturbance all through the rest of the time when someone found a book among his belonging to someone else and passed it to its rightful owner with much ostentation. Caven was furious of course but never thought of blaming us guilty ones as we had mixed up our books among the rest.

Friday, April 6, 1894
Ch'town, P.E.I.

We had a scrumptious time in Cicero hour to-day. A huge Government committee came down at nine to inspect the buildings and Dr. A. was absent the whole hour showing them over the premises. We kids were left to our own sweet devices and the boys nearly tore the place down.

This evening when Mrs. MacMillan, Alec, Mary C. and I were in the sitting room and Florrie and her beloved Jack Whear in the parlor the doorbell rang. Mary M. made a dive for the door, as if she expected someone for herself but if so she got rather left for she had to come back in a moment and

Jack. X

announce "John Sutherland to see Maud"—at the same time looking at Mary C. as if she thought it should have been she he asked for. You see, there has been a curious state of affairs here for some time. Away back in last term Florrie and the McMillans got it into their heads that Jack Sutherland was going with Mary C. Goodness only knows how they came by the idea for, until to-night I don't suppose Jack and Mary had ever exchanged a dozen words in their lives. Once or twice last term Mary went to see a friend of hers in town and said friend's brother who is, like Jack, an unusually tall fellow, saw her home, we suppose that MacMillans who are always watching and prowling saw him in the darkness and jumped to the conclusion that it was Jack S. Anyhow, they began to tease Mary about Jack in the rather nasty way of which they are past masters. Mary and I were dying for some mischief so we took it up and contrived to keep their belief alive in various different ways. We have kept it up religiously with such good luck that Florrie and Alec and the MacMillans will probably go to their graves with the firm conviction that Mary and Jack were terribly sweet on each other during her college year. We have resorted to many dark and devious devices—mysterious appointments, mock notes, imaginary invitations etc. When Mary and I came home from anywhere in the evening I always came in before her and Mary walked around the block before coming in. Result—the folks here thought *I* had come home alone and Jack with her. If poor Jack knew I fear he would put me down as a hopeless reprobate. But we never *said* one word that wasn't *true* in the whole matter. If the MacMillans and Florrie chose to interpret our mysterious remarks and hints in the light of their own prepossessions that was surely their own affair. Mary C. and I have got more fun than enough out of this awful farce.

To return to our mutton:—I ran out to the hall and there was my tall cousin with his bewitching smile. I towed him into the sitting room with a significant grin at Mary C. for the benefit of the others. Mrs. MacMillan got up and went with unusual alacrity. We expected Alec would follow suit but do you think he did? Not he! The idea never entered his skull. There he sat and told his silly little stories and cackled away until I could have taken him out in the back yard and unostentatiously murdered him.

But it wasn't Mary C. who went to the door with Jack and had such a delightful little chat with him before he said good night. Oh, dear no! And somehow I don't believe it was Alec either.

Saturday, April 7, 1894

Mary and I were out for our customary "constitutional" this evening and on our way home we met Jamie Stevenson and Stuart Simpson at Crabbe's

Corner; they smiled with such unusual expansiveness that we wondered what on earth was wrong with us. On arriving here however we discovered the cause—they were coming here to board. We are rather glad as it will likely be good fun.

Monday, April 9, 1894

Dear me, are you sure it is April? I should really suppose it to be December. Such a howling snowstorm as it has been all day—and is yet! There'll be "foots" of snow in the morning. College as usual. Hedley McKinnon wants me to write another article for the next *Record*. I didn't make any promises and I wish I could squirm out of it, for I haven't the faintest idea what to write about.

Wednesday, April 11, 1894

Same old routine. After tea we came up to our books. It is past nine now and I have stopped for a breathing spell but must begin again at ten. Mary has succumbed and is lying across the bed sound asleep. Coming exams are already being dolefully discussed in college circles. Whenever you see a little knot of girls over a radiator you may be sure they are canvassing that subject. I scribbled something for the *Record* this evening and succeeded in getting off a spurt entitled "Extracts from the diary of a Second Class Mouse." Ida says Norman Hunter told her Dr. A. said that "The Usual Way" was very cleverly written. A compliment like that from the doc is worth having.

Thursday, April 12, 1894

Mary and Ida coaxed me to go to the Bazaar[1] at the Kirk to-night but I wished I had had sense enough to stay home for we hadn't a bit of a nice time. There was a busy crush, and no one we knew; everybody looked tired and we both felt it and looked it.

Now for geometry until 11. But I don't feel in very good trim for it.

Friday, April 13, 1894

Another college week has flown by on wings of wind. This last day of it has been dull and cloudy and yet one of those days when I am unaccountably

---

1.   Sale of fancy-work and baked goods by the ladies of the Presbyterian church.

haunted by vague dreams of a breeze-swept, mossy hillslope on a cool summer afternoon with short, golden grasses silvering in the wind and a spruce tree tossing its green boughs over an old wandering fence with its longers bleached a silvery gray and with clusters of wild everlastings and blue asters in its corners, a few mossy, grass-grown sticks scattered here and there, and a blue-bird perched on the point of a picket.

Mary and I have tried to study to-night but it was too cold to stay in our room so we did not get on very well. There is such a ceaseless racket going on here all the time. It is a poor place for college students to board.

Sunday, April 15, 1894

Mary and I went to Zion this morning and evening. After evening service we went down to Aunt Mary's and stayed until nine. When we came home and toddled into the sitting room there sat Jack S.—and everyone looked at Mary C. to see how she took it!

Slowly the others melted away and Mary and I were left to entertain Jack. We had a jolly time.

Mary and I are now ready to go to bed. I hope we will not have the experience we had last night. We had just got into bed when we remembered that we had not put up the window. Mary hopped out to attend to it and having done so came back on the run and landed with a flying leap on the bed. An awful sound was heard and the bed-tick promptly collapsed. We lost no time in getting out to explore the damage and investigation revealed a slat broken in two. Here was a fix! If the MacMillan's discovered it we would never hear the last of it. We yanked off the clothes, put a slat from a pile of slats belonging to another bed and kept in our room, in the gap and hid the broken pieces of the other in my trunk. Then of course we sat down and laughed until our faces ached.

Monday, April 16, 1894

Alec is going home. I don't suppose anyone will miss the poor little monkey much, but Mary and I will miss him a little to poke fun at.

Prof. Harcourt had a skeleton in Hygiene to-day—such a weird looking thing. I'm sure I shall dream of it to-night.

After we came home we tried to study but since the boys are moved up into Alec's room we don't get much work done, as they are in here every minute to tease or talk. Jim is a fearful tease and when he gets one of his wild fits on nothing can be done with him.

About 8.30 Stewart S. called up to us that Jack and Will S. were downstairs. We wouldn't believe him but finally rushed recklessly down thinking he was only joking but to our dismay they were really in the hall, and Howard Leslie and Ed McFadyan were at the door with Jim.

As soon as we recovered our wits we whisked Jack and Will into the room while the others went upstairs. The boys stayed for an hour and of course we had lots of fun.

Thursday, April 19, 1894
Ch'town, P.E. Island.

Prof. Caven informed me to-day that I must write an essay for commencement. I'd much rather not but I know very well I will have to do it.

Stewart and Jim are both out to-night and so we are left in peace and quietness. Jim was in here all the afternoon pretending to cram Roman History but he effectually prevented both us and himself from learning anything.

Sunday, April 22, 1894
Ch'town, P.E.I.

Mary and I went to Zion this evening but came straight home after service as we thought Jack S. might come in with Stewart on his way home from the Kirk. So we came up here and sat down in the darkness by the window to watch and amuse ourselves by all the side-shows to be seen on the street. It was nearly nine and we had just confided to each other our firm belief that he was not coming to-night when he came and Stewart came running up for us. Down we went and got a most energetic handshake from our "Prince of Good Fellows."[1] All the rest soon went out, leaving Jack to our tender mercies. We were pretty good to him however.

Monday, April 23, 1894

We had a sort of social earthquake at 187 Fitzroy St. this morning. You see, when Jack went away last night I went to the door with him as usual. He kissed me good-night—also as usual, I admit—and as he stepped out said,

---

1. Phrase historically applied to King James V of Scotland.

"Good-night, *dear*." Now, Florrie, who was, as always, stuck in the parlor with Jack Whear, and Mary MacMillan who was airing herself at the room window above, heard that unlucky kiss and "dear," which seems to have impressed them very much. Mary C. went downstairs this morning before I did, unfortunately, and Mary M. at once demanded, "Who went to the door with John S. last night?"

Unsuspecting Mary, true to our policy of always telling the strict truth when cornered, and never supposing it mattered much anyhow, answered "Maud" and thereby gave away the whole affair completely. When I, all unconscious of this, came tranquilly down to my morning repast—Mary C. having gone to an early class—the guns were opened and I more than "caught it" from Mary M., Florrie, and Mrs. Mac. Fortunately, the boys were not down or I should have died on the spot.

The fun of it is, however, that MacMillans don't quite see it all yet and are under the extraordinary impression that Mary C. is their co-sufferer. *Such* a drubbing as I got from Mother MacMillan for "*deceiving* poor Mary C. into thinking John S. was coming here to see *her* when it was *me* all the time." Fancy! You should have heard Mary C. howl when I told her. We both feel rather cheap, however. But I suppose we are properly punished for putting up such a hoax on MacMillans. But then they were all *so* deliciously gullible.

Tuesday, April 24, 1894

When I came home from college to-day I registered a vow that henceforth, exams, or no exams, I'm not going to kill myself studying as I've been doing all the term. I'm pretty well up now, anyhow and am not much frightened about anything except the geometry and chemistry, and I *am* worried about those.

College is full of dread rumors of coming exams—exams first, exams last and exams between. Hedley McKinnon coolly informed me to-day that they want me to write a couple more articles for the May and June *Records*. I don't know where the time is to come from or the gray matter either.

Everyone is out of the house to-night except us students. Stewart and I are down here studying in the sitting room while Jim and Mary are in co. upstairs—quite the reverse of the usual arrangement.

Friday, April 27, 1894

The last hour to-day was French, and it was such a lovely day that Fannie Wise and I resolved to skip class and go for a walk. We succeeded in dodging Caven and Dr. A.—not altogether an easy task—and off we went. We had a spluxious time and got back to the boys' gate at two. We didn't dare go in by our own gate for fear the doc would nab us and Dr. A. doesn't love truants at all. As we went in we saw Caven standing by his window and knew that he might turn and see us at any moment. I flew wildly across the campus while Fan sneaked around by the fence, and we both got in without being seen.

Fannie Wise

Saturday, April 28, 1894

Ida, Nell, Mary C. and I went to-day and had our beautiful selves photographed in a group to preserve as a "screwveneer" of P.W.C. days. We had no end of fun fixing up and getting posed. I expect we will all have a grin a yard wide on.

Mary and I spent the evening at Aunt Mary's and had a lovely time. Jack S. was also there.

Tuesday, May 1, 1894

Mary and I overslept this morning and had to dress on the double quick but made out to get to college on time. Air full of exams! Nobody knows how sick I am of the word.

Dan MacMillan arrived home this evening as dirty and cranky as ever. Evidently his sojourn in the rural districts hasn't improved him any. He and Mary M. fight everlastingly, especially at meal time.

Wednesday, May 2, 1894

B. Faye Mills,[1] a noted evangelist, is at present holding meetings here and the place seems wild with excitement. I had not been to hear him before

---

1. The two-week visit of this American evangelist dominated local newspapers.

but to-day Mary and I went. The meeting was held in the opera house this afternoon. The house was packed: we had to sit behind the speaker on the stage. Mr. Mills did not impress me as being much of a speaker but there is something very magnetic about him. Ida "got converted," as they say—how I hate the expression!—and I imagine Mary C. was pretty hard hit.

I went up town after the meeting and met Selena who is in for her vacation. Mary whisked off to the meeting again this evening but I declined to go and spent the time reviewing Greek instead.

Thursday, May 3, 1894
Ch'town, P.E.I.

Exams are constantly talked of in college to the exclusion of every other topic. Aunt Mary and Nettie Montgomery[1] called here this evening and wanted me to go to the meeting with them. I couldn't, but I promised to go tomorrow night.

Sunday, May 6, 1894

This afternoon Mary and I went to the Big Brick for the 2.30 service. We got there early enough to secure a seat in the gallery, just below "the Prince" from whom we got several very broad smiles. Mr. Mill's address was very fine and made me do some thinking. I have been feeling rather dissatisfied with my life this past week or so. Besides, I knew Mary Campbell really wanted to "come out" but was a little afraid of me—my sarcastic tongue and unfailing and unsparing raillery. I knew if I came out she would, too; if I turned away so would she. The responsibility was one I did not care to assume and the result was that we both signed the prayer cards when they were passed around.

After all, I hardly know whether I've done a wise thing. There are some things I find it very hard to believe.

The farewell service was held to-night in the Big Brick and 2700 people were present. The meeting was certainly very thrilling. But *feeling* and *belief* are such very different things—at least, after we begin *really* to think.

When we struggled out through the crowd we discovered to our dismay that it was raining. We had on our new spring hats—and we had no umbrella; a nice predicament! But John Sutherland came gallantly to the

---

1. A second cousin, daughter of Donald Montgomery and Nancy Anna Campbell of Alberton.

rescue of two such distressed damsels with a stout arm and a sheltering umbrella and brought us safely and dryly home—bless his heart!

Monday, May 7, 1894

Mary and I sacrificed our dearly beloved morning nap this morning in order to get down to the station to see B. Faye Mills off. A huge crowd was there for the same purpose.

College to-day was quite lively. We have an exam in English Thursday. *That* doesn't frighten me much but next week may some benign fate watch over me for we have French, Roman History, Xenophon and Latin Composition! Just imagine how we'll have to hustle!

Saturday, May 12, 1894

Today was a pearl among days. But poor I had to shut my eyes most resolutely to all the outdoor freshness and begin to "cram" Roman History as soon as possible after breakfast. And from that until tea time I read and re-read and scribbled notes until the very sight of the book was hateful. At dusk I took an hour off and then tried to persuade myself to begin on French but the more I tried the more repulsive the idea seemed and at last I made the awful resolution not to look at it—no not even if we had forty exams in it on Monday. Mary and I went out for a walk and when we got back Will S. and Jack S. were up in the boys' room. Soon they all came into ours and we had a lot of fun and laughed until the cobwebs of study were swept out of our brains.

Monday, May 14, 1894
Ch'town, P.E. Island.

I went to college this morning with anything but a good conscience, seeing that I had never looked at the French. The exam began at eleven in Dr. A.'s room and was pretty hard but I think I'll be all right in it if an accident that occurred doesn't get me in wrong with Caven.

Will Sutherland sat across from me on the other side. He sent a note over to me asking a question *re* the 4th section of the paper. While I was scribbling an answer Dr. A. came in and sat down at his desk where he was concealed from my view as I from his by the blackboard. I finished the note, folded it carefully up and passed it to Sam Willis who in turn passed it to Ethelbert

McDuff. Then the catastrophe came. The doc pounced like a hawk on the unfortunate McDuff and ordered him to bring the missive to his desk instanter. I don't say of course that the doc expressed himself in just such classical language but that was the gist of it. McDuff had to prance up with the note, while Will and I exchanged horrified glances. I expected nothing short of an earthquake but the blessed old doc simply threw the note into the waste basket without so much as looking at it and sent McDuff back to his seat. I drew a long breath of relief and went to work again. But alas! As soon as the doc went out that old sneak of a Caven hunted out that note and read it. Of course no name was on it, and the writing was so atrociously bad that I hope he won't recognize it as mine. He

Prof. Caven

cross-questioned McDuff closely but got small satisfaction from him. McD. assumed his blankest look and didn't appear to know anything—where the paper came from or where it was going. I don't know what the outcome of it will be I'm sure. Nobody, except Willis and McDuff, and two or three girls in my immediate vicinity, knows anything about it and they won't tell, but I'm afraid Caven won't rest until he has ferreted the matter out. Stewart and Jim nearly drove me frantic with suppressed laughter at dinner time discussing the rumpus and wondering who had written the note. I didn't give it away for I think the fewer who know of it the better.

Tuesday, May 15, 1894

Our exam in Roman History began at 9 to-day and lasted till 2—five mortal hours. That sounds pretty bad—but it wasn't so hard after all, in spite of its quantity.

Just imagine, we have another boarder—a Mr. McMann. He is a middle-aged man and a Catholic and has a wife somewhere down east whom he expects here soon. He is an Irishman and a carpenter and altogether seems to be a very rough and boorish sort of person.

Thursday, May 17, 1894

We had our Latin Compo exam this morning and it was quite easy. I think I'm all right in it—surely at least I did better than last time. *That* was too disgraceful.

But after the exam came my long-expected earthquake. I had heard no more of that unlucky note since Monday and had almost forgotten it and hoped everyone else had, too. But alas, when I came over from the Normal, after chemistry, Caven met me in the hall with a brow like the traditional thunderclouds and whirled me into the doctor's room. I saw that wretched note in his hand and knew what was coming.

"Did you write this?" he demanded, dramatically holding out the accusing scrawl.

"Yes, sir, I did," I answered humbly, for I knew my wisest course was to throw myself on his mercy.

"You did! Well, you are the last girl on this side of the grave I would have suspected of doing such a thing," he said violently. "I would *never* have thought it of you. Now, who was it for?"

I had employed the time of this outburst by rapidly thinking what to do. I was bound I wouldn't betray Will. He was working for a diploma and to lose it would be serious. I could not get a diploma, owing to being here only the one year, so Caven might pour out the vials of his wrath upon me if he chose.

"I cannot tell you," I said firmly.

"Had it reached its destination?" demanded Caven.

"No, sir," I replied promptly, glad that I could at least exculpate poor McDuff.

Caven cross-questioned me severely but I would not tell him and at last he said,

"Well, then I will punish you since you will not tell me the real culprit. How will you like to have that whole section struck out of your paper?"

I wouldn't like it at all, that was flat. It would mean a loss of at least 25 marks. But I stood firm and then he dismissed me. I felt blue all the rest of the day. But after all I think Caven will forgive me when his anger cools. I have been his favorite pupil and I don't think the old man will harden his heart against me for long. At least I hope not.

Friday, May 18, 1894

I think Prof. Caven has got over the crisis. He was quite nice to me in French class to-day.

I wrote several drafts of applications for schools this evening but didn't write any real ones as Jim was in here all the evening writing an application for a position in the bank and driving us half distracted with his nonsense.

Oh dear, just think! A month from to-day all will be over. I cannot realize it. In one way it seems barely yesterday since I came to P.W.C. and in another it seems an age. I've had so much fun and made so many nice, new friends.

Mr. McMann's wife arrived on the scene to-day. She is an odd-looking personage.

Jack S. was down to-night and we had such a nice chat. Dear old Jack, he is simply the nicest fellow in the world—so chummy and simple and jolly, without any sentimental nonsense about him.

Wednesday, May 22, 1894

No exam to-day—but we shall pay up for that on Friday when we have both Chemistry and Greek Composition. I am dreadfully frightened of the Chemistry.

Caven informed me to-day that he had decided to "forgive me completely" and I am quite reinstated in his good graces.

Thursday, May 24, 1894

As this is our "Gracious Queen's"[1] birthday we were blessed with a holiday from exams—and I wish I could add from studies as well but they seem to be irrepressible. I "crammed" Greek Composition and chemistry all the forenoon. After dinner Mary, Nell and Ida went to the park.[2] They coaxed me to go too but I said, "Get thee behind me, Satan," and buried myself in formulas and chemical properties until three o'clock. Then I hopped up, threw the chemistry across the room, dressed on the double quick and set

Entrance to Harbour, Charlottetown, P.E. Island.

Prof. Shaw

1. Queen Victoria; her birthday is a national holiday in Canada.
2. Victoria Park, on the harbourfront, was a civic centre because of its cricket, football, and baseball clubs; tennis courts; cycling paths; militia training grounds; and promenade.

off for the park. Everybody and his sister were there and I had quite a hunt before I found the girls. We went and sat down on the harbor shore. It was charming. The water was such a pale, ethereal blue and the little capes and headlands were hazy purple. Professor Shaw and a Mr. Matheson came along after awhile and sat down beside us and we had such fun, discussing exams[1] and such agreeable topics in a very light-hearted way. When we came home we had tea—such as it was—and then Mary and I came up here and had a snack of candy. I finally finished up my loyal celebration by studying English literature.

Friday, May 25, 1894
Ch'town. P.E. Island

We had our Greek Compo. exam this morning and it was quite easy. I made at least three pretty awful mistakes, though. Still, I think my average in Greek will be fair.

But if the Greek was easy the chemistry more than paid up for it. Such a horrible paper! It is a wonder my hair did not stand straight up on end. It *was* pretty badly disordered before I got through. I answered all the questions in some sort of a way but goodness only knows what I put down—*I* don't. Thanks be, it's over anyway.

Old McMann and his wife are a terrible couple. They fight like cat and dog. All the time he is home she is quarrelling with him and when he isn't she stays in her room and cries. She has just had a spell of it now.

As I was too tired to study to-night and was all alone I recruited my shattered nerves by getting out and reading over a lot of old trash—old time rhymes, such as "Dahlias," "A Concert" etc. How vividly they seemed to bring back all those dear old schooldays! They recalled memories of Mollie and Nate and Jack. Dear old Mollie, what chums we were! If Nate, loitering along the green roads on his way home from the post-office, saw "Mollie" coming around the corner he knew "Pollie" wasn't far off and if "Snip" came whistling up the hill "Snap" was generally within earshot.

Mary is out to-night and I miss her so. Dear me, we have very little longer to be together—a brief three weeks. Thus it goes. Just as soon as I meet and learn to love a friend we must part and go our separate ways, never to meet on quite the same ground again. For, disguise the fact as we will, when friends, even the closest—and perhaps the more so on account of

---

1. Each exam ran four to five hours; immediately after completing college exams, students wanting a teacher's licence wrote three exams a day for five days.

that very closeness—meet again after a separation there is always a chill, lesser or greater, of change. Neither finds the other *quite* the same. This is only natural. Human nature is ever growing or retrograding—never stationary. But still, with all our philosophy who of us can repress a little feeling of bewildered disappointment when we realize that our friend is not and never can be just the same as before—even although the change may be an improvement?

Monday, May 28th, 1894

I went to college with chill forebodings which were more than fulfilled when I saw the algebra paper. It was a *beast*! I did all the sums except two but I can't for the life of me say whether I did them right or not. The exam lasted four hours and left me feeling limp.

The climax of the McMann-MacMillan affair came tonight. Old McMann and Mrs. MacMillan had a really dreadful fight. He said everything to her—and gave her some pretty good hits, too, it must be confessed, although they were not conveyed in very classical language; then he discarded his weeping wife altogether, packed up his goods and chattels and departed, his last words to Mrs. MacMillan being some curt advice to change her ways and "do the square thing by her boarders." I am really not a bit sorry for Mrs. MacMillan. She deserved all she got for taking in such people in the first place.

Mrs. McMann soon sneaked out also, bawling down the stairs, and it is to be hoped we have seen the last of the amiable couple.

Tuesday, May 29, 1894

I verily believe that 187 Fitzroy has a monopoly of the queer things that happen in this town. Last night, just as Mary and I were getting ready for bed, the bell rang. I lifted the blind and peeped out. Below was that forlorn Mrs. McMann, in company with a strange man.

"Who is there?" I asked.

"It's me. Mrs. Mullen," she wailed, evidently taking me for our gracious landlady whom she invariably called "Mullen"—and the unknown supplemented this by saying,

"I found this lady wandering around lost in the park and I brought her home as she said she lived here."

Meanwhile, Jim Stevenson, having heard the commotion, had run down and let her in and she came upstairs sobbing and wringing her hands and said she would have to stay here all night. I went into her room and she was going on at a fearful rate. Mrs.MacMillan refused to get up and Mary C. wouldn't go near her, so I had to do the best I could to calm her. She had followed McMann, she said, "far into the woods," and only turned back when he threatened to kill her. Then she lost her way and was found by some man and brought home.

Well, *such* a time as I had trying to soothe her and get her to go to bed! She hadn't a cent or a friend in the world she declared. I said everything I could to cheer her up, gave her lots of good advice about how to manage men—Jim and Stewart, who were listening to it all on the stairs, have never given me any peace since!—got her to bathe her face and go to bed. Then I left her. Of course, after all this excitement I didn't sleep for half the night. Mrs. McMann decamped this morning before we got up and it is to be hoped we have seen the last of her.

To-day was beautiful. Summer is really here now and all the trees have donned a misty green. But this spring I have no time to enjoy the beauty of nature. Nothing but exams for me! I'm so tired of them. We had our geometry to-day and it was rotten as Shaw's exams always are. Tomorrow School Management will finish the college exams.

Thursday, May 31, 1894
Ch'town, P.E.I.

We had our college groups photographed to-day and took the School Management exam in the afternoon. It was very long—8 questions and all with several divisions. I answered them all in some sort of way, making up what I didn't know. I have been revising Cicero all the evening for the License, although continually interrupted by Stewart and Jim who have had one of their wild fits on. Jim has won the medal. It has been a stiff pull between him and John Riley, a lank, ugly, unpopular academic but Jimmy has won out at last.

Jim S.

John R.

I have to write an essay to read at Commencement and feel rather creepy over the thought. I am going to write it on the character of *Portia* in the play[1] we have been studying.

Everything is now in a continual flutter at college over the License exams. I have got back most of my college papers and have led in several subjects.

Tuesday, June 5, 1894

Five more days of worriment over! To-day was perfect, with blue skies and sunshine and the tender sheen of young leaves. But all this beauty was lost on us poor miserable creatures.

This afternoon while I was revising Latin Jim came up and began tormenting me about the valedictory. He wants me to write it for him, simply because he is too lazy to do it himself. I don't feel as if I had the time to waste on it. But I wanted to oblige Jim so I finally took a sheet of paper and scribbled down a few standard platitudes.

Wednesday, June 6, 1894

Had toothache all night and when I got up this morning all the left side of my face was swollen into a big puff. Such a looking object as I am! Whatever shall I do if it doesn't get better before Friday night when Commencement comes off in the Opera house[2] and I have to read my essay?

I went to college, astonishing everybody by my vast amount of *cheek*. The doctor gave us our license exam numbers. I am no. 8. We also got our license time-tables. Three exams on Monday—English, History and Agriculture.

I came home and plunged into algebra. In the middle of it Jim came up again about that wretched valedictory. So I had to toss my problems aside and help Jim with it—or rather write it and compel Jim to give an opinion on the most important points. I finally got it done in some fashion. Jim will have the *kudos* of it and I the grind. Well, what's the odds! It doesn't hurt to be obliging.

Just think, this night fortnight I will be in Cavendish! I cannot realize it. It does not seem to enter into my calculations at all. My vision cannot pierce beyond the darkness of next week. It is completely bounded by the gloomy shade of "License Exam."

---

1. LMM's essay emphasizes the wit of Portia, heroine of Shakespeare's *The Merchant of Venice*, as well as her tact in handling suitors, seeing her delicacy in love as less important than her intellectual power and eloquence.

2. Theatre in the new Masonic Temple, opened in October 1893.

Thursday, June 7, 1894

Got up at five this morning to study. My face is better but is far from being presentable yet. College closed today. I felt so sorry. My pleasant P.W.C. days are all over. Very sadly I gathered up my books and passed out—as hundreds have done and as hundreds more will do. But no one ever left or ever will leave that olde college with deeper and more genuine regret in her heart than did I.

Friday, June 8, 1894
Ch'town, P.E.I.

The curtain is down and the lights out—on my college year as well as on the stage of the Opera House where we spent such a delightful time tonight.

When I got up this morning my face was terribly swelled—worse than ever—and I was in despair. I determined just to let it alone—and then the contrary thing, seeing I wasn't going to coddle it, began to get better of its own accord and did so so rapidly that it was quite presentable after all by night time.

The "cream challie"
[L.M. Montgomery]

Mabel Fielding and Nellie McGrath came down in the afternoon to hold a Council of War about the License Exam. About four the dailies came out with the honor lists.[1] I have five firsts and three seconds. We also got our Commencement programmes and they are very cute.

After tea we dressed in a flutter of excitement. I wore my cream challie[2] with a bunch of pansies. Ida came along and we set out in great state for the Opera House. We got there, went on the stage—where there was a formidable array of vacant chairs—and by various dark windings found our way down to the dressing rooms where everybody was prinking. Then we came up and took our seats. The house was well filled and John S. was in the gallery smiling as a basket of chips.

My essay came after the first chorus and somehow or other I got out in front. I felt awfully scared, but didn't show it and got through all right.

---

1. LMM had top marks in both English courses and in agriculture, tied for first place in school management and in essay-writing, and was in the top five in teaching.

2. Challis is a very fine cotton or woolen fabric.

Louise Laire also read an essay and songs, speeches and presentations of diplomas filled up the programme.

But the most delightful time must end. We sang, "God Save The Queen" and it was over. In a few minutes the stage was empty and the lights out. As they vanished, leaving us in semi-darkness, I mentally said good-bye to my happy college life and turned with a sigh to the unknown future.

Jack S. came down with me and said all manner of nice things to me.

Saturday, June 9, 1894

Jim went out before breakfast this morning and got a *Guardian*.[1] He passed it over the table to me with the remarks that there was a very high compliment in it for me. There was a "puff" of about half a column over my essay and I felt pleasantly tickled. This afternoon the editor of the *Guardian* called to get the essay to print.

Monday, June 11, 1894
Ch'town, P.E.I.

Well, this much dreaded day has come at last, and moreover has passed and left me in a tolerably satisfied frame of mind, for everything so far has gone pretty well. Mary and I got up at five and studied until 7.30. At 8 we went down to the college. We larked around, laughing at everything and were hysterically gay with the recklessness born of nervousness.

Nine o'clock found us all in Dr. A.'s room waiting our doom breathlessly. We first Class girls and a number of the Second were left in the room. Our English paper was a snap. Roman History was pretty stiff but I did it all. Then we had Agriculture and I think I got along all right in it, too. But that *awful* geometry comes tomorrow and I *know* it will be the death of me!

It was a real pleasure to come home to-day and stack away a big pile of books as *done with*. That dear old English class will always have a warm spot in my memory. Roman History, too, was always pleasant and interesting. As for Agriculture, I never liked it or the Professor who taught it. I have too many dismal recollections of getting out of bed in the dark and cold to go down at 8 the first term.

Just imagine. This night week I'll be in Cavendish—delightful thought! But—just imagine, this night week I'll be away from Charlottetown! Horrible thought!

---

1. Both Charlottetown papers praised the essay and the performance.

Tuesday Morning, June 12, 1894
Ch'Town P.E.I.

Mary and I took it quite easy this morning and didn't get up till six. We are cramming Hygiene now. To-day will decide my fate. If I get through the geometry alive I'm not much afraid of anything else. May some kind fate protect me!

Night

Well, as I am still alive you may infer that some kind fate *did* protect me. Our geometry paper was quite easy. I did six out of eight, so feel at rest. But if the geometry was easy the French paper more than made up for it. It was *fiendish*. I think I made a fair percentage but it was a close call. The Hygiene was easy—I'm all O.K. in that.

I'm *so* glad the geometry exam is over. I can hardly realize it. It has been hanging over my head for a whole year. Thank goodness most devoutly that it is disposed of.

Wednesday, June 13, 1894

Another of the dreaded five days has passed. We had Latin this morning and I got on finely. But the English Literature was very hard. School Management was easy. Tomorrow will be the hardest day—Chemistry, Algebra, and Greek. I think I'll get through all night in Greek but I'm shaky about the other two.

Thursday, June 14, 1894
Ch'Town, P.E. Island

Well, thank goodness!

The most dreadful day of the list is over and I think my head is still above water. Went to college this morning with dire forebodings which seemed to be shared by everyone. Everyone you met had some new and startling report about exams, examiners and "examinees." The Greek was not hard but the Chemistry was nasty and the algebra floored us all. It was the hardest paper I ever saw. I hope I made enough to float through but I have my painful doubts. I am so thankful the day is over. We have only one exam,— Academic English—tomorrow and it is the last.

Friday, June 15, 1894
Ch'town, P.E.I.

I am F—R—E—E !

What a delicious sensation! We had English this morning and it was pretty hard but my foot is on my native heath with English.

After it was over Dr. A. came in to say good-bye to us all. Everyone was crying and for awhile I felt as if life would not be worth living away from the dear old college. Finally it was over and we all scattered as sheep without a shepherd. I cannot realize that it is all over.

Mary and I cleaned up our room this afternoon and had an enormous pile of rubbish to burn—all the notes, scribbles etc. which have seen so much honourable service during the term.

Saturday Morning, 8.30
June 16, 1894

It's a wonder that I'm alive to tell the tale for I've been having an exciting time. Last night, Annie Moore came down and proposed that, since we hadn't seen Professor Caven to bid him good-bye, she and Fannie Wise and Mary and I go to his house to see him. We went and he was so pleased to see us. We had a very jolly call but oh, my goodness, when we were leaving didn't the old fiend kiss us all round! I am sure I shall never be the same girl again—he was so whiskery and tobacco-y! I was sorry to leave him, though, for he has been a good friend to me during my college year.

Then we decided to celebrate the evening. We all met at nine and went to Carter's[1] where we invested all our spare cash in caramels. Then we roamed about town until we were tired. Annie and Fan came down to stay all night with us, so we took off our boots on the doorstep, sneaked in, and tiptoed in single file to our sky-roost. We lighted a lamp, divided our caramels, and got on the bed to eat them. Such fun as we had! And we laughed until it was a wonder the caramels didn't choke us!

Then came the problem of how to stow ourselves for the night. It was finally agreed that Fan and I should have the bedstead and the chaff tick, while Annie and Mary were to have the feather bed on the floor. Fan and I took the sheet—there was only one—and a blanket and the bolster and let them have the quilt, the other blanket and the pillows. We had no end of fun and carried on half the night. We wanted to go down to the train at 7 to

---

1. A general store on Queen Street.

see some of the crowd off and resolved to get up at 5.30 but the first thing I knew was Annie's voice saying, "Girls, it's 6 o'clock." We all made one frantic leap out of bed and then such a scrimmage for clothes and brushes and combs! In a brief time we were ready and, scorning to wait for anything so commonplace as breakfast, we rushed to the station.

It was a delicious morning—clear, fresh and cool—and for the first time this spring I felt at liberty to enjoy the beauty of the world. The glorious arch of blue sky above us was no longer one vast concave on which to work geometrical problems, and the rustle of the leaf-laden trees no longer suggested only books and foolscap.

Later On

I've had a very busy day of it. For one thing I went and had my tooth extracted and took ether. It was quite a funny experience and not at all unpleasant.

Norman came in for Mary this evening. I felt very blue to see her go and when they left I was just on the point of tears. I *didn't* cry however, for Jim had told me that John S. was coming down to say good-bye and I wanted to save my complexion for that. So I ran upstairs to dress and togged myself up just as nicely as possible. But Jack has never come yet and I don't believe he will now. I could just cry! The mean thing! I don't suppose I'll see him at all now to say good-bye and I don't care! If he thinks no more of me than that he can just stay away. I'm going straight to bed for I'm too cross to do anything else!

Sunday, June 17, 1894

But I was crosser still this morning when I found that Jack *was* here last night after all. While I was dressing I had heard the bell ring but hadn't my blouse hooked, so it was a couple of minutes before I could run down. When I got there I found only the milkman and supposed it was he who had rung. I cried myself to sleep last night, thinking all sorts of hard things about poor Jack and when Jim said this morning,

"You went out after all last night,"

I said rather snappily, "No, I didn't!"

"Well," said Jim, "John came down and Mrs. McLeod next door told him everybody was out."

Just fancy how provoked I felt! I could have clawed Mrs. McLeod. Why couldn't she have minded her own business? I went to church in a very unchristian frame of mind but John was there and I contrived to explain the matter to him.

And this is really my last night in Ch'town! I am not sorry to leave MacMillans but Ch'town and Charlottetonian friends and days will always have a warm spot in my heart.

Monday, June 18, 1894
Cavendish, P.E.I.

Here I am in green old C. again. Grandma came in for me this morning. We had a charming drive home and got here about eight.

Wednesday, June 20, 1894

There are meetings every night in the church now and I went to-night with Pensie.

Grandma

The result of the exams came out to-day. I am 6th on the list. Not too bad for one year! But dear me, they must have poured fire into them for out of 120 only 49 passed.

I had a letter from Mary. She is going to teach in her own school. Dear knows where I shall be teaching—if I can get a school at all. I fear it is not going to be easy.

Friday, June 22, 1894
Cavendish, P.E.I.

The school exam came off this afternoon and Mollie and I went because they are going to rebuild the school and it will never be "our old school" again. Ches, Austin, Nellie and Lu were the sole remaining four of the old classes. The rest were simply "kids." Sitting there, there came to me a sudden chill realization that I was "grown up" and the knowledge was not half so sweet as I had once dreamed it would be. And yet it seemed so *very* short a time since Mollie and I had been there in those seats ourselves, thinking school examinations occasions of state. Every old memory of school days came back to me.

But once my musings got an unexpected shock. Into the schoolroom popped *Nate*! Do my best, I can never suppress a start of surprise when I see him. He has such a faculty for appearing unexpectedly.

He is not as nice looking as he used to be—he has got thin and scrawny. I wonder if he is to be home long.

Monday, June 25, 1894

I have begun systematic study again—mapped my day off, so much time for such a thing. But I reserve the evenings for amusement. I spent the afternoon to-day at Pensie's. We had lots of fun. Mamie Simpson was there dressmaking and in the evening Alec harnessed up a prancing little mare—he has sold "Doctor," alas!—and took her and me for a drive. We had a merry one.

Uncle Leander and Eric[1] arrived to-day.

Alec

Thursday, June 28, 1894
Cavendish, P.E.I.

I went over to Mollie's yesterday afternoon and stayed all night. Had a very pleasant time. This evening Lu, Mamie and I went to prayer meet-

Mollie's home

ing. Coming home we three and Pen were together as far as Uncle John's gate, when Alec and Will Bulman[2] came up. Will, of course, dashed after Pen while Alec announced his intention of going home with us three. We had a good deal of fun and at the barn gate Alec ceased to trouble himself about the other two and came down with me, having our usual difficulties with the many intricate and obstinate gates with which this place abounds.

Sunday July 1, 1894

This evening I was rummaging among a lot of accumulated rubbish and came across an old box filled with a curious medley. As I had some time to waste I sat myself gravely down and looked over it. The first thing that turned up was the picture of a peculiarly hideous and grotesque monkey, I had to grin

---

1. A first cousin, son of Uncle Leander and brother of Murray Macneill.
2. Will Bulman (1871–1947) married Penzie Macneill in 1898.

over it. Jack Laird sent that down to me one day in school "for a valentine." I at once retorted, "Oh, thank you, Jack. I've always wanted to have one of your photos and this is *such* a good one."

Jack didn't seem to appreciate the joke. Then came a note from Alma Macneill[1] and two manuscripts written in an angular school-girl hand, entitled "To Maud from Alma." What a host of memories they conjured up! What fun Alma and I had over those rhymes, sitting up on the old "side bench" together! Jim MacLeod[2] trained the shooting ideas[3] of Cavendish school then and of all his mischievous pupils Alma and I were most constantly in disgrace. The main reason for this was our inveterate habit of getting out on that old bench and writing "po'try" on our slates when we

Alma (later in life)

should have been sharpening our intellect on fractions. Of all those wonderful productions few are now extant. We began first by writing "acrostics" on each other's names. Fragments of them haunt my memory still. One of hers I remember ended thus,

> Up in the apple tree, under the boughs,
> Daisy screeched after them to bring her the cows.

From this we advanced to burlesquing our schoolmates—at least, those whom we did not like—whose unconscious ears must have tingled more than once. One of Alma's on Charlie McKenzie ran thus,

> Have you ever heard of young Charlie Mckenzie?
> If you have not just inquire of Pensie.
> You will find him going to see Mag McLure,
> Or driving old Jack o'er a pile of manure.

From scholars to teachers was a natural transition and one day we agreed to "write up" in stirring rhymes all the teachers we had had, including "Jim" himself. I might observe in passing that we called the reigning pedagogue "Jim"—behind his back!! Of this "Dunciad"[4] not a line can I now recall. Mine filled my slate; two verses were allotted to each teacher and the two about

---

1. A third cousin, daughter of George W. and older sister of LMM's classmate Clemmie; she moved to Massachusetts in 1893.

2. Teacher in Cavendish, 1884–87.

3. Witty misquoting of James Thomson, *The Seasons*, "Spring" (1728), "to teach the young idea how to shoot."

4. A mock literary satire by Alexander Pope (1688-1774), first published in 1728.

McLeod were not at all flattering. Alma and I were gleefully comparing them when "the master" himself, who was sitting before us, with his back to us, hearing a class, suddenly turned around and took my slate out of my paralyzed hand. Horrors! I stood up, firmly believing that the end of all things was at hand.

But Jim did not read it. Why in the world he didn't is a mystery to this day. It may be he had a dim suspicion of what it was and wanted to save his dignity. Whatever his reason he handed the slate silently back to me and I sat down with a gasp, sweeping off the accusing words as I did so, lest he might change his mind.

Then Alma and I decided to write poems addressed to each other. They were such successes—in our own estimation—that we wrote two more. We praised each other extravagantly. I gushed over Alma's golden hair, blue eyes, pink cheeks and dimples. She really was a very pretty girl but hardly the tremendous beauty I pictured. But "the poetic license" etc. She painted the lily very freely in my case also—in especial did she rave over my "wondrous braids of nut-brown hair." Well, I always had plenty of hair! In the wind-up she prophesied that I would marry Jack Laird! I wedded her to John Bell!

Underneath these productions of youthful genius I came across a tiny knot of yellow fur wrapped in a paper labelled "Carissima." Poor Carissima, where is she now? In the Happy-Hunting-Grounds, let us hope. When I spent that winter at Park Corner Frede C. had a little pet cat—a spotted gray-and-yellow affair whom I named *Carissima*. As this was the Italian for "Little darling" Frede added the French version "Mignonette" and the cat became known to fame as "Mignonette Carissima Montgomery Campbell."

View of Uncle John C.'s house from back

Whether it was the heavy dignity of such a name, or the amount of petting she got from us all, or the late hours she kept with various felines—whether for any or all of these reasons, "Cariss" began to fail in health and went down so fast that we began to fear she was destined to fill an untimely grave. She did not die, however, for many a long day afterwards, but she continued to look as if she had been pulled through a key-hole.

"Cariss" was always getting herself and other people into scrapes. One night when Clara C. and one of her admirers were coming home from church they fairly stumbled over "Cariss" and one of *her* admirers carrying on a most energetic flirtation at the door. On another occasion when I was sitting up late to entertain a beau "Cariss" who had been snoozing under the stove, got up and going over to the door began to answer loudly and unashamedly the yowls of a serenader outside. Guess my mortification! Then, too, whenever anyone was in, she would inevitably climb on a chair in the most conspicuous part of the room and fall to licking herself *all* over with great assiduity.

Next to "Cariss" came a scrap of black fur from "Mephistopheles." This once formed part of the hirsute adornment, not of his Satanic Majesty, but of a little black kitten in P.A. which Edie S. and I made a great pet of. It was a demoniacal-looking animal, black as a coal, with long sharp ears and goblin-like green eyes—hence his name. We always shortened it into "Mephis" however. Sometimes on a particularly cold night we would smuggle him upstairs and let him sleep with us, a proceeding he gloried in, cuddling down at our feet and purring vociferously. Alas for poor Mephis! He became subject to fits and his doom was sealed. He disappeared one day and no questions asked.

At the bottom of the box was a sadly rumpled and stained sheet of paper. It contained a "pome," called "A Moonlight Walk." It is my production, is not finished, and never will be. Such a lot of trouble as I had over that unlucky rhyme in by-gone days! One March day in the winter of 1889 Mollie was to come home with me from school and stay all night. During the day in school we planned what we expected to do and among other things we decided we would have a moonlight walk. When we had planned this I began scribbling verses on my slate for fun. I had quite a run of "inspiration" and got about half the "pome" done, describing an imaginary "Moonlight Walk" and the ludicrous incidents thereof—likewise imaginary. Then I copied it down on a sheet of paper. This I left in my desk, intending to finish it later on, but I never thought of it again.

One day, several weeks after, I was sitting by the school stove at noon recess, reading a novel called "Zanoni"[1] when Jack Laird came along, peeped over my shoulder and said, "'Zanoni'? Was that the fellow you took *the moonlight* walk with, Pollie?"

Something in his tone made me look up and I saw a teasing twinkle in his eye.

"Jack," I exclaimed indignantly, "you've been rummaging in my desk! What business had you?"

Jack's only reply was a grin and "The spring calf was out late that night, wasn't it, Pollie?"

---

1. *Zanoni* (1842), Edward Bulwer-Lytton's occult novel about the love between a Rosicrucian who has lived since ancient times in Babylon and an Italian opera singer (who is also loved by a stalwart Englishman).

Then he dodged, just in time to avoid "Zanoni" which I threw at his head.

Later on the murder came out. Jack and Nate had both read the thing and had more over told all the boys of the literary gem they had discovered. Copies of it have been turning up at intervals all over Cavendish ever since. I thought I should never hear the last of it. They poked fun at me all winter—for nothing could convince them that the absurd adventures related in the "pome" were not narratives of actual facts.

When I got through the box I carried it to the kitchen stove and dropped its contents in. Life is too short to moon over rubbish. I *did* preserve that blessed "Moonlight Walk" however.

Monday, July 2, 1894

Mamie came to sew for me to-day and this evening we set off for a stroll. We went to the school first. It is being torn down and is in a state of ruin fearful to behold. It made me feel so badly I was glad to hurry away and go down to the brook. There we sat on a log and discussed old school day reminiscences. It was dark and dim and shadowy. The maple trees hanging over the brook waved their branches with a sweet, sibilant rustling. Finally we came home through the dew-wet meadows where the fire-flies lit their starry lamps.

I had a letter from Ida to-day. She is teaching.

Thursday, July 5, 1894
Cavendish, P.E.I.

Prayer-meeting to-night and after it a drive with Alex. It was as perfect an evening as can be imagined—intensely calm, with a dim golden light irradiating the land. It was delicious driving through the woods, so dark and rustling and mysterious. This evening before prayer-meeting I had a delightful ramble through the fields, starry with clover and buttercups, climbing old mossy fences, brushing through spruce copses, and startling blue-birds from their nests.

I was re-reading "Last Days of Pompeii"[1] to-day. Its charm never fails. I wish I could have lots of books. I teach myself to hope that such good fortune may be mine some day, but at times I weary of saying "Patience and Perseverance." It is so hard not to see all at once the results of those estimable virtues.

---

1. *Last Days of Pompeii* (1834), highly coloured novel by Edward Bulwer-Lytton (1803–73) about decadence of the Roman Empire in the first century, ending with the eruption of Vesuvius.

Sunday, July 8, 1894
Cavendish, P.E.I.

I went for a walk to the shore this evening at sunset. It was so beautiful. The sea, lapping lovingly, as of old on the silver shores, was blue and rose and shining calm. The air was very still, the sky high and ethereal.

Seashore framed by rocks

My room

I am up here in my own room now. The window is open and softly on the still night air is borne the gentle rustle of the poplar trees outside, and then, silver, fluting voice of a solitary frog—the subtly sweet "voices of the night." The pasture is dotted with sheep, dimly white in the gloom. Oh, night, thou art Sublimity's self! Wild and storm-tossed indeed must be the soul which beneath the shadow of thy mighty wing feels not its near kin to the Eternal Night, under Thy coldly-solemn stars, passionless watchers at the portals of Infinity, we realize the littleness of time, the vastness of Eternity.

Saturday, July 14, 1894

Nellie McGrath is teaching at the Western Road, Nellie Rodgerson at Marie. Everyone but poor me can get a school, it seems. Dear knows, I've tried hard enough. I have sent applications for a score of schools, but so far the result has been discouraging silence. I cannot get to apply to the trustees in person and so I have a poor chance. Other girls' fathers or friends drive them about to apply for schools but grandfather will not do this for me, or let me have a horse to go myself, so there is nothing for it but letters, which are generally not even answered.

I was reading "Vanity Fair"[1] to-day. I didn't like it. The good characters are inane, sickly-sweet things and the bad ones are so clever and interesting that it is vexing to see their downfall.

Tuesday, July 17, 1894
Cavendish, P.E.I.

I went out for a stroll to-night and met Maggie and Chesley out driving. They invited me to go, too, and we went down the big lane and away up the shore. We had a magnificent spin. The sky was pink and gold and its fairy hues were reflected in the sea which was a calm expanse of silvery blue. When we got back to Cawnpore the big full moon was just rising and we flew up the lane and in along the Cavendish road as far as Robertsons. We had a lovely time.

The *Ladies World* came to-day with my "violet" poem in it. It looks quite real.

Thursday, July 26, 1894

Well, I have got a school[2] at last and it is away up at Bideford. I got the word to-day, and will have to go Saturday. I feel immensely elated, for I had almost given up hope of getting a school.

I had a letter from Laura to-day and I believe she will soon be engaged to Andrew Agnew. He keeps on going there and I begin to think that his perseverance will be crowned with success.

Friday, July 27, 1894
Cavendish, P.E.I.

I am all packed up and ready to start in the morning. Lu and Pen are going to drive me to the station. And so this is my last night in dear Cavendish for awhile and I go forth to-morrow to a new life among new people. I don't know how I will succeed but if hard and persevering work can bring me good-fortune I am resolved that I shall attain to it.

---

1. William Makepeace Thackeray's novel (1848) traces the rise and fall of a fiercely ambitious young woman.

2. LMM went as a Second Class Teacher to Bideford with a base salary of $180 a year, plus a supplement of $10, a school house allowance of $20, and contingent expenses of $20.

Saturday, July 28, 1894
Bideford,[1] *P.E.I.*

"Here I be!" Amen!

Lu, Pen and I started gaily off at five o'clock this morning. It was blowing a hurricane but nevertheless we contrived to have a very jolly drive. We got to Hunter River in lots of time and when the train came I said good-bye to the girls and took my departure. Had a very

Ellerslie Station

pleasant ride and reached Ellerslie station which is about two miles from Bideford—at 10.30. I was met by Bayfield Williams,[2] a young law student and his fiancée, Miss Edith England, a fair, rather pretty girl. They told me I

Nettie Millar

was to go to Mr. Millar's, one of the trustees, who would accommodate me until I found a boarding-house. We passed the school on our way down. It is large, about as artistic as a barn, and bleakly situated on a very bare-looking hill.

Mr. Millar's place, where I am at present domiciled, is rather pretty. There is a large family, among whom are no less than five of my future pupils. There is also a Miss Schurman visiting here. After dinner Miss S., Nettie Millar and I went for a walk to the river shore which is quite handy here. The

Sewing Circle met here this afternoon—Miss England, Daisy Williams, Emma Ellis, and Maud Hayes—the latter a girl nearly twice as tall as myself who yet is to be one of my pupils. She is really the tallest girl I have ever seen.

Sunday, July 29, 1894

To-day was breathlessly hot. We did not go to church. There is a very nice Methodist church in Bideford. The nearest Presbyterian church is at Tyne

---

1. A north-shore fishing village about 66 miles (106 km) west of Cavendish in a protected bay famous for oysters. Founded in 1814 by William Ellis and his apprentices, Williams and England; in 1860 Alex Millar established the Bideford flour mill. Descendants of these families still dominated Bideford life in the 1890s.

2. Descendant of one of the founding families of Bideford, he had preceded LMM as teacher, 1892–93, before leaving to study law.

Valley, about three miles away. I passed most of the day reading and eating the cherries which the Millar children bring to "teacher." What a comical sensation it gives me to hear that name applied to me! I suppose I shall be an object of curiosity around here for awhile. To-morrow I must take the plunge into "schoolmarming." Will I come bravely to the surface and strike out for the fair shores of success, or sink helplessly beneath the billows of failure?

Monday, July 30, 1894
Bideford, P.E.I.

This morning Mr. Millar drove me up to the school and I went in, feeling forty different ways at once and rather frightened into the bargain. The school is rather big and bare and dirty. There were about twenty children there, from six to thirteen years, and I called them in, said a few words to them and took down their names, feeling as idiotic and out of place as I ever did in my life. I have plenty of namesakes for there are three Mauds in the school.

Some of my Bideford pupils under another teacher

I had a rather hard time all day. It was so fearfully hot and there seemed so much to be done. The children seem quite bright but are shockingly behind hand in their lessons and apparently have no idea how to learn. Looking back now, I really think I got on pretty well for the first day, but it was very trying, and when four o'clock came I was so tired I could have sat down and cried. I just felt discouraged.

It is over two miles from the school to Mr. Millar's and when I got here I was nearly at my last gasp. But after I had had my tea and got bathed and rested I plucked up fresh courage.

After tea Josh Millar drove me up to Mr. Estey's, to see if they would take me to board. He is the Methodist minister and his

The Parsonage

family consists of himself, Mrs. E. and one little girl, Maud, a sweetly pretty little maid of seven, who is one of my pupils. The parsonage is a nice house with pretty grounds, about half a mile from the school. Mrs. Estey[1] seems like a very nice woman and was not at all averse to taking me but said she must first consult Mr. Estey who was away. She promised to let me know to-morrow. I do hope she will take me for there is no other nice place near the school where I have any chance of getting. I am so unsettled in this homeless condition that I am perfectly muddled.

Tuesday, July 31, 1894
Bideford, P.E.I.

Had another very hot, hard day but a shade more satisfactory than yesterday. On my way home from school I called to see Mrs. Estey and was delighted to find that she would take me. But I cannot go until Friday, as she is to be away.

Wednesday, Aug. 1, 1894

"Schoolmarming" gets a little easier every day but I haven't come to liking it yet. I do get so horribly tired and then I can't keep from worrying about my work.

I helped Nettie Millar pick cherries to-night and then went for a long walk in the twilight. Bideford is a very pretty place but seems to be a very quiet one.

I am to move up to the Parsonage Friday night and I am heartily thankful. I want to get settled down. Besides, although the Millars are very kind their cooking and table are simply awful.

Friday, Aug. 3, 1894

I really believe I am learning to like teaching. But this week has seemed as long as a year.

After tea I came up to the Parsonage. I have a great big room—too big—commanding a lovely view of the bay. Mrs. Estey seems very nice, but I am not greatly taken with Mr. E. Still, I am sure I shall like it here. But the night

---

1. Ada Estey, wife of Rev. John Estey, once mixed liniment into a cake, suggesting one of the adventures in *AGG*.

was close and rainy and oppressive and I took the worst spasm of homesickness and loneliness and discouragement I've had yet. Down came the tears in a shower. In the midst of my blues Gertie Moore called to see me. She is Annie Moore's sister and is teaching over at East Bideford across the river. Her call was not much of a consolation. She is the fastest, most unceasing talker I ever listened to.

Mrs. Estey

Saturday, Aug. 4, 1894

I have had no time for lonesomeness to-day at all for I have been on a jamboree. A big crowd, including the Millars went on a blueberry excursion up to "Lot 11" and I went, too. We left at ten, all in a big truck wagon, and had the roughest and jolliest drive imaginable. We made a day of it and had dinner and tea in the barrens, and laughed and talked and had a fine time. We had a merry drive home and were a rather tough-looking sunburned lot.

Sunday, Aug. 5, 1894
Bideford, P.E.I.

I have heard enough preaching to-day to last a month with care and economy.[1] This morning I went to the Methodist church. It is small but very pretty. I went down with Nettie Millar and went with them to Presbyterian service in Tyne Valley in the afternoon. We heard Rev. William MacLeod preach—or rather jump and rant and howl. I was heartily glad when he finished. Shrieve Millar[2] and I drove up to Lot 11 in the evening and heard him again. It is a nice drive but Shrieve is a nincompoop.

Wednesday, Aug. 8, 1894
Bideford, P.E.I.

I am really getting on splendidly now and enjoy my work—so different from last week when I was so tired and discouraged and hopeless. To-day I had

---

1. Phrase perhaps quoted from Albert Hastings Markham's *Life of Sir John Franklin and the North-west Passage* (1891).

2. Shrieve Millar (1875–1970), a successful Bideford farmer.

a lovely time. Mr. Williams' folks, who live just across the road from here, invited me to a picnic to Indian Island, which they had in honor of the boys, Arthur and Bayfield, who are home on their vacation. Quite a crowd went with us. We got on board a big scow at Richards' wharf and had a delightful sail to the Island. We had a jolly time all through and after tea we had a dance in a house with an Indian[1] playing the fiddle. We had a most delicious sail home but when I got back to the Parsonage I found the house locked up and deserted. I was sitting gloomily on the veranda when Shrieve Millar came along and took me for a drive. So I have had a pretty gay day and am tired enough to sleep soundly.

A. Williams and E. England

Friday, Aug. 10, 1894

I'm just as sleepy as when I left off. Yesterday it poured rain all day but cleared up at night and Daisy Williams came over to ask me to go to a party with them at Mr. Seaman's. I had just a lovely time. There was quite a crowd there and we danced to our heart's content. Luther and Arthur Williams were there and I had lots of fun with them.

Daisy Williams

I like boarding here so much and consider myself very lucky to have got here. Mrs. Estey is so jolly and just like a girl.

I'm going on another expedition to-morrow but I don't expect much pleasure from it. Shrieve Millar, Austin Ramsay, Nettie and I are going up to visit friends of theirs at O'Leary.[2] I didn't want to go at all but Nettie did and her mother wouldn't let her go unless I did so I consented. I know I will have an unpleasant time for I don't like either Shrieve or Austin Ramsay.

---

1. First Nations peoples (largely Mi'kmaq) inhabited villages on the north shore of PEI.
2. Village near the west end of PEI, centre of potato farming.

Monday, Aug. 13, 1894
Bideford, P.E.I.

My forebodings were correct—I had a horrid time. We left Saturday about one. We had a pleasant drive but it is 26 miles up there and I was tired out when we arrived. We stayed with the Smallmans. They are nice enough but uninteresting. Sunday was very slow. We went to preaching at O'Leary and heard that miserable MacLeod again—he seems to be ubiquitous. We left for home after tea to my devout thankfulness. We had a nice drive and got home about ten.

School goes on well. I have 38 on the roll now and am getting fond of them all. They are a nice little crowd and very obliging. Some of them bring me a bouquet every day, so that my desk is a veritable flower garden. I think they like me, too, from some encouraging reports I have heard. My favorite pupils are Jack Millar and Maud Estey.

Thursday, Aug. 16, 1894
Bideford, P.E.I.

I was invited to a small party at Mr. Williams' tonight and had a lovely time. They have a nice house and are such nice refined people. Arthur W. walked home with me. He is going away to-morrow.

Maud Estey

Wednesday, Aug. 22, 1894

Who should pounce down on me to-day but Inspector Campbell! Of course the exam was necessarily mainly in the last teacher's work and so was not very satisfactory. I am resolved it shall not be so next time.

John Dystant,[1] a young Methodist minister, was here to tea to-night and I had to entertain him while Mrs. E. was at work. He is quite nice.

I have a most wretched cold. What a horrid thing a cold is! Whatever induced that poor, unlucky Pandora to open that fatal box and thereby let loose so many ills on our ill-fated race?

Will Montgomery, a second cousin of mine, who lives over at Port Hill, came to see me this evening. He is real nice and is coming over for me some Friday night soon.

---

1. Brother of Lewis Dystant. Studied at Mt. Allison and was ordained Methodist minister; the University of Illinois awarded him a doctorate of divinity at the end of a distinguished career.

Thursday, Aug. 30, 1894
Bideford, P.E.I.

I was to tea at Mr. Wm. Hayes[1] yesterday evening and had a very pleasant time. I left at 6.30, walked smartly home, dressed, and walked down to Mr. Millar's; for I was invited to go with them to a party at Gordon Ramsay's at Tyne Valley.[2] We walked down to the Valley, danced till two, and then walked back to Mr. Millars—having walked about nine miles all told since school "let out." You may be sure I was ready for bed when I reached Mr. Millar's. I was abominably sleepy all day in school. I was never so glad of anything as when school came out. I came home, went at once to bed and slept until 8.

Sunday, Sept. 2, 1894

Will Montgomery came over Friday evening and took me back to Port Hill. It is a very pretty drive over there. Will lives with his mother and two sisters, Maggie and Louisa, both of whom are rather staid spinsters. Saturday morning we all went over to Bird Island to pick cranberries. We left at nine and drove to the shore where we all embarked in a leaky flat which wobbled painfully and alarmingly. Nevertheless, we all got over in safety and tumbled out on the Bird Island cranberry beds. I had never seen cranberries growing before and didn't exactly feel as if I were pining to see them now, but I couldn't stand around all day doing nothing, so I went to work rather half-heartedly. It might have been good fun if I had been dressed for the part but of course I had my good clothes on and they don't agree with cranberry beds. I kept up a pretence of picking until after dinner and then I sat down in a little hollow and talked to Will about books and Russia's foreign policy[3] and education for the masses!! Will is interested in world doings and it was good to have a real conversation again with a man of some brains.

At about three we concluded to go home and started for our boat. Imagine our dismay at finding that someone—probably a prowling Indian—had stolen one of our oars. A nice pickle! Stay on Bird Island all night—cold, tired, and hungry! I mentally vowed that, let me be but safe on the mainland once more, neither sail nor picnic should tempt me off terra firma again in a hurry. Finally the men got a pole and after an awfully long time poled us over to Indian Island. Will went on shore and after another long dreary wait,

---

1. William Hayes, owner of a carriage-making business and postmaster.
2. Village just south of Bideford famous for its oyster beds.
3. Russian imperialism in this period was widely criticized, e.g., in Kipling in *Letters of Marque* (1891).

he reappeared with a doubtful looking oar he had made himself. We started again and *did* get home finally... but it was just as much as ever. This morning I felt decidedly stiff enough.

We went to the English church in the morning and after dinner drove to the Presbyterian church at Lot 14. Will brought me home this evening.

It is very like the fall now—chill, high coloured skies, mournfully-sighing winds, coldly purple seas, shorn harvest fields, all speak of vanished summer.

Tuesday, Sept. 4, 1894

Prince of Wales opened to-day. Wouldn't I have liked to be there! I can just see them all and hear the dear old doctor haranguing them. My college year was the happiest of my life and I never expect to have such a good time again.

I was busy writing letters all the evening. I love letter-writing. To be sure, all my correspondents are not equally interesting. Some are dull and it is rather tedious to write to them. I have never heard from Edie Skelton since last November. I am sorry, for, although her letters were not of much account, I had a warm love for the girl herself and did not wish her to slip out of my ken. Alexina is rather dry, but Laura and Will are O.K. Mustard is a by-gone. I stopped writing to him last winter for I simply could not be bothered any longer with him. I suppose he is a full-fledged Reverend now. Hattie Gordon's letters are always capital and so are Selena's. The absence of Lem's letters wouldn't worry me at all. Mary C.'s letters are interesting but may cease to be so as our interests slowly cease to be mutual. Amanda's and Lucy's letters are generally interesting because they give so many details of home gossip. Pensie and Clara cannot write worth-while letters. Clara C. by the way, is in Boston now, working out as a domestic servant. It is absurd. Clara herself never had any lofty ideals or ambitions but I simply cannot understand her parents, especially Aunt Annie, permitting such a thing. If she wanted to earn her living they were quite able to afford to educate or train her to some occupation which would not have involved a loss of social caste. The idea of Clara Campbell "working out"! It would be laughable if it were not so tragic.

Thursday, Sept. 6, 1894

I gave the fourth class a written exam in grammar to-day—the first of the kind they ever had. Really, it was tough. I feel quite worn out. I suppose they thought they had a hard time but it wasn't as hard for them as for me! I remember when *I* used to grumble at exams and think the teachers imposed them on us out of pure malice. But I have a clearer insight into my former teachers' trials now. I may be teaching my pupils something but *they* are teaching me more—whole tomes of wisdom.

Saturday, Sept. 8, 1894

Mrs. Scott, a friend of Mrs. Estey's came last night, for a visit. She is a stout lady with very black hair and eyes and a merry, ringing laugh.

To-day was placidly uneventful. In the afternoon, Mrs. E., Mrs. S., Maudie and I played croquet. I don't care for croquet—there isn't enough "go" about it to suit me. I lounged around the lawn, pounding the yellow clover blossoms and watching the mellow September sunlight falling over the trees and golden brown sward and over the river and bay, deeply, darkly blue.

Edith E. and Daisy W.

I was invited up to Mr. England's this evening. Daisy Williams went, too, and we had a very nice time and came home under a hazy September moon, while the glow of a far off wood fire painted a page of glory on the sky.

Sunday, Sept. 9, 1894
Bideford, P.E.I.

Preserve me from a rainy Sunday. It is tolerable when there are a lot of folks in the house with you, but in a quiet place like this it is distractingly lonely. I did not get up till ten which broke the back of the day at any rate. There was no preaching here to-day. After dinner I put on cloak, rubbers, and an indestructible old hat and sallied forth for a tramp. I went up to Seaman's corner and struck into a lane I have been longing to explore. It is called, I believe, Lover's Lane, but it is certainly not in the least like *my* Lover's Lane at home. It has a beauty of its own, however. As I tramped along my spirits rose—I felt fresh and free and energetic. The lane was green and grass-grown, with here and there along the fence an old gnarled spruce tree or a copse of young saplings. There was a sense of companionship in their dark green boughs. I love trees. I felt like a new creature, bodily and mentally when I got back.

Monday, Sept. 10, 1894

"Harvest is ended and summer is gone."[1]

I realized that to-day when, walking home from school in the mild hazy September air, I looked over at a maple grove and saw a blood-red branch waving triumphantly among the green uniforms. It was the flag of autumn's vanguard. Oh well, "it is not always May"[2]—and possibly it is a very excellent arrangement that it is not.

It is a perfect evening now and as I sit here at sunset by my broad, low window I can see as fair a scene as ever delighted an artist. The sky is a faintly-flushed heliotrope, the rivers and creeks are calm as glass, and the little purple points, the fringing spruces and the far-off islands are mirrored perfectly in the pale azure and rose waters, over whose surface several sailboats are gliding as gracefully as gulls. A soft lemon-hued light falls over hill and creek and island, and it seems as if tired old Nature had fallen into a chance nap at eventide.

Thursday, Sept. 13, 1894
Bideford, P.E.I.

To-night was brilliantly moonlight, with a sparkle of frost in the air—an ideal night for driving if one only had an ideal companion! Shrieve Millar came about eight and we went to George Sharpe's[3] at East Bideford—a mile, as the crow flies, several miles around by the road. It is a very pretty drive and I enjoyed it exceedingly, as we drove past sheets of water sparkling with starry brilliancy, past clearings where the light cast sharp black shadows among the stumps, and through still woods mysteriously dim in the white radiance.

Friday, Sept. 14, 1894

Really, when September feels in a gracious mood and smiles on her eager lover, Autumn, she can be royally beautiful. To-day was a symphony in azure, pearl-veiled skies, peaceful fields, opal skies and cricket songs. However, the symphony was all *outside* the schoolroom.

---

1. Misquoted from "The harvest is past, the summer is ended, and we are not saved," Jeremiah 8:20; quoted again in *AGG*, *Chronicles of Avonlea*, and *Anne of the Island*.
2. From a poem with that title by Henry Wadsworth Longfellow, *Ballads and other Poems* (1842).
3. George Sharp (1839–95), married to Martha Ellis.

Mrs. Estey and Mrs. Scott came up to the school at three to hear the recitations. The kiddies did well, and really we had quite an amateur concert, very like those we used to have "lang syne" in the old Cavendish school. How short a time it seems since I was a little schoolgirl, trotting to school o' mornings and finding a world of wonders all around me. And now here I am, a genuine live school teacher myself! I can never get used to that fact and wouldn't be a bit surprised if the kiddies were to rise in open rebellion and refuse to obey me. I wonder if the teachers I used to think such marvels of learning and dignity really felt as I do. I daresay they did.

Saturday, Sept. 15, 1894

I was down to Mr. Millar's this afternoon, as the Sewing circle met there. I got a cute little gray kitten, whom I mean to call "Coco." I carried it home in a basket in company with Daisy and Rebie Williams, and we had an awful time with the little wretch and laughed until we were breathless.

I went with Shrieve to a magic lantern show at Ellerslie this evening. The views were very good but the showman was a bungler and my pleasure was spoiled by two clowns who sat behind me and kept up an endless stream of senseless, would-be funny comments on every picture.

I must really drop Shrieve. He is quite impossible as an escort.

Sunday, Sept. 16, 1894
Bideford, P.E.I.

The outside world was so beautiful to-day that after dinner I set out for a walk to a grove of spruce and maple in Mr. Williams' field. I was so warm and tired when I got there that I lay down in a mossy hollow among the ferns under the maples and fell asleep before I knew it. I slept for a couple of hours. I should have had fairy-like and sylvan dreams but as a matter of fact I did not dream at all.

Tuesday, Sept. 18, 1894
Bideford, P.E.I.

Ugh! Autumn must have played September false and she is weeping the tears of her widowhood.

Mr. & Mrs. E., Mrs. Scott, Maudie and myself went down to the shore at dusk. A thick pall of mist hung over the waters through which the opposite shores and the little points loomed phantom-like and unreal. A good natured oysterman took us for a row. The water was glassy-still and the lights along shore twinkled through the mist.

To-day, while I was hearing the primer class, I was rather appalled by seeing two lank, freckled, rough-looking lads stride in and sit down. They seemed rather formidable, but I hid my trepidation, recognizing the need of firmness from the start, for one was George Howells, the traditional "bad boy" of the district. He is the grandson of a man who served a life sentence in prison for shooting another man. It happened in Malpeque when I was a small child and as it was a "*cause celebre*" in those days I heard it much talked about. Let us hope George will not prove to be a case of atavism. His principal adornment is freckles.

His companion was George Murphy. They swell the roll to 48.

I dismissed school at recess, as I wanted to be home in time to see a wedding which was to come off in the parsonage at three o'clock. The party were up to time and for dress and behaviour were the funniest I've ever imagined outside of a comic recitation book. The whole performance was as good as a play. The groom was badly scared and his attendants were drunk. Mr. Estey received the huge sum of one dollar for tying the knot and the whole party drove off, singing "Nearer, My God, To Thee,"—which I suppose they thought appropriate. I had to sign their name to the marriage certificate as neither of them could read or write.

It is a regular fall rain now—a night wild enough to suit any novelist in search of suitable weather for a murder or elopement. Tried to play "logomachy"[1]—"Methodist casino"—this evening but as Mrs. E. was tired, Mr. E. more than usually satirical, Maudie peevish, and Mrs. Scott and myself rather indifferent the game was not a notable success.

Friday, Sept. 21, 1894

Such a tear-splashed world as greeted us this morning! Nature's face looked like some stained, swollen child's, half sullen yet and undecided whether to smile or cry again. After pouting and scowling half the day she finally concluded to brighten up and blew away all her vapors.

Work in my little absolute kingdom went on as usual. What an undisputed sway I exercise, supreme mistress of half a hundred restless little souls, pilgrims on the weary road to knowledge!

---

1. A word game, ironically called "Methodist casino," since Methodists disapproved of all card games, including the then-popular casino.

Saturday, Sept. 29, 1894
Bideford, P.E.I.

I spent most of to-day reading MacCaulay's essays.[1] His sparkling pages are never dull and he can invest the dryest details with interest and charm.

This evening I went to the P.O. for a walk. It was cold and chill; the sky was overcast with wrinkled gray clouds, save along the north where a strip of yellow sky gleamed palely. No living creature but myself seemed abroad and the cold gray shadows settling down over the withered fields lent to the landscape an aspect inexpressibly dreary and mournful. It made me feel hopeless, and as if the best of my life lay in the past. Externals have a great influence on me—too great, perhaps.

I have been reading this evening and petting "Coco," who is shamefully spoiled by everybody in the parsonage. It made me think of poor old "Topsy."

She is still alive at home and I have a warm corner of my heart for that old gray-and-white cat down in the old barns surrounded by the dark spruces where I used to play and dream, and romp with my pussies, regarding them as very important denizens of my small world.

And those old autumns when we picked apples among the fallen leaves on frosty mornings while the cats made mad rushes around us and the hens clucked slyly under the big sweet-apple trees.

Where we picked apples

Is it really the same world I saw then that I see now? It seems so very different. The "coloring of romance" is gone. *Then*, everything was invested with a fairy grace emanating from my own imagination—the trees that whispered nightly around the old house where I slept, the paths and lanes where I loved to stray, the fields, each individualized by some oddity of fence or shape, the sea whose murmur was never out of my ears—all were radiant with "the glory and the dream."[2]

---

1. Misspelling for Thomas Babington Macaulay, author of *The Lays of. Ancient Rome* (1842) and *A History of England* (1849).

2. From William Wordsworth's "Ode: Intimations of Immortality from Recollections of Early Childhood" (1807).

Monday, Oct. 1, 1894
Bideford, P.E.I.

Mrs. Capt. Richards[1] called on me to-day. The Richards are old people and very wealthy. He is a ship-owner and builder, and has a fine, old-fashioned place down by the shore. She is very nice and invited me down.

Fred Ellis[2] began to go to school to-day. He is a tall 17 year old and I feel ridiculously insignificant beside him. But that is not the worst. Nettie says Josh is going to come and that she heard Luther Williams was too. I can't credit that last for he must be over 20. I am none too well-pleased at any of them coming as they are all over age, so don't count in the average.[3]

Saturday, Oct. 6, 1894
Cavendish, P.E.I.

I closed school yesterday for vacation and came home. When I got here I found a letter from Will awaiting me which was quite a surprise. He is in Winnipeg at St. John's college[4] and is going to study law. He couldn't have chosen any profession which would suit him better. Will is just cut out for a lawyer.

Home again

Sunday, Oct. 7, 1894

What glorious aspects October can assume when she pleases! To-day was perfect.

I was in Sunday School this afternoon. It is quite appalling to see the number of "kiddies" who have shot up into big boys and girls since last year.

---

1.   Local usage of assigning to the wife her husband's status-title as in "Mrs. Doctor Blythe" in *Anne's House of Dreams*.

2.   Fred Ellis (b. 1880), a young member of one of the founding families of Bideford.

3.   School students past the age of compulsory education were not considered in assignment of funds.

4.   St. John's was officially opened in Winnipeg, 1866, reviving an earlier school at the Red River Settlement. In 1877 St John's College, St Boniface College and the Manitoba College became the founding colleges in the University of Manitoba.

It really made me feel awfully old and "grown-up" to see them in the places my old mates and I used to fill.

After S.S. I went down with Pen and had a very nice time. In the evening Alec took us into the Baptist church.

B. Church.

Thursday, Oct. 11, 1894

This evening was deliciously moonlight—Lu and I went down to Pensie's. I never spent a pleasanter evening. Alec, Pen, Lu and I sat in the parlour and laughed until the walls re-echoed. What a dear old place it is to go to! Always the same and always certain of a good time!

Friday, Oct. 12, 1894
Cavendish, P.E.I.

What a delightful employment picking apples is! It was a real pleasure to me to-day to prowl among the old trees, each possessing its own unchanged individuality. What an enormous number of apples we kids used to consume long ago. I couldn't begin to do it now. But there are lots of things I couldn't do now—and wish I could, alas! Why can't carefree childhood last forever? Now that I have written that down in cold blood it strikes me as a very silly question indeed and I feel a sneaking shame of it.

Tuesday, Oct. 16, 1894

Oh, why can't—but no, I won't! I closed with a silly question last time and I won't begin again with one—otherwise I intended to ask why couldn't pleasures last forever. I suppose it is better that they can't, or what would we accomplish in life? But I've been having such a perfectly jolly time—I've been to town and Mary C. was in, too. I went in on the train Saturday evening and was met at the station by Bertie and Lew and Mary C. Mary and I had a most rapturous reunion and I expect we made perfect geese of ourselves. Nettie Montgomery is boarding at Aunt Mary's and going to college. She is rather affected but very nice and full of fun.

After tea Mary and I went down to see Norman—who is going to college again—and then went for a walk around town. How delightful it was to be in town again!

It was late when we got back so we went straight to bed and talked all night. Sunday morning we went to dear old Zion. Really, it was delightful to be there once more. John and Will S. were there, too, and looked as natural as life.

After dinner Mary and I went down and made a brief—a very brief—call on MacMillan's. They don't seemed to have improved any. In the evening after church John S. and Jack Gordon—a second cousin of mine who is in the bank here—came down and we had a jolly evening.

Monday Mary and I visited the dear old college. It was so lovely to be there again. We saw all the professors. Dr. A. and Caven are as nice as ever. I saw many familiar faces but alas, more unfamiliar ones. Monday evening John was down again and we had so much fun.

To-day I spent shopping. Grandma drove in for me and we came home in the evening.

Wednesday, Oct. 17, 1894

I spent this afternoon at Mollie's. In one way it was nice to be there. But someway, Mollie seems changed from what she used to be. There seems to be a slowly widening distance between us which it is hard to bridge. Our interests are ceasing to be in common. Well, our long friendship of thirteen years shall not fade if I can help it.

Chesley Clark

Monday, Oct. 22, 1894

It is appalling how events pile themselves up when they once begin! Here I have whole oceans of news—some of it quite graphic, too. To begin with, I was at a party at Charley McKenzie's Friday night and had a splendid time—nearly danced my feet off. Ches drove us home and I danced the rest of the night in my dreams. Saturday morning Pen, Lu, and I started off for a cruise to Park Corner and Malpeque, and you may be sure our drive was a merry one. We got to Aunt Annie's at eleven-thirty and had dinner. But oh dear, how lonesome it was there! The girls are both away—Clara in Boston and Stella at P.W. College. I had never before been there without them and I felt like crying all the time I missed them so. After tea we went up to Malpeque where we remained until church time the next day. We had a very nice time. From church we drove back to Aunt Annie's and after dinner Lu and Pen went to visit their respective relatives and I went to see Aunt Mary Cuthbert with whom I stayed till dark. I had just got back to Uncle John's when Lu came back and with her *Lem*.

Geo. H. Cook,
CHARLOTTETOWN, P. E. I.

Lem (seated on left)

The instant I saw *him* I took a creepy fit. I don't know how or why it was but I felt instinctively that Lem's visit would not be as harmless as usual.

We spent a pleasant evening, but finally the others all drifted away and left me to my fate. I was desperately resolved to do my utmost to prevent Lem from speaking out. And until the very last moment I flattered myself that I would succeed. I laughed and joked and teased poor Lem. I was quite

The parlour at Park Corner

nice and chatty but if he became sober—which he did with alarming frequency—I would invariably give the conversation a frivolous turn which would quite rattle poor Lem and leave him precisely where he was when he began. It began to get very late and Lem kept saying he must go, but, like Harry in the song "he didn't." Finally, however he did get up to go and I rose, too, rejoicing, for I thought all danger was past.

But Lem was not out of the house yet. He followed me over to the table and put his arm around me.

"I suppose you'll go away up there to Bideford and forget all about me," he said.

"Oh, no, I won't—I never forget anyone—I have a remarkable memory," I answered flippantly.

I have this advantage over Lem—he can never tell when I'm in earnest or when I'm not. It was the case now. He tried several more baits but as I only laughed at each and wheedled him a little nearer to the door each time he did finally get there. I stepped to it with alacrity—a moment and he would be gone!

Then suddenly Lem stepped back, took me in his arms again and said seriously,

"Maud, I came up here to-night to say something. I haven't said it yet but I will now. I've been thinking about this—I've been going with you for a long while now and I've been thinking that perhaps I'm keeping you from going with somebody else you'd like better. But I love you and won't it be all right?"

I stammered, blushed and finally gasped in confusion, "Oh Lem, don't be foolish."

But Lem wouldn't take this sensible advice at all and went persistently on being foolish.

"I thought I'd speak now, for fear there *was* somebody else you liked better and"—"No," I broke in desperately, "there is no one else"—and then I stopped, conscious that *that* wasn't exactly the wisest thing to say. I tried to be cool, but I am bound to say the attempt was a miserable failure for I wasn't in the least prepared for such a scene.

"Then, Maud, if you'll just say 'yes'" —

But this was just what "Maud" couldn't say, so she broke in desperately.

"Oh, Lem, don't! I like you ever so much but I'm not thinking of anything of *that* kind, Lem. All I *am* thinking of is getting an education and"—

"Yes, and when you have got it will it be *all right*?" he asked again.

"I can't make any promises, Lem," I said more composedly, beginning to get my wits back again, "I'm too young"—

"Yes, and I'm young, too," he said. "But I'm in earnest, Maud, indeed I am. And I hope you'll consent some day. Anyhow, I wish you may win success in everything. I wish you well indeed, I do."

We went out then and I stood dumbly and rather unhappily and held the lamp while he got his coat and hat. When he was ready to go I held out my hand.

"If you'll just say *one word*, Maud," he said.

"Good-bye, Lem," I said hastily, drawing *away*. There were a dozen soothing things I wanted to say but somehow I could get nothing out but that ungracious farewell.

"Good-night, dear," said Lem. "Perhaps we'll see it in the same light some other time."

And then he went away—to my huge relief. It is an abominable business—this telling a man you can't marry him. I went to the room, where the girls were asleep and quickly got into bed. Perhaps you think I did not soon go to sleep after my exciting interview, but I did, for I was tired out.

Poor Lem, I'm sorry things have turned out so. He is a good, manly fellow and I've always liked him. But I can't give him anything more than friendship. I don't know much about love but I *do* know I'm not a bit in love with Lem and never could be. I don't mean to feel badly over this, either. Lem will not be broken-hearted. He is not of the type that cares deeply or takes things hardly. He will be a good deal disappointed, but he will soon be looking for another "girl." "Love" with him means that he is quite fond of a tolerably good-looking girl whom he could feel proud of as a wife. He has an aptitude of a certain sort of business but he has no brains, culture, or breeding. So he is out of the running on every count. I've always been frank and friendly with him but I've certainly never pretended to be anything else. He cannot accuse me of having deceived him in anyway.

Wednesday, Oct. 24, 1894
Cavendish, P.E.I.

This afternoon I had a long ramble and went back to "Sam Wyand's field," and the woods around. I think I walked miles and fairly drank in the beauty of those wild places.

This evening Pen, Lu, and I went up to Darnley Clark's. We had a very nice evening and Ches came home with us. We all went down with Pen and on the way out Everett and Jack Laird who turned and went back with us. We had a merry time and larked at Pen's door for nearly an hour.

Saturday, Oct. 27, 1894
Bideford, P.E.I.

Here I am again. Pen, Lu, and I drove up to Kensington yesterday afternoon and spent the night at Mrs. Pidgeon's.[1] In the evening several of our friends came in— Lem among them. We spent a very pleasant evening playing whist and

Kensington Station

logomachy. The train left at nine this morning and the girls saw me off. Nettie Montgomery was on the train and I was glad of her company, even if

---

1.   James Pidgeon was a partner with William Cousins in an early ship-building business in Bideford.

she did fill up the greater part of the time detailing all her many aches and pains and sicknesses. She is one of those people who seem to take a gruesome pleasure in that sort of thing.

Mrs. E. and Maudie met me at Ellerslie. Have been working hard all the afternoon unpacking and getting settled down again. Having accomplished it I am so tired that I'm only fit to go to bed.

Tuesday, Oct. 30, 1894

After all a return to work is not unpleasant and teaching, though it has its pains, has also its pleasures. I am very much skimped for time these short hours but still I manage to make both ends meet and I have got the school pretty well organized now.

Wednesday, Oct. 31, 1894
Bideford, P.E.I.

A new kiddy started to go to school to-day and such an oddity as he is! His name is Amos MacKay and he disturbed the school work not a little by his naive goings on.

Edith E., Daisy W. and I were invited down to Capt. Richard's[1] this evening to meet their cousin, Miss Richards from Wales, and we enjoyed ourselves very much. Miss R. is very nice but she talks with such a decided accent that it is difficult to understand her.

I am getting on beautifully in school now and am even feeling encouraged about the fourth class. Ever since I came here that class has been the problem of my existence. I never imagined such a set of stupids. But they actually seem to be wakening up.

Monday, Nov. 5, 1894

"Guy Fawkes'"[2] night—and I've been having a very pleasant time. The Orange Lodge[3] at Ellerslie had a supper in the hall to-night and Lewis Dystant came

---

1. Captain Richards (b. 1819), a wealthy ship-owner and builder in Bideford. Captain Richards' home, built in 1864, was selected a hundred years later as the best house of its vintage in PEI.

2. Until well into the twentieth century many Canadians lit bonfires to celebrate the defeat of the "Popish plot" of 1605, designed to overthrow the British government.

3. Protestant fraternal society, very strong in rural Canada, commemorating the victories over the Irish in 1690 by King William III (William of Orange).

out and took me. He is an Ellerslie youth who sings in the choir here; he
seems nice and is quite nice-looking.

We had a fine time at the supper. There were about 50 there and as I'm
getting pretty well acquainted with the people around here now I enjoyed
every minute of the time. We came home at 12 and I promised to go with
Lew D.[1] to a week-night preaching service at Tyne Valley tomorrow night.

Tuesday, Nov. 6, 1894

Lewis Dystant

Tyne Valley preaching indeed! Here is one who
wasn't there. It has been a raging snowstorm all
day. Only eight pupils were in school and time
dragged woefully. I assure you my walk through
the keen wind in the snow and slush made me
think of my sins—a foretaste of coming pleasures
this winter no doubt.

I had a letter from Jack Sutherland to-day,
thanking me for my photo. Dear old Jack, what a
lot Mary C. and I used to think of him—and talk
of him!

Sunday, Nov. 11, 1894

It is true November weather these days, dull, cold and gray. All summer
brightness and autumn glory has departed and there is yet no sparkle of frost
or purity of snow to supply its place.

I went to "class meeting" with Mrs. E. tonight. It was a beautiful moonlight night and quite a number were out, Lew Dystant among them. He
walked home with me.

Tuesday, Nov. 13, 1894
Bideford, P.E. Island

Rev. Mr. Corbett preached at the Valley tonight and Lew D. came out to
take me. It was a perfect night, clear, crisp and moonlight, and the drive
seemed all too short. After the service we went for a drive through to the

---

1. Lew Dystant. LMM changes the spelling to "Lou" on further acquaintance. He eventually moved
    to Summerside.

station. Lew is a nice fellow. That is, he does very well for somebody to drive me about.

Friday, Nov. 16, 1894

For a change to-day was lovely—haze-veiled rivers, pearly blue skies, softly whispering west winds.

Last night there was a social at Tyne Valley. Lou took his sister Sadie and me. We had a very fair time although there was too big a crowd for real fun. Lou bought a cake for me. It will do nicely for snacks at odd hours.

Tuesday, Nov. 20, 1894

A wretched sort of day—bitterly cold and blowing a hurricane. I'd really thought I'd freeze going to school.

This evening Daisy W. and I went to a practice at Mr. England's. We are going to get up a concert for Xmas. We are to have three dialogues and I am in two—"Cinderella" and "The Irish Love Letter." "Cinderella"[1] is quite a pretentious dialogue, as there are several scenes in it, with costumes, music, and dancing.

Sunday, Nov. 25, 1894

I went down to dinner at Mr. Millar's this morning as per invitation, but was in misery all the time because just before I left home Mrs. Estey unexpectedly asked me to take the organist's place at church to-night, Mrs. Currie, the regular organist being away. I felt dreadfully nervous but consented. When I went to church this evening I felt as if I were going to immediate execution, but I got on all right in spite of my dismal fears.

Tuesday, Nov. 27, 1894
Bideford, P.E.I.

Our house has a new inmate. Lula Gamble[2] from Fifteen Point came here to-day to stay for a few months and go to school. She is about 12 and is so

---

1. LMM's scrapbooks show that she played one of the sisters; Edith England played Cinderella. "The Irish Love Letter" appears as "The Old Settler's Story" in a program preserved in LMM's scrapbook.
2. Lula Gamble (1882–1981) became a teacher and moved to Massachusetts and later Connecticut.

far advanced that I hardly know where to place her. She is a nice little thing and is to room with me.

There was a practice at Mr. Williams' tonight and we all turned out in full force. We are to have a basket social in connection with our concert.

Tuesday, Dec. 4, 1894

I am so busy these days that I seldom have a moment's spare time. I have begun to prepare for my exam and intend trying to get up a little programme. I have spent most of the evening writing out that old dialogue "The Rival Orators" for Frank Grant and Willie Cannon. It brought back old times very vividly when we were busy in the dear old school getting up our first concert and Nate and Ches were preparing this very dialogue. As I copied it tonight it seemed to me that I could almost hear them going over it. Time and place faded. I was no longer the prim (?) teacher of Bideford school but again a light-hearted school girl beside Mollie at our old desk while Nate and Ches were up on the floor "going through" that old dialogue. Well, there have been many changes since then!

Thursday, Dec. 6, 1894

Last night about six Lou Dystant's sleigh-bells jingled through the frosty air as he came to take me to a lecture on "Prohibition"[1] up at Lot 11, the lecturer being no other than my dear old teacher Mr.—now Rev.—Fraser. We were soon flying up the road in a dazzle of frost and moonlight. I never enjoyed a drive more. The night was bewitching, the roads were like gleaming stretches of satin ribbon, there was a white frost that softened the distant hills and woods to a fairy dream, and the moonshine fell white and silvery over all. Earth looked like a cold, chaste bride in her silver veil, waiting to be waked by her lover's kiss to warmth and love and passion. I was sorry when we got up and had to go out of the moonlit dazzle to the stuffy little church with its rows of commonplace, hum-drum people.

But the lecture was neither commonplace nor hum-drum. It was splendid.

To-day was hard. The attendance at school is large now and it makes the work much more difficult, for there are not half enough seats and the children are so crowded. I like teaching but I do get dreadfully tired some days.

---

1. In 1901 Prince Edward Island would become the first province to legislate prohibition of sale of alcohol. In Island schools "Scientific Temperance" was an examination subject.

Dear me, this time last year I was a gay college girl discussing approaching exams with my chums—and now here I am, a sedate Bideford "schoolmarm" well versed in the mysteries of rod and rule!

The dialogue practice was at Mr. Millar's to-night and Lou D. came out and drove me down. He is really a nice *handy* person.

Sunday, Dec. 9, 1894
Bideford, P.E.I.

After service this morning I went down to Mr. Millar's and went with them to the afternoon service at the valley. Tonight was a beautiful night and I went up with the Millar boys to preaching in Lot 11. We had a splendid drive there and back even if the same sermon we had at the valley was sandwiched in between.

Friday, Dec. 14, 1894

Oh, I'm tired! My worries over my exam programme are hammering nails in my coffin. It is hard work training those kiddies. Most of them have no idea how to do anything right.

I wrote a long letter to Mary C. tonight. Dear old Mary, how I wish I could have a jolly good racket with her as of old. It would clear away the cobwebs from my brain. But patience—patience—patience! I am sick of the very word. I would just like to tear around and be as impatient as I liked for awhile.

Sunday, Dec. 16, 1894

Yesterday afternoon I spent at Mr. England's and had a splendid time. They have a lovely house and are very nice people. In the evening we went to practice at Mr. McDougall's[1] and after we had disposed of the dialogue we wound up with a dance which lasted till ten. I stayed all night with Edith and we talked till nearly three o'clock. Today was a quiet, drowsy one. Lou and I stayed there all day and we all read and cat-napped alternately, only waking up thoroughly to eat a roast goose.

I must go back to work tomorrow. Ugh!

---

1. The McDougalls were descendants of John ("the Yankee") Ramsay, one of the first settlers in Bideford; they had intermarried with the Ellises.

Monday, Dec. 17, 1894

After all, work isn't a bad thing to go back to when you've had a good sleep and feel in excellent trim. After school I went to Robert Hayes—a place I've never been yet. Had a poky time. Lou came in the evening and drove me home in mud to our eyes.

I heard today that Uncle John Montgomery has had a stroke of apoplexy and is very ill. I am very sorry.

I made my basket for the concert tonight—it is of apricot crepe paper and is very pretty. The affair is to come off Xmas night and I sincerely hope it will be a success.

Monday, Dec. 24, 1894
Bideford, P.E.I.

O—o—o—oo! If it is as cold as this tomorrow night we'll all freeze to death, for that Tyne Valley hall is a barn-like place and was simply awful tonight. We were all down there for a "dress rehearsal."

I am invited to Mr. Millar's to dinner tomorrow and to Mr. Dystant's to tea. I must go to bed now and get my beauty sleep for so many social functions.

Tuesday, Dec. 25, 1894

Well, my goodness!—or somebody else's goodness if mine isn't substantial enough!

This morning was dull and gray; it was blowing a hurricane and spitting snow. I went down to Mr. Millar's and had a very dull time—which was just what I had expected—and at noon it began to rain and poured down in bucketsful. Of course I knew Lou wouldn't come out for me and at three Jack Millar drove me home. Night closed in with a downpour. No concert of course. Isn't it all aggravating?

Friday, Dec. 28, 1894

My, I'm tired! Last night I went over to a Masonic supper[1] at Port Hill with Edith E., James Richards, and Bayfield Williams. It was a simply fearful night

---

1. The Freemasons' secret society owned the hall or temple, which was a centre of social activity in many villages.

of wind and rain and darkness. There were not many there and the whole affair was terribly flat and dull. It was three when we got home and after nine when we woke. They drove me to the school. It was a wet, unpleasant day but the kiddies all came and in the afternoon my dreaded first school exam came off. Twenty-three visitors came and I was delighted. The children acquitted themselves very well in both lessons and programme. Then, of course, came the usual "speechifying" which was very gratifying as all present concurred in expressing thorough satisfaction. Mr. Millar moved a vote of thank to the teacher "for her trouble" and I had my first experience in receiving a vote of thanks and making a little speech in reply. Then we sang "God Save the Queen" and dispersed. I came home very happy and most fearfully tired.

Sunday, Dec. 30, 1894

Our wonderful concert is over at last and that is much to be thankful for. It didn't look much like it all day yesterday for it blew and poured and froze but it cleared up at dark and there was an excellent audience and everything went off finely. Our programme was a big success. Then came the sale of baskets. Mine went the highest—Lou bought it. I stayed at Mr. Millar's all night and John drove me home this morning. The world was fairly lovely with a white frost.

1895

Wednesday, Jan. 2, 1895
Bideford, P.E.I.

I had a taste of some of the pleasures of my profession this morning. The drifts were terrible. The road to the school was full to the fence-tops. Mr. E. drove us up and we got upset and I froze my fingers.

Ephraim Phillips called this evening to get the loan of my Greek text-books. He is attending P.W.C. and is home for the holidays. We had a chat about the dear old college and professors. It did me a world of good—pulled me out of my rut and made me feel keenly alive once more.

Sunday, Jan. 6, 1895

I felt lazy today so when the rest were all off to Sunday School I settled down by the fire with Tennyson and some doughnuts and was all ready for a cosy quiet time when I heard a knock at the door. I knew it was Lou and would just as soon it hadn't been; but we had a nice jolly chat—although it wasn't as good as Tennyson and doughnuts!

Monday, Jan. 7, 1895
Bideford

Maud Hayes[1] began to go to school today. She intends to study for P.W.C. and is pretty well advanced. I shall have to hear her lessons after school.

Maud Hayes

I heard today that poor Uncle John Montgomery is very ill and the doctor thinks it is a tumour on the brain. I feel terribly sorry. Dear old Uncle John—he was so kind and jolly and good.

The week-of-prayer meetings began tonight; it was rainy and disagreeable but I had to go and play. I am organist most of the time here now and I hate it, for there is no regular choir and all is at sixes and sevens in that respect.

---

1. Born 1878, Maud Hayes eventually attended Prince of Wales College and MacDonald Institute, Guelph. She became vice-principal of Summerside High School and principal of Montague High School before returning to Bideford in 1896 and teaching there sporadically until 1908.

Wednesday, Jan. 9, 1895

Tonight was lovely—moonlit and sparkling. Lou had a team and after prayer meeting we went for a spin along Ellerslie way. It was a glorious drive and served to clear away the effects of playing the organ tonight—a performance that is swiftly and surely bringing down my gray hairs[1] with sorrow to the grave.

Saturday, Jan. 12, 1895

I spent this afternoon and evening at Maud Hayes'! Got nearly drowned walking through, too, for it is a big thaw. But I like to go there and I enjoyed myself, even if I did have to promenade around in a pair of Maud's stockings while my own were drying. Maud is by no means built on the fairy plan and I could almost have drawn them clean up to my ears.

Monday, Jan. 14, 1895
Bideford, P.E.I.

Today in school—I had a horrible time getting there through the slush, by the way—I happened to pick up my old "Hamblin Smith"[2] and opened it at a fly-leaf. And there was a lot of nonsense. Selena had scribbled on it one day in school when *I* was a pupil. As I read it over, the memories of that pleasant year when Selena taught in C. came back with a rush. It *was* such a jolly year.

Daisy, Edith and I were invited down to Captain Richard's tonight and had a very nice evening.

Thursday, Jan. 17, 1895

Lou came here after prayer meeting—for the meetings are still going merrily on—and brought me a novel to read. He brings me a new one every time he comes, which is a blessing, as of course novels are not among the plentiful furnishings of a Methodist parsonage. To be sure, the poor chappie is not the best judge in the world of an interesting story—sometimes he hits it, sometimes he doesn't; but anything does to fill up a tired or idle hour. I have

---

1. Jacob's words in Genesis 42:38.

2. Hamblin Smith (1829–1901), author of over sixty textbooks, including *Elements of Geometry* and *Elementary Algebra*, many of them adapted to Canadian schools in the 1880s. New editions of Hamblin Smith are still used in the US and UK, as well as Canada.

a very pernicious habit of going to my room after Lou departs and reading for all hours. I am so crazy about reading that I *can't* let a book drop until I see its end, even if it is as dull as a cookery recipe. I am always making good resolutions anent this—and breaking the same just as soon as I get a novel in my clutches.

Thursday, Jan. 24, 1895

Today was *perfect*! As I plodded home from school this evening I refreshed my wearied senses drinking in the chaste beauty of the landscape. It was very calm and still and the declining sun cast chill pure tones of pink and heliotrope over the snow. There seemed to be an abundance—not of *color* but of the *spirit* of color. There was really nothing but pure white but you had the *impression* of fairy-like blendings of rose and violet, blue and opal and heliotrope.

Sunday, Jan. 27, 1895

I had a delicious time this afternoon reading. Reading is a luxury I don't have a great deal of time for now so that when I do get a quiet uninterrupted hour to sit down to a book I duly appreciate it. The first half hour I gave to Longfellow's poems—poems which never lose their witchery for me. There are undoubtedly many greater poets than Longfellow—many stronger, grander, deeper; but he is full of sweetness and tenderness and grace.

Then I read Hawthorne's wonderful "Scarlet Letter"[1] over again. It is a marvellously powerful book, both in style and analysis. What a power of character-painting—and *such* character—such deep, stormy, passion-wrung character. The hero is a *man*, the heroine a *woman*, and the true portrayal of such must ever appeal forcibly to the great heart of humanity, throbbing through all its varied phases of passion and pain.

Tuesday, Jan. 29, 1895

Will Montgomery came Saturday afternoon to take me down to Malpeque to see Uncle John Montgomery who is very near his last. We crossed the bay that evening in a big snowstorm and found a houseful there. It was

---

1. Nathaniel Hawthorne's novel (1850), set in a Puritan New England village, presents the tragic consequences of a sexual relationship outside of marriage.

a sadly changed house. The life and soul of it was gone. I went up to see poor Uncle John. Could that haggard wasted creature be the big, hearty uncle of yore, with the ringing voice and the laugh that shook the house? The mental change was a great and pitiful as the physical change—the blurred eye, the indistinct speech, the clouded intellect.

Uncle John Montgomery's house from the bay

We came back to Port Hill last evening and Will brought me home this morning. We nearly froze in school today as the supply of wood ran out so at two I dismissed school and came home, vowing deadly vengeance on the trustees.

Wednesday, Feb. 6, 1895

Such a storm and snow blockade! Yesterday morning we got up to find Chaos apparently lord of the elements. Such a white whirl! Lula and I did make a crazy attempt to get to the school but a half smothering in the first field soon sent us back sadder and wiser. How I detest these terrible storms! I always feel as if I were smothered in them and could never get out into air and life again.

This morning the storm was over. When the sun rose from the purple hills beyond the bay and his golden fingers stretched over white, icy plains and snowy hills the world looked beautiful. But the drifts prevented anyone from stirring out.

Monday, Feb. 11, 1895
Bideford, P.E.I.

What can have happened to poor February to sour its temper so terribly? When in school Friday afternoon another big storm came up and when a team came for the Ellerslie pupils I dismissed school, as Lula and I were the only ones from Bideford, and went down with Maud Hayes to spend the night. Saturday was fine but the navigation was not open so we had to stay, and as Sunday was again stormy I did not get back to the parsonage till today.

Wednesday, Feb. 13, 1895

Tonight Lou came out to drive me to prayer meeting. We started but couldn't get near the church on the cutter as the road wasn't broken. I was not going to wade in through snow up to my knees, so we just went to Tyne Valley for a drive. I expect Mr. Estey would think I was lost to grace for deserting the prayer meeting in that fashion; but he is not very obliging to me and I am somewhat out of patience with him.

Monday, Feb. 18, 1895

On Friday Edith E. sent down word for me to go up and when school was out I waded up over the banks. I had a lovely time there as usual. Saturday evening Lou came out and took me through to his place where I stayed till Sunday night. The drives over and back were very pleasant but I can't say I enjoyed myself very much while there. Sadie is very insipid—one of those jelly-fish sort of girls—and Mrs. D. worries you to death with fussy kindness—or what she means for kindness.

Sunday evening, as we drove out, was perfection—clear and sparkling, with lemon lights in the west and one great lucent evening star gleaming like a liquid jewel on the hectic cheek of dying day. It grew darker as we drove along over the white fields—the velvet sky was powdered with stars, and the spruces took on their mystic gloom!

Poor Uncle John M. is dead. They telephoned it over to me from Port Hill. It gave me such a shock although I had been expecting to hear it.

Monday, Feb. 25, 1895

I had promised Nettie Millar that I would go down Saturday, so I went, although I do not really enjoy going there. I always feel bored—and they do have such terrible meals! Lou came out and drove me down. We went to the post office first where I got my letters, among them one from Selena.

Sunday was an intolerably dull day and it was a relief when I was able to go. I suppose it is a little ungrateful of me when they are all so kind and seem to like me so well. But they are *rough* and their cooking is abominable. Such meals as I get there are a serious impediment to grace!

Tuesday, Feb. 26, 1895
Bideford, P.E.I.

I was really almost worn out when I got home from school today. This has been
a very hard month. The road is always so bad that when I get down here I feel
more dead than alive. Nevertheless, when I had got my tea and got thoroughly
warm—a condition I seldom am in while in school—I planned a good evening
at fancy-work and books. But presently a jingle of bells announced Lou. So
off I went for a drive and we had a charming one. Lou has the dandiest little
mare—I have named her "Miss Flo." She can go like a bird.

Sunday, Mar. 3, 1895
Bideford, P.E.I.

Today was beautiful. There was preaching at the Valley this evening and
Lou took me down. It was just sunset when we left. The west was a sea of
glory—fleecy crimson clouds, vast lakes of amber and pearl, bars of fire. The
air was clear and the roads like satin.

It was so nice to be in a Presbyterian service again. I like the Methodists
but to get the real "at home" feeling I have to get into a Presbyterian church.

Thursday, Mar. 7, 1895

Yesterday morning Edith sent me word that she was going in to Mrs. Dystant's
today to help Sadie make a dress and wanted me to go in in the evening and
the two of us would stay all night. But I had my own personal reasons for not
wishing to stay there all night, so I resolved not to go—especially as it was
prayer-meeting night and Mr. Estey wouldn't get over it for a week if I didn't
go to prayer meeting and play the organ. So when Lou came out to take me
in I told him I couldn't go and we started in all good faith for p.m. But on
the road Lou coaxed me to go in, saying he would bring me out that night.
On that condition I consented and we went. Had a fairly nice evening and I
went home with Edith and stayed all night.

Sunday, Mar. 10, 1895

Friday night after school I went up to Edith's and stayed all night. I always
enjoy myself there. I almost envy Edith E. her lovely home. It seems to me
she has everything heart can wish for.

And yet, after all, I would not change places with her. In fact, with all my little trials and tribulations—of which I have always had my share—I have never yet met with anyone with whom I *would* exchange places—that is, if a change of personality were included, too.

Thursday, Mar. 14, 1895
Bideford, P.E.I.

There was a social in aid of the Valley church at Mr. Millar's last night and Lou and I were invited. I bade adieu to my books and fancy-work somewhat regretfully—for I knew we'd have a dry old time—and went.

Arriving there, I made my way through rooms already lined with blank faces and escaped upstairs to the spare room, where half a dozen girls were prinking and, without waiting to remove my wraps, sat down to inspect some letters Lou had brought me out. One was quite a delightful surprise for it was from the Editor of the Toronto *Ladies Journal*, accepting a poem I had sent it, "On The Gulf Shore,"[1] and adding a few complimentary words. They don't pay for poetry, however, so that the "honor" is all the recompense.

After reading my other letters I took off my hat, fluffed out my bangs, and went downstairs. As music was being called for I filled the gap until I got tired, and then I settled myself between Maud Hayes and Lily Dalton. Everyone was evidently on his and her good behavior—at least, it seemed a penitentiary offence to speak and a capital crime to smile. As we knew we'd have no fun unless we made it ourselves Maud and I began making all the reckless speeches we could to each other and we laughed at our own wit until the old dames looked askance at us. For downright stupidity these church socials "take the cake." People look primmer and more hopelessly uninteresting there than at any other time, rooms are hot and stuffy, and everyone seems in everyone else's way. The main things to do seem to be,

1. Sit prim.

2. Look demure or disapproving according to your age.

3. Hang back and act cranky in any game other people try to get up.

4. Cram yourself with a lot of indigestible stuff, the effects of which will be ever present with you for a week.

I escaped the last number of this programme at least by becoming a waiter. Of course I tired myself out carrying cakes around with a fixed, sickly,

---

1. The Blue Scrapbook dated 1893–96 contains this poem by "Maud Eglinton," published in February 1895, and "When the Apple Blossoms Blow" by "Maud Cavendish," published in the *Ladies' Journal*, July 1895. This Toronto magazine bought ten more poems and two stories from LMM before 1900.

won't-you-have-some smile, but that was infinitely preferable to loading my protesting stomach with a lot of sweet stuff and going home with a violent headache and a malevolent temper.

After supper kissing games[1] were started and flourished where all others had failed. As I do not play them I carried Lou off promptly and we left. If I thought I would have the moral strength to keep it I'd make a vow never to go to a church social again!

Wednesday, Mar. 20, 1895

We have been having a perfectly dreadful time. All last Saturday and Sunday it snowed and blew and drifted. Mr. E. was away and Mrs. E. and I were penned up here in big white banks the whole time. Monday and Tuesday were rough and the walking to school as bad as it could be—no trace of a track and knee-deep in stiff drift all the way. We had no mail for a whole week and I never felt so desperate in my life. Lou got over tonight, however, and we went for a drive. The roads were bad, but we got along and it was a relief to get a glimpse of the outside world again.

Sunday, Mar. 24, 1895
Bideford, P.E.I.

Nettie Millar came up Friday and I went down with her and stayed all night. Rev. Mr. Kirby,[2] who exchanged pulpits with Mr. E. today arrived here yesterday afternoon. Lou and I had planned to go for a drive in the evening and it would have been a perfect night for the same; but Mrs. E. wanted me to stay home as she had a lot of work to do and couldn't talk to Mr. Kirby, so I agreed and when Lou's knock came I flew down to inform him. *He* didn't like it either, but went and put his horse in meekly enough and we had a stupid evening all round. Mr. Kirby seemed to be under the impression that he was that third party who is a crowd and that therefore it was his duty to obliterate himself as far as possible. So he buried himself behind a newspaper, while Lou and I talked disjointedly and wished ourselves out on the starlit roads behind "Miss Flo."

Today was lovely—oh, I am so glad that spring is really coming. The winter has gone quickly enough in one way but these last two months have been so stormy that they have been very hard on me physically.

---

1. Young people are paired by blind chance in games such as spin the bottle and post office.
2. Originally from NB, now the Methodist parson on the Bedeque circuit.

Thursday, Mar. 28, 1895
Bideford, P.E.I.

We have been having delicious spring weather. The roads are getting sunken and slushy, the brows of the slopes are peering out barely from their crown of snows, little pools of water are lapping the feet of cold white banks which are gradually assuming a pitifully violated appearance; the hot kisses of that old libertine, the sun, have desecrated their virgin purity.

All this is poetry—but it is really very prosy prose to slush around ankle deep whenever you set foot outside the door.

I spent this evening at Mr. England's. One reason why I like to go there is that you can make yourself so thoroughly at home. They don't persecute you to distraction trying to "entertain" you. You are allowed to enjoy yourself in your own way.

Monday, April 1, 1895
Bideford, P.E.I.

Time honoured date! I anticipated a wild time in school with the kiddies playing tricks on each other but they were very good on the whole.

Lou came out Saturday evening and took me in to spend Sunday with them. I had a nicer time than last. Sadie was away so I had to sleep alone and nearly froze to death. And yet when good Mrs. D. asked me in the morning if I had slept well I was hypocrite enough to murmur feebly, "Oh, y-e-es." But then she had fussed so much about that bed, putting hot irons in it and airing the blankets etc. If after all her trouble I had confessed that I was cold she'd never have got over the shock.

Saturday, April 6, 1895

This week has been a hard one, owing to the mud and slush. Thursday evening Mrs. E. and I drove over to Mr. MacKay's at East Bideford and met there—Inspector Campbell. As he would visit my school the next day I felt pretty nervous. I went early to school yesterday morning, had it swept and garnished, and drilled up the kiddies. In due time he came and things were not too bad. The children did well and the order was excellent. He professed himself satisfied and gave us a half-holiday.

Thursday, April 11, 1895

I really do not think I am killable by natural causes or I would never have survived this week. On Monday a big April freshet[1] set in—a serious thing in this part of the country where the land is so flat. Tuesday and Wednesday I was nearly drowned going to school and got there wet to the waist. I was completely exhausted when I got home and was so tired I couldn't sleep. It froze last night, however, so today was better, and as tomorrow is Good Friday my tribulations are over for this week.

Friday, April 12, 1895
Bideford

The Grand Division[2] met at Ellerslie today and I had promised to recite at the public meeting tonight, so Lou came out after me. The hall was crowded. I recited "Caleb's Daughter" and for an encore "The Schoolmaster's Guests."[3]

Edwin Simpson was there from Bedeque, where he is teaching, and we had a short chat.

Monday, April 15, 1895

Last night we had our Easter Missionary service in the church. I recited and read a selection. Lou came down with us, and as the walking was vile Mrs. Estey made him stay all night. Rev. E. was away or she would not have dared to extend the courtesy. When Mrs. Estey got up this morning she found every door piled high with logs of wood! I discovered today, that it was done by Fred Ellis, Jas. Miller and Cliff Williams, thinking, I suppose that when Lou went home he would have a picnic getting out. But as he did not go at all that little scheme fell flat and it was poor Mrs. Estey who had to open the doors when she got up this morning.

Saturday, April 20, 1895

This has been an uneventful week—one day just like another. Lou was out Thursday evening and again tonight and brought me my letters. One was

---

1. A flood resulting from a spring thaw.

2. Regional meeting of the Sons of Temperance.

3. In this recital piece by Will Carleton, published in *Bell's Standard Elocutionist*, the district fathers dress down the young teacher—one of them is spokesman, the others mutter, "Them 'ere is my sentiments tew!"

from the Rev. Mr. Liang of the Halifax Ladies' College,[1] to whom I had written concerning going there. He wrote that I was so far advanced that he thought I had better take a selected course at Dalhousie[2] if I did not care to enter as an under-graduate. "Care to enter." There is nothing on earth I would like so much but there is no use in thinking of it, for I could not afford to complete the B.A. course. I shall likely take the selected course if I decide to go at all. I am anxious to spend a year at a real college as I think it would help me along in my ambition to be a writer.

I shall be heartily glad when vacation comes for I need it. I get wet every day and naturally keep up the worst sort of a cold. I do not feel well at all.

Sunday, April 28, 1895
Bideford, P.E.I.

Spring is really here. This morning Cliff Williams sent me over a bouquet of the first May flowers—delicate pilgrims from the shores of Summerland. How I kissed their pink and white buds and how their subtle aerial perfume recalled old days of Cavendish springs. Friday night I went up to Edith's and stayed there till tonight. Saturday evening Fred England, Charlie Hayes, and Lou came out and we had such fun.

Tuesday, April 30, 1895

Just as I had called school in after dinner today and was hearing Amos MacKay "count up to fifty" Frank Grant came in from the P.O. and handed me a letter. It was from Laura, so I had to open it at once and the first thing I saw was, "My own darling:—*I'm engaged*!!!"

It quite took my breath away. She wrote at one o'clock at night, just after "he" had gone, and I was the first person to be told. I have been expecting it for some time. Agnew has loved her long and faithfully and he is a fine, good fellow. Dear Laura, how glad I am that she is so happy. I hope she will ever be so through all the future years.

---

1. A residential school in Halifax, NS, founded in 1887, on Pleasant Street (now Barrington) at Harvey. In 1894–95 there were ninety-two students, most of them in the College's Conservatory of Music. Halifax is the capital of NS, and the cultural and financial centre of the Canadian Maritime Provinces; in 1895 it had a population of around forty thousand. Halifax appears as "Kingsport" in Montgomery's *Anne of the Island* (1915).

2. A university in Halifax, founded in 1818. In 1895 it granted degrees in Arts, Science, Engineering, Law, and Medicine, and enrolment was just over three hundred. The University was housed in the Forrest Building, on College Street. Women had been admitted to Dalhousie since 1881.

Monday, May 6, 1895
Bideford, P.E.I.

Earth has not forgotten how to be lovely nor spring how to charm. It was delicious today. After tea Mrs. Estey and I walked over to the station and called at the P.O. on our way back. I am going to board there after vacation. Mr. and Mrs. Estey leave for another circuit early in June, so it is necessary for me to look for a new abiding place.

Lou came along as we left the P.O. and we all sauntered home in the cool, lovely twilight. Getting here, Lou and I did not go in but went around to the corner of the veranda where we perched ourselves on the railing and chatted for an hour. It was a simply delicious night. The moonlight fell in a misty golden shower over trees and grass, and the bay before us shimmered in glory. The wind was as soft as a wind of June and the frogs were singing. All my cares and worries melted away in sheer happiness and joy of living. I felt as light-hearted and care-free as a child.

Tuesday Morning, May 10, 1895
Bideford

This has been a very busy week as I have been preparing to go home for vacation. Last night I packed up. Then Mrs. E. and I had our constitutional to the P.O.

This morning is lovely—so sunny and warm. The water in the bay is sparkling like a sea of diamonds, the grass is growing green and the willows are out in all their spring bravery.

Monday, May 13, 1895
Cavendish, P.E.I.

Back in my old niche again! It fits me as snugly as if I had never slipped out of it. Will it ever grow too small, I wonder.

Saturday morning Mrs. E. drove me to the station and at 1.30 I reached Kensington where grandpa met me.

Cavendish is as pretty as ever with the faint mist of green over all its groves and gardens. I took a walk

A nook in the school woods

through the school woods this evening. They are but little changed from what they were in the balmy spring days when "the old crowd" haunted their green shades and ferny dells. What fairy realms of beauty and romance those old woods were to my childish imagination! Roaming through them it is hard to imagine that I am a child no longer. I can almost cheat myself into believing that the past five years have been a dream from which I have awakened to find myself still "sweet fifteen" with long braided tresses hanging over my shoulders and strange fancies of coming womanhood hovering around my path.

Thursday, May 16, 1895
Cavendish

Went to prayer meeting tonight. When I got home Ches was here for the mail and we had a long jolly talk over old schooldays—and especially the day we all cleaned the school and Jack L. undertook to put the fire out by pouring a bucketful of cold water upon it. I shall never forget that scene.

Sunday, May 19, 1895

Mollie came over yesterday afternoon and as it rained at night she stayed here until morning. Mary Campbell and Joe MacPherson came down today and we had a gay time. Mary is as jolly as ever. We chattered about mutual friends and old rackets until our tongues were tired and then we went to the shore. It was grandly beautiful. The surf rolled in foamy wreaths on the rocks; the sandshore stretched away into silvery mists, while through the gaps in the dunes smiled glimpses of ideal beauty—velvet-green fields and groves, wooded hills and blue ponds.

We went to church this morning and after service Mary and Joe left for home.

Thursday, May 23, 1895
Cavendish

This week has been very quiet and pleasant. This evening Lu and I went to prayer meeting and as we were too early we went for a walk in along the road. It was lovely. The trees and fields are a delicate fairy green, purple violets are peeping out of the grass under the spruces, and at evening the setting sun tints pond and bay and ocean until they are "a sea of glass mingled with fire."

Pensie was up at prayer meeting and asked us down tomorrow.

Tuesday, May 28, 1895
Cavendish, P.E.I.

I am just back from a visit to town and feel pretty tired after all my junketing about. I went up to the station on Saturday with the mailman and had a very wearisome drive. I got to town about six and went at once to Aunt Mary's. After tea Mary Campbell appeared, much to my surprise and delight, for she had written me

Market Square, Charlottetown

that she was much afraid that she would not be able to get in. We went to Norman's boarding house, got him to escort us around town and had a jolly walk. Sunday morning we went to Zion. I certainly do love that church. We had hoped to hear Mr. Sutherland preach but he had been suddenly taken ill and his place was supplied by an imposing youth from Kensington Hall. He was so short that we could barely see his thin pompadour above the pulpit and his grammar was barbarous. His text, as he announced it, was "the 16th chapter of the 11th Psalm"—Echo answers "Where"!—and his treatment of this problematical text was quite in keeping with its undiscoverable nature.

After dinner Jack S. came down to see me. In the evening Norman and I went to church together and afterwards had a nice walk up Prince St. Monday morning Mary and I spent shopping and at noon went down to the college. We found the dear old doctor superintending an Academic exam in his room and he was delighted to see us. We sat and chatted with him for nearly an hour. I told him I was going to take a selected course at Dalhousie next year and then he told me I had "great literary talent" and ought to cultivate it, and went on to give me some good advice how to do it and said he had no doubt of my ultimate success. Words like those from such a man as Dr. Anderson are indeed encouraging.

Then we went to see Mr. Caven—who is as rubicund and jolly as ever—Mr. Robertson and Mr. Shaw, and then we left. Mary had to go home on the afternoon train.

After tea Selena Robinson called and we had a jolly chat. Jack and Will S. and Jack Gordon came down and spent the evening and we had a most hilarious time.

This morning I had to rise with the lark to catch the early train. The ride out to Hunter River was charming. The country is a veritable "Garden of Eden" now, with all the blossoms out. This evening Lu and I went for a walk up Lover's Lane, which is bewilderingly sweet now with wild cherry bloom.

Thursday, May 30, 1895

Last evening Lu and I went up to Darnley Clark's. We didn't have much fun as Ches was away but he came back in time to walk home with us. It was a glorious moonlight night and we had a very jolly walk. Ches has taken a position in the Stanley cheese factory.

Murray arrived today—to no delight of mine! I went to prayer-meeting this evening and had a drive with Alec afterwards.

Lover's Lane

Saturday, June 1, 1895
Ellerslie, P.E.I.

Lu drove me up to Kensington this morning. The train left at 10.30. Gertie Moore and several other teachers I knew were on board and Gertie almost talked me to death. As we had a three hour's wait in S'Side I was very tired when I got to Ellerslie. Maud Hayes met me and I came out here to my new boarding house. It seems strange not to be going out to the Parsonage.

Sunday, June 2, 1895

Lou came out this afternoon and took me for a drive. We had a fairly pleasant one although it was so cold we almost froze. In the evening we walked out to church and I had to take my old position on the organ stool. It is real nice to be back in Bideford again.

Wednesday, June 5, 1895

Monday I began work again, with a turnout of 33 pupils, half of whom were in the primer class, so the amount of work was considerable. After school I went down to the Parsonage for tea. It seemed like home again. After tea Mrs. E. and I went to the Valley and had a pleasant drive. Tuesday evening I spent at the Millars!

Thursday, June 6, 1895
Ellerslie

I have *the* experience of my life to chronicle—at least, I am very sure that one such experience is enough for a lifetime. Every tale must have a beginning, no matter how it is spelled, and I'll have to go back to my first arrival here to come to the root of mine. Soon after I came to Bideford I noticed on a hill not far from the P.O. a large, old-fashioned house of a very "shabby genteel" appearance, situated in once beautiful but now sadly neglected and overrun grounds. On inquiry I found out that said house had once belonged to a well-to-do family; but reverses came to them and after several changes, all tending downward, the property had passed into the hands of the present possessors, who, I was told, were a by-word for oddity and dirt. When Amos MacKay came to school I found that he lived at this place, old Mr. and Mrs. MacKay having adopted him. Well, last Tuesday morning Amos appeared with a letter addressed to me. I took it with inward misgiving, expecting to get a going-over for some sin of commission or omission in regard to Amos; but this is what I read.

> Miss Montgomery:—
> As you have never been to see us since you came here I wish you to come and visit us and let us know by the bearer of this note when you will come.
> Yours truly,
> Archibald MacKay.

Well, of course I had to go, so I sent word that I would go Thursday evening. To make things pleasanter Maud Hayes and all the rest immediately began to prophesy what I would get to eat etc. etc., and really among them all they succeeded in nearly driving me wild.

After I came home from school this evening I dressed and went over, wishing myself a thousand miles away. When I knocked at the front door there was a great hurrying and scurrying and whispering! The door was opened and I stepped into a large dim, *dusty* hall where I was met *en masse* by the whole family, down to Amos, who came sliding along the wall, looking like a small goblin in the extraordinary garments he wears. The first to greet me was the mistress of the mansion herself—a withered old dame with her hair twisted around her ears in the fashion of 50 years ago. I was really frightened that she was going to kiss me but I escaped this by hastily dropping her hand and extending mine to her lord and master, who was literally a hideous old creature, all whiskers and rags. Bringing up the rear were son and daughter who did not greet me at all effusively—probably for the excellent reason that they are deaf mutes!

I was pushed, pulled and cornered into the dining room where Mrs. MacKay took my hat and left me to talk to old Archie while she got the tea. He kept up a steady stream of questions in a mumbling indistinct voice and while I floundered through my answers I kept my eyes on the table, mindful of Maud's dismal prophecies, and saw to my dismay that "the half was never told."

Words fail to describe my feelings as I sat down to that meal! *Did* they really expect me to eat such stuff? I wished the floor would open and swallow me up but as it didn't, I grimly threw myself into the fray, determined to eat something or perish in the attempt—and I rather believed I would do the latter.

The old lady poured out tea in cups which looked as if they had never been washed since the day they were bought. Inside and out they were liberally daubed with ancient tea-stains. I tried vainly to find a clean spot to drink from and, failing, shut my eyes and took a wild gulp, the taste nearly finishing what the sight had begun, for it was an atrocious brew with huge lumps of *sour* cream floating sound like ice-bergs in a muddy sea. As soon as I had partially recovered from this dose I opened my eyes and examined the contents of my plate to see what I could dare eat. It was nearly filled with a huge lump of—well, I suppose it was intended for pie. Peering out timidly was a leathery edge of thick brown crust. Inside this was a slimy mass of pale green stuff—presumably stewed rhubarb, although Maud insists that it was burdock!!—and a huge spoonful of coarse brown sugar, mingled with *sour, lumpy* cream was spread over this. This inviting mixture was furthermore crowned by a huge splurge of "cranberry sarce."

Well, *that* was hopeless! I did take one spoonful but had death been the penalty I could not have swallowed another. So I took a huge slice of bread fully an inch thick, plastered on some butter—*such* butter! I found three hairs in it:—and washed down each mouthful by a gulp of tea. I actually ate a whole slice and then, choked down a "patty pan." Honestly, I was afraid I would vomit at every bite. I shall *never* forget that awful meal. I would not have minded the food being poor and badly cooked if it had only been *clean*!

When all was over we went into the parlor where I had to sit for the rest of the evening and talk to my host and hostess. The floor was covered with hideous red mats and the chairs with equally hideous crocheted tidies—all of which, the old gentleman proudly informed me were "Maggie's work." Dirty lace curtains hung in the windows and the walls were adorned with a marvellous assortment of newspaper prints, cards, almanacs, prize pig cuts, etc.

Would that I could depict our conversation! But one example must suffice.

"D'ye understand *Lating* and all that?" demanded the old gentleman.

"Oh, yes," I responded, glibly and rashly.

"What's that?" he asked darting a very dirty finger at the newspaper I held. "What's that in *Lating*?"

"This?" I gasped feebly, wondering if he expected me to translate the whole sheet off into "Lating" *extempore*.

"Yes. What's 'newspaper' in Lating?"

Now, considering that newspapers are rather more modern than the empire of the Cesaers I might be pardoned for not knowing but old Archie could not be made to understand this and my reputation for classical learning was at stake. But I solemnly aver that every word of Latin I ever knew fled from my memory except "papyrus" and I blurted it out as a drowning man might clutch at the proverbial straw.

But it answered the purpose for poor old Archie thought it was simply wonderful and remarked "De-e-arr, de-e-arr," in a tone of profound marvel at my erudition!

But everything comes to an end sometime, if you only live to see it, and at last I got away and crawled home. Verily, we schoolmarms have troubles of our own. And I have acutely realized the truth of Pope's line,

"A little learning is a dangerous thing."

Thursday, June 13, 1895

This week seems to have flown on wings of wind. Sunday afternoon Lou and I drove to Pres. service in the Valley and in the evening we walked out to Bideford church to hear his brother John preach. Then we spent an hour or so at the parsonage. Monday, Tuesday and Wednesday I stayed with Mrs. Estey, as Mr. E. was away and we had a jolly time. Today

Bideford Meth. Church

was very hot and 37 little squirmers in school didn't make it any cooler. Fred England and Lou were in tonight and we had lots of fun.

Monday, June 17, 1895

Went to preaching yesterday morning—and that is the last sermon I shall hear in Bideford church for Mr. Estey goes to conference tomorrow. It gave me a start to hear the announcement for it made me realize how brief my time here is getting. I have been too busy to think much about it but it came home to me very suddenly just then and with a sharp pang, too. I shall be so sorry to leave. I have had such a nice time here and have so many friends.

This evening Lou and I, George Walsh and Bertie Williams, Charlie and Maud Hayes all drove up to Lot 11 to preaching and had a merry drive. They are an odd-looking crowd up there. The most extraordinary people put on the most extraordinary clothes in the most extraordinary way, and the result is super-extraordinary.

I had 40 kiddies in school today—I have over 60 on the roll now—a pretty heavy school.

Mr. and Mrs. Estey went away today. How sorry I felt to bid Mrs. Estey good-bye! She has been so kind to me.

I have had a story[1] accepted by the Toronto *Ladies Journal*. No pay yet—but that may come some day.

Wednesday, June 19, 1895

Last night they had their annual school meeting. All expressed regret at my resignation and said if I stayed they would vote me a higher supplement.

Clara Grant brought me the dearest bunch of "pink-pinks" to school today and their delicate bells recalled visions of Lover's Lane with its cool shadows, green arches, and whiffs of wood scents.

Lou, John D., and Fred England spent the evening here and we had such fun.

Lover's Lane

---

1. "A Baking of Gingersnaps" by "Maud Cavendish," published July 1895.

Saturday, June 22, 1895
Bideford, P.E.I

I have been busy making P.P.C. calls.[1] Was at Mrs. McKenzie's today. She said she was so sorry I was leaving as Maudie[2] was getting on so well. She said everyone spoke well of me and there wasn't a person who had a word to say against me. It is so nice and I am very glad, for I have worked hard and tried to do my best for my pupils.

Monday, June 24, 1895

So it has come—my last Monday in Bideford school. Shall I ever forget the *first* Monday? One chapter of my life is nearly closed. Time's unseen fingers are already turning the last page. And it has been a varied chapter of pleasure and toil, hardships and joys. I shall be sorry to part with the children. Most of them have crept into my heart.

John Millar has been my favorite pupil—a fine manly little fellow he is. Arthur Millar is also nice but dreadfully mischievous and Gordon was an urchin I never liked and who has given me a good deal of trouble. Alice Millar is only a "kid," thin, sunburned, a thorough tomboy, always running with the boys, not particularly lovable at all. Little freckled Maud McKenzie with her elfin head of short silky red curls and "cute" face is a nice little thing. Fred and Lottie Ellis were two pupils I never liked although they gave me no trouble. I never felt at ease with them. Emma Ellis was the worst pupil I had and gave me more trouble than all the others put together. Claud and Rebie Williams, Reagh Gorrill and Maud Estey were all dear pupils. Then there are the "yard" children, poor and ill-bred for the most part; yet some have a promise— never, alas, likely to be developed—of better things. The two little McArthur boys, Arthur and Cornelius, are two perfect imps and shame dulness personi- fied. They simply could *not* learn. Belle and Garfield MacArthur were slightly brighter, however. Belle and Lizzie McFadyen were very pretty girls and nice pupils. Maud and Annie MacDougall were quiet and commonplace. Then, coming over to Ellerslie, Maud, Bertie, Clifford, Irene and Ella Hayes were as nice pupils as a teacher could wish. Willie Cannon and Aldred England were two nice smart lads, while Frank Grant was a clever, conceited, restless, bully- ing boy—an extremely *wearing* pupil. A whole drove of Murphys, Sudsburys and Howells may be catalogued *en masse* as "fair to poor," and there are a few

---

1. Some schools on PEI had started the first pupil–parent conferences in the early 1890s.
2. This Bideford student later became LMM's music pupil in Halifax.

others who are a compound of faults and virtues—as indeed, when it comes to the last analysis, most of us are.

Thursday, June 27, 1895
Bideford, P.E.I.

Yesterday the Sewing Circle bazaar came off. I took a half holiday and Maud and I presided in the lemonade and candy booth. It was a very flat affair and not a great many people came. Still, I had a rather good time. In the evening we had a little dance at Mr. McDougalls.

Today was a busy one for I had to give all the kiddies a final drilling on my exam programme. Now I am sitting by my window writing and must soon go and dress—for tonight will be the last meeting of "the Club," by which name we designate the informal little gatherings we frequently hold in Mr. Hayes' cosy little square hall, the "members" dropping in on evenings they feel like it—Charley, Maud, Bertie, Fred England, George Walsh, Lou and John Dystant and myself. We have had lots of fun and I hate to think that this will be the last.

Later on

"The Club" had a most successful meeting. Fred England was initiated into the "second degree"—i.e. the lunch after the newer members leave.

Friday, June 28, 1895
Bideford, P.E.I.

"The sceptre is departed from Judah"[1]—I am no longer teacher of Bideford school. But I feel so badly that I half wish I had never resigned. This morning I went early to school. Every child brought a bouquet for decoration and the boys got huge armsful of ferns with which we adorned every adornable place, and the old school blossomed out into unusual splendor. Seventeen visitors came and the exam went off splendidly. At its close my pupils presented me with an address and a very pretty little jewel box of celluloid mounted in silver. The girls were all crying and so was I, and so were most of the women present. Then we sang "God Save The Queen" and I went down to Mr. Williams to tea. On my way home I called into the deserted

---

1. Genesis 49:10: "The sceptre shall not depart from Judah."

school to say good-bye to it alone. As I stood there I thought of the first day I had crossed its threshold—a trembling confused young thing feeling scarcely less childish than the children I was to govern. This has been a very happy year for me and I shall never think of this old school without a very kindly feeling.

Tuesday, July 2, 1895
Cavendish, P.E.I.

It is all over—and I am glad for I have been having a rather miserable time of it these last few days.

Saturday I spent making farewell calls and went to Mr. Dystant's for the night. After dinner on Sunday Lou and I went for a drive up the Fourteen Road, which is a very pretty one, and then we went to Mr. Millar's for tea.

After tea I bade them good-bye and we came up to class-meeting.[1] At its close came a shower of good-byes, some of them very hard to say, and then we went down to Mr. England's for a brief call.

Mr. Hayes' house

When we got back to Mr. Hayes' everyone was in bed, so we sat down in the front hall. I felt decidedly uncomfortable and didn't know just what to expect. I have driven about with Lou for a year, but I certainly, most certainly never gave him any encouragement whatsoever to think that I cared anything for him except as a friend. On the contrary I have put myself to considerable pains, in all the indirect ways permissible, to *discourage* him. Still, I could not tell how he might have deceived himself and he has been terribly blue and depressed for these past few days.

I was sitting on the lounge when he came over to me and one look in his face was enough!

We had a very dreadful talk about which I do not care to go into details. Lou said he loved me but admitted that I had never encouraged him and that he never supposed I cared for him, although he could not help coming to see me. I felt very much cut up. I never thought Lou would care half so much but he seemed simply distracted. I told him he would forget me in time and find

---

1. Methodist Bible classes for young adults.

somebody else better suited to him—but in common with all lovelorn suitors he couldn't seem to take that view of it at all. He did finally go. I felt very sorry for him—but really I think he might have displayed a little more dignity. His abandon of feeling was rather disgusting, to speak the plain truth.

I got up at five the next morning to finish packing. I felt tired out, and my head ached. Maud Hayes was going into S'Side[1] to take her entrance exam and we left Ellerslie at 8.15. Lou was also going down on business and came with us. I watched the old school until it disappeared and then turned around with a sigh. Lou was sitting opposite to me, looking haggard and dreadful. *I* wasn't at all hilarious, so that Maud was the only cheerful one of the trio.

Everything was deserted at Kensington, as it was Dominion Day. As grandpa met me in a truck wagon I had a most wearisome, hot and dusty drive home, and arrived here almost worn out. I have been most wretchedly lonesome ever since—as homesick for Bideford as I was homesick for Cavendish my first week there.

Saturday, July 13, 1895
Cavendish, P.E.I.

The days are crawling by slowly—each one seems as long as three ordinary days. Thursday I went to the Stanley Church tea. I don't know what possessed me to go for such affairs always bore me to tears and I never enjoy myself at them. Alec was there and took me driving in the evening. This passed the time but wasn't particularly interesting.

Sunday, July 21, 1895

I am just beginning to get over my lonesomeness—I have been really half frantic. This afternoon Pensie, Alec, and I went to church at New Glasgow. We had no end of fun laughing—of course, after we came out—at poor Mrs. Albert Laird who came sailing down the aisle and plumped herself down in front of us with a sewing needle and a yard of white thread hanging from the crown of her bonnet down over her back. Every time she twitched her head—and she is noted for her twitches—the needle would fly. It did look perfectly ridiculous and the comments of a pewful of boys behind us on "the latest style in millinery" were hard to bear.

---

1. Entrance exams for PWC were held in several regional centres such as Summerside. LMM consistently uses capitals within the abbreviations, as in "S'Side," and "Ch'Town."

We went to Mamie Moffats for tea and in the evening went over to the Baptist church at New Glasgow. It was a delicious evening for driving and I enjoyed that part of it quite well.

Thursday, Aug. 1, 1895
Cavendish

I spent this afternoon at Mollie's and had a very pleasant time. It is the most conservative old place— nothing ever seems to change. It is really restful to go somewhere where time seems to stand still. The old garden, sloping down to the pond, where huge wil- lows droop over the still water, is a charming spot. Gnarled apple trees bend over plots of old-fash-

The old garden at Mollie's

ioned flowers—thickets of sweet clover, white and fragrant, beds of mint and southern wood, pansies, honeysuckles and blush roses. And there is an old mossy path bordered with clam shells running up to the ivy-grown front door steps.

Sunday Night, Aug. 11, 1895

I spent yesterday afternoon with Pensie and had a nice time. In the evening Alec took me for a drive and we started off in the hazy purple gloaming with a full moon of reddish gold creeping up her cloudy stairway to her star-sen- tinelled throne. By the way, just suppose I had made the foregoing remark to Alec! What *would* he have made of it. He might have understood the word "moon" but he would have thought the rest of it was a Latin outburst. We drove all the way to New Glasgow.

This evening Pensie and Will Bulman and Alec and I started for the English church[1] at South Rustico, but as it began to rain we went to the Baptist church instead. After service we went for a drive around Rustico and got caught in another heavy shower.

---

1. In Canada, usually called Anglican Church or Church of England; LMM uses the American form, Episcopalian.

Monday, Aug. 12, 1895

Selena has been here and we have had so much talking to do that there has been no time for anything else. We are up in my room now. Selena is sitting

My room

The orchard

by the window, reading a novel, and I am scribbling on my trunk. Selena arrived Friday night and we went in to the Baptist church where a crowd of Ch'town campers, who are rusticating at the shore, gave a concert. We had a fine time, especially "between the acts." When we got home Selena and I went to bed and talked until the clock struck three.

On Saturday afternoon we coaxed a horse from grandpa—the hardest thing to do in the world—and drove up to Stanley to see the cheese factory. Ches works in it and he showed us all over it, and we had lots of fun.

This evening about dark Selena and I were out in the orchard when Alec and Will Stewart drove up and asked us to go for a drive. We had a merry time, four in one buggy, and as I had to drive that wild horse perched up on Alec's knee my position was a rather precarious one.

Friday, Aug. 16, 1895
Cavendish

Selena and I have been having a pleasant time. On Wednesday Uncle Leander came, bringing with him his new bride—his *third*, no less. She is not ill-looking, but has a rather *common* face. Her best point is her fine complexion and bright golden hair. She seems kind and pleasant but not at all intellectual—quite the reverse in fact. She appears to be quite uneducated and makes bad breaks in ordinary grammar—on the whole rather an odd bride for clever, fastidious Uncle Leander. But then I suppose a double widower with a large family of none-too-"easy" boys cannot pick and choose—if marry he must!

Selena goes tomorrow and I shall miss her horribly.

Saturday, Aug. 17, 1895
Cavendish

Aunt Mary[1]

This is a lonely house tonight. There was a wholesale exodus this morning. All Uncle L.'s went and Pen and I drove Selena to New Glasgow. I miss her so much—our jolly rackets, our confidential talks, our little plots and designs. I think I'll go to bed and have a good cry.

Sunday, Aug. 25, 1895

I have had a very busy week. Last Monday Vinnie MacLure came to do my sewing for me and we have been at it steadily ever since. Vinnie is a very jolly girl and we have any amount of fun, skylarking round a bit in the evening when our work is over.

Thursday, Sept. 5, 1895

Another fortnight has gone by very rapidly. I have had considerable mild, diluted fun, warranted not to hurt in any dose. Saturday evening Mollie came over at dusk and I went a piece with her. On the way back I fell in with Alec and Pensie jaunting airily around in a road cart and I got in with them. Whether or not the road cart jolted all our fun to the surface I don't know but we were all very witty and laughed wildly.

On Sunday, service was in the forenoon and I went from church with Pen. After dinner she and Alec and I went to English church in South Rustico.

---

1. Uncle Leander's new wife. His first wife, Jane Perkins, was the mother of all his children. His second wife was Annie Putnam.

I had a letter from Perle Taylor[1] of Ch'town this week. She was at Halifax[2] Ladies' college last year and wants me to room with her next year. I presume I shall although I don't know her at all. But then I know nobody else there and one stranger is as good as another. Perle is the daughter of Dr. Taylor of Charlottetown.

Perle Taylor

Sunday, September 15, 1895
Cavendish, P.E.I.

This is my last night at home for another while—I start for Halifax tomorrow and have been very busy all the week getting ready. I feel tired and worried and discouraged—not a bit hopeful or expectant. Nobody seems really to sympathize with my going to Halifax. Grandmother is willing for me to go because I wish it so much but not because she has any understanding of my reasons for wishing to go. She is going to help me a little financially too as the hundred dollars I saved while teaching out of a salary of $180 is not quite enough for board at H.L.C. and tuition at Dalhousie. Grandfather has shown no interest of any kind in my going. Cavendish people generally show a somewhat contemptuous disapproval. Not a great many of them voice it but Mrs. Albert Macneill—who never cares what she says or how she says it—expressed their opinion in her own vulgar fashion when she remarked to me the other day, "I don't see what in the world you need with any more education. Do you want to be a preacher?"

Now, I don't care a snap for the opinion of Mrs. Albert or any of her ilk—with my mind, that is. But I like Mrs. A. with all her shortcomings, and there is something in me that feels hurt and bruised by this attitude of old friends and acquaintances. Others are jealous and sneering. A thousand pin-pricks can cause a good deal of suffering. If I had just *one* friend, whose opinion I valued—to say to me "You are right. You have it in you to achieve something if you get the proper intellectual training. Go ahead!" what a comfort it could be!

---

1. Perle Taylor (1877–1957), daughter of Dr. Francis Perle Taylor of Charlottetown, studied at Prince of Wales College and Halifax Ladies' College; in 1914 she married Murdock Mackinnon, farmer and Conservative politician who was appointed Lieutenant-Governor of PEI in 1919.

2. The capital of Nova Scotia, and the cultural and financial centre of Canadian Maritime provinces; in 1895 it had a population of around forty thousand. Halifax appears as "Kingsport" in Montgomery's *Anne of the Island* (1915).

Monday, Sept. 16, 1895
Ch'town, P.E.I.

This morning grandma and I drove in and I had a busy day. Grandma went home in the evening. I had several callers. Lou Dystant came down to see me off and Norman Campbell and John S. also came in and we had a very nice evening.

HALIFAX SEPT. 17, 1895

Ladies College, Halifax, N.S.

The date is surely worthy of capital letters! For the past four years the day when I should write that heading in my diary has danced before my eyes, an alluring will-o'-the-wisp of ambition and hope. It is come at last and I truly do not know if after all it is really worth all the toil and self-sacrifice and struggle that I have expended in bringing it about. I suppose there is a good deal of truth in that old proverb about anticipation and realization.

Anyway, I am here—at least, as much of me as has survived my tossings to and fro and my journeyings hither and thither upon the earth this day. This morning I was up early and Lou Dystant and Lou McIntyre went to the boat with me. I crossed in the St. Lawrence, a wobbling old tub of a boat. It was quite rough but at first it was pleasant enough. The sun, pouring through ragged, sullen clouds changed the water to burnished copper and the land came out from between its misty curtains. Later on, I was a little seasick and had to lie down until we got to Pictou Harbour.[1] We changed cars at Stellarton and again at Truro.[2] We arrived in Halifax about 7.30. Miss Clark,[3] the L.C. housekeeper met me. She seems very nice and is engaged to Arthur Williams. When we got to the college she took me to Perle Taylor's room. Perle seems friendly and rather nice but it did not take me ten minutes to perceive that her brains are *nil*.

---

1. Ferry-boat terminus on north shore of Nova Scotia.
2. The old Intercolonial line to Halifax.
3. Bertha Clark, engaged during this year to Arthur Williams (1869–1973), who had been known to LMM from her days in Bideford.

After I had my dinner I felt less tired, so went up with Perle to the Assembly room to watch the calisthenic exercises.[1] Then we came back to our room with a troop of girls to be treated by Perle to a "feed" which I need not say is decidedly illicit. They are gone now and the room is quiet. I am too dazed and weary to know what I really think but I imagine I shall like it here. I daresay it would be pleasanter to room on "the third—and-a-half," as the floor where the other Dalhousie girls boarding here room is known: but I am too tired to speculate so here goes for the narrow-little iron cot, two of which the room contains.

My old acquaintances, Edith and Marian MacLeod, are here and I am very glad.

Wednesday, Sept. 18, 1895
Ladies' College, Halifax

This morning Perle's alarm clock awoke me early and I got up and dressed, meanwhile absorbing information from Perle as to H.L.C. etiquette. Then we went down to breakfast. The dining room is a long, plain, bare room, lighted by 16 huge windows, and with the walls wainscotted in yellow. It is really a hideous and depressing apartment.

After dinner I interviewed the principal, Miss Ker,[2] an elderly Englishwoman, unpacked, and then went up for my shorthand lesson. Miss Corbin is the teacher. There are three others in the class. I think I shall like shorthand very much.

I must now stop scribbling and get ready for bed as the rule is "Lights Out" at ten. If I roomed on the Third-and-a-half I would not have to fall in with this, but with Perle I must. Dalhousie opens tomorrow and I must gird up the loins of my mind and pitch in. Excuse my mixed metaphors.

Thursday, Sept. 19, 1895
H.L. College

It seems like a year since last Thursday. This morning I went up to Dalhousie.

Dalhousie College, Halifax, NS

---

1. Swedish-style gymnastic exercises were performed in most women's colleges. The LMM scrapbook has a cartoon—"Vassar, '94, doing calisthenics"—of two girls exercising, to the horror of an elderly aunt.

2. The principal of Halifax Ladies' College, a graduate of Girton College, Cambridge, England.

My companions were Bessie Cumming[1] and Elena Baker[2]—Seniors—and Rita Perry,[3] a sophomore. I did not take a violent fancy to any of them and they certainly did not try to help the stranger within their gates very much in her new departure.

It is about half a mile to the college which is a large ugly brick building in bare ugly grounds. When we went in

Entrance to old Dalhousie

we were greeted with terrific cheers from a crowd of freshmen who were singing glees[4] on the staircase. As soon as possible we went to Dr. Forrest's[5] room and were registered. Then we came home. By this time I was tired, bewildered and lonely and could hardly keep the tears back. In fact, I was just going to curl up on my bed and have a good comfortable *howl* when Miss Clark came in and asked me to go for a walk. We went out to the Park.[6] It was beautiful—so quiet and natural. Miss C. is very nice and jolly and we found plenty to talk about.

I felt like a new person when we came back at six. We were late for dinner so Miss C. asked me to wait and have dinner with her; we went into the parlor and finished out our chat. I am getting more settled here now and I think by next week I'll feel quite contented.

That eternal piano practice is going on as usual. It rings in my ears day and night. They tell me that after you are here awhile you get so used to it you never notice it. The gods grant this be true!

---

1. Bessie Cumming (1874–1953), daughter of a Nova Scotia minister, had spent a year out of college between first and sophomore year, graduated with a B.A. in 1896; returned for a year of post-graduate training to teach in The School for The Blind in Halifax; married Rev. A.F. Robb in 1901; and went with him to Korea as a missionary teacher for over thirty years. Many of her seven children were born in Korea.

2. Elena Baker (b. 1874), graduate of Pictou Academy, B.A. in Arts from Dalhousie in 1896. Later taught at North Sydney High School, appointed vice-principal in 1898 and in 1901 succeeded Bessie Cumming at The School For The Blind before moving to British Columbia and eventually marrying the inspector of public schools in Vancouver.

3. Marguerita (Reta) Perry came to Dalhousie in 1893, but left without graduating.

4. College songs, sung by freshmen, in defiance of sophomores; see Montgomery's *Anne of the Island*.

5. John Forrest, D.D., was president of Dalhousie from 1885 to 1911.

6. Point Pleasant Park lies between the Northwest Arm and Halifax Harbour.

This is prayer meeting night at home. They are probably gathered in the church now. It is only a week since I was there but it seems like a year. I *am* homesick, that can't be denied, and I feel pretty blue by spells.

Friday, Sept. 20, 1895
Halifax Ladies College

This morning I went up to Dalhousie and got my Latin class certificate. There was nothing else to do so I came home and studied shorthand till lunch. In the afternoon I went up to Dalhousie again to see about my German class. The Professor is an old German by the name of Leichti[1] and there are not many in the class.

Jas. McIntyre

James McIntyre is in Halifax now and he called this evening and we had a pleasant chat.

Saturday, Sept. 21, 1895
H.L. College

This morning I travelled over half Halifax hunting for some books and got only one I wanted. This afternoon Jim called for me to go to the Park with him and then we went to the Public Gardens[2] which are lovely. But I feel very tired after so much tramping.

Tuesday, Sept. 24, 1895

Today has been a pleasant one—or would have been if I had not been troubled with an intermittent headache. I got some letters in the morning that cheered me up. I had only one class in college today—French at two.

---

1. James Leichti, M.A., a Swiss Lutheran, had taught French and German in Halifax Grammar School before coming to Dalhousie; he became McLeod Professor of Modern Languages (1866–1906).

2. Sixteen acres of trees, flower beds, and fountains, including a bandstand, in central Halifax, the oldest formal Victorian gardens in North America, established 1841, officially opened 1867.

I have got acquainted with a Miss Shatford who lives in the city and who seems to be a nice girl. She is taking a special course like myself. So far I do *not* like the Dalhousie girls.

I had to come home in company with Reta Perry whom I cordially detest. This morning I studied Cicero—"Kikero," they pronounce it here. They use the Roman Method and I don't like it at all. It seems like a new language and actually gives me a curious homesick sort of feeling for old P.W.C. days and dear old Dr. A.'s careful watch over our pronunciation.

I'm homesick tonight—there is no denying that. It is a *horrible* feeling

Wednesday, Sept. 25, 1895
H.L. College

Latin class today was splendid and so was Second English. We had to write a theme in the latter and the subject was "My Autobiography." Our English professor, Dr. McMechan,[1] seems very nice, but is, I think, rather a weak man.

PROFESSOR MCMECHAN.

Miss Amy Hill,[2] a Dalhousie girl, called on me today and I am invited there to a party tomorrow evening. I smiled a little in my sleeve over her call and her invitation. I think I know the motive. She is reputed to have quite a fancy for Murray Macneill and I suppose she has an idea that she can curry favor in his sight by showing a little attention to his cousin. This is amusing, in view of the cordial dislike Murray and I really feel for each other. He, by the way, is attending Dalhousie in the Senior year, but he has never even called on me since I came here. This of course does not matter to me at all. But considering the fact that he has been a guest almost every summer at my home one would imagine he would at least show the outward forms of politeness for his own self-respect. But Murray cannot forgive me for not bowing down to him and worshipping him—something which he demands from all feminine creatures. That is the plain truth. So I fear poor Miss Hill will not advance her hopes much by her attention to me.

1. Dr. Archibald McKellar MacMechan (1862–1935), educated at the University of Toronto and Johns Hopkins University, had taught at Dalhousie since 1889 and published many books including editions of Thomas Carlyle (1896, 1901). Later mentioned LMM in *Headwaters of Canadian Literature* (1924), a landmark in nationalist criticism.

2. Amy Hill (1873–1937), student at Dalhousie between 1891–92 and 1904–5, graduated B.L., 1896. Her hospitable family home was on Robie Street.

I had a long letter from Edith England today. She is at Sackville college,[1] taking music and painting—likes her work but hates the place. That, however, is probably mere homesickness and will soon wear off. Edith has been a petted only child, surrounded by luxury all her life, and the contrast must be rather hard for her.

Friday, Sept. 27, 1895
H.L. College.

I preface my remarks with a yawn—I am terribly sleepy. Yesterday I had two classes at Dalhousie and went to French with Miss Shatford.[2] After dinner I came up and dressed for the party. There were several there but really it was a poky time— not half as much fun as a jolly country dance at home. We played games all the evening but I was glad when it was over.

PROFESSOR HOWARD MURRAY.

I was horribly sleepy this morning and had to plod up to college in a pouring rain. I am getting to feel quite at home in the college now and like it very much, especially the English classes. Professor Murray of Latin lore is nice but a little slow. Old Prof. Leichti who teaches French and German is very nice and a perfect example of the "old school" gentlemen but he is absolutely no good as a teacher.

Saturday, Sept. 28, 1895

After lunch Jim McIntyre phoned up to ask me if I would like to go the matinee and of course I "liked." The opera was "Olivette"[3] and was amusing but the company is a rather poor one. Jim goes to New Glasgow N.S. on Monday and will not be back for sometime. I am sorry, for cousins are convenient things.

---

1. Mount Allison College, at Sackville, NB—now Mount Allison University.

2. Charlotte, or Lottie, Shatford (1876–1946) came from a wealthy family; her father was Warden of Halifax County. She later married Edward Francis Handy from Dublin and moved with him to British Columbia with their four children.

3. Comic opera, *Les Noces d'Olivette* (1879) by Edouard Audon, English adaptation by H.B. Farnie.

Monday, Sept. 30, 1895
H.L. College.

Today after English it poured rain so I did not come home to lunch but stayed in the library and read George Elliott's[1] biography, and also had a chat with an old acquaintance of mine, a Mr. Rodgerson,[2] who used to teach in Rustico.

Miss Ker had a fit of innovation tonight and changed all our places at the table. I am at her table now between Jessie Morris[3] and Edith MacLeod.[4]

Thursday, Oct. 3, 1895

It is a very pretty walk up to the college. The grounds about the hospital and poorhouse[5] are lovely. The trees are turning golden brown and the fresh morning air is odorous with the woodsy smell of frosted leaves. I am beginning to feel at home in the big rooms and long halls of the college and to recognize a face here and there in the groups and clusters. Our English classes are very nice.

Sunday, Oct. 6, 1895

This morning, Mr. Williams, Miss Clark, and I went to Fort Garrison[6] church where the soldiers go. It is a very "high" church; the sermon didn't count for much but the music was fine and it was a sight to see the soldiers marching in, in all their scarlet glory. When we came out whom should I meet but little Maud MacKenzie of Bideford. I was so surprised I could hardly believe my eyes. She and her parents are in Halifax for the winter.

---

1. Probably the standard biography by George Eliot's husband, J.W. Cross, *George Eliot's Life as Related in Her Letters and Journals* (3 vols., 1885).

2. J.A.C. Rodgerson (1871–1925) appeared earlier in the Journal as "Mr. Rogerson, a school-teacher in Rustico." He graduated from Dalhousie 1896 and was gold medalist in medicine, 1900; after working at Victoria General Hospital, Halifax, and on the S.S. *Gulnare*, he returned to PEI, practicing at Vernon River and later at Hunter River.

3. Jessie Morris (1873–1901), business school student.

4. Edith McLeod (1877–1936), mentioned in a Charlottetown entry, October 18, 1891; a young woman born in Georgetown, PEI, now a student in Halifax.

5. A hostel for the "indigent" at the corner of Robie and South Streets.

6. Fort Massey Presbyterian Church, established 1871 on the site of an old garrison on Tobin Street at Queen.

Wednesday, Oct. 9, 1895

Lottie Shatford asked me to go down with her last
night. She is living with her married sister here and
the latter is away at present so that Lottie is alone.
They live in a very pretty cottage on the Park road
and Lottie and I had a lovely time.

In Second English today Prof. McMechan gave
us back our "autobiographies" with criticisms. He
told me mine was particularly good and interesting.
Then we had to write an account of "My Earliest
Recollection." Mine happens to be that of seeing my
mother in her coffin and of putting my tiny baby
hand on her cold face.

Lottie Shatford

Saturday, Oct. 12, 1895

How fast "the moon of falling leaves"[1] is slipping away! This morning Miss
Chase[2] and I went down to the Greenmarket, partly because it is considered
one of the "sights" of Halifax, partly because we have to write a theme on it
in class next Wednesday. It was worth seeing. In the afternoon Chase and I
went to see the football match between Dalhousie and the United Service.[3] I
never saw a football game before and as I didn't understand it at all I didn't
find it particularly interesting.

Thursday, Oct. 17, 1895
H.L. College

Last Tuesday I went home with Lottie from college and stayed all night.
Yesterday afternoon Miss Clark and I went to Lem Dystant's to tea. He is
Lou's older brother and lives in Halifax. Mrs. D. seems a nice little woman
but rather "common." Arthur W. came out for us after tea and we had a nice
evening and a pleasant walk home.

---

1. From Isabella Valancy Crawford's poem "Malcolm's Katie" (1884), II, 61.

2. Margaret Hawthorne Chase from Onslow, NS, daughter of Rev. J.H. Chase (who had been Dalhousie's
    first graduate in 1866), graduated B.A. in 1899, then went to California with her father, graduating
    with an M.A. in 1915 from the University of California, and eventually became assistant director of
    California Polytechnic School.

3. Army and navy team.

Sunday, Oct. 20, 1895
H.L.C.

This is Sunday morning and I am sitting up here in bed when almost every-one else is away at church. I don't feel at all well.

Friday evening I went to the Philomathic Society at Dalhousie. It was good. Papers were read on "Present Day Authors."

Yesterday afternoon I went with Arthur W. and Miss Clark to see a big foot-ball game between Dalhousie and the Wanderers, in which the latter won.

I had a letter from Laura yesterday. She is to be married next spring. How funny it seems to think of Laura being married! She wishes I could be her bridesmaid! Oh, if I only could! But it is impossible.

Monday, Oct. 21, 1895
H.L.C.

This evening Lottie and I went to the opera. It was "Billie Taylor"[1] and I did not care for it at all, although the music was excellent. But the "living pictures" at the close were beautiful and well worth seeing.

Sunday Oct. 22, 1895
H.L. College

I am getting shockingly dissi-pated. It is nearly midnight and I am not yet in bed. But then one *can* go to bed every night and one *cannot* go to the opera every night, and that is where I have been again.

After Senior English today Lottie and I went for a walk in

the public gardens because we have to write a theme on them tomorrow. It was a delightful evening, clear and crisp. The gardens seem lovely and deserted now but are sadly beautiful even in their desolation. The gray

---

1. A "nautical comic opera" (1880) by Edward Solomon. Programs for *Olivette, Iolanthe, Billie Taylor, Faust,* and *The Beggar Student,* preserved in LMM's red Halifax scrapbook, are reproduced in Epperly's *Imagining Anne.* Operas were put on at the Academy of Music on Pleasant (Barrington) Street, near the HLC.

paths were littered with whirls of crinkled leaves. The horse chestnuts were splendid amber-gold, and the lakes and ponds were calmly silver in the dusky light.

The opera tonight was "Iolanthe" and was very pretty. Coming home I happened to fall in with Miss Clark at the door and we came in and had a feed of crackers and gooseberry jam in the kitchen. That's what it is to be on the good side of the housekeeper.

Sunday, Oct. 27, 1895

I really don't know what has got into me. I am never well now for two days at a time. I have had a fearful headache and *eye*-ache all day.

Reid[1] and Perry and I went to a missionary lecture at Dalhousie this afternoon and to Fort Massey church at night. They are to have a social at the latter place Wednesday evening and I intend to take it in.

Monday, Nov. 17, 1895

Truly, "there's many a slip 'twixt the cup and the lip." Who would have guessed when I laid down my pen that Sunday evening when I would take it up again, or what that "headache and eye-ache" of which I complained portended?

I have had *Measles*—and thereby hangs a tale! Several of them, in fact.

On the Monday and Tuesday succeeding the 27th I suffered everything from "a cold in the head"—as I supposed—but I went out as usual. I felt miserable enough, but I never thought of measles, which was odd, because they were in Dalhousie and I might have been suspicious. On Wednesday I felt worse than ever but went to college. Perry had also developed "a cold" and she felt so ill she stayed in bed.

When I came up from lunch I felt so badly that I went to bed, hoping that a good sleep if I got it might make me feel well enough to go to the Fort Massey social. I dozed fitfully all the afternoon and was dressing for dinner when Miss Claxton[2] came in with a mysterious expression on her thin, inquisitive little face. Miss Claxton,—commonly known as Clack—is the matron, an Englishwoman, and a fussy meddlesome Englishwoman at that. I will confess I dislike her heartily and so I did not hail her entrance with frantic delight. Nothing daunted by my cool reception, however, Miss Claxton

---

1. Alberta Victoria, a Dalhousie student who, like three out of four women students at the time, did not graduate.
2. The Halifax 1901 census lists a Miss Constance Claxton (b. 1856).

spoke, "few and short were the words she said," but alas, how crushing to my hopes! They all tumbled down like a castle of cards.

"Miss Perry has the measles and I am afraid you have them, too."

If she had informed me that Miss Perry had attempted to blow up the college with dynamite and accused me of being an accomplice I could not have been more thunderstruck. By the time I had rallied my scattered wits Miss C. had scrutinized my neck, found rash and decreed my doom. I was ordered at once to Perry's room and went, with no very pleasant emotions over the prospect of being shut up for an indefinite period—and with Rita Perry at that—a girl whom I dislike extremely.

Margaret Perry

"Clack" had sent for Dr. Lindsay who came, looked wise, pronounced it measles, and assured me I couldn't possibly be hungry when I was simply ravenous. The unkindest cut of all was that I had been caught before dinner—and it was roast beef night, too. Not a thing would that hard-hearted being let me have to eat but ordered us to be at once removed to the college hospital and quarantined there for three weeks.

The next thing was a nurse—a Mrs. Fraser, who was quite a dear old soul but earned her six dollars a week very easily I think. Speaking of money, the measles have made quite a sad hole in my scanty funds, alas!

We were whisked off to "the hospital"—a bare, barn-like set of apartments in a remote part of the college. Here we were put to bed. I was by now pretty sick and all that night and the next day I was quite ill and my eyes were very bad. But on Friday I was much better and from that out I improved rapidly.

But oh, how terribly dull and wearisome it was! The Dal girls sent us amusing letters every day and Mrs. Fraser read us immaculate stories out of "Leisure Hours" and kindred publications but in spite of this the time dragged fearfully. I dislike Perry and she *must* dislike me quite as bitterly, for there is something in our very natures that is antagonistic to each other. She is one of the people on whom my soul declares war at sight. But we have always been civil to each other on the surface and now as we were companions in misfortune, we made the best of things, buried the undeclared hatchet and got on excellently well, talking freely of cabbages and kings—and men! *And* things to eat!

We were simply half starved most of the time for they would give us nothing but abominable "invalid's diet"—weak tea, toast, and various "slushes" were all we got for the first two weeks. I soothed my hunger pangs and whiled away some of the time composing a serial "pome" on our experiences, entitled "When Perry and Mont had the measles."

On the next Friday they let us get up and I never was so glad to get out of bed in my life before. As soon as our eyes could stand it we got books and papers, but still the time was long. Of course we had some fun. Plenty of funny things happened and we invented two or three brand new jokes every day. Then the girls would come to the bathroom window of Corridor 3—which was just across the court from us—and talk to us from there in the dumb alphabet, giving us news of the outside world. On Tuesday they let us go out for a walk and you may be sure we enjoyed it. After that we went out every day but were not allowed to meet any of our friends. Mrs. Fraser left on Wednesday and then it was duller than ever. How we counted the days until we would be free!

At last Monday came. This morning we were disinfected from head to heels and came down, reeking with cinnamon, but happy beyond words. And I assure you I've had a busy day. I am to room on the Third—and—a Half until the week is out. How delightful it is to be back in civilization once more! But I'll have to study hard now, for of course I'm fearfully behind hand in everything.

My letters have piled up since I was ill. Letters from home tell me that Mr. Archibald has accepted a call to Sunny Brae, N.S. and leaves C. this week. I am very sorry. It will be a great change and it will seem very strange to have another minister in C. He has been there for eighteen years.

Saturday, Nov. 22, 1895
4 o'clock P.M. H.L. College

I am sitting here by the window in Reid's room—Perry being home for Thanksgiving. Reid is asleep on the bed. It is a very dull, gloomy day—has snowed and rained rawly. 'Tis the time of bleak skies and chill winds; and yet it seems only yesterday that I was pinning pink-and-white mayflowers in my hair on the parsonage veranda and laughing a welcome to the spring.

On Thursday night I went with Lottie to the Academy of Music to see *Faust*.[1] It was put on by

Vic Reid

---

1.   Gounod's opera (1859) based on Goethe's story of the man who sold his soul to the Devil.

an excellent company and was grand. The fourth act in especial—the revel of demons and witches on the *Broken* on *Walpurgis* Night—was grandly horrible. I only wish I could see it all again. I never enjoyed anything so much.

Sunday Morning, Dec. 1, 1895

I was glad enough to get back to college last Monday. In the morning Rob MacGregor asked me to write a paper on Ian MacLaren[1] for the Philomathic[2] on Friday night. I didn't want to, for I've so much back study to catch up with, but he urged me so hard that I consented and was promptly stuck up on the bulletin board—at least my name was— between "Crockett on Crockett" and "Simpson on Barrie."

2. Window of my room; 1. Window of Reid's and Perry's room

Perle as a gypsy at masquerade

I've "set up housekeeping" on my own account now. Miss Ker told me on Monday that she thought I'd find it nicer to room up here on the Dalhousie flat for good. I do not always agree with Miss Ker but in this instance I emphatically did and moved joyfully up. I have a cosy little room all to myself and feel as independent "as a pig on ice." I never liked rooming on Corridor Three.

Perle is a nice soul enough but we have absolutely no interests in common. She is very deaf and this makes her rather tiresome. She has only three ideas in her head—to get something good to eat, something fine to wear, *and* a beau! I like all these in due proportion myself

---

1. Pen name of John Watson (1850–1907) a "Free Kirk" Presbyterian minister and author of the bestseller *Beside the Bonnie Brier Bush* (1894), a nostalgic story of life in a Scottish rural parish.

2. A literary and philosophical society, founded 1891; *philomath* means a lover of learning. All faculty members were honorary members, and all past and present students could join for an annual fee of fifty cents. Montgomery's *Anne of the Island* cites ideas presented at the Philomathic as the best learning acquired at college.

but I don't allow them to crowd everything else out. No doubt I bored Perle as much as she bored me so we are much better apart. Here I am as happy as a queen and can stew and putter round as I like without interfering with anyone or being interfered with.

I wrote my paper on Thursday and last Friday night Lottie called for me and we went up to Dalhousie together. There was a big turnout of students and I was a little nervous, but I think I got on all right—at least, folks appear to think I did.

Tonight we went up again to the Missionary meeting of the Y.M.C.A.[1] as Reid had to read a paper before it.

Sunday night

This evening after preaching—really, it has been so long since I was in church that it had all the sensation of a novelty—it was too delightful to stay in the house, so Mr. W., Miss Clark and I walked out to Lem Dystant's. Lou's sister Annie whom I never met before was there. She seems like a nice, simple girl but very uninteresting.

Wednesday, Dec. 4, 1895
H.L. College, N.S.

This has been one of my "blue" days. I have felt dull and stupid and discouraged and tired. This state of mind has probably been induced by late hours of hard study. The weather, too, is so dull now—so cold and gray. I wonder if a good night's sleep will unravel the kinks of my existence—I think I shall go to bed early for once and try it.

Sunday, Dec. 8, 1895

I spent this afternoon with Lottie and had a very nice time. Clifford MacLean,[2] a friend of Lottie's came in in the evening. When I left, poor Cliff was in duty bound to see me home, of course, and we started. I tripped serenely down the front door steps and then, totally forgetting the terrace flight, I stepped

---

1. The Young Men's Christian Association, established in Halifax in 1853 by Samuel Cunard; the original building at the corner of Granville and Prince Streets was replaced by the Pacific Building in 1911.

2. Clifford MacLean (1876–1955), a Nova Scotian who graduated from Dalhousie University, became a teacher and in 1916 joined the Canadian army as a lieutenant.

just as serenely off the edge and got to the bottom rather more quickly than I had expected. Cliff came tearing down to see if I were killed but, beyond giving myself the cramps laughing, no evil consequences ensued.

Lectures at Dalhousie close on Wednesday. I must put in some extra licks of study if I mean to do anything at exams. There is no need for me to take them at all of course but I want to do so just to see what I can do against the Dalhousie competitors.

Thursday, Dec. 12, 1895
H.L. College

I spent most of today writing a thesis on "Character in Paradise Lost."[1] I hated the subject and put off the evil day as long as I could but had to settle down to it today. I did not make a brilliant success of it at all. The subject is too big for me to tackle.

Tonight I was invited to a social at Mr. Gandier's[2] — Mr. G. is the "eloquent and popular" minister of Fort Massey church. I wore my cream crepon dress with a pink silk crush collar and a fillet of pale pink silk ribbon around my hair. The girls assured me that I looked "out of sight," whatever that may mean. I had a fairly pleasant evening—not dangerously exciting at all. Manse socials, where the guests are invited according to their position in the alphabet and are mainly unknown to each other, are not apt to be.

Monday Morning, Dec. 23, 1895

Exams began last Monday. We had Latin and French. The Latin was easy but the French very hard. Tuesday I had no exams, so studied hard all day for the three that came on Wednesday—Roman History and Second and Senior English. I did pretty well in the first two, I think, but am afraid I didn't do much in the last. The exam seemed to be mainly in work I missed when I was ill with measles. It is something new for me to go down to defeat in English!

Thursday afternoon John Dystant,[3] who is spending his holidays at Lem's, called. I was glad to see John, who is a nice fellow, but I was *not* glad to hear

---

1. *Paradise Lost* (1667), an epic by John Milton, recasting the Bible story of man's first sin in order to "justify the ways of God to man."

2. Alfred Gandier, D.D. (1861–1932) came to Fort Massey Presbyterian Church in 1893. He left in 1900 for Toronto, where he became principal of Knox College, 1909–25, and later of Emmanuel College.

3. John and Lem were brothers of Lewis Dystant, LMM's suitor from Ellerslie. John was now a Methodist minister, and Lem worked for the Halifax Bakery and Confectionery Company.

him say that Mrs. Lem had sent him in to take me out there for the afternoon. There was no decent way of getting out of it so I had to go. They wanted me to stay all the evening, too, but I had to go to the "Break-up Concert" at Dalhousie. There was an enormous crowd there and it was rather amusing but not very enjoyable. Perhaps I was too tired. The torchlight procession was rather good fun however.

On Friday morning the general exodus took place. All the girls went home and I confess I felt rather blue to see everyone going home and poor me left behind. My fare home would not cost any more than my board here but grandma wrote that she thought I had better not go home for fear the roads might be bad for getting to the station etc. I know what that means. Grandfather doesn't want to be bothered meeting me or taking me back.

Miss Clark did not go until this morning. I shall miss her more than all the rest put together.

Evening

This afternoon about four I resolved to go for a walk, so I betook myself out to the Park and sat down on "Greenbank"[1] to look over the harbor. It was

very lovely. On my left lay the city, its roofs and spires dim in their shroud of violet smoke that drifted across the harbour and stained the fair blue of the sky darkly, as if some fell angel had spread his murky pinion across the calm beauty of heaven. George's Island loomed out of the mist and the water lay before me satin smooth in sheen and silver gray, while the gentlest of wavelets lapped against the granite crags. Far to my right stretched the harbour taking on tints of rose and coppery gold as it reached out into the sunset until it lost itself in banks of dull, fire-fringed clouds. The sails of several pleasure boats gleamed whitely afar off and their long reflections wavered in the gray water. The tiny dark headlands cut the creamy expanse and the opposite shores, softened by the mist, folded into each other in hill and valley of dark and light.

---

1. The fortress on George's Island appears as "William's Island" in Montgomery's *Anne of the Island*, chapter 6, with interesting changes from this journal entry.

A mingling of sounds came through the ripe air. On George's Island the light-house beacon flared through the smoke like a baleful star and was answered by another on the far horizon. And far above all, in a concave of stainless blue, where no soil of earth could reach, shone a silver-white half moon with a maiden veil of pearly vapor drawn chastely over her pure face.

Tuesday, Dec. 24, 1895

Really, this is a somewhat monotonous existence. An account of one day's programme will furnish a pattern for all the holidays here. Holidays? Bah!!

Eight o'clock found me sleepily dressing—for early rising rules are in abeyance during vacation—and 8.30 found me sitting at the breakfast table with as prim and proper expression as my somewhat vivacious physiognomy can assume, hardly daring to smile. We have our meals in the library now, as the heat is shut off the dining room. In severe state at the head of the table sits Miss Ker. Nature must have meant Miss Ker for a man and got the labels mixed. She might have made a fairly good one, but as a woman I consider her a woeful failure. She is guiltless of corsets and her dress is in strict con-formity with the rules of hygiene and ugliness. Her iron-gray hair is always worn in a lop-sided coronet and she possesses a decided moustache. She is a "Girton" product and no doubt very clever. But she has not one atom of charm or magnetism.

Opposite Miss Ker sits Miss Claxton who is her very anti-type. Miss C. is a fussy, nervous little old maid, with a hooked nose, an inquisitive expres-sion and a thin rattling little laugh that sets my nerves on edge.

Miss Tilsley is another English lady of uncertain age, but rather more like other people. She is dark, black-eyed, and *very* "English." Miss O'Ellers[1] (pronounced Erlers) the German teacher, is really the best-hearted and most nearly human of the lot, though she is very ridiculous in some ways. Miss Ker dislikes her and is always snubbing her most undeservedly, whereupon I feel that I would like to take Miss Ker by her lop-sided braid and shake her violently. Miss Notting[2] is a kindergarten teacher and is an aggravated specimen of old maidism. She could never have been very likeable even when a young maid. Miss Whiteside,[3] the elocution teacher, is a Canadian,

---

1. Margarete Karoline O'Ellers (1860–1923) taught both German and French at Dalhousie. In July 1896 she married Gunther Gustav Von Der Groeben in Toronto and moved to Erie, PA.

2. Martha Annie Notting (1856–1904), kindergarten teacher from Yarmouth, NS, after training in Toronto opened a private school in Halifax in 1895. She was admired for her bravery in teaching after one arm had been amputated.

3. Maud M. Whiteside, A.T.C.M., taught elocution and calisthenics.

however, and besides is young and very pretty and I am not so much afraid of her as of the other grim cats. I am really frightened to speak for both Miss Ker and "Clack" seem to be lying in wait to pounce on any unguarded word or expression—and a snub from either of them is a rankling thing. They seem able to instil such cold venom into it. If I were a Ladies' College girl they would be within their rights, however ungracefully exercised, but as I am of Dalhousie and merely a boarder here, I rather resent their "bossing." I *did* get square with Miss Claxton the other day, though—beautifully square. I went into the teacher's parlor and seeing Miss Whiteside and Miss Tilsley there alone, as I supposed, I said, "Isn't this a lovely morning, girls?" Up popped Miss Claxton from a low chair where she had been squatted unseen. "You should not call us girls," she piped frigidly. "It is not respectful." "Oh, I beg your pardon, Miss Claxton," I said politely. "I did not see you there. Of course I would never refer to *you* as a girl." Miss Claxton liked it very little, for she does not relish an allusion to her age anymore than ordinary people, but she had to take it, for my apology was perfectly courteous in tone and matter and she had no excuse for resenting anything in it.

Breakfast over, we wait for the mail which is the chief event of the day here. After that, I read, write, study, crochet, or prowl forlornly around until late in the afternoon when I go out for a walk. Dinner at six is another formal affair and the evening is a repetition of the afternoon.

Wednesday, Dec. 25, 1895
H.L. College

This Christmas, which I expected would be very dull, has been a rather pleasant one after all. I got a number of pretty gifts and some delightful letters. We had a goose repast at night and a pleasant evening in the parlor afterwards.

Monday, Dec. 30, 1895

Amy Hill telephoned down today asking me up this evening. A few other Dalhousians were there and we had a nice evening. "Poley" Hill,[1] who is one of the "famosities" of the college walked home with me and was mildly entertaining, even if he scarcely comes up to my shoulder.

---

1. Probably Amy's younger brother Allan Massie Hill (1875–1943), B.A. Dalhousie 1896, D.D. Author of work on Nova Scotia history, he eventually moved to Verdun, QC.

Tuesday, Dec. 31, 1895

I'm really getting dissipated—here I am just home from another party at Dr. Mackays. I did not enjoy it frantically as I found myself set to play whist[1] with a partner who preferred to talk very diluted fun to looking after the game. Anyway, parties where everybody is a stranger to one are not apt to be surpassingly delightful.

---

1. Before bridge developed in the twentieth century, the most popular partnership card game, with no bidding for trumps and no "dummy," but high cards taking tricks in each hand.

1896

Wednesday, Jan. 1, 1896
H.L. College

Welcome '96! It has been a glorious day as far as weather is concerned. The other day Ruth Simpson[1] called and invited me up to dinner there tonight. So, although I had my own private opinion of her long delay in calling, I went. Besides Ruth my hostesses were her aunt Mrs. Simpson and the latter's niece, Miss Stewart. Frank S. came in later on and was fairly entertaining. I enjoyed the evening fairly well but would have done so to a much greater extent had it not been for the habit in which they all seem to indulge—that of picking every unfortunate caller to pieces as soon as the door shut behind him. I had the uncomfortable and paralysing conviction that they would do the same kind office for me when I left.

Tuesday, Jan. 7, 1896

All yesterday and today there has been nothing but arrivals, and the climax was reached tonight when the Dalhousie girls returned, all that could be heard was racing and chasing and kisses and yells of welcome on corridors and stairs. College opens tomorrow and I am not a bit glad. I've got lazy and contented in vacation and don't like the idea of starting in to struggle again. It must be, however, so I have religiously set my alarm clock for seven and intend to "buckle to" with all due "grit."

It has been gruesomely cold these last three days. I believe winter is really upon us at last and the next two months are likely to prove mortifying to the flesh. Well, well, I suppose I must give up my novels and my morning naps and all the other vacation indulgences and return to hard, systematic work.

Wednesday, Jan. 8, 1896
H.L. College

A cold bath may be unpleasant to get into but after the first plunge you don't mind it. So it is with a return to work after holidays. You shut your eyes, take a resolute header, and find yourself quite reconciled to it.

The results of our Latin exam were announced in class this morning. They follow quite a different method here from that which they use at P.W.C. Here no professor stalks in with a huge bundle of papers under his arm which he proceeds with malicious deliberation to dispose of according to

---

1. Ruth Simpson (1879–1905), daughter of Jeremiah and M.A. Simpson.

value. The malicious deliberation is here to be sure, but for the rest, the Professor simply reads out the list in each "class"—viz. "First," "Second" and "Pass." Those whose name is not called read their fate in silence. I *got* a "First" both in Roman History and Latin and led the class in the latter. It was a pretty good showing and as I've worked hard for it I enjoy it.

Friday, Jan. 10, 1896

I got a "Second" in French—much to my surprise—and a first in English. Was down to a turkey-feed in Perle's room tonight and if noise and racket constitute a good time we must have had one.

It snowed heavily today and I suppose we must make up our minds to face winter in earnest now. I hope I won't have to wade through snow as I did last year. But then I'll not have the sleigh drives either. Poor Lou, he certainly did give me some lovely ones.

Saturday, Jan. 11, 1896
H.L. College

I went to see Mrs. McKenzie and Maudie this afternoon. They live on Maynard St. away on the other side of Citadel Hill.[1] She wants me to give Maudie music lessons. I hesitated at first for it is a long way out and I detest giving music lessons. But in the end I consented for it will mean five dollars and every cent has to count with me. I am to go Wednesdays and Saturdays.

We have a new Dalhousie boarder—Nina Church.[2] She is a thin, nervous-looking girl and I know nothing about her either to like or dislike yet. Perry and Reid cordially detest her—to be sure, that is no guide. But Miss Clark does also, so there must be some good reason.

I have been fooling away my time tonight—first with the MacLeod girls, then with Miss Clark; and then all we Dal. girls sat in Reid's room and discussed love-letters and similar weighty and grave subjects. We are a happy-go-lucky crowd, I must say, and have a gay little world of our own up here on this flat. I am not very intimate with any of the girls but I like them all well enough except Perry. Miss Chase is my favourite, Reid next. Bessie Cumming and Elma Baker I do not quite fancy. But we all get on very well together and have lots of fun.

---

1. Historic site of the old fortress and barracks on the high mound at the centre of Halifax.
2. Nina Church (1869–1968), B.A. Dalhousie, 1896; went on to Radcliffe College, M.A., 1903 and Ph.D., 1914. She taught at Wellesley College and became the dean of women at Oklahoma University.

Monday, Jan. 20, 1896
H.L. College

The "itch for writing"—I forget how it is spelled or I would write it in Latin—
is upon me tonight, so I must e'er get out this long-suffering old journal and
scribble in it.

This morning Latin class came first. We have a very nice one. Professor
Murray[1] is charming, although I thought him a bit stodgy at first. I have
got used to the "k" way of pronouncing Latin and once in a while prevail
on my tongue to say "Kikero" when I mean Cicero. We are at Virgil now
and are in Book V of the Aeneid[2]—we studied the VI at P.W.C. with Dr.
Anderson keeping us in the straight and narrow path of good Latinity.
Latin is one of my favourite studies now. Little did I think I would ever
become so when I first began to learn it in that old white schoolhouse
under Miss Gordon's watchful eye. What fearful messes I used to make
of my declensions and conjugations! I was quite sure I could *never* learn
Latin; but time works wonders and there are harder things than Latin to
be conquered after all.

The hour between Latin and English I spend in the library, browsing
among books—and getting more real good than I do in classes. 'Tis a nice
old place that library, with several tables where students read, a cosy corner
here and there, and a bust of Cicero surveying the scene from his exalted
position over the classics department. I wonder if it really looks one bit
like Cicero.

It is a spot for chance gossips and the only place where a boy and girl dare
chat together—always in a cautious undertone of course, for it is one of the
rules of the domain that no loud talking is permitted, so that sounds there
are none, save subdued whispers, rustling of leaves, tip-toeing footsteps and
echoes from the outer halls.

English hour is generally an interesting one. Lottie and I sit on a front seat
next the wall, beneath a picture of Titania[3] and her fairy court, with a long
row of Shakespeare's heroines staring us in the face. We are reading *Romeo
and Juliet*[4] now and as sentimental scenes are Prof. McMechan's forte it suits
him admirably.

It is always a nuisance to go back to Dalhousie after lunch for German,
because I feel that I am not getting one spark of benefit out of that class. Go

1. Howard Murray (1859–1930), McLeod Professor of classics, and dean of the college.

2. LMM had studied Virgil's epic in 1893 at Prince of Wales College.

3. Queen of the fairies in Shakespeare's *A Midsummer's Night's Dream*.

4. Shakespeare's tragedy of star-crossed lovers.

I did, however, and put in the hour reading "Old Mortality."[1] Very dreadful, do you say? But not so. It is part of our Senior English work.

Midnight

We had a "picnic" up on "Pandemonium Flat" tonight. It is one of the new rules that they have sprung on us Dals. this year that we must put out our lights at eleven, ostensibly to protect our health but in reality to save "Daddy Laing's" precious gas. Well, I needn't say that this rule isn't always strictly observed and less so than ever since the holidays. So that it was five minutes on the wrong side of eleven when I, standing before the mirror in a classic undress and brushing my hair, heard a faint tap at my door.

"Come," I called out, as unconcerned "as a pig on ice," for I supposed it was one of the girls. But you could have demolished me with the traditional feather when our austere principal herself poked her head in at the door.

"Aren't you going to bed?" she asked in a tone that conveyed her impression that I had some deeply rooted design of staying up all night.

"Yes," I gurgled faintly—"I—I—didn't notice that it was after eleven"—which was strictly true, for I hadn't troubled myself about the matter at all!

"Well, you *must* notice," said Mother Ker acridly, as she rustled away.

As soon as I dared I slipped out to see if anyone else had been lagged.[2] Chase, Baker and Cumming had all been caught but, as the devil looks after his own, Perry and Reid had just turned theirs out before she passed.

Margaret Chase

Well, Chase and I resolved to stay up as long as we pleased, even if we had to do it in the dark, so I turned out my gas and went into Chase's room where we larked and laughed till nearly twelve.

Wednesday, Jan. 22, 1896
H.L. College

I have to read a paper before the next Y.M.C.A. on "The Educational Phase of Missions"—I think the title is bigger than the girl. So it dawned upon me

1.   Walter Scott's novel (1816) about the Covenanters of Scotland.

2.   Slang: caught.

today that I'd better get a wiggle on. I've got it about one half written and it is a dry as one would expect from the name. I can't get any life into it. I know nothing of the subject at first hand naturally and all the material I could get was very juiceless.

Saturday, Jan. 25, 1896
H.L. College

I had a letter from Alexina McGregor this morning. She wrote to tell me of her engagement to Mr. Wright, a young P. Asian[1] who is—of course—the model man! Bless us!

A big snowstorm raged all day and made my walk over Citadel Hill to give Maudie McKenzie her lesson quite exhilarating. It cleared off a little at dark and they telephoned down from Pine Hill that the Y.M.C.A. would be held, so Reid and I went. It came off all right and I read that blessed paper.

Sunday, Jan. 26, 1896

This evening Reid and I stayed home from church as it was wet and we had colds and as we were passing along the corridor we happened to glance into Chase's room, her door being open. Now, Chase is notoriously untidy and had left her room as usual in a state resembling original chaos. Reid and I were ripe for mischief, so we waded in—not to make things worse for that was impossible but to give a piquant arrangement to them. We succeeded admirably—you should have seen that room when we had finished. Then we dressed a broom and pillow in Chase's clothes and stood it up by the window. It was "flee for your life" when Chase got home.

Miss Clark

Midnight

I suppose Miss Ker would have a kitten fit if she knew I was out of bed at this hour. About nine of the maids came up to say that Miss Clark wished to see me. I hurried down, suspecting why I was wanted. Miss C. had confided her story to me before and I knew that the relations between her

---

1. From Prince Albert.

and Mr. Williams were strained almost to the yielding point. When I went in she was crying and simply held out her ringless finger to me. She has broken her engagement at last. She was driven to it. Williams has treated her shamefully and the poor girl is almost heart-broken. I am sorry for her but I think she is well rid of him. I don't think there is a spark of principle in him and I feel sure he would never make her happy.

Tuesday, Jan. 31, 1896
H.L. College

Tonight all we Co-eds[1] gave an at home to the Seniors and Juniors in the Munro room. We have been thinking and talking of nothing else for a fortnight and it has been a brilliant success. We had dear little "Topic" programmes,[2] and my five topics were taken by Cliffie MacLean,[3] Mr. Crockett, Mr. Mackay, Mr. Burchell and Mr. Hattie, the last of whom saw me home. He is mortally slow.

Monday, Feb. 3, 1896
H.L. College

This evening Perry, who is writing a philosophical essay, was around getting our "number forms"—that is, the form in which we see the figures from 1 up to 100 in our "mind's eye." I never thought of the subject before but all the girls thought my number form was very peculiar. The appended diagram roughly expresses it.

---

1. Young women admitted to academic institutions; woman students had been graduating from Dalhousie University since 1881.

2. In lieu of dance cards on which young men could sign up for a particular dance: these "programmes" assigned a conversational topic for each succeeding partner.

3. After graduating from Dalhousie University, Clifford McLean (1876–1955) became a teacher and in 1916 joined the Canadian army as a lieutenant. Other partners at the at-home included Albert Edwin Crockett (1871–1958): after graduating from Dalhousie he moved to Rochester, NY, where he eventually became secretary of the chamber of commerce; Charles Jost Buirchell (1876–1967), a student from Cape Breton, NS, who became a lawyer after graduating and worked with the High Commission for Canada in England and Australia; Mr. (Robert) Hattie (b. 1879): he and Albert Crockett became editors of the Dalhousie *Gazette* in 1896–97. After graduating he remained in Halifax, working as a newspaperman, and by 1911 had become publisher and president of Maritime Merchant Limited.

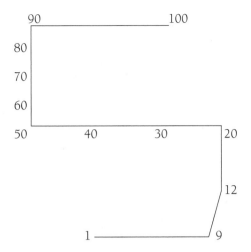

It cannot do so perfectly because I do not see them on a plane surface. From 1 to 4 are on a plane; from 5 to 9 they go down just like the steps of a stair, so that I see 9 on a much lower level than 4. From 9 to 12 are on a level: then from 12 to 20 they climb up like a stair. 20 to 24 are level, 25–30 drop down in steps. 30–34 level, 34–40 steps, 40–44 level, 44–50 steps. Then 50 seems to be away up in the air above 49, without any connecting steps. 50–54 level, 54–60 steps, so that 60 is on a level with 49. From 60–90 the levels and steps alternate as before. At 90 the numbers turn at right angles, 90–94 are level and 94–100 are steps.

Most of the girls saw the figures 1–100 in a straight line. Chase saw them in circles of tens—something like this

```
     9   1
  8         2
 7    10    3
  6         4
     5
```
and so on.

Wednesday, Feb. 5, 1896

This afternoon it was as much as your life was worth to cross Citadel Hill for at every step you risked being swept into limbo by a coasting sled. Scores of kiddies were there and I really envied them. The coast is a splendid one—even better than those famous ones of lang syne days, in our "big field" and down Pierce's hill.

Maudie M. is getting on only fairly well. I don't think she practises half enough. I can hardly blame her, but her mother should see to it. Any child dislikes practising naturally. I used to hate it myself when I first began. I had no organ of my own then so I had to go down to practise on George R.'s. How well I remember that snug old parlor, no longer in existence, as Geo. R. tore the old house down a few years ago and built a new one. It was such a neat little spot with vines clambering over one window and a big willow kissing the other with lithe tips. And there were wonderful tidies[1] on the chairs and gay mats on the floor and books and cards carefully arranged on a round table and vases of dried grass on the mantel piece and some coloured chromos[2] on the walls. And there was a tiny spare bedroom opening off it, with a marvellous green and white patchwork quilt on the bed.

Friday, Feb. 7, 1896
H.L. College

The bottom fell out of Halifax sometime last night. Getting across the big slough on the campus this morning forcibly reminded me of some of my adventures in Capt. Richard's bog last April. Tonight however, I borrowed a pair of rubber boots and heroically splashed up again to the Philomathic for was not Mr. Hattie to read a paper on "Mesmerism" and Frank Currier,[3] Pine Hill theologue, Dal. librarian and the biggest "comic" ever born to read one on "ghosts"?

Bert Hattie's was 80 pages long and exceedingly dry. But Currier's was the most excruciatingly funny thing I ever listened to. There wasn't the "ghost" of sense in it from beginning to end but it was such exquisite nonsense that every sentence in it was hailed with shrieks of laughter.

When we came out "Little George" sidled up to me.

"Little George" is one of the "famosities" of Dalhousie. Very clever, a perfect gentleman, of irreproachable morals, he is the most hopelessly, painfully, incurably bashful fellow that ever walked its classic halls. "Little George's" passages with his lady friends are regarded as rich morsels at Dalhousie. I was introduced to him in the library one day when the Y.M.C.A.'s were hunting for victims to write their missionary papers. Mr.

---

1. Antimacassars or doilies to protect chairs from soil.
2. Vintage photographs, using time-lapse technique.
3. Frank Allison Currier, M.A. Dalhousie, 1896.

McRae introduced him as "one of the shining lights of the Y.M.C.A.," and then went off, leaving poor George standing before me, trembling from head to foot, afraid to remain and equally afraid to flee. He made me so nervous that I wanted to laugh so I got myself out of the way with all possible speed.

I heard no more of or from "Little George" until the day of the missionary meeting when he paused about six feet away from me in the library one day with such an appealing look that I was sure he wanted to say something, as I stopped to give him a chance. Trembling and shifting from one foot to the other, he stammered out something which I took to be a question about my paper, so I answered that it was ready and got me away at once. Then, two or three days after the meeting I was reading in the library one morning when "Little G." came in, stole cautiously across the floor to a remote corner, and sat down. There he sat the whole hour, eyeing me stealthily the most of the time until the bell rang and I gathered up my books for exodus. Little G. evidently thought that it was then or never, so he took his courage in both hands and sneaked over to my table when he contrived to stammer out the formal thanks of the Y.M.C.A. for my paper.

So, of course, I was amazed when Little G. came up to me tonight. The amount of courage he must have employed would be worthy of a hero and I felt that I could do no less than reward him by a gracious assent when he asked under his breath if he might see me home. So down we came, wading the bogs and slithering along the icy streets with a brisk wind on our backs. The gutter kept "Little G." from edging clear out of sight and I talked on perseveringly. I was extremely thankful when I got home and dismissed him. I certainly hope poor G. will never think it his duty to attempt anything of the like again.

Saturday, Feb. 15, 1896

My head is quite giddy—I've had an extra streak of luck today. In January the *Evening Mail*[1] offered a prize of five dollars for the best letter on the question "Which has the more patience under the ordinary cares and trials of life—man or woman?" The letters poured in and the best of them were printed in the Mail every evening. At first I took small interest in the contest, but Lottie—whose bother-in-law is on the paper—urged me to send in a letter and finally I did. I was tired of the usual strain as I tried to

---

1.   One of four Halifax daily newspapers.

produce something more original and wrote a short allegory representing guardian angels seeking boons from the Great Giver etc.:—This is a copy of the letter.

> It was the day when all the guardian angels came to
> the Benign Giver to ask a boon for each several charge.
> One by one they came in bright procession, and departed
> rejoicing; but one stood apart with drooping wings and
> veiled face.
> Last of all he, too, approached the Giver and knelt
> in reverence before Him.
> "Oh, Benign Giver," murmured the sorrowing spirit.
> "I am woman's guardian angel, nor know I what boon to
> crave for her who needeth all. From cradle to grave her
> path is through sorrow and pain and self-sacrifice. She
> brings man's children forth in agony, she rears them
> in anxiety, she gives them up to the world in bitterness
> and anguish of heart. Daily she is beset with
> unnumbered trials. Grant then, Most Benign Giver, some
> boon to compensate and strengthen."
> He ceased. All heaven was hushed. Through the
> silence sounded the Giver's voice.
> "Sad spirit," He said tenderly, "take from my hand
> this most precious boon for women, this boon bestowed
> on none other of My creatures—the gift of long-
> suffering, all-forgiving divine patience."
> Then the guardian angel unveiled his face and passed
> from the shining multitude with joy on his radiant brow.
> Enid.

Mr. Weir showed this letter to Lottie—of course he didn't know it was mine as all the letters were signed with a nom-de-plume—and said it was the prettiest thing sent in but that it wouldn't take the prize because it wasn't an argument. I ruminated another while and one night I arose in the middle of the night to write down the following verses:—

> As my letter must be brief
> I'll at once state my belief
> And this it is, that, since the world began,
> Since Adam first did say
> 'Twas Eve led me astray

A woman hath more patience than a man.
If a man's obliged to wait
For someone who's rather late
No mortal ever got in such a stew,
And if something can't be found
That he's sure should be around
The listening air sometimes grows fairly blue.
Just watch a man who tries
To soothe a baby's cries,
Or put a stovepipe up in weather cold,
Into what a state he'll get,
How he'll fuss and fume and fret
And stamp and bluster round and storm and scold.
Some point to Job with pride
As an argument for their side!
Why, it was so rare a patient man to see
That when one was really found
His discoverers were bound
To preserve for him a place in history.
And while I admit it's true
That man has *some* patience, too,
And that woman isn't *always* sweetly calm,
Still, I think all must agree
On this central fact—that she
For general, all-round patience bears the palm.

I signed this effusion "Belinda Bluegrass" and sent them in. The competition closed on the 7th and the letters were handed to Professor McMechan who was to be the judge. This morning Lottie suddenly appeared on the Third-and-a-Half and exclaimed breathlessly,

"Oh, Maud, I believe you've won the prize! Dr. McMechan has sent the best and second-best in. Both are verse and one of them is by 'Belinda Bluegrass' but I'm not sure which is first."

So I was in suspense all day. Tonight when I was coming home from Maudie's lesson I bought a *Mail* from a newsboy. But I did not open it then. No, I scuttled home, flew upstairs, and dressed for dinner. Then I opened the paper and the first thing I saw was "Prize won by Belinda Bluegrass." Of course I was pleased! Moreover, my first letter won honorable mention on account of its literary merit.

Thursday, Feb. 20, 1896

I had another very pleasant surprise this morning. Sometime ago, I sent a short story called "Our Charivari"[1] to a Philadelphia magazine—"*Golden Days*"[2]—and today I got a check for $5 for it. Isn't that lucky! And so encouraging, too. I feel so happy over it.

I went uptown to invest my *Mail* prize money today. I wanted to get something I could keep always and not get tired of, so I got Tennyson, Longfellow, Whittier and Byron. They are nicely bound and I've always longed to have them of my own.

Dear me, how quickly the winter is slipping away! It has not seemed like winter for it has been very mild and fine for the most part. How different from last winter in Bideford where we were surrounded by such huge drifts in the dear old parsonage. I wonder who has my old room this winter.

Happening to glance up just here my eyes fell on a card on the wall in front of me with several views of P.A. on it—nearly all well-known spots to me. There is the "River Road" where Will and Laura and I went walking in those wonderful western twilights when the sky was rose and gold and crimson over far dim prairie slopes and the river waters mirrored back the colours in fairy-like shadings save where they were deep and dark beneath the thick poplars on the banks. What a witchery there was in a prairie twilight! And we three would loiter along the dim path, laughing and chatting in careless mirth. Then there is a view of the station and the long platform where we used to promenade when waiting for the train; and the thick poplar bluffs and purple-misted hills behind it, with beyond them winding trails and sheets of prairie sunflowers and blue-bells, and gleaming, gem-like lakes.

I wonder where all the High School Scholars of that year are now. I have half forgotten their very names. Poor Frank Robertson is dead. Then there were the Jardine boys and "Nitchie" Tom Clark and Harry Oram, whose face was never clean, and John MacLeod and the MacKay boys and that peculiar youth, Douglas Maveety, and Willy McBeath. I forget the others—except Will P. of course. How will I remember that first morning he came to school and sat behind me! I don't think we were ever introduced—just scraped up an acquaintance. The first remark I remember his making to me was a droll statement that he "couldn't study with such beautiful hair in front of him." In any other boy it might have sounded silly or impertinent but in Will P. with

---

1. Originally misspelled "Charavari." Like Montgomery's *The Golden Road* (1913), this story is written from the point of view of a young boy visiting his PEI family farm.

2. A long-established juvenile magazine, published in Philadelphia, 1880–1907. LMM changed the order of her successes when she retold the story of this fortunate fortnight in *The Alpine Path* (see note on entry for August 1, 1892).

his ingratiating smile it seemed just the thing to say! Then followed pleasant days in the old "council room" where we wrote notes and exchanged our books and laughed over our jokes and afterwards walked home from school together. How like a dream it all seems now!

Tuesday, Mar. 3, 1896
H.L. College

This afternoon I went to Mrs. MacKay's to tea and afterwards to hear Mr. Gandier lecture on his trip to Naples, Pompeii, and Vesuvius. It was very interesting although Mr. G. can never resist the temptation of tucking a snug little moral into every paragraph. He is as fond of morals as the *Duchess* in Wonderland. As for his jokes, they are so carefully built that you forget to laugh in wondering how he did it.

Saturday, Mar. 7, 1896

Oh, how tired I am! But there is "no rest for the wicked" for I have to stay up for two hours yet and read extra English, having got permission from Miss Ker to keep my light for that purpose. Lottie came up this morning and we began work on our thesis for distinction—or *extinction* as I rather think mine will prove before I am through with it. Mine is the metre in "Comus"[1] and hers is the same in *Romeo and Juliet*, and we ploughed along, discussing "end-stops" and "runovers" with all the wisdom of people who knew nothing about it. I wish the thing were done. It has been hanging over my head like a sword of Damocles ever since the term began.

Saturday, March 14, 1896
H.L. College

This has been an extra busy week. Last night I felt dreadfully. I wore myself out attempting to do too much and had to go to bed at 9. I tossed and tumbled about all night, dreaming fearful dreams, and woke up at two in a high fever, with a sore throat and a raging headache. I at once concluded that I was taking scarlet fever—it is around—and—totally forgetting that I had the scarlet fever when I was a child—I got up in a panic to hunt up a treatise on infectious diseases and read up the symptoms. I couldn't conclude I

---

1. A masque (1637) by John Milton praising virtue, in a variety of lyric rhythms.

had them *in toto* but I had enough to worry me unpleasantly. However, I ate a cracker and crawled into bed again where I soon fell asleep. I felt seedy enough this morning but as I have remembered having scarlet fever once I don't think it's likely I'm in for it again.

I have been pegging away at my thesis all the week. It is tedious, uninteresting work, and I cannot see what possible good there is in it for anybody. Tuesday, I had a letter from Mr. Dennis,[1] the editor of the *Herald*. He is going to get out a special Dalhousie edition and wants me to contribute an article on "The Experiences of a Girl Student at Dalhousie."[2] I want to do it but the request couldn't have come at a more inconvenient time.

Saturday, Mar. 21, 1896
H.L. College

I have had grippe most of this week and haven't been able to do anything worth while. I can't realize that the term is so near its end. The way time flies at college is appalling. Last Monday morning I got a cheque for twelve dollars from *The Youth's Companion*[3] for a poem I sent them, called "Fisher Lassies."[4] The editor also wrote some pretty nice things about it. It is such an encouragement because *The Companion* uses only the best things.

Saturday, Mar. 28, 1896

Another busy week. Last Sunday evening I went to Chalmers church with Mr. Rodgerson. We went to hear the noted Dr. Sexton[5]—whom I consider an old fraud. I was disappointed for I expected something good but apparently all he could do was quote poetry. Friday night I was at a Conversazione at Pine Hill[6]—a big affair, over five hundred being invited, and very dull.

---

1. William Dennis, news editor since 1882 of the Halifax *Herald*, founded by J.J. Stewart. Dennis became Stewart's partner in 1897 and owner in 1907 after Stewart's death.

2. Published as "A Girl's Place at Dalhousie College," includes grateful comments on the objects and values of a university education for working girls and for wives.

3. The leading American magazine for young people; published in Boston, circulation of 540,000 in 1900.

4. A poem in nine rhyming quatrains, by "M.L. Cavendish" romanticizing the girls ("joyous, lithe-limbed, as the sea-birds free"). The rhythm echoes Charles Kingsley's grimmer "Three Fishers Went Sailing" (1851).

5. A Presbyterian minister. A more famous Dr. Frederic Sexton, founder of the Nova Scotia Technical College, was only sixteen years old at this time.

6. An evening of intellectual talk at the Halifax theological college.

I finished both of my thesis and the *Herald* article to boot this week, and it was a huge relief. I have been studying doggedly the whole week in spite of feeling ill, hating it all the time and longing to pitch the book away.

Thursday, April 2, 1896
H.L. College

I can't study tonight. A restless mood is on me and I *cannot* settle down to my books. May Taylor has just been up here for a chat. She is a Ladies' College girl, very nice and clever—a great contrast to the usual run of H.L.C. girls who, like Perle, seem to live only for dress, beaux and eatables.

Today I had another pleasant windfall—a cheque for three dollars from *Golden Days* for a poem "The Apple Picking Time."[1]

Last Sunday night Edith MacLeod came up and slept with me. We both slept in the one bed and as the H.L.C. cots are rather

May Taylor

narrow it was a work of art to keep in. Nevertheless, we had a "scrumptious" time and a real good old-fashioned talk. Monday night I went down and slept with her. I am going to sleep with Isobel Morrison tonight—it is Easter Holidays here now, hence all this sleeping around, which of course is not permissible at other times. Isobel is up here now, sewing buttons on her garters. She is a Cape Breton girl and very jolly.

Tuesday we had our last French lecture and our last in Senior English. I was very sorry to be done with English. I have enjoyed that class so much and got so much benefit from it. We had our last Latin lecture yesterday and I regret that, too. There is only one more lecture for me at Dalhousie—Second English on Monday.

Sunday, April 5, 1896
H.L. College

Last night Dr. Anderson lectured for the Philomathic. I went of course—the spectres of a dozen exams could not have frightened me into staying at

---

1. Published as by "M.L. Cavendish" in *Golden Days*, October 1, 1896.

home. The lecture was on "MacBeth" and was capital. This afternoon all the Island girls were invited to meet Dr. A. at afternoon tea at Mrs. McInnis'.[1] We had a lovely time.

Wednesday, April 8, 1896

Last night Mr. Dennis sent me tickets for the opera. Miss Clark and I went. The opera was "The Beggar Student"[2] and was very pretty. I enjoyed myself immensely. I always do. I think opera is delightful. It has no bad after effects on me—never disgusts me with homely, workaday life; on the contrary, it sends me back to it with renewed zest and spice.

Friday, April 10, 1896
H.L. College

I went up to college this morning feeling rather unprepared for the exam. We had it in the law library. The paper was hard and I expect I put down some fearful howlers. From it I went to French and it was fearfully hard. I was completely disgusted with life by the time I had finished and went flying to the ladies' room in a doleful mood. It made me tireder than ever to find I was "gazetted"[3] with Rodgerson. This was the brilliant item, doubtless supposed by its perpetrator to be a joke.

> J.A.C.R. loves to recite,
> "Ye banks and braes and streams around
> The castle of—"[4] (We suppress the last word out of deference to his modesty.)

Whoever got that up deserves a leather medal!

Saturday, April 11, 1896

This morning Isobel M. and I went for a long walk through the park. It was beautiful. We just rambled on, past mossy-floored pine aisles and watched the pearly waters of the harbour cream and shiver beneath the silvery mists floating over them.

---

1. Probably Mrs. Hector McInnes (Charlotte Mary McNeill, B.A., 1887) who had married into a family prominent in Dalhousie circles; her husband was on the board of governors.

2. Comic opera by Carl Millöcker (1842–99).

3. Noted in the college newspaper as being involved with Mr. Rodgerson, a theology student.

4. These lines from Burns' "Highland Mary" end with "the castle of Montgomery."

When I came back I had to begin packing up because I am going out to spend a fortnight with the Lem Dystants as my room is wanted for another girl. My poor room—it looks sadly dismantled and forlorn now—pictures, books, nic-nacs all gone and only a few stray garments and necessaries scattered around. My poor little room where I have been so happy! I wonder if old dreams can haunt rooms—if, when one leaves forever the room where she has dreamed and thought and joyed and suffered and laughed and wept, something of her, intangible and invisible, yet none the less real, does not remain behind like a voiceful memory.

Friday, April 17, 1896
Halifax

I have been domiciled at No. 5, Chestnut Terrace this week. Monday morning I had two English exams and I think I did all right in them. Yesterday afternoon I went in and took the extra French. Then this afternoon I went up and took the extra English exam—and it is not only the last exam I shall have at Dalhousie but probably the last exam I shall ever take! I remember the first one I ever had—it was in history, when Mr. Fraser was teaching in Cavendish. And between that time and this stretch twelve long years each of which has flourished its separate quota of exam papers before my weary eyes. First in that dear old schoolhouse of vanished childhood. What a fuss we used to make over our exams! At home in a tiny drawer of my upstairs room I keep a big bundle of those old exam papers. How anxious we were to do well—how gravely we discussed the questions afterwards—how proud or otherwise we felt when the teacher announced the results! Then there were the exams at P.W.C. before which Mary and I used to sit up half the night and cram. And oh, that dreadful, never-to-be forgotten "week of horrors"—the week of the License Exams! I don't believe anything could induce me to live that week over again.

Prof. MacMechan told me today that I had handed in a splendid Senior English paper.[1]

I am having a nice *restful* time out here, reading, walking and chatting with Mrs. D. I have a nice little room with chestnut boughs stretching across the window, their big fat buds swelling on them. How ever new and delicious it is to watch the leaves coming out in the spring from the first sappy brown bud, through all the stages of tender green mist to a full-leafed luxuriance. How I love trees!

---

1. LMM wrote on "Metre in Milton's *Comus*." The thesis was an optional addition to senior English, necessary to finish with distinction.

Saturday, Apr. 25, 1896
5 Chestnut Terrace, Halifax

I was at a rather nice little party at Amy Hill's Thursday night. Yesterday and today I have been very busy. I am going home Wednesday, as are most of the Island students. Convocation[1] is going to be something of a fizzle. George Munro,[2] the great benefactor of Dalhousie has just died and out of respect to his blessed memory they are not going to have a public convocation. It is too vexing, after I've waited over a whole week on purpose.

Tuesday, April 28, 1896—

has been and come and is almost gone, and with it the end of my Halifax sojourn. I came into town this morning leaving Chestnut Terrace unregretfully. I had a nice rest but oh, dear, it was awfully *slow*. Half the time I didn't know what to do with myself.

After lunch we girls all went to Convocation which was held in the college law library. The place was packed and the programme quite interesting. Elma, Bessie and Nina got their B.A.'s.

Most of this evening I spent with Bertha Clark. I shall be so sorry to part with her.

Wednesday, Apr. 29, 1896
Ch'town, P.E.I.

"Back to my native land again"—it seems as if it must have taken more than a day to bring me here. This morning my alarm clock wakened me at 6. I hopped out, dressed, and got my breakfast in solitary majesty. At 7.45 my cab came, so I said my farewells and left, taking a last look at H.L.C. as I drove out of the gates through the misty gray morning.

A few minutes after I got on my train Mr. Rodgerson appeared and stuck to me all the morning. I wished him anywhere else because I simply cannot endure him and that is all there is about it!

At Pictou we took the *Stanley*; it was cold and rough crossing over but I was not seasick and we reached Ch'town at five. Laura and Harry met me

---

1. Graduation ceremony.
2. A generous benefactor of Dalhousie University, though not himself a Dalhousie graduate, Munro (1825–96) had endowed several professorships and provided scholarship funds.

and I came up to Aunt Mary's. This evening Jack S. and Jack Gordon came down to see me and we had one of our merry old times.

Friday, May 1, 1896
Cavendish, P.E.I.

A charming May day truly—blowing a hurricane and temperature below freezing point! I came out to Hunter River and had a most unpleasant drive home. The roads were frightful and I was very cold. Got here at dark. It is nice to be home once more. Everything seems pretty much the same.

Tuesday, May 5, 1896
Cavendish, P.E.I.

Have been busy seeing old friends. Was in church Sunday. It seemed very strange not to see Mr. Archibald there. His substitute, Mr. George, preached fairly well. He is only here for a time.

Tonight, having nothing better to do, I went upstairs and read a lot of old letters—Nate's among the number. How vividly they brought back those dear old schooldays. I almost fancied myself a schoolgirl once more, going to the old school with my classmates, now so widely scattered; and a strong longing swept over me to go back to those dear old merry days when life was seen through a rosy mist of hope and illusion and possessed an indefinable something that has passed away forever.

"Where is it now, the glory and the dream?"

Gone—gone with the lights and shadows of those olden years—gone never to return. The freshness of early dawn comes but once and nothing can ever recall its vanished splendors.

Saturday, May 30, 1896

This afternoon Jack Laird came in for mail and we had a lively chat. We were having a No. 1 time when old Mrs. Wyand[1] came in and sat down. Neither Jack nor I were pining for her society but

An old green field

---

1. Probably Margaret, Sam Wyand's wife (1828–1904).

she appeared to fancy we were for she stayed until Jack got up and made his exit in disgust. I went for a long walk after that through the old green fields by myself. Finally I lay down in the grass by the fence and watched the clouds drift over the blue sky above me. It was so beautiful.

Wednesday, June 3, 1896

This was Laura's wedding day. By now she is the bride of Andrew Agnew. How I wish I could have been present at her wedding. But that was impossible. I wish and hope for her every happiness.

Andrew and Laura Agnew

Monday Morning, June 8, 1896

Saturday afternoon Lu and I and Wellington MacCoubrey[1]—the teacher here—drove up to Darlington to visit Mary Campbell. We had a fine time all through. Mary and Lu and I slept together and we laughed ourselves sick to hear Mary mimicking old Gaelic women talking. She can do it to perfection. Sunday morning we all went to Brookfield church and in the afternoon we drove to Strathalbyn. The latter place is Lot 11 over again. We came home in the evening and had a merry drive.

Sunday, June 14, 1896
Cavendish, P.E.I.

A country Sabbath is suggestive of rest and peace and quiet—sleepy blue skies, shadows golden and green, sunny fields, and the pink and snow of apple blossoms. June is at her height of radiant loveliness now. What a pity it lasts such a short time!

A corner of my room

---

1.   Wellington Maccoubrey (1874–1950), LMM's contemporary from New Glasgow, PEI.

I am here in my old room—my little absolute kingdom. Here I read, write and dream. My favourite pictures adorn the walls, my well read books are on their shelves and my clock ticks me cheerful company.

Tuesday, June 30, 1896

Grandpa and grandma went to town today and so "Monty" kept house alone in great state and glory. When they came home I got a few trifles I had sent for—among others, a dotted cream veil with a distracting border. I have a decided weakness for dainty veils. A woman who has the right sort of a veil and knows the right way to wear it can always appear well-dressed. But the veils some women wear! *And* the way they put them on!! When I see a woman with a limp, skimpy, dragged-out veil barely reaching to the tip of her nose and clinging there for dear life I long to reach over and claw it off and hold it up to derision and contempt. A woman who dons such a veil really commits a social crime and I contend that it would be justifiable *veilicide*.

Wednesday, July 8, 1896
Cavendish

This afternoon Kate and I went back to the woods to look for berries and visited "Kentucky" and Wyand's stumps. We got our bowls full but we worked for it, scrambling through brush, climbing dreadful fences, and getting roasted in the hot sun.

Nate is home now and was down today on his bike. We had a pleasant chat. He looks very thin and had a genuine *moustache*. It gives him a grown-up look but I don't think it becomes him at all.

I got a five dollar check from *Golden Days*[1] today for a short story. People envy me these bits of success and say "It's well to be you," and so on. I smile cynically when I hear them. They do not realize how many disappointments come to one success. They see only the success and think all must be smooth travelling.

---

1. *Golden Days* published "Our Practical Joke" in July 1896 and "A Missing Pony" in September 1896.

Saturday, July 20, 1896
Cavendish, P.E.I.

This afternoon who should come in but Alma Macneill—dear old Alma not a whit changed from the days of yore but still the same golden-haired Alma with the dimpled cheeks and the sweet smile. She went to Boston three years ago and this is her first visit home.

In April I sent a story to the MacClure Syndicate[1] and it has just been accepted and printed in the Chicago *Inter-Ocean*.[2] The cheque ought to come soon—hope it will be a good fat one.

Alma

Sunday, July 26, 1896

I suppose I must go and get ready for evening service—somewhat against my inclination for I was out this morning and I honestly think once is enough to go to church on any Sunday.

Sunday is supposed to be a day of rest but in reality it is as hard worked a day as any in the week. We cook, eat, and wash dishes galore. We dress with weariness to the flesh and tramp to church in the heat, sit a long and mostly very dull sermon out in a stuffy pew and come home again not a whit better than we went—not as good indeed for we have got a headache and feel very vicious for our pains.

I have an ideal Sunday in my mind. Only, I am such a coward that I cannot translate it into the real, but must drift on with the current of conventionality.

But I would *like* to go away on Sunday morning to the heart of some great solemn wood and sit down among the ferns with only the companionship of the trees and the wood-winds echoing through the dim, moss-hung aisles like the strains of some vast cathedral anthem. And I would stay there for hours alone with nature and my own soul.

I think that would really do me great good. But how dreadfully unorthodox and *odd* it would be. The local spinsters would die of horror.

---

1. S.S. McClure, founder of *McClure's Magazine* (1893), started the first newspaper syndicate to reprint previously published material by well-known authors such as Kipling, Stevenson, and Rider Haggard.

2. Respectable magazine that pioneered colour printing on rotary presses in 1892; published "In Spite of Myself" July 1896.

Wednesday, July 29, 1896
Cavendish, P.E.I.

I spent this afternoon with Alma and had a lovely time. They have such a delightful old garden and an immense willow in it that is my envy.

In the evening Mollie came over and wanted me to go back with her and stay all night. We had a very jolly time.

Alma's garden

Saturday, Aug. 1, 1896
Cavendish, P.E.I.

Under the birches

This evening at dark I flung a cape over my shoulders and went down to the school for a walk.

I felt lonesome and a wee bit blue; and leaning over the gate thinking over various perplexing problems didn't tend to raise my spirits any.

It was very cool and fresh and dewless: the light of sunset was still in the west but all the land was dark.

Just as I was coming back I met Jack Laird under the birches. We sat down on the dyke and had a jolly chat. I felt quite like myself again after it.

Tuesday, Aug. 18, 1896
Park Corner, P.E. Island

I came up here Saturday afternoon. Saturday morning Edwin[1] and Alf Simpson called at our place. Ed has been teaching in his own school at Belmont[2] this

Uncle John C.'s house

---

1. Edwin Simpson (1872–1955), a second cousin (his grandmother was a Macneill, sister of LMM's grandfather). When leaving school teaching to study law (later changing to theology), Edwin, like Gilbert Blythe in *AGG*, helped the lady he favoured to find a teaching job.

2. A village on Malpeque Bay about 40 miles (64 km) from Cavendish.

summer but is going to college in October. I had applied for the school and he called to tell me I had got it. I was very glad for I have been feeling fearfully discouraged over my chances of getting any kind of a school.

Uncle Robert Sutherland's

Yesterday morning I went with Stella to her school, stayed there until noon and then went on to Uncle Robert Sutherland's. Jack was home for a flying visit and we had a jolly time. He expects to go to Ottawa soon to take a position there.

I stayed there until this afternoon and was sorry to leave. It is such a lovely place—an ideal country house, big, roomy and delightful; and they are all so nice.

Thursday, Aug. 20, 1896
Park Corner

I have just been having a siesta on the sofa and have wakened up feeling rather stupid. So I think I'll try to work it off by writing—sitting by the kitchen table on the old blue chest.[1] How very much like old times it seems!

Stella

George

Tuesday morning I went over to see Aunt Eliza. The call was more of duty than pleasure, for I am not frantically fond of Aunt Eliza. Yesterday afternoon George and Stella and I drove up to a picnic at Malpeque church—rather a tame affair. When we came home we drove down to Howatt's, where we found Lem and Ella MacLeod. Lem is home for his vacation now. We

---

1.   This appears in Montgomery's *The Story Girl*.

came home about nine and had an exhilarating drive, for we laughed and sang comic songs the whole way up. And after Stell and I went to bed we began talking events over and "making speeches" and I laughed until I ached.

Monday, Aug. 24, 1896
Park Corner

Stella and I were up to a choir practice at Pensie Cousins' Thursday night; and Saturday afternoon we were invited up to Mrs. Ramsay's and had a very nice time.

In the evening we went down to Captain George's. I fancy our reception and entertainment were rather cool—it is impossible to say why; so we did not outstay our welcome and came home early.

It is very dull here today, for Stella is away at her school and it is pouring rain. I have read everything that is readable in the house, including several "shilling shockings" by Bertha M. Clay[1] and others of that ilk, so you may realize to what straits I am reduced.

Friday, Aug. 28, 1896
Park Corner

Today I went with Aunt Mary to a picnic at French River and had a very nice time. Saw Lem and had a friendly talk with him. Then Mattie Sutherland and I had a lovely drive around the river shore.

Sunday, Aug. 30, 1896
Cavendish, P.E.I.

Saturday morning Lem arrived at Uncle John C.'s to spend the day and he and Stell and I had lots of fun. I expected George to take me home in the evening but he couldn't so Lem offered to bring me down. Stella came too and we had a very jolly drive. They went home today.

---

1. Bertha M. Clay (1836–84), author of cheap romantic fiction (called "dime novels" in the US), such as *A Mad Love* and *The Duke's Secret*.

Tuesday, Sept. 8, 1896

I had a delicious walk this morning through Lover's Lane. It was an ideal September day— sunless, dreamy mellow, with a low cricket symphony running through all like a faint minor accompaniment. The air was resinous with the breath of ripened fir and the woods were decked out with the advance flags of autumn's vanguard—here and there a flaming maple bough amid the tawny green.

Lover's Lane

Saturday, Sept. 19, 1896
Cavendish, P.E.I.

It is a regular autumn storm out tonight—pouring rain and blowing hard. And it *is* autumn! It is hard to realize it. Summer always goes so quickly. But I love the fall although the hints of coming decay are saddening enough.

I got a check for ten dollars from *Golden Days*[1] today for a short story. It was for and about boys. I like writing that kind of a story best and so far I have succeeded best with them.

Tuesday, Sept. 29, 1896

Today was an exquisite autumn day. Grandma and I were in town as I had a good deal of shopping to do.

Fannie Wise has taken the school here now and is boarding at Uncle John's.

Jack Laird was in tonight. He is home for vacation now and we had a discussion of professional woes.

I have written a good deal lately in the way of stories and poems. I love the work and it is my dearest dream to do something worth while in this line some day.

Thursday, Oct. 15, 1896

My poor little "den" is lonely and forlorn now—for I am leaving home tomorrow. Its walls are stripped and bare, my clock is gone, and the resultant

---

1. A weekly children's story paper from Philadelphia (1880–1907).

silence impresses me as something uncanny—as if some living presence had gone. I am all packed up and am very tired.

Fannie was over all night last night and we had a good "college" talk. What fun it is to compare old P.W.C. reminiscences!

Wednesday, Oct. 21, 1896
Belmont, P.E.I.

Friday afternoon Lu and I left for Kensington. It was showery and we had a rather chilly and disagreeable drive, but got up about four and stayed all night at Mrs. Pidgeon's. Saturday morning I took the train to Miscouche where Mr. Simpson,[1] Ed's father—known among the clan as "Sam" Simpson—met me.

Belmont is five miles from Miscouche and it is a rather pretty drive but the roads were mud to the axle. Belmont is a rather pretty place, owing to the bay scenery but I have a creepy, crawly presentiment that the natives as a general thing are not so pleasing.

I am stopping at Mr. Simpson's until I find a boarding place. They live too far from the school for me to board here. Mrs. Simpson—who was also a Cavendish Simpson and married her cousin as a matter of course—seems like a kind, mild woman but of a somewhat melancholy disposition.

Aunt Mary Lawson[2] is here on a visit, which makes me feel quite at home.

There are three boys home now—Fulton,[3] Alfred and Burton. None of them is very good-looking—Ed would seem to have absorbed the good looks of the family. Fulton is a perfect giant, with the most enormous hands I ever saw on a man. He is a Simpson to the back bone—the concentrated essence of Simpsonism. Alf seems to be the nicest of the three. He is jolly and not so "Simpsony" as the others.

I can't make much of Burt. He is another all-over Simpson but possesses one characteristic that is *not* of the Simpsons—he is very quiet.

There is one girl Sophy aged 15. She is the most lifeless mortal I ever came across and I can make absolutely nothing of her. I really don't think

---

1. Samuel Simpson (1835–1909), whose father had moved from Bayview to Belmont, halfway between Cavendish and Bideford.

2. Mary Lawson (1827–84), another great-aunt, younger sister of LMM's grandfather Alexander Macneill; a favourite relative and a repository of family stories. *The Golden Road* (1913) is dedicated to her memory.

3. Fulton (1877–1955) remained on the farm, as did Alfred (1874–52); Burton (1876–1914) became a minister; Sophie (1881–59) never married, and remained at home; another brother, Milton (1879–1952) became an English professor at Kalamazoo, MI.

she is quite normal. Aunt Mary says it is "too much of the one breed"[1] and I fancy she is right.

On Sunday it poured rain all the morning. After dinner it did hold up a little and Fulton proposed that we go up to the Presbyterian church at Central Sixteen,[2] about three miles away. We started and as soon as we did down came the rain again viciously. You can imagine what a nice agreeable drive we had!

Monday morning it was still pouring rain and Fulton drove me to the school. On the way we called in at a certain Simon Fraser's to see if I could board there.

It is a fairly decent-looking place about a quarter of a mile from the school. I can't say that I was greatly taken with the people though. All that I could extract from them was that they would consider the matter and let me know by the end of the week.

The school is situated on the bleakest hill that could be picked out. The view from it is magnificent, looking out over the headwaters of Richmond Bay.[3] The building is very small and only fairly well furnished.

A forlorn sight greeted me on my entrance. The trustees were putting up the pipe and the children were huddled around. I waited dismally and damply for what seemed an endless time; finally the pipe was up, a fire built; my papers signed and the trustee gone. I drew a long breath, and "hoed in."

I have taught three days now. Owing to the abominable weather the attendance has been small, not exceeding sixteen. In spite of the fact that the last teacher, Mr. Fraser, was considered a great gun I find the children terribly backward. They are a scrubby lot of urchins, too, and I don't believe I shall ever like them very well. Most of them come from rather poor homes.

There are a good many large girls going. One of them is Marie Monro, who is a new scholar, having only recently come to the settlement. She lives with her uncle, Dan Campbell, *the* trustee of the school, according to all accounts. Marie has passed the P.W.C. entrance and now intends taking up the Second Class work.[4] This doesn't suit me at all. There is more than enough work to be done in an ungraded school without doing work that is supposed to be done in P.W.C. However, there is no help for it. Marie impresses me as an odd girl—clever but eccentric. Her first greeting of me was "I shall expect a great deal of you for ever since I can remember you have been held up to me as a paragon."

---

1. Samuel Simpson had married a first cousin Eliza Simpson.
2. Central Lot 16 is a village inland from Bentinck Cove.
3. At the junction of the Grand River and Malpeque Bay.
4. Like LMM when she studied Greek, Marie Munro intended to bypass the Third Class work and enter PWC with advanced standing.

I must confess I found no reply to make to this—I was really too much amazed. I had never heard of her in my life and none of her connections that I can guess at ever knew me. So why or how or in what fashion they have held me up as a "paragon" to her is something I do not know and not likely ever shall know—for I certainly won't ask Marie.

This morning I enjoyed the pleasant sensation of being locked out of my own school. After my weary tramp of two miles I arrived there to find that the school was not open and after much investigation into the mysteries of cause and effect I found that the boy who was to make the fire had gone to Summerside and taken the key with him. The result was that we had to wait until nearly eleven while Willy Campbell went home for a duplicate key. We were nearly chilled stiff.

Thursday, Oct. 22, 1896
Belmont, P.E. Island

This morning I called at Mr. Fraser's determined to extract a decided answer from them one way or another. They have finally agreed to board me. I don't know how I shall like them but it is simply "Hobson's Choice"[1] for there is nowhere else to go. They keep the post-office, which will be a convenience at least.

There are only, two mails a week in this forsaken place. How letters cheer me up when one is a stranger in a strange land, grubbing away for a living in a dead-and-alive country district like this! I loved teaching in Bideford but I do not believe I shall *ever* like it here!

Sunday, Oct. 25, 1896
Belmont

This has been another terrible day of wind and rain. But it cleared up at night and Fulton, Sophy and I drove up to the Methodist church at Central. No minister turned up however, so we left and went to a house where three maidens of the name of Campbell live. The youngest of them will probably never see forty five again but they are very nice and kind, if a little odd.

I am to move to Fraser's tomorrow. I know I shall be lonesome. I only hope the people will turn out better than I expect.

---

1. No choice at all: from an anecdote in *The Spectator* (1712), about a liveryman named Hobson who made each customer take the horse nearest the door.

Tuesday, Oct. 27, 1896

Well, they have—though goodness knows there is plenty of room for improvement yet I am here—fairly settled down and trying to feel contented.

I came here from school last night, and as I am now a member of this family circle a word or two of description will not be out of place.

Imprimis, then, the oldest of "us" is an aged crone, well down the treacherous slope of the eighties, deaf, almost blind, wrinkled and tottering, who nevertheless, poor old soul, thinks herself in duty bound to entertain me by quavering remarks about the weather and "the bad cold going round." I wouldn't mind her if she would only leave me alone but when she persists in talking to me it makes me woefully nervous.

Then come mine host and hostess—Simon Fraser and wife. Simon and his fair bride, although only a few years married, are long past their first youth and, never very comely, have grown markedly less so with advancing years. Of Simon I have as yet seen little but I believe he is rather intelligent and has a leaning to scepticism which even good Mrs. Simon's rigid Presbyterian proclivities cannot straighten out. Mrs. Simon herself is "fair, fat and forty-odd." Her grammar is excruciating and her manners not at all highly polished. She acts as if she were dreadfully in awe of me, but she is very kind.

This promising couple have one daughter, Laura, a spoiled, blue-eyed little monkey of four.

Then there is Dan, Simon's brother, a confirmed old bachelor whose state I assuredly shall not attempt to change. Simon himself could never pose as an Apollo but compared to Dan he is "Hyperion to a Satyr."[1] Poor Dan's lack of manly beauty is, I understand, attributable to the fact that when he was a child his father threw a stump at him. Dan never recovered from the effects of this gentle missile. He is post-master and evidently considers the position one of great responsibility.

Then there is a Miss Fraser, yclept[2] Jessie, whose state of single blessedness has not prevented her from becoming a mother. She gravitates equally between here and the home of her daughter, Mrs. McLaurin.

At present I have for a room one of those detestable little "off-the-parlor"[3] places hardly big enough for a closet. There is no table in the room—nothing save a tiny washstand above which is suspended a looking glass in which I see myself as I devoutly hope others do *not*. My trunk swallows up all the

---

1. *Hamlet* I.ii.140.

2. Archaism: named (used mock-heroically).

3. A small ground-floor bedroom, usually reserved for an elderly person.

space left vacant by the bed and there is only one nail in the whole apartment on which I can hang anything.

I have my meals in solitary state in the sitting room. So far the table has been fair and, greatest of all boons, *clean*. Mrs. Simpson is a most estimable woman but she hasn't the faintest idea how to cook or serve.

My "den" has one redeeming feature. The view from the windows is exquisite. We are only about twenty yards from the bay shore and I can look out on a sheet of pearly shimmering water over to the misty purple coasts in the distance.

All this, however, did not prevent me from nearly freezing to death last night in bed. Just in time to save my life I remembered a fur coat—presumably Simon's—which I had noticed hanging on the parlor wall. I crawled out, got it, and spread it on the bed, and finally went to sleep under it.

Wednesday, Oct. 28, 1896
Belmont, P.E.I.

This morning I sat resolutely down to write some verses. I am not surrounded by a poetical atmosphere at present but I forced myself to do it. After tea I went up to Mr. Simpson's for a walk and found Fulton laid up with a severe pain in his side. He seemed very ill.

Sunday, Nov. 1, 1896
Belmont, P.E. Island

Have just got home from Mr. Simpson's to find everybody in bed—at eight o'clock! I went up there Friday evening and found the doctor there. Fulton has peritonitis and is very ill. I stayed up until tonight to help them. I was at Mr. Campbell's to tea Saturday night and enjoyed myself very much. May, the eldest daughter, is a very nice girl.

Wednesday, Nov. 4, 1896

I feel tired out tonight. Marie Monro makes the school work so heavy for me. She has so many sums she can't do and as I have absolutely not a scrap of time to do them in school I have to do them at home and I worked three hours over

Marie Monro

them this evening. But on the whole I rather like Marie in spite of her odd-ities. There is a clever streak in her. I don't object to *her* but to the extra work she makes—and goodness knows there is no need of extra work in an ungraded country school.

·I am trying to do a little literary work now but it is under such difficulties that I am half discouraged. I am "cabined, cribbed, confined,"[1]—and can never lay my hand conveniently on a thing. Moreover, I have to keep every-thing locked up as this family, so I have discovered, are given to ransacking my room and possessions when I am away. Blessed be he who invented locks and keys!

Saturday, Nov. 7, 1896

I have just come in from a walk to Gull Point. It cleared up perfectly this evening for a wonder and at sunset I ventured out. From my window I had looked at Gull Point every day—a long red spit running sharply out into the bay. Its tip was generally white with gulls. So I determined to go there.

It was almost dark when I left the house and hurried down over the long stretch of gray, marshy fields until at last I reached the point and walked out on its wave-rippled sand to the end.

The scene before me was a witching one. Away to the south were heaped sullen, purplish-gray masses of rain-clouds but the west was a clear lake of saffron and elfin green and ethereal blue, where floated the shallop of a thin, curved new moon slowly deepening from lustreless white to gleaming silver and then to burnished gold, and attended by one solitary, pearl-white star. The vast concave of sky above was of flawless violet and the wind-rippled water was of that perfect lustrous blue only seen in the mellow afterlight of a rare evening. Little crisp puffs of foam blew over the point like elfin things and the pools of water along the reedy shores gleamed like mirrors of pol-ished jacinth. Far out, dusky islets lay in the shadows of the clouds along the dim horizon, and a fresh wind was blowing down the bay.

I came home with a sense of refreshment and encouragement. I needed it, for this has been a dreary week—rain every day and nothing but mud and mist. I did not expect Belmont to be a lively place but I did not think it would be such a realm of dull hopeless isolation as it is. There are no nice people in it except Mr. Simpsons', Mr. Campbells' and Alan Frasers'. The rest are all rough, poor and illiterate.

I had a letter from Ed Simpson today asking me to correspond with him. He wrote quite a clever letter and I think I will agree to an occasional

---

1. Slightly misquoted from *Macbeth* III.iv.

correspondence as it will keep me in touch with college life and lend a little spice to this dead-and-alive sort of existence.

The *American Agriculturist*[1] has accepted a poem of mine.

Friday, Nov. 13, 1896
Belmont, P.E.I.

As usual this morning I wrote an hour before going to school. My brain is too weary for literary work after the wear and tear of school hours, so I give my morning freshness to it, scrambling reluctantly and shiveringly but resolutely out of bed at seven o'clock, just as the red sun is rising from the purple hills across the bay, and a long, dull-crimson banner falls across the water.

I dress as quickly as possible, arrange my box of a room, and sit down to lose myself for one happy hour.

When schooltime comes I put away all my fancies—as it were, locking them up and leaving them so utterly behind that I seem to be stepping into another life. But this week's toil is over and I am free for two blissful days.

Saturday, Nov. 14, 1896

I really have to come to you, old journal, for a little comfort. I am badly in need of some. By the way, would it not be a pat idea to call this my "grumble book" instead of my journal?

Never mind! I do all my grumbling here and it never gets outside your covers.

My especial cause of complaint tonight is that I'm half frozen and haven't been really warm for one minute today. It has been bitter cold, with a piercing wind that goes through this crazy old house as if it were made of paper, for not one of the doors or windows will shut squarely or tight. Cold seems to shrivel me right up. I can endure nearly everything else but if I get cold I am no good for anything, physically or mentally.

Friday, November 20, 1896
Belmont, P.E.I.

Another week put in, thanks be! I *did* manage to exist through last Saturday night. Sunday afternoon I fled up to Mr. Simpson's where I got thoroughly

---

1. Founded 1842, published in New York, a weekly magazine since 1894; published "Home from Town" in November 1896 and "Riding to Church" in February 1897.

warm for the first time in 48 hours. Yesterday evening I went up to Mr. Campbell's and stayed all night—*getting warm* again! That comprises my highest ideal of earthly bliss at present!

When I went to school this morning there was no fire on and when we did light it, it sulked the whole morning. It was bitterly cold. I am half frozen this very minute and I shrink from the thought of the coming night.

I cannot say that this family have improved very much from closer acquaintance. They do not seem to be in such awe of me now and in some ways this is all right but in others not. For one thing, we often have our meals together now and I do *not* like that. No, I am *not* overly fastidious. If you only knew how rough and uncouth and *dirty* the men are you would wonder how I could eat at all.

The food still continues to be fair, however, and if I could only be warm I would not grumble over the other unavoidable ills of my existence. Why, last Sunday night it snowed and my pillow was actually *covered with snow* that drifted through the window!

Tuesday, Nov. 24, 1896

I am going to scribble something—not because I have anything worth scribbling but merely because I haven't a single thing to read and am too tired to work. So, as I am decidedly lonesome, I shall pour out my woes to you.

I have not so many as usual however as I've had rather an easier time of it since my last entry. I went up to Mr. Simpson's Saturday evening and stayed there until Sunday night. Fulton is going about but is not able to go out yet. Sunday night Alf drove me home. Actually, that was the first sleigh-drive I've had since I left Bideford, for I was never in a sleigh the whole of last winter.

Thanksgiving. Nov. 26, 1896
Belmont, P.E.I.

Hum! I rather think I've put my foot in it; someway or other. At any rate, I feel rather uncomfortable—partly, it may be, from the effects of too much Thanksgiving goose and partly from the events of last night—although I am sure I am not to be blamed for them.

To go back a bit—on the Sunday night that Sophy and Fulton and I were up at the Miss Campbell's they asked him to bring me up some evening and he said he would and I said "all right." He took sick almost immediately afterwards and I never thought anything more of the matter.

The night Alf and I went up to the Methodist church we called in there and they asked *us* to go up some evening; and on Sunday night as we came home Alf said, "If the snow lasts suppose we pay that visit up to Campbell's on Wednesday night."

Of course I assented. I knew that Fulton was too ill to go out for weeks yet and it seemed to me a very unimportant thing who took me up. And besides, Alf and I had been invited on our own account, quite independent of anybody else.

Last night Alf called for me on his way home from Summerside and I went on down to his place with him. Fulton was all right when I went in, but when he found out where I was going—for of course I told his mother when she asked me to take my wraps off—he went into the room and shut the door. Aunt Mary came out and told me he had gone in, mad as a hatter, and made quite a scene, saying very nasty things to Alf.

Naturally, I felt horribly uncomfortable and was glad to get away. We drove up to the Campbell's and found they were not at home. So we drove back. Alf wanted me to go home with him for Thanksgiving but of course I didn't feel like it after Fulton's behaviour, so I came home. Thanksgiving has been a dull, gloomy day and I've been dreadfully lonesome. What a wretched old hole Belmont is! What a difference between it and Bideford!

Wednesday, Dec. 2, 1896
Belmont, P.E.I.

I am frozen up once more and remember you in my hour of tribulation. Last Saturday afternoon I was invited up to Mr. Campbell's and stayed all night. Sunday I ventured down to Mr. Simpson's, with no little trepidation.

Fulton was very stiff at first and also very doleful because he is not getting well very fast. However, I acted just as usual and he eventually thawed out.

When I left Monday morning Alf waylaid me at the front gate to ask me to go up to see the Campbell girls on Tuesday evening. So we went and had a woefully dull time. I was nearly frozen coming home and the roads were awfully rough.

To-day was *beastly* cold—down to zero and a bitter wind blowing. I am half ice now and must go and warm my poor little toes before I become utterly defunct from suspended circulation.

Saturday Morning, Dec. 5, 1896
Belmont, P.E.I.

Well, I have managed to exist so far and as the cold snap is about over for this time I have hopes of surviving after all. But I assure you I've had a rare week of it.

This has been my daily programme.

Get up at seven and contrive to dress and do my hair by dint of running out every few minutes to thaw my numbed fingers at the fire. Then eat my breakfast, shivering all the time, and next, arrayed in jacket and gloves—for my room is too cold to endure it otherwise—make my bed and snug up my den.

This done and once more thawed out, I sit down and write till school time, when I muffle up and scud to school in the teeth of a biting wind.

After school I come home, get warm, and have a *comparatively* comfortable time until nine, when I begin to shiver again in anticipation of going into my ice-box of a bedroom and crawling into a cold bed.

However, after innumerable shrinkings of the flesh I do get in, get warm, and finally sleep, thus ending the day.

Yesterday evening May Campbell and I went up to Allan Fraser's. They are rather nice—as people go in Belmont anyhow.

Monday, Dec. 7, 1896
Belmont, P.E.I.

Saturday afternoon I set off[1] reluctantly enough to make another promised visit. I had asked Sophy Simpson to go to Mr. Lyle's with me. To go anywhere with Sophy is bad enough but to go alone to Lyle's was worse, so of two evils I chose the least.

We got there in due time. It was a lovely day—a stray bit from our lost Indian summer—but the walk was so long that I was tired out. And as for the afternoon I never put in a more doleful time. Mrs. Lyle is one of those women who speak in a wailing dolorous voice—you are nervously expecting her to burst into tears every moment. She gives you the impression that life is indeed to her a vale of tears, and that a smile, never to speak of a laugh is a waste of muscle and time truly reprehensible.

Her daughters are all painfully quiet. Sophy is the reverse of vivacious, and although it is very seldom I cannot make some kind of small talk, yet today I was undeniably stuck and you can imagine what a lively time we had.

---

1. In the typescript of the Journal, LMM changes this to "I went."

Burt and Alf came for us in the evening and I went to Mr. Simpson's to spend Sunday.

As I slept with Aunt Mary I found out a few amusing things. Among others, Fulton has taken a terrible spite against Alf—we will not inquire the reason?—and moreover is terribly cranky and childish. He does not seem to be getting much better and I suppose his slow recovery is trying to him. Anyhow, I'm completely disgusted with him of late. No gentleman would act as he has done.

Sunday was a dull, quiet day. There was preaching at the Methodist church in the evening and Alf asked me to go. As I was honestly afraid Fulton would make a public scene if I went alone with Alf I got Sophy to go too, though Alf was anything but pleased at the idea. When Alf drove me home after service he told me he was coming over, weather permitting, to take me to a concert at St. Eleanor's next Tuesday evening. I was delighted for it seems to me that I have been buried alive for the past seven weeks. I simply hate Belmont and all that pertains to it.

Wednesday, Dec. 9, 1896
Belmont, P.E.I.

It really seems to me that I never was so tired in all my life before. I feel just fagged out, hopeless, and dispirited. I used to work hard enough in Bideford school but it wasn't a circumstance to Belmont.

Yesterday Edmund Campbell began going to school, thereby just doubling my already too great amount of work. He is going to study for the entrance. He is not far advanced and does not seem very bright. If Marie were not also going to school I could get along fairly well but as it is I shall have a winter of downright drudgery.

Alf came along about four last night and I forgot all my tribulations for the time being when we were finally on the road. The evening was perfect—calm, slightly frosty, clear as a bell, with a wealth of delicate aerial colour in earth and sky and water; and the roads were splendid. We went right into Summerside[1] and it is such a pretty drive.

And oh, it was so delightful to get out of Belmont—for awhile, to get back into the world, to realize that there were places after all where existence was not an unvarying treadmill. I have almost felt as if I were simply atrophying away here but my jaunt last night has convinced me that there is plenty of life left in me yet.

---

1. Second largest city in PEI. Presumed to be the model for the city where Anne served as a school principal.

When we left Summerside we went out to St. Eleanor's. The concert was A1 and very enjoyable. Then we had a delightful drive home through the calm, star-lit night, and got back to Belmont about 11.30.

Then, of course, my troubles began again. Firstly, when I came in, numb with cold, do you think I could find a solitary match? Not I! And as I did not like to wake anyone up I was compelled to go to bed in the dark, cold and hungry and cross.

I thought I should never get to sleep. I was so cold—and when I did it seemed no time till I was awakened up at seven and had to tumble out in the dark. I got up and after breakfast I wrote two verses of "po'try"—which, seeing how wretchedly out of sorts I felt, I consider a genuine exhibition of modern heroism!!!

Then I went to school in a pouring rain, up to my knees in slush, for it had snowed in the night. There were thirty one children in school and what with them and Marie's and Edmund's classes I had to "hustle" until when school came out I felt like something that had been dead a thousand years and had just been resurrected.

Well, I'm going to read some magazines now and forget all my perplexities and tribulations, roaming in an ideal world.

Monday, Dec. 14, 1896
Belmont, P.E.I.

Yesterday morning I went up to Mr. Simpson's—per invitation, I may say, as I don't go there unless I *am* invited. Fulton is ill again with pleurisy and he is simply an awful crank. His mother has a dreadful time with him, and indeed the whole household comes in for a share. Aunt Mary generally lets me into the sidelights of the subject.

Hitherto, Fulton has kept his crankiness pretty well out of sight when I am there but this time he didn't. I can make a good deal of allowance for the effect his tedious illness and long confinement indoors has had on him, but still he need not be so absurdly unreasonable and sore.

He is simply furious with Alf and suspicious of everybody and everything. Poor Alf cannot drive away on the most innocent errand without Fulton rushing up to the garret window to see where he is going; and if Alf drives in the general direction of Fraser's—Fraser's house itself cannot

Aunt Mary Lawson

be seen—then the Simpson household pays the penalty for the rest of the day. I suppose if Fulton were well he would not behave in such an idiotic manner. I am sorry for his mother. Aunt Mary said Fulton told her (Aunt M.) that he "didn't care whether he got well now or not, he had been so wounded and disappointed." Pray, does Fulton imagine that because I talked pleasantly to him, drove to church once with him and his sister, and promised to visit a couple of harmless old maids with him, that I was bound to him for the rest of my life, to the exclusion of all other men, brothers or non-brothers. He surely can't be so ridiculous—and yet what else has he to complain of?

But I know this—I am out of all manner of patience with him and henceforth when I am there I shall simply ignore him unless he behaves with some decency.

Thursday, Dec. 17, 1896
Belmont, P.E.I.

Yesterday and to-day have been bitter cold and blowing a hurricane.

Yesterday evening I was invited up to James Simpson's to tea. His son Judson is married to Myra Arnett, a cousin of Edith England. I met her in Bideford: they live with the old folks.

I wonder how some people live at all—they seem to get so little out of life. It must be a bare, starveling existence for a vast number.

James Simpson seems to be the black sheep of the family. At least, his other brothers don't seem to have much to do with him. I think he is an aggravated crank—though to be sure they are all that more or less. He married beneath him, and his family are all very rough and their housekeeping is ditto. I did not enjoy my visit at all and was heartidly glad when I got away.

Saturday, Dec. 19, 1896
Belmont, P.E.I.

Here I am—stranded! I had intended to go up to Mr. Campbell's this evening but a rainstorm has washed away my plans. I am all the more to be pitied because I hasted to-day and did all I had to do so that I might go gadding with a clear conscience—and now I have nothing to do and—worst of all—nothing to read. So I have to fall back upon my usual *dernier resort*—scribbling.

I gave my "den" its regular Saturday "sorting out" this morning. It is such a little hole of a place; but I have got it fixed up a bit and a few pictures pinned around the walls to gladden my eyes in my solitude.

How I love pictures. But I wish you could see some that adorn the walls of this mansion! There is one abomination in particular hanging on the wall of the sitting room that fairly gives me the nightmare. It is a "chromo" of the most aggravated description and if I go suddenly insane some day "know all men by these presents" that it is that picture which has caused it.

Monday Dec. 21, 1896
Belmont, P.E.I.

Something dreadful will really happen to me soon if this cold snap continues! I verily believe the *air* in my room is frozen!

But "grin and bear it"—"summer *will* come again"—and meanwhile my "pedal extremities" as Norman Campbell used to say, are icy cold, and out in the kitchen Simon is moaning most piteously with a sprained back. Truly "this world's a wilderness of woe"—but it isn't half bad in spots after all.

I spent yesterday at Mr. Simpson's as usual. Milton, the youngest son, is home from P.W. College. He is a nice little fellow. Charlotte Macneill of Bayview is also there—who is neither little nor nice!

Poor Fulton is in a pitiable condition. He is again laid up—this time with an abscess in his side; the doctor says it will be two months before he can stir out. He wasn't quite so cranky with me this time—indeed, he was very nice but seemed extremely dispirited. This softened my heart towards him of course and I was also as nice as Nature permits me to be. I really want to be friends with him, for it is not pleasant to be "out" with a member of any family where one visits often. On the other hand, I am afraid to be as friendly with him as I'd like to be lest it again inspire him with hopes or wishes that are quite impossible of fulfilment. I think it was really a special mercy of Providence for me that Fulton fell ill so soon after I came here. If he had not and if I had gone driving about with him as I would most likely have done his mad infatuation might have deepened into an intense passion, and I tremble to think what might have happened when he found that I could never care for him. William Clark of Cavendish went insane and hanged himself—it was said because my mother would have nothing to do with him. And Fulton Simpson with his intensity of feeling and lack of ordinary self-control impresses me as a man who might do anything in some overwhelming spasm of disappointment on thwarted passion.

It was bitterly cold in school to-day. I dread the night inexpressibly. I do not sleep at all well at nights now and I think it is because the room is so cold.

Monday, Dec. 28, 1896
Belmont, P.E.I.

Well, I've been having a lovely time—the old schoolday adjective of "scrumptious" if the only one which will fully express it. Of course I've been out of Belmont to have it!

Edith England invited me to spend Christmas with her and I accepted if she could send anyone for me. I knew there was no one she could get except Lou D. so I told her she might send him and he arrived along at 11.30 on Wednesday. We started for Bideford at two. It was cold but the roads were good, so we got on finely. Lou was nice but very quiet. When we reached Tyne Valley the road began to get interesting. The old Valley and the road up to Mr. Millar's all seemed so natural and it was real nice to be on it again. We reached Mr. England's about four and Edith and I had an ecstatic reunion.

They were going to have a concert at Ellerslie that night and I was to recite. The concert was merely a Sunday School affair and was rather flat but I had an exciting time meeting old friends and pupils. Then Edith and I went home and talked all night.

The next afternoon Lou took us for a drive on the ice. We had a splendid spin and called at Mr. Williams' on our way home.

Christmas night there was a service in the church. Lou came home with us and came in. The poor boy hasn't got over his folly yet. He was very quiet all the evening and seemed dispirited. I was very sorry for him but I could do nothing better for him than treat him with merely courteous friendliness.

In the morning I went down to see Mr. Millar's and in the afternoon Lou came out and took Edith and me in to see his mother. As we passed the school I ran in to see the old room. It was the only thing in Bideford that seemed strange to me for I have grown used to the much smaller Belmont room.

In the evening Clifford and Luther Williams and Wesley MacKinnon came in and we had a very jolly time. Wesley is an East Bidefordian who is home from the States on a visit. He was not around in my time. Edith seems to be carrying on a very marked flirtation with him, in spite of her engagement to Bayfield Williams. She told me all about it. She is really quite infatuated with Wes—who is not at all her social equal—but realizes that he is impossible for anything serious. He is crazy about her; so, in Bayfield's absence, they are snatching what they dare of the sweets of love-making. It would be a dangerous game for some types but Edith will not go too far. She will give Wesley a kiss or two and some walks and drives together and they will have a rather tragic parting scene when he goes back to the U.S. Both will forget and Bayfield will never know. That seems to be Edith's way of looking at it. Not that Bayfield deserves anything better. He is a notorious flirt himself. What I cannot understand is how Edith can care at all for a man like Wes MacKinnon.

Sunday was a bitterly cold day with the air full of flying frost. Lou and I started for Belmont in the evening. It was just sunset, clear, calm and crisp, delightful for driving; but as poor Lou seemed very low-spirited and I was dull over going back to Belmont we did not have a very exhilarating drive.

Edith had told me that Lou had been drinking hard—something he never used to do. So I twisted up my courage to speak of it. He denied it but in an evasive way that rather increased than banished my suspicions.

He said also that his love for me had ruined his life. I cried, foolishly enough, and told him he would think differently by and by.

"I might if you were any ordinary girl," he said, "but I shall never meet anyone like you again,"

"You will meet someone far better suited to you," I said, a little impatiently—for there is a certain something about Lou when he begins to bewail his fate that disgusts me. His lack of birth and breeding betrays itself then.

We reached Belmont about 7.30. Lou stayed all night and went home this morning, while I betook myself to my school. I must say it ground hard to return to drudgery. Visiting is all very well while it lasts but the day of reckoning is sure to come.

Wednesday, Dec. 30, 1896

What can be going to happen? Yesterday and to-day have been deliciously mild and April-like. I have been working slavishly in school of late for I am going to have the semi-annual examination tomorrow. It won't be much of an affair, I suppose, for I have no programme. I simply had not the time or strength to prepare one. I don't expect many will come as I believe they never turn out well here.

I was up to Mr. Simpson's this evening. Fulton has had his side lanced and seems much better in some ways.

In the evening Alf, Milton, Charlotte, Sophy and I all went up to Mr. Campbell's. Sadie and Olive Fraser were there and we had the merriest evening imaginable playing "Apes and Angels."

It was eleven when we got back to Mr. S.!—a highly respectable hour. I should say. But Fulton seemed to regard it as a terribly improper one and this morning aired his views on it, asserting that every house should be locked up for the night at ten. I rather pity his future family.

1897

Saturday, Jan. 2, 1897

Can it really be '97? The century is growing old—only three more years for it to live.

Thursday afternoon I had my exam and got it well over. After school I made up my report—a tedious piece of business—and then I went to a party at Caleb Lee's. We had a rather nice time, although of course in that strictly Baptist household there was no dancing.

We broke up about one and of course as soon as I got home my troubles began. I was chilled to the bone when I went to bed; I remained so all night and didn't get a wink of sound sleep the whole time.

New Year's day was glorious—clear, sparkling, sunny. I was invited up to Mr. Campbell's for dinner and had an enjoyable time.

After dinner I went down to Mr. Simpson's for we had planned a drive over the ice to Hamilton. Alf, Milton, Charlotte and I were going. When I turned in at the gate Aunt Mary suddenly appeared at the front door and beckoned me in that way with a mysterious expression. She towed me into the parlor and shut the door as softly as if I had been dynamite. Then she told me in a conspirator's whisper that they didn't want Fulton to know I was going with the crowd. He is sick again and worse than ever, and she and Mrs. Simpson had decided to intercept me at the gate and smuggle me out again by the front way when the pung had driven around out of view of the kitchen windows. This proceeding was carried out and I suppose it saved Fulton an afternoon of jealous agony.

We had a nice drive over the bay. The ice was in splendid condition, all sparklingly blue and white, and the fair, cold expanse of the bay was gemmed with dusky purple islets, like jewels on the breast of a fair woman, and rimmed in by misty violet coasts. We enjoyed every minute of the time and reached our destination. Mr. William Simpson's—about 4.30. Charlotte stayed over but the boys and I came home at dark.

I slept with Aunt Mary and we had a good talk. They are almost worn out with Fulton. He is simply intolerable—sulky, jealous, meddlesome, querulous. In fact, I really believe his illness and sufferings have affected his mind or he would never say the things he does. He has the wildest, most unearthly look about him and keeps tormenting his mother by telling her that he doesn't want to get better and won't try to. He never speaks to Alf except go quarrel with or result insult him. He was very nasty to me this time, too—this morning I mean, when he discovered I had been to Hamilton. But I took his nastiness very coolly. He must learn that that sort of thing does not worry me, when I have done no wrong to him.

Monday, Jan. 4, 1897
Belmont, P.E.I.

Well, this *is* a "spell of weather!" I have been grumbling so long at the cold that for very shame's sake I dare not turn around now and grumble at the rain, mist and mud! Otherwise—but I will heroically refrain!

Saturday was perfect—*overhead*—mild as May, with misty horizons and the bay ice as glare as glass. But *underfoot*—well, the less said about that the better for my resolution!

There was preaching in the Baptist church yesterday morning for the first time since I came. Mr. Baker, an evangelist, has come to hold meetings here. On principle, I do not approve of "revivals," but anything is welcome to vary the deadly monotony of life here. He preached twice yesterday. I have to be organist—much against my will. But I wanted to oblige Mr. and Mrs. Simpson—or rather, the latter, for I do not care very much for "Sam." The Simpson flavour is so woefully strong in him. But I do really like Mrs. Simpson and she has been very kind to me.

I was up there to dinner yesterday. It is an understood thing that I spend Sunday there, and I should really die of loneliness here if I didn't. Besides, as long as Aunt Mary is there it is a great pleasure to go, although the fact that two of the boys are on bad terms because of me always makes me feel uncomfortable. And I never know what outburst may come from Fulton. He continues poorly and cranky, but seems to be slowly gaining.

To-day was rainy and muggy and horrible. I nearly got swamped going to school.

Went to "meeting" tonight. Simon hitched up a cart and took us all—not a fashionable conveyance at all but a perfect boon to a weary "schoolmarm" who comes home from school tired to death, with small taste for turning out again in the dark to walk half a mile through mud and water ankle deep.

Monday, Jan. 11, 1897

Yesterday morning I went down from church to Mr. Simpson's as usual. Fulton does not seem very well yet and is too cranky to live. I had no pleasure in my visit.

To-day was a perfect one and tonight was glorious—too glorious by half. Mark my words, we will pay for it very soon.

Saturday, Jan. 16, 1897
Belmont, P.E.I.

My prophetic remarks came true. Last Tuesday morning we awoke to see a regular "old-fashioned blizzard" on the rampage. There was no school and no meeting at night. But Wednesday, Thursday, and Friday nights we had full meetings, to all of which we went in Simon's "one-hoss" wood-sleigh.

After dinner to-day I togged myself up and set out for pastures new. There is a certain Mrs. MacGregor who lives in Belmont a short distance up what is called—for reasons deponent knoweth not—the "Tory" Road. The said Mrs. MacGregor is a widow and, having been a "schoolmarm" before her plunge into matrimony, when her hubby died, she turned her eyes back wistfully to the green—where far-off-pastures of professionalism, and betook herself again to the cultivation of young and shorting ideas in what is known in Belmont vernacular as "the Sou'-Wes' School," coming home to her farm every Friday night.

Recently she has had a cousin visiting her—a Mrs. MacDougall, a young widow of about 30, nice and jolly, with whom I have become quite friendly. So Widow No. 1 invited me up this afternoon to have tea with widow No. 2.

Hence it was that I started off this shimmering blue afternoon and invaded the solitary precincts of the Tory Road. Most of the way led through a thick growth of young spruce and cedar. The woods were placidly still and calm. The thick ranks of young saplings were snow-laden and white, save where a warm golden shaft of light from the low-hanging sun pierced through, tinging the dark bronze-green of the spruces and the grayish-green streamers of moss with vivid beauty.

I had a pleasant afternoon and went to the meeting at night. It was a glorious moonlight night all misty with white frost.

Monday, Jan. 18, 1897
Belmont, P.E.I.

Yesterday was a dream—a poem—a symphony—a what you will so that your definition expresses the ethereal revel of colour, the thrilling glory and splendor of the wonderful day that came in roseate and golden across frost-rimed hill and crept away at night in an elf-land of moonlight.

I went down to Mr. Simpson's after morning service. After I came down from taking off my wraps Fulton was glaring out of the room window.

I said amiably,

"How are you getting on, Fulton?"

He threw a black glance over his shoulder and grunted surlily,
"I'm improving."

I shrugged my shoulders, exchanged a smile with Aunt Mary, and betook myself to more congenial company in the parlor. I did not speak to Fulton again, nor did he speak to me, although he watched me with such cat-like and stealthy vigilance that it made me nervous. As far as health goes he does seem to be "improving," but the same can't be said regarding his manners.

We went to afternoon service and there was quite a number to tea at Mr. Simpson's afterward. Then we went to service in the evening. Alf drove me with his wild gray mare "Maud" (*not* a namesake!) Fulton did not speak when I said a general "good night" but as we drove out of the yard I saw him silhouetted in the lighted kitchen window peering out—no doubt trying to discover whether Alf and I were alone or were properly chaperoned by Sophy. Evidently he could not make it out, for when we drove down the lane in front of the house he was pasted up against the parlor window and must have sprinted through the hall with considerable celerity to get there so quickly.

The church was so packed tonight that I had to sit on the organ stool the whole time and it nearly broke my unfortunate back.

Today it poured rain all day and things were on a rampage of disagreeableness.

Monday, Jan. 25, 1897

Talk about the society for the prevention of cruelty to animals! There ought to be a society for the prevention of cruelty to school teachers, especially in the matter of icy rooms, and cold schools. I wonder that every drop of blood in my veins hasn't turned to ice long ago. I think it must be getting very thin.

I have been rushed off my feet this week. The meetings are still going merrily on and seem likely to do so for an indefinite time. I'm getting tired of them for a steady thing. I have to go every night, as I am organist, and I'm getting behind with my own work.

Last Monday we had a huge thaw and rain. But Tuesday morning there was a change—well, rather! The mercury down to 25 below zero is no joke, and that is what it was all Tuesday and Tuesday night.

I got to school without being frozen but some of the children were not so lucky and we had such a time getting them thawed out—the poor, half-clad little souls.

It was too cold for a meeting at night, so we hugged the fire until ten o'clock and then I crawled shrinkingly off to bed.

Thursday I had a letter from *The Ladies' World*[1] accepting a poem called "In Haying Time."

Saturday morning was fine and pleasant and Alf and I went in to Summerside. We had a nice drive and it was a treat to see a place where people *lived*.

Wednesday, Jan. 27, 1897
Belmont, P.E.I.

I have been through all sorts of adventures of late. "Listen to my tale of woe."[2]

Tuesday evening Alf and I started over the bay to attend a meeting of the Grand Division at Port Hill. It was rather frosty and windy, but we got over to Will Montgomery's all right. There we found Fulton, William Simpson of Hamilton, and my especial pet among the Simpsons, Arthur Simpson of Cavendish, who had all gone over in the morning. No Grand Division, you understand, could possibly get along without the Simpsons.

Speaking of Fulton—he really seems to be getting quite well. Monday afternoon he came to the school after Sophy—just poked his head inside the door and called "Sophy"—didn't deign to notice my existence at all. So I was expecting to find him more grumpy even than usual if that was possible; but—perhaps owing to the general effect of company, or maybe not wishing to make an exhibition of himself before my relatives and his own—he was positively amiable and even seemed able to endure Alf's presence calmly. I do hope he has come to his senses at last.

At the hall I fell in with Edith England and Lou Dystant, besides several other Bideford people, and I had lots of fun.

After the concert we all went up to Will's for supper—and a good satisfying Montgomery meal it was! We left about eleven—three sleighs of us. Fulton stayed over. It was fine and calm all the way down to the ice but we had hardly driven a mile on the lattern when suddenly there came up a blinding snow squall. In the twinkling of an eye we were enveloped in a white whirl so thick that we could not see from one bush to another.

We couldn't keep the road, though we hunted for the bushes for nearly half an hour. We got completely bewildered and at last, having driven long enough to get to Belmont twice over we pulled up to hold a council of war.

How those three men did howl and yell through the storm, all talking at once! Each one had a different opinion and plan, and each was positive he

---

1. Illustrated five-cent magazine, founded 1897 in New York; discontinued 1904.
2. A popular college song (1884) by Hubard Smith.

was right. When Simpsons disagree who shall decide? As they couldn't agree on any plan of action we just stayed where we were for half an hour to see if it would clear off. Alf held the buffalo around me so that I did not feel the cold so badly.

Finally, as the squall continued as thick as ever, we decided to take the wind in our faces and start. *If* the wind had not changed—a rather momentous "if"—this would take us across to Cape Malpeque. *If* it had—well, we might drive straight into the channel.

In no very long time, however, we reached land. At first the men thought it was Cape Malpeque but after driving along it for sometime they found it wasn't, but couldn't make out where we were.

At last we caught a faint glimpse of a light away over the fields and decided to steer for it. There was no use in looking for a road—we just had to make one. We turned slap up the bank, tore a gap in a fence and drove across two fields. The going here was fair, but the next field was a swampy one where the sod had been heaved up into huge hummocks by the frost and however we got through that *awful* place without smashing everything up is more than I can tell. I expected every moment to hear the runners go smash. I was half frozen and wholly frightened but I shook with laughter to hear Arthur Simpson shouting without any cessation, "Where are you taking us, Alfy? Where are you taking us, Alfy?" As he was well in advance of us and tearing madly onward it didn't look as if "Alfy" was taking him anywhere! The horses were terrified by the bumping of the sleighs and were neither to hold nor bind.

But in the end we did get through and the next thing we struck was a dyke. The other two horses went over all right but "Maud" balked and jumped and finally kicked. Our traces broke and I had to scramble out and wait while Alf fixed them and lifted the sleigh over the dyke—still in a blinding white of snow. I got chilled to the marrow but eventually we got underway again and reached that blessed house in ten more minutes.

Where do you think we were? At John MacArthur's at Fourteen, not half a mile from where we started. The wind had changed with a vengeance! And all the time we had thought we were going straight for Belmont!

We had to stay there all night. I didn't sleep a wink—I was too tired and cold, and besides the accommodations were very poor. We started early in the morning and soon got home not much the worse of our adventure.

I almost wish these meetings would come to an end, for I have got fearfully behindhand with my work. Still, they enliven up the place a bit. Two or three a week would be all right.

Baker[1] did not speak tonight. A Mr. MacLeod did and he is a narrow, uncultured fanatic of an intensely disagreeable type.

Saturday, Jan. 30, 1897

Well, this morning something happened. Mrs. Simon, with an important air said that the upstairs room—that long-promised, almost despaired—of room—was ready for me and I might move up at once if I liked.

You may be sure I *did* like. If there is one particular spot on this planet I detest it is that ice-box where I have been sleeping ever since I came here.

The upstairs room is a fairly nice one as rooms go in Belmont. It is a good size, warmed by a pipe, has a table, a clothes closet and a mantel piece. I spent this morning "flitting" and by noon I had everything as neat and cosy as possible. I feel like a new creature.

Tuesday, Feb. 2, 1897
Belmont, P.E.I.

Yesterday I received a letter which surprised me more than any I ever received in my life—a letter from Edwin Simpson. I have written him two or three times since he asked me to correspond with him and have received three letters from him—quite interesting and clever ones, somewhat tediously involved in style.

Yesterday's letter was a long one of several closely written pages. It began innocently enough with comments on my last letter, college news, and an account of his visit to Halifax during the holidays etc., etc., down to the middle of the 5th page. Then he suddenly broke off abruptly with the statement that he felt impelled to tell me why he had asked me to correspond with him—that he had intended to tell me at Xmas had not eye-trouble compelled him to go to Halifax instead.

"Then," he wrote, "I could have told you personally what I now feel I must tell you. It is that I love you."

I was so amazed that I nearly dropped the letter. Ed went on to say that he had thought of me ever since our first meeting and that our old friendship of five years ago in Park Corner was still fresh in his memory—that he never forgot the impression although circumstances threw us apart so widely; and although he made no effort to meet me it was because he felt that it would be

---

1. Baptist evangelist who had been preaching at the Grand Division revival meetings.

absurd for a person situated as he was to make any such advances. But now he "sees his way clear into 'life's field of action'," and his "former fancy has deepened into an uncontrollable passion."

I don't seem able to believe that this has really happened. Other men have loved me and I have always guessed it long before they told me but it never entered my mind that Edwin Simpson cared anything for me. We have been almost strangers for the past four years. In the old Park Corner days our little "affair" meant nothing to me—I did not like him as well as Lem then. Even when he asked me last fall to correspond with him I thought it was merely because he knew I could write pleasant amusing letters and give him all the home news. His mother is his only other correspondent here and *her* letters certainly can't be amusing or gossipy!

Edwin Simpson

I must answer his letter tomorrow although I don't fancy the task at all. I can only make the one answer for I don't love him. I've had no opportunity to learn to care for him.

When he was at our place this summer I found him interesting and thought he had very much improved. But I never thought of anything more. I *might* learn to care for him. He is a handsome fellow, clever and educated; our tastes in many respects are very similar, and *if* I cared for him it would be a very suitable arrangement.

I know my family would not approve—at least, grandfather and grandmother. They hate all the Simpsons; grandfather is rabid against second cousins marrying; and Ed is a Baptist. For my own part, neither of these considerations would weigh against a real affection. But there is no use flying in the face of your family for anything less.

Wednesday, Feb. 3, 1897
Belmont, P.E.I.

I determined to stay home from the meeting tonight in order to get time to answer Ed's letter. I wonder if Mr. Baker would consider it a valid excuse!

I told Ed frankly that his letter had surprised me greatly and that I certainly did not love him, never having thought about him in that way at all. I said I *might* learn to care for him if he were willing to wait awhile and take the chances but if he wanted a final answer at once it would have to be "no."

I'm very glad the letter is written for it wasn't an agreeable task at all.

Sunday, Feb. 7, 1897

The meetings are still going on. Baker is evidently determined not to leave a sinner in Belmont. Everybody will have to "get good"—to quote Mrs. Simon's cultured phrase!

I have no use for Mr. Baker after last night. In the "after meeting" he came out with a narrow, bigoted preachment on immersion.[1] I was secretly furious. Week after week I've gone up there and played the organ for him and I consider it an insult that he should say such things in my presence. Evidently he *did* feel some small pin-prick of shame for when he concluded he cast a rather deprecating smile at me and said "Of course I suppose you are all Baptists here. If you are not, you ought to be."

I gave no answering smile. I looked as dour as my Scottish Presbyterian great-grandfather himself could have done. If Baker thought he was addressing only Baptists, why speak on immersion at all? *They* did not need to be convinced of that.

I went to the meeting again tonight, however, for reasons of my own quite unconnected with Baker or Baptism, and Alf and I got a fearful upset coming home. Just where the road turns in at Gamble's gate there is a bad slew and then a snowdrift. We were going at a terrific rate and when we slewed against the drift the sleigh tipped neatly over and spilled Alf and me and the furs in a heap. It was a fortunate thing that sedate old "Lady" was in the shafts and not that harum-scarum "Maud," or dear knows what would have happened. Alf and I scrambled to our feet to the tune of derisive yells from a crowd of "kids" behind us, righted the cutter, got in, and drove off, the whole affair having passed in ten seconds.

Saturday Morning, Feb. 13, 1897
Belmont, P.E.I.

This week seems to have been conjured away by magic, it has gone so fast. Wednesday morning Edgar Lyle[2] called at the school to ask if I would care to go up to the Central church that night to meeting. I would have much preferred not to, for I do not like Mr. MacLeod but I thought it would look badly to refuse to go to my own church, so I went.

It was bitterly cold. Edgar Lyle is a bore—a sentimental goody-goody chap. He wanted me to go again tomorrow night but I said "no" plainly.

---

1. Baptist conversion ceremony entailing submerging the whole person in water.
2. Edgar Rochford Lyle (1875–1958) came from Indian River, PEI.

Aunt Mary has gone away and I miss her horribly. Most of the pleasure in going to Mr. Simpson's is gone for me.

Wednesday, Feb. 17, 1897

Monday night there was no service here so Bert, Alf and I went up to Central. Mr. McLeod had a magic lantern—the latest dodge for revival meetings!— and the place was packed. His pictures were quite wonderful—especially one showing the heart of the unconverted man—a large red affair sliced open down the middle and filled with a lively assortment of snakes, hyenas, wolves and other unpleasant creatures. If the austere Teacher of Galilee had seen it and heard McLeod's hysterical yelps about it, I wonder what He would have thought.

Tuesday night Alf and I went to a "Birthday Social" in S'Side. We had a delightful drive and the social was rather enjoyable. We had a wild drive home for Alf and Woodland Simmons raced all the way. Woodland and Alf have both been "converted" through Baker's ministrations, and the former testifies vociferously every night. But neither seems reconciled to be beaten in the matter of horse-flesh because of this. "In honour preferring one another" doesn't hold good when your favourite trotter is in question. For my part I expected every moment to be tipped out, skimming over those fields of glare ice and missing the other sleigh by a hairsbreadth in the narrow gaps.

This evening Mr. Baker held his farewell service. He goes from here to Cavendish—where he will find a far less impressionable crowd, if I mistake not.

Alf and I had a glorious spin afterwards.

Tuesday, Feb. 23, 1897

To-day was very stormy. There were only 16 pupils in school and it seemed like play. But I simply detest teaching here. It is such hard work and most of the children are stupid, ignorant and rough. This is not surprising, considering the kind of homes they come from. It is all so different from Bideford where I had such pleasure in my work.

To-night I wrote a long letter to Mollie. I haven't any chum in Belmont and I miss that more than all else. How far away now seem those dear old days of our early teens—half childhood half girlhood. And yet, I do not really think if the choice were offered me that I would go back to them. I believe I am happier now than I was then, despite my hardships. Every age has its own troubles. My childhood and early girlhood had them and they were just as real and worrisome to me then as those of today are now. So after all I do not really want to go back, though at times I do grow desperately weary of struggling and striving, with not much prospect of anything better ahead.

Monday Morning, Mar. 1, 1897

I am sitting here half frozen for another cold snap is on and the mercury is down to 20 degrees below zero. I have just finished my hour's writing at my new story and my fingers are so cold and cramped I can hardly hold the pen. Verily, I have to pursue literature under difficulties. I dread going to school to-day for I know the room will be frightfully cold.

Friday evening they had choir practice at Mr. Simpson's and I had to go as organist. Nobody knows how I hate it. I stayed all night. Fulton started off to Cavendish on Saturday for a cruise. I hope he will take a good long one. He and I have been carrying out a policy of "masterly inactivity" of late and "never speak as we pass by." I grew tired of being insulted undeservedly, so I just ceased to take any notice of him, the ill-bred boor.

Well, I must be off to school. I only hope I won't freeze stiff before night.

Night

No, I haven't frozen stiff, but I've come so near it there was no fun in it. However, school is over for to-day and I am sitting here trying to get warm before going on with my work.

I had a letter from Ed tonight. He said he would *not* accept my answer as final but would wait and hope for a more favourable one in the future. He begs me to continue the correspondence and not let this incident have any effect on our friendship.

Monday Morning, Mar. 8, 1897

Last evening Alf and Bert and I went up to Central to hear "Roaring Billy" hold forth. He *did* hold forth for something over an hour and a half on the absorbing analogy between a railway train and a Christian—according to *his* definition.

Yesterday morning Mrs. Simon and I drove ourselves up to hear Mr. Higgins preach in the Baptist church. Mr. H. is a marvellous creature from a physical standpoint. He seems to be made out of remnants all put together wrong end foremost! But he is not such a bad preacher.

After dinner I went down to Mr. S.'s, per invitation, driving with Alf, Bert and Sophy in the box sleigh. Sophy was in one of her very frequent "moods" and wouldn't even speak. She is the weirdest bit of humanity I ever came across. I am never comfortable when she is around, even when she is in good humor. However, I chattered away to the boys, who are never afflicted with spasms of silence.

In the afternoon Alf and I went to S'Side. The day was delightful and we had a lovely drive. We had tea with some friends and went to the Presbyterian church in the evening. We got home at ten after a lovely moonlit drive.

But the fires were out and I was compelled to go to bed in a chilled condition. As a consequence I was cold all night, slept wretchedly, and felt seedy this morning. I suppose, though, one must always pay some penalty for her pleasures. *I* always have to anyhow—sometimes double.

Alf and I are planning a trip to Cavendish next Friday if weather and roads permit. Lu is going to have a party that night and I want to take it in.

Tuesday Night. Mar. 9, 1897

I am *fearfully* tired. Tuesday and Thursday are always hard days in school but this particular Tuesday has seemed possessed of seven devils, if a day *can* be possessed.

I had two acceptances of stories to-day, however, and that has heartened me up a bit. One was from *Arthur's Home Magazine*[1] and the other from the *Philadelphia Times*.[2]

Oh dear me, *is* life worth living? Not when one is as tired as I am at present.

Monday, Mar. 15, 1897

Friday afternoon Alf and I started for Cavendish, although recent rains and thaws had left the roads in a very problematical condition. However, we got on very well and reached Clifton at three, where we had tea at William Montgomery's. It was just dark when we got home. Our arrival was a great surprise as I had not sent word I was coming.

---

1. A popular women's magazine like *Godey's* until 1898; published "Goose Feud" in April and "Strayed Allegiance" in July 1897.

2. A pulp magazine, founded by McClure in 1878, publishers of an annual almanac; bought out by *New York Times* in 1901; published "A Prize in Elocution" in March, "Extra French Exam" in May, "Detected by the Camera" in June, "The Violet Challie Dress" in August, and "Gold Link Bracelet" in September.

Then we went over to the party but I can't say I really enjoyed it. Alf doesn't dance—thinks it the unpardonable sin, I believe—and I didn't like to leave him alone among strangers with nothing to amuse him. So I didn't dance much either but played croquinole[1] most of the evening and was bored to the point of tears. I *love* dancing and I loathe croquinole.

We left Cavendish on Sunday afternoon and went to Park Corner where we stayed all night at Uncle John C.'s. This morning we had to make an early start. It was fine but very cold and as it snowed a good deal last night the roads were very heavy. By the time we got to Malpeque it began to blow and we had to drive over the bay in the teeth of a biting northwester and a drift that was as bad as a snowstorm. I was half frozen when I got here but no rest for the weary in Belmont. Had to hurry right off to school and put in the day feeling like something the cats had brought in.

Wednesday, Mar. 17, 1897
Belmont, P.E.I.

I have felt very lonesome and homesick since coming back this time. This household seems coarser and more vulgar than ever after my sojourn in Cavendish. I often wonder what these people I board with have to exist for. They seem to get no pleasure out of life—yet they seem contented enough. I suppose a man born blind never misses his sight.

There is Simon himself—the man seems to have no enjoyment or variety whatever—not even as much as falls to the lot of his neighbours. He works like a slave but he is poor. He never goes anywhere, not even to church. They never have company here and never visit elsewhere. His days are spent in an unceasing round of drudgery.

Mrs. Simon is the feminine counterpart of her liege lord. As for Dan, I hardly believe he is a human being. If he ever had any soul it must long sure have atrophied away.

With such people I naturally can have nothing in common. I live among them—eat, sleep, and talk—but I am not of them at any point of contact.

Monday, Mar. 22, 1897
Belmont, P.E.I.

Saturday evening just at sunset as I was moping by myself in the dusk Alf came along with gray "Maud" and took me for a dandy drive to Miscouche.

---

1. A game played with checkers on a round board.

Yesterday I experimented with three denominations. In the morning I went up to the Baptist church to hear Mr. Robinson of S'Side. Then I went down with Mr. Simpson and after dinner we all piled into a pung and drove up to Central to hear Mr. Sutherland of Zion church preach. After tea we wound up our religious orgy by going to the Methodist church.

Monday, Mar. 29, 1897
Belmont, P.E.I.

Friday last was a play day. For the first time since I came here no advanced pupils were in school and the work seemed so easy. Saturday morning Mrs. Simon, Jessie and I drove into S'Side. The roads were *awful*—all slush and water. But we got in, got our shopping done, and

Aunt Emily's

left for home at four. After a horrible drive—or more properly *swim*—we got home at six. I had just got my tea when Alf came to take me down to Malpeque.[1] As we went on the ice from Simon's door right to Aunt Emily's we had a perfect drive and another one as lovely coming home yesterday evening. Really, I don't think there is anything more delightful than a spin over good ice on a clear March evening under a sunset sky.

Monday, April 5, 1897
Belmont

Everything now is mud and slush. Saturday afternoon Will Montgomery came and took me over to Port Hill. At night we went to a meeting in Fourteen Church. That fanatical McLeod—who seems literally to pervade this part of the country—broke all his previous records for absurdity to pieces and I never was so tired of anything in my life. Also I had another dose of him Sunday morning. Sunday evening I spent discussing theological questions with Will who is a very clever and thoughtful fellow.

He brought me home this morning on the ice and we had a charming drive. There were only a few in school today so I had an easy time and don't feel as tired tonight as I usually do.

---

1. Village on the north shore of PEI where LMM's Aunt Emily and Uncle John Montgomery lived.

Monday, April 9, 1897
Belmont

I am heartily glad this school week is ended for it has been such beastly walking—or rather *wading*—that I feel fagged out. I suppose there is a long spell of it before me yet and I am ready to groan in agony of spirit, as I am sure I shall be intolerably lonesome. So no more sleigh drives for me, that is evident.

I have made up my mind that I will not teach in Belmont another year.[1] The work is too hard and I simply cannot exist another year here at Frasers'. I hate Belmont. The people, with the exception of three families are perfect barbarians. I suppose I shall have a dreadful time to secure another school but there is no sense in wrecking my health here. I have been very nervous lately, I sleep badly and I seem to have constant colds—the result of doing two teachers' work all winter and being half frozen most of the time.

I am still pegging away at my writing.[2] The road of literature is at first a very slow one, but I have made a good deal of progress since this time last year and I mean to work patiently on until I win—as I believe I shall, sooner or later—recognition and success. I am up in my room now and I think I will jot down a description of it just to help preserve its appearance in memory.

On the door—a dark brown with lighter trimmings—are tacked a pink duster bag, a beaded clothes brush pocket, and a medley of pictures clipped from magazines. On the wall above the mantel hangs a small photo of Jack Sutherland and a calendar of Uncle Leander's church. The mantel itself is decorated with an odd assortment—"sunbeam photos," a China dog given me by Well Nelson years ago, a vase, boxes, bottles, crimpers,[3] thimbles etc. On the next wall hang three fancy calendars, a needle book, a curling tongs holder and some photographs. On my little table below are a few books, a stand mirror, a Madonna and my jewel box.

In the corner is a curtained shelf behind whose draperies of startling red calico hang my dresses. The top shelf is filled with hats and the lower is crowded with magazines and schoolbooks. The window is curtained by a lambrequin,[4] also of Turkey red, and in front of it is my washstand with the appurtenances thereof. The window looks out directly on the roof of Simon's

---

1. The typescript of the journal adds that the Campbells had objected to her intimacy with the Simpson family and put pressure on her to resign.

2. LMM now began recording in a literary scrapbook the writing and publication dates for all her poems and stories. She wrote "From a Gable Window" and "The Light in Mother's Eyes" in April.

3. Small irons for pleating.

4. Short curtain across the top of a window or draped on a mantel piece.

kitchen but beyond it is a beautiful glimpse of harbour. A 12 x 6 mirror hangs at one side and on the other above my bed hang a watch pocket and another calendar—my friends run much to calendars at Xmas times. At the foot of my bed is my trunk.

Thursday, April 15, 1897
Belmont, P.E.I.

I have been much shocked and grieved to-day. I have been wondering for the last three months why Will P. hadn't answered my last letter. To-day I received a letter from Laura[1] telling me that Will had died on the second of April!

It was a great shock to me. Of course in these past busy years Will and I have grown away from each other but we have corresponded right along and I have always felt a comrade's affection for him. I cannot realize that *he* can be *dead*—he, so full of life and fun. He died of long and painful complications resulting from an attack of influenza some time ago. Laura says his sufferings were terrible and he was quite resigned to die although he wanted so much to get better and fought hard for his life. Poor Laura is heart-broken and his parents are crushed by the blow. Will was a model son and brother and his family fairly worshipped him.

When I had my cry out I went to my trunk and took out that old ten year letter of Will's. It is only six years since it was written but the understanding was that in any such event as this—but how little we dreamed it would happen—the letters were to be read.

I cannot describe my feelings as I opened the envelope. The letter seemed like a message from the dead—from the world of spirits. It was a letter of love, speaking more plainly than he had ever ventured to do in ordinary letters, and oh, how it hurt poor lonely me to read it!

Willie dead! And buried in his grave on that faraway prairie! It *can't* be! Wasn't it only yesterday that we sat in the old High School and wrote our notes and laughed over mutual jokes and walked home from school together in the winter evenings? Wasn't it only yesterday that we sauntered by the river in the purple June twilights or roamed over the prairies gemmed with bluebells? And wasn't it only yesterday we spent at the Maiden lake picnic and cut our names together on the old poplar by the lake?

Alas, no, it is six long years ago! And Will is *dead*! How Laura will miss him! They were so devoted to each other.

---

1. Laura Pritchard had married Andrew Agnew in Prince Albert on June 3, 1896.

Monday, April 19, 1897 .
Belmont, P.E.I.

I wrote a long letter to dear Laura Friday and the writing of it comforted me so much. To-day was spring warm and sunny, with a mellow southwest wind blowing. The ice has all gone, leaving the bay blue and sparkling, and tiny green things are poking their heads up in garden nooks.

JOURNAL

JOURNAL
Volume II[1]

L. M. Montgomery

April 25, 1897–February 7, 1910

Rt. Hon. Cecil Rhodes[2]

---

1. Here begins the second of LMM's handwritten journals.

2. LMM was a great admirer of Cecil Rhodes (1853–1902), businessman, statesman, and empire builder of British South Africa. She kept a picture of him in her room.

Sunday, April 25, 1897
Belmont, P.E.I.

This is Sunday afternoon and I am curled up in bed, writing—a drowsy, sleep-flushed specimen of humanity, for I have just wakened out of a post-prandial nap and feel rather stupid. I have nothing to do so I purpose scribbling some nonsense in my journal to keep myself out of that mischief which his Satanic Majesty is popularly supposed to find for all idle hands.

This morning was one of April's darling days—warm south wind, hazy horizon mists, general summery feeling in the air. If the ground were only a wee bit drier I would start off for a walk—although Belmont is not a good place for solitary rambles at any time. There are no leafy lanes or secluded fields here as in Cavendish or Bideford. The only place is the bay shore and that is rather damp and boggy just now for promenading. One must be content to drink in from a distance its new beauty of sparkling blue waters and violet-shrouded coasts.

I wonder how dear Laura is to-day. Somehow, she always seems nearer to me in these wakening spring days of breeze and blue—for it was in the spring of that far western land that our friendship out-blossomed to fullest flower. How her memory and Will is linked with the remembrance of green, violet-spangled prairie slopes, far amethystine hills, tranquil blue lakes, sunset hours by the river with its fringing curtains of budding leaves, parks of white-skinned poplars and sunny trails. Alas, I suppose the prairie violets are now blooming over Will's grave and never again shall we roam together by the blue river in the twilight or loiter side by side over blossoming prairies of far away.

The cherry trees down the lane

In a little vase on my table I have a couple of willow sprays thickset with silvery catkins. They remind me of the old willow tree in the "Haunted Wood" that used to bud out so bravely every year, and the poplar in the front orchard with its wealth of pussy willows. How I love trees! Often and often, when I am alone in the woods I will put my arms tenderly about some old, gray-lichened trunk and press my face to it, feeling its life and balm flowing through every vein in my body as if it and I were one. There are some trees down home that I love so well that I would almost as soon have one of my fingers cut off as see one of them cut down—the old birches around the garden, the tall balsam poplars behind the house, the old spruces back of the well and the cherry trees down the lane.

I remember while in P.A. what an unspeakable comfort in my lonely moments was the one tree our lawn could boast—the leafy western maple at the gate. And out on the prairies I always had a wild feeling of kinship with the white-stemmed poplars,—as if some of their sap were mingled with my life-blood. Perhaps—who knows?—it was. Perhaps I *was* a tree in, some other state of existence and that may be why I love trees so and feel so utterly and *satisfyingly* at home in the woods. I have always had a sort of leaning to that old doctrine of transmigration. It is hard *not* to believe that I have lived somewhere before.

It is almost time for the mayflowers. I long for the sight of them—little pale pilgrims from summerland, with *their* memories of olden springs when we went rambling through "the barrens" for mayflowers, coming upon plots of them, sweet and fragrant and sky, hidden away in the spruce nooks and hollows.

Monday, May 3, 1897
Belmont, P.E.I.

I am a forlorn mortal to-night. I have the most wretched cold again—as diabolical as a cold in the head *can* be— and I feel totally depraved and "fit for treasons, stratagems and spoils."[1] Last week was enough to drive one distracted. It began to rain on Tuesday and kept it up all the rest of the week—mist, mud, and misery—alliterative agony. Friday night I annexed the aforesaid cold and since then I

Old Baptist Church, a very jolly walk

have done nothing but sniffle, sigh and sneeze—I am getting more alliterative than ever!

I had a letter from Ed S. today. He expects to be home in six weeks. I rather dread his coming. I shall have to decide a certain matter once for all—and I am finding it hard to decide.

---

1. Shakespeare, *The Merchant of Venice* V.i.

Friday, May 7, 1897

I am "a free nigger." By that refined and classical expression I mean to convey the information that I closed school today and can look forward to three blissful weeks of rest and freedom. This week has seemed dreadfully long but it *has* come to an end at last.

I had a note to-day from the editor of the *Philadelphia Times*, accepting a short story I had sent him and saying he would be pleased to hear from me again.

Cavendish, P.E.I.
Wednesday, May 12, 1897

I came home last Saturday. The train was "full of schoolmarms and politicians," as I overheard someone say. Grandfather met me at Kensington and we had a cold drive home. Sunday I went to church. I find that I am beginning to feel a good deal like a stranger in Cavendish church now. Sunday evening I went in to the Baptist Church to hear Mr. Baker. He has been holding meetings here for some time now but, as predicted, is not finding the C. people as impressionable as the "Sixteeners." Monday night I went again and Jack L. came home with me. We had a very jolly walk.

Friday, May 21, 1897

Last Saturday I went to town. Just before starting I got word from Laura that she is the mother of a little son. I am so glad for her. But how funny it is to think of Laura with a baby!

Aunt Mary's have moved further uptown. Lewis was away in New York but Bertie was home for her vacation. Mary C. could not go in; so things seemed very much changed— no Lew, no Mary, no "dear old Prince" even, for Jack S. is in Ottawa now.

I came home yesterday afternoon. Mollie came over and we went to prayer meeting in the evening. This afternoon I spent with Pensie.

By the way, my poor old pussy "Topsy" seems to have gone to the shades. She disappeared in the winter and has never been seen since. I miss her not a little. She was a part of my home life so long—it's over ten years since she was a little kitten.

Laura's baby,
Willard Victor Agnew

Tuesday, May 25, 1897

Sunday afternoon I took one of my old-time rambles through the school woods and Lover's Lane. The trees are mistily green and thousands of tiny wood things are springing up under the spruces.

After I came back Fan and I went to the shore and up as far as the lobster factory. From that we went up to the road by way of Charlie Simpson's lane and so home—a four mile tramp that quite satisfied my passion for walking.

Yesterday afternoon Fannie and I went up to John C. Clark's and were bored to tears.

Lover's Lane

Thursday, June 3, 1897
Belmont, P.E.I.

Saturday morning I left home and reached here about five. I was fearfully tired—so tired that I could not sleep but tossed restlessly about all night. In the morning I went to church and down to Mr. Simpson's afterwards.

Monday morning I went back to school. As the key had been lost in the winter the doors and windows had been nailed up and as nobody was there to open them we could not get in. We had to wait for nearly an hour in a pouring rain before we could get in. I was disgusted and am devoutly thankful that it is my last term here. Finally we got a window pried open, got in and got to work.

When school came out I started for Miscouche. I had a letter I was very anxious to mail as soon as possible and as there is no mail here before Thursday I resolved to walk over to Miscouche and mail it there. As Miscouche is five miles away this involved a ten mile walk but I set off briskly. It was a fine evening and I walked so smartly that I was back here at 7.30 having covered the whole distance in a little over two and a half hours. But of course I was very tired—too tired to sleep and I thought the night would never end. Wednesday evening I went to the shore with a crowd of young folks, expecting to have a sail but it proved too rough. Last night I *did* get a good sleep and felt more like myself today. This evening I had a delightful ramble over the fields and enjoyed it to the core of my heart.

Wednesday Night, June 30, 1897
Belmont, P.E. Island.

It seems years since I laid down my pen at the close of that last entry. Between then and now stretches a century of suffering and horror, "counting time by heart-throbs." The girl who wrote on June 3rd is as dead as if the sod were heaped over her—dead past the possibility of any resurrection. I cannot realize that *I* was ever *she*. And indeed, I was not. What or who I am now I do not know. I only know that I have made a terrible mess of things and am the most miserable creature on the face of the earth. It is all my own fault—and I wish I were dead!

I seem to have been in a horrid dream and to have lost my own individuality completely. I feel as if I were in an unknown world where *everything*, outward and inward, seems hopelessly changed. *I* am not Maud Montgomery at all. I feel as if *I* must have sprung suddenly into existence and *she* were an altogether different person who lived long ago and had nothing at all in common with this new *me*. I have been an utter, complete, wretched little fool. I see it all now plainly, when it is too late.

I do not know if I can write down a lucid account of the events and motives that have led me to this, but I shall try. Perhaps it will help me if I write it all out.

To go back, then, to that letter which I received from Edwin Simpson last winter asking me to marry him and which I answered with a conditional "no." During the winter I thought a good deal about it off and on for I knew the matter would probably come up again when we met in the spring. The more I thought of it the more I was inclined to think that I might as well accept him.

I knew I did not love him but I thought I *could*. I had never *really* loved anyone although I have had several violent fancies that did not last very long. And having come so far in life without experiencing anything except these passing fancies I had almost concluded that it was not in me to love as *some* people seem to do in real life and *all* in novels. I had thought so much about Ed that I had come to feel a queer impersonal affection for him, as for some imaginary lover of dreams. Intellectually, he was more congenial than most men I have met and than any who have ever made love to me. In short, I thought life with him would be a very satisfactory existence. Ed was clever; he was studying for one of the learned professions and consequently his wife would have a good social position and a life in accordance with my tastes. He had no bad habits or traits of character. Above all—and in my lonely life this carried great weight—*he* loved *me*. I wanted love and protection. Life at times lately had worn a somewhat sombre aspect to my forward-looking eyes. The thought of a settled home and position was very alluring. My health had not been at all good all this spring and I felt tired and discouraged. I had had to work far too hard in school all winter and I was run-down and inclined to take a rather morbid view of my prospects. Hence, I was all the more tempted to grasp at what promised to lift me out of my Slough of Despond.[1]

Of course, I knew that in deciding to marry Edwin Simpson I was probably making considerable trouble for myself. I knew my people would not favour the match for two reasons—Ed is a Baptist and is also my second cousin. These things were not a serious objection to me although I would have preferred them otherwise. But I knew that grandfather and grandmother would consider them almost as serious as if he had been a Mohammedan—especially grandfather who has an almost morbid hatred of relations marrying.

However, the upshot of it all was that I decided if, when he came home, I thought I could care enough for him I would accept him.

The Saturday night after my last entry—the fifth of June—I heard Simon Fraser say that Ed had arrived home. I went to church the next morning feeling somewhat excited for I knew he would be there too. He was on the platform addressing the Sunday school when I went in. He looked well—spoke well. "Certainly" I thought, "it will not be hard to care for *him*."

When church was out he came over and shook hands. Mrs. S. asked me to go down to dinner and Alf, Ed, and I walked down together. Ed and I talked of college and Browning and a score of similar non-combustible subjects during the walk and afternoon. In the evening we all walked up to the Methodist church and I spent the night at Mr. S.'s! Ed was very attentive—I was pleased—flattered—God knows what—anyhow I fell quite sure I could care for him.

Tuesday night came—June 8th—a date that marks the boundary line between two lives for me. I went up to prayer meeting and Ed walked home with me. It was a lovely moonlight night. We talked as usual of books and studies. I did not expect him to say anything that night and I was flatly taken by surprise when, as we turned into Fraser's lane, Ed said abruptly,

"I suppose you were surprised to receive that letter of mine last winter?"

Then I knew what was coming—and I felt dizzy. If Ed had only *not* spoken then—if he had left it for a fortnight or even a week I believe I would by that time have realized that I could never care for him and all that has come upon me would have been averted. But he *did* speak—and I sealed my folly.

I don't remember with any degree of clearness just what we did say. We walked up and down the lane and talked confusedly enough; finally I managed to stammer out that I thought I cared for him and that I would be his wife.

---

1. A metaphorical bog from John Bunyan's allegory *The Pilgrim's Progress*, into which the character Christian character sinks under the weight of his sins and guilt.

He kissed me and said "Thank you." We came in then. I took off my hat and cape in a daze giving Ed, at his request, the flowers I wore. It all seemed like a dream. I was conscious of no emotion whatever, either pleasurable or painful. We sat down by the window, with the June moonlight shimmering on the bay below and talked of the future and the past. When he went away I went upstairs and sat for a long time in thought. I did not feel at all unhappy—but neither did I feel happy—certainly not as a girl should feel who had just parted from the man she had promised to marry.

The next evening was Wednesday. A number of us met at the lobster cannery and went out boat sailing—Olive Fraser, May Campbell, Marie, Miss Campton, Alf, Burt, Sophy, Edmund, and others were in the party. Ed, of course, was there. I could not help seeing some faults in him that night; they were very glaring—and unfortunately they were the very ones I dislike most in a man—the faults common to so many of the Simpson clan. I thought he was far too self-conscious, too fond of saying and doing things for effect, and—in plain English—far too *conceited*. However, I reminded myself that I could not expect to find him perfect when I was a very imperfect creature myself. I told myself that character counted—not little flaws like that—a very proper and common-sensible view of the matter, as anyone would say. But I was yet to realize that there is a higher law than commonsense after all—the law of natural instinct which I had utterly disregarded in my practical arrangement of matters.

We walked home together across the fields. Ed came in and stayed late. I continued to feel emotionless and matter-of-fact. Of course he kissed me often. Those kisses roused absolutely no more feeling in me than if another girl had been kissing me. When he went away I went sleepily to bed, dully reflecting that this sitting up with one, even if he were my lover, is a very stupid performance, which left me feeling drowsy and incapable the next day at work.

I did not see him again for a couple of days. Then I went up to a choir practice at Mr. Simpson's and he walked home with me. That night it struck me what a restless, nervous mortal he was; it seemed impossible for him to sit still for a moment. Hands, fingers, and feet must be perpetually moving, lifting, twitching. I was tired and fagged and this habit of his had an absurdly exaggerated effect on me. I felt as if I must *scream* if he didn't sit still. When he went away I actually felt as worn out as if I had passed through some tremendous physical strain.

Of course, we had discussed several details in the course of our conversations. We decided that as our engagement must be a long one it would be best to keep it a secret for a time at least from all save a few intimate friends. On this account I declined to wear an engagement ring for awhile.

I felt decidedly ruffled when I learned what Ed's plans really were. I had supposed and he had in his letters certainly led me to believe that he intended to go in for law or else a college professorship. Now I found that he meant to enter the ministry. I would not have minded this so much—though I certainly think the life of a minister's wife is a rather hard one in many ways—if he had been a Presbyterian or indeed any denomination but a Baptist. But to marry a Baptist minister would necessarily involve my re-baptism by immersion—a thing utterly repugnant to my feelings and traditions. Of course, Ed said that, if I had any *insuperable* objections to his choice of a profession, he would give it up. But he did not try to conceal the fact that such a giving-up would seriously "inconvenience" him, and I, on my part, felt that I had no right to impose arbitrary restrictions to his choice in so serious a matter and that such a course on my part would be very selfish indeed. So I finally resigned myself to it and told Ed so as cordially as possible.

By the middle of June I was beginning to recover from my strange feeling of unreality. My numbed sensibilities were, alas, reviving. Vague doubts and fears and perplexities began to disturb me. I remember the night of the 17th of June with especial distinctness because it was the first night I became conscious of feeling a *dislike* of Ed's caresses. Hitherto I had accepted them unemotionally. Now they seemed to irritate me—my former torpor was replaced by a distinct sense of *physical repulsion*. I reproached myself for this and carefully concealed it; but my feelings were beginning to alarm as well as puzzle me.

On Thursday evening, June 17th, I went up to Allan Fraser's after school. I felt tired and bored with things in general. After tea Olive and I went botanizing in their swamp. Olive, in common with the rest of Belmont, was devoured by an unholy curiosity regarding Ed and myself and threw out numberless hints which I parried mechanically. I was amazed to discover that it *annoyed* me to be teased about Ed!

He had promised to meet me there and at sunset he came. We spent the evening there. I was dull and languid—Ed as voluble as usual. He has the Simpson habit of talking too much. When we left and walked together down the dark road he kept on talking until I felt tired of the sound of his voice. When we reached home he came in. As for me, I was suddenly in the clutches of an icy horror. I shrank from his embrace and kiss. I was literally terrified at the repulsion which quivered in every nerve of me at his touch. It seemed as if something that had been dormant in me all my life had suddenly wakened and shook me with a passion of revolt against my shackles. When Ed went away I rushed upstairs and flung myself on my bed. My God, what had I done? Was it possible I had made an awful mistake? I shiver yet at the remembrance of that terrible night. The veil seemed to be torn at once and completely from my eyes. I looked—and saw that I could not *bear* the mere touch of the man I had promised to marry!

This awful visitation seemed to me utterly inexplicable then. Looking back now, I can clearly see that my feelings that terrible night were merely the climax to an unconscious process that had been going on from the very first night of our engagement. It was the sudden revolt of my whole nature from the false bonds which I, ignorant of their real nature, had imposed on it.

My martyrdom had begun. Since then what have I not suffered?

How I got through the next day I don't know. I worked slavishly in and out of school—it was my only relief for it kept me from thinking, thinking, thinking!

There was a choir practice up at Major MacKinnon's at Central in the evening and I had to go. Ed and Fulton—who by the way is remarkably civil to me now—called for me. I grimly reflected as I pinned on my hat before the glass that Ed would not feel particularly proud of his fiancee's appearance that night. A more wretched-looking creature it would have been hard to find. I was as pale as a corpse, with black circles under by dull tired eyes. My head throbbed painfully. We called for Olive. The laughter and conversation of our little crowd gave me a certain stimulus and so helped me to keep up appearances at least. But when I found myself walking home alone with Ed, under the glistening stars, down the dusky, sibilant spruce road, all my depression returned. I wondered that he didn't notice it but he did not—he simply talked on and on.

When we reached home we sat down by the window. Ed put his arm about me and kissed me. Suddenly I felt as if that kiss scorched me with an intolerable shame. When he bent his head again I sat up abruptly and pushed his arms away; if he had kissed me again at that moment not all the resolution in the world could have prevented me from betraying my repugnance.

I moved away from him; he took this to be simply a bit of coquetry on my part and leaned back, looking at me with a quizzical smile. In a few moments I had recovered my self-command. Ed was perfectly unsuspicious. I was thankful for this. If he *should* suspect it seemed to me that it would be an unbearable humiliation for me. He thought me very quiet that night and said so but ascribed it to fatigue after our long walk. His belief in my weariness did not lead him to curtail his stay however. I thought he would *never* go. He lingered on—and kept talking of our future *together*. If he had been trying he could not have invented a greater torture for me. I writhed in soul at every word but I kept myself rigidly in hand. I did not again turn my cold, unresponsive face from his kiss; but when he had gone I went up to my room saying under my breath "God help me."

Somehow I got through Saturday and Sunday without breaking down. I went to Mr. Simpson's because I had no excuse for not going and was rained in for the night. That day brought to me a final conviction that not only I did *not* love Edwin Simpson but that I *never* could.

Monday morning was rainy and Ed drove me to school. He little dreamed what thoughts were seething through the brain of the pale girl at his side. Ed, like all the rest of the Simpsons, has not a great deal of perception. He is one of the men who are generally so busy talking about themselves that they fail to notice moods and tenses on the part of others. I was thankful for this just then—it necessitated less forced animation on my part. I had then no thought of trying to break the engagement—I was *afraid* to do it. Remembering Fulton's all but insane behaviour I did not dare to speculate what Ed's might be, or what effect such a thing would have on him. I clung to the hope that in time I could conquer my physical loathing of him and be at least content. Happiness I no longer hoped for.

Engaged only a fortnight and in such a state of mind. There is, no doubt, a ludicrous and absurd aspect of the case but I am unfortunately incapable of seeing it. I see—and feel—only the tragedy of it.

The Tuesday after that rainy Monday was a holiday, being the Queen's birthday. May Campbell had arranged a picnic to Curtain Island.[1] The picnickers were the Lyles, the Simpsons, the Campbells, Frasers and myself. We set sail at nine. It was a fine day but blowing hard and we had a distinct exciting sail over. The exhilaration of the motion and the physical delight of skimming over the waves and through the spray lent me a sort of spurious animation. After all—perhaps I had been morbid—perhaps things were not so bad after all.

Arriving on Curtain Island we started on a tramp through the woods to the other side, from which we emerged tattered and torn to an alarming degree. After dinner Ed took me off to a grassy headland where we sat and had a long talk which I desperately anchored to books, studies etc., for I could not have endured a personal element. If marriage meant only a series of conversations on intellectual subjects I could marry Ed very well. I enjoy talking with him on such subjects. But just as our chat was veering towards personalities, in spite of me, a timely thunderstorm came up which compelled us all to take refuge in a tiny lobsterman's hut. It rained almost continuously for the next two hours and we all got into a state of muddiness and dampness and general stickiness. The wind had died away when we started for home and the bay was like glass. The sail back seemed to me

---

1. Now called Courtin Island, used as a setting in "The Curtain Island Mystery," published in the *Star Monthly*, October 1902.

interminable. I was in the deeps of depression and my condition was almost one of collapse. My appearance must have been ghastly for everyone commented on it and asked me if I were ill. I could only reply that I was tired to death. Ed knew this perfectly well but it did not prevent him from asking me to go to prayer meeting with him. I assented as I would have assented if he had asked me to walk to Summerside with him. It seemed to me that I must do everything he wished me to do in order to atone in some small measure for the wrong I was doing him with every breath I drew.

I do not want to do Ed any injustice. I admit that he is good, fine-looking and clever. *If* I loved him I suppose I would not notice his faults and imperfections—at least they would not jar on me so harshly. But I do *not* love him and sometimes I fear I will soon find myself *hating* him! What wonder that I hate and despise myself?

I wonder if I shall ever get *rested* again. I feel *so tired* all the time. It is such a hard task now to keep up with all my old-time everyday duties. I seem to loathe them. I cannot get up any interest in them and merely drag myself through them in a mechanical way.

The outer world about me is fair—very fair. Yet I care nothing for its beauty. A veil seems to have dropped between my soul and nature. This is hardest of all to bear.

Wednesday and Thursday passed in much the same way. In the evening Ed came. What a nightmare it seemed! There was only one thing that nerved me to endure it—and that was the fact that it would be the *last*, for a time at *least*, for Ed was going away on a visit to Nova Scotia on Saturday and I would be gone from Belmont before he returned. This was my one ray of comfort. If he had but known, as he lamented our approaching separation how *I* longed for it! But he did not know. He judged my feelings by his own and took them for granted.

I am, and always have been, a proud woman. It would have killed me if any outsider had guessed my state of mind, to sneer or pity. I know that no one has done so. To all in this household I have appeared my usual self, though quieter and graver. In society I have been my usual self also. I have laughed and jested and talked small nothings, wrapping the cloak of my pride over my gnawing fox as gaily and smilingly as did ever Spartan boy.[1]

The day following that night I had my school examination. I took little trouble with it for I felt no interest in it and I dismissed the scholars apathetically, not caring in the least that it was the last time. I have never liked the scholars here, but even if I had I would not have felt the parting just then. One does not mind a pin-prick when a limb is being wrenched away.

---

1. Legendary child martyr: rather than cry and betray his family the boy let a fox gnaw his breast.

Of course, there were a few of the children whom I liked, but the majority were very unlovable— rough, ignorant, lazy. A long and unregretful fare-well to them!

That night we were invited to a small party at Mr. Campbell's. We had a stupid time for most of the

Myself and the pupils of Belmont School

guests seemed dull and tired. As for myself, I had reacted into a wild, fever-ish fit of gayety. My eyes were burningly bright, my cheeks hot and crimson. Ed bent over me on our walk home—I spent the night at Mr. Simpson's as Sophy asked me and it was really too far to walk home so late—and whis-pered that he had never seen me look so beautiful and that he would carry with him forever the remembrance of my face that night. Such lover-like flattery ought to have seemed delightful to me; but instead I grew chill and cold and shuddered away from his arm in agonized repulsion.

Saturday morning I got up, listless and distrait, with the hot, defiant pas-sion of the previous night burned out to dull white ashes. When I left Ed, who was going to the shore, walked with me as far as the cannery road, and there we stopped to say good-bye. I gave him my hand passively and coldly lifted my face for his farewell kiss. "Good-bye, my darling," he said as he turned down the shore road. I drew a long breath of *relief* and walked on. *What* a relief it was! And how horrible that it should be so!

That evening I went to Miscouche and took the train to Alberton[1] where I was going to attend a Teacher's convention[2] and visit Nettie Montgomery. I had no pleasurable anticipations of the visit—I seem to have lost the power of feeling pleasure in anything.

Before me on the train two teachers were sitting—McIntyre and Trowsdale. They had both taught in Park Corner when Ed was attending school there and by a curious coincidence they were discussing him. They did not notice me behind them or if they did, would not have supposed that I had any special interest in their conversation. They did not like Ed, it was evident, and they said such things of him that even I grew angry and could hardly help flying out at them in his defence. Then I laughed miserably to myself at my mental picture of their amazement and consternation if I were to do any

---

1. North-shore town, 40 miles (64 km) west of Belmont, near the western tip of the Island.

2. Professional development conference: a school holiday.

such thing. But, for all my anger, the things they said of Ed were *true*; "he was clever—*but*"—seemed to be the essence of their comments. He seems to affect most people precisely as he does me.

Nettie met me at the train and I remained there until this afternoon. I felt very tired and ill all the time but my depression lifted somewhat in such cheerful society. Monday evening Nettie and her father and I went out for a drive. The horse became frightened, ran away, and threw us all out. Fortunately none of us were much injured—Nettie had a slight cut on her cheek—but I felt the shock severely and have not yet fully recovered from it.

I left Alberton to-day at 3.30. I had a tiresome ride down to Miscouche and my head ached continually. When I finally got off at Miscouche I declare I just felt like sitting down and crying childishly. But that would not do, so I left my valise at the office for the mailman and started spiritlessly on my five mile walk to Belmont. It soon began to rain and I plodded doggedly on through it, until about half way here John and Nettie Lyle overtook me and drove me to Fraser's gate. When I got here all my old gloom and depression settled back. I think this place has a wretched influence over me—I feel worse the minute I step inside the door. The people are so queer, the surroundings so coarse and rough that they jar on every fibre of my nature which is just at present strung-up to a peculiarly sensitive pitch of nervousness.

I got upstairs to my room, flung myself on the bed and cried my heart out. The tears were a distinct relief—the very first I have shed in all this dreadful time. I cried and cried until I felt utterly exhausted but the mental relief was unutterable. I felt as if something had been cleared away from my brain and for the first time I felt able to take up my pen again and write in this journal.

I am going home Saturday. I am sitting here in my poor old room. I shall be sorry to leave it—it is the only place in Belmont I *will* be sorry to leave—as I always am to leave an old room. A room where one sleeps and dreams and grieves and rejoices becomes inseparably connected with those processes and acquires a personality of its own. This room is not a pretty or dainty one but it has always been a retreat for me, the one spot in Belmont where I might be alone and possess my soul in quietness, the world forgetting. And now I must leave it and go out elsewhere. How many rooms I have left so and how many more am I fated to leave yet in my wanderings!

I wish I were home. I want to rest—rest—rest! At present I am utterly incapable of thinking calmly and dispassionately on any subject or coming to any abiding or rational decision. My mental balance has been too rudely shaken to recover its normal poise very readily.

I cannot express the self-contempt I feel when I think of my folly. I am in a gulf of self-abasement and humiliation and remorse, mingled with an unsubduable rebellion against the fate I have brought on myself. I see clearly now where I made my primary mistake. It was in ignoring the law which ordains that without real love any intimate bond becomes a galling and hated fetter and engenders hate and bitterness of soul. That I sinned in ignorance is small comfort and no aid.

Looking back over the past three weeks I wonder how I have lived through them without going mad. The physical effects are plainly visible. I am thin and pale, hollow-eyed and nervous. As for the mental and emotional detriment who can judge or measure it?

Oh, what shall I do? And there is no living mortal to whom I can go for advice or help. I must dree this wind[1] alone. If only my mother had lived!

It is strange to think that Ed never suspected anything—never noticed my altered manner. Verily, "those whom the gods wish to destroy they first make blind"—as in my own case. But as for me, my days of blindness are over. Too clearly and plainly I see now and the sight is one which might well blast my soul's vision forever.

Up to this spring I have had a *fairly* happy life and what cares and worries I have had—and I have never even in childhood been free from them—did not weigh me down unbearably. Life looked to me fair and promising; I was young and ambitious. Now everything is changed and darkened.

To-night Ed is far away and I suppose he is thinking lovingly of me—wretched, wretched me! And I? I could strike my reflected face there in the mirror—I could lash my bare shoulders with unsparing hand to punish myself for my folly. It would be a relief to inflict physical pain and thereby dull my mental agony. Sometimes I drop my pen and walk wildly up and down my room with clenched hands. Outside the rain of a moist odorous June evening is falling on the roof. I hear mare's voices calling to each other in the gloom of the barnyard. Afar off, the bay looms grayly through the curtain of rain and twilight.

In the morning I will dress and do my hair and go down with a smile to exchange greetings and tell about my visit and make business-like arrangements for my departure. But in this one precious little hour of solitude I can throw aside the mask and look on my naked soul, knowing that no prying human eye gloats over the revelation.

I know I am writing wildly and distractedly. But it is such a relief to pour out my misery in words, I am so tired. It seems a century since I was light-hearted and gay and ambitious.

Ambitious! I could laugh! Where is my ambition now? What does the word mean? What is it like to be ambitious? To feel that life is before you,

---

1. Scottish dialect: endure this fate.

a fair, unwritten white page when you may inscribe your name in letters of success? To feel that you have the wish and power to win your crown? To feel that the coming years are crowding to meet you and lay their largesse at your feet? I *once* knew what it was to feel so!

I have been pacing the floor again—I can't sit still for any length of time. It is dark outside now and the rain is beating on the pane like ghostly fingertips playing a weird threnody. Oh, *do* other people suffer like this? If they do, how can they live?

Perhaps when I am once home in my dear old room I will find something of peace and calm again. Perhaps when I lay my head once more on the pillow of my girlhood its spell may charm me back to paths of tranquillity and murmur "Peace be still" over the stormy waters of my troubled soul. Here to-night no such sleep will visit me. I will lie in the darkness and gaze out into it for hours—and then when the gray dawn comes up over the bay I will fall into the dull heavy slumber of absolute exhaustion of thought and feeling, to wake again in the golden morning sunshine and feel that in a world of beauty and gladness I am only a black unsightly blot of misery.

I am cold and tired and worn out!

October 7th, 1897
Cavendish, P.E.I.

"Harvest is ended and summer is gone."[1]

I have got out this journal at last. I have neglected it for months, for I *could not* write. The summer is over now. It is October and autumn. We are having delightful fall days, misty and purple, with a pungent, mellow air and magnificent sunsets, followed by the rarest of golden twilights and moonlit nights floating in silver. Maple and birch are crimson and gold and the fields sun themselves in aftermaths. But it is autumn and beautiful as everything is it is the beauty of decay—the sorrowful beauty of the end.

In one way this summer has seemed long—in another short. I have not been happy or at peace. I have suffered continually—and it has done me good. I have *grown* much in some respects and I think I have gotten a great deal nearer to the *heart* of all things. I was a *girl* up to last spring—now I am a woman and I feel acutely that girlhood is gone forever. I have learned to look below the surface comedy of life into the tragedy underlying it. I have become *humanized*—no longer an isolated, selfish unit, I have begun to feel myself *one with my kind*—to see deeper into my own life and the lives of

---

1. Compare "The harvest is past, the summer is ended, and we are not saved." Jeremiah 8:20.

others. I have begun to *realize* life—to realize what someone has called "the infinite sadness of living," and to realize how much each of us has it in our power to increase or alleviate that sadness. I understand at last that "no man liveth to himself."

Home

I came home the first of July, leaving Belmont with no regrets. I did hate that place bitterly. I have been home all summer as I did not succeed in getting a school. It is always hard for me to get a school as I have only my own unaided efforts to rely on. Grandfather has always been opposed to my teaching—not for *my* sake, indeed, but simply because he has an absurd prejudice against teachers as a class, dating back to the time one who boarded here quarrelled with him and left. She *was* a detestable creature but he was quite as much to blame for the quarrel as she was and put himself very much in the wrong. He suggested once this summer that I go into a store at the Creek but I simply would not do that. He will not let me have a horse to take me to interview trustees personally so I have to depend on letters, a very poor plan when teachers are so over-plenty and the personal applicant stands the best chance. But at last I have obtained the Lower Bedeque school[1] and I go in two weeks time to take charge of it.

Cavendish has been very quiet this summer. Uncle Leander and family were over for a month. Chesley Clark and Jack Laird have both gone out west and I miss them considerably.

I have heard from Laura only once this summer. When I opened the letter I found in it a tiny packet enclosing a little gold ring worn almost to a thread—the ring I gave Will six years ago and which he had always worn to the day of his death. I slipped it once more on my finger and thought of all the changes that have been, of all that has come and gone since last I wore it. It seemed like a golden link between me and my lost self, between the present and the past. Poor little ring! I shall always wear it in remembrance of those dear old days. Its circle is the symbol of eternity and eternal friendship. Surely, surely, those who knew each other so well and dearly here will meet again in some fair Hereafter.

Aunt Annie, Uncle Leander's second wife, gave me that ring long ago when I was twelve years old. It was never off my finger till I gave it to Will

---

1. On the Dunk River, which empties into the Summerside Harbour bay, on the south shore of Prince Edward Island. The Aboriginal name means "the hot place."

and it never will be again until it is worn out. Aunt Annie wore it when she was a girl, so it is very old.

The only *social function* we have had this summer was prayer meeting, that faithful old standby. The prayer meeting of today however is very different from its predecessor. It has evolved into a "Christian Endeavor Society."[1] I can't say I approve of the change.

Looking back on my past life I think I have had a rather peculiar spiritual experience. I am not "religiously inclined," as the phrase goes, but I have always possessed a deep *curiosity* about "things spiritual and eternal." I want to *find out*—to *know*—and hence I am always poking and probing into creeds and religions, dead and alive, wanting to know for knowledge sake what vital spark of immortal truth might be buried among all the verbiage of theologies and systems.

When I was very young—about eight or nine—I began to think of these things very deeply and passed through a great many bitter spiritual struggles, of which I could not have said a word to those about me. My theology was very primitive and I took everything very literally. I supposed heaven was a city of golden houses and streets, where we would always walk around with harps and crowns and sing hymns all the time and where it would be "one endless Sabbath day." I could not help thinking it would be dreadfully dull. *One* Sunday on earth *seemed* endless—how then would it be with one that really *was* endless? But I also thought that this was very wicked of me—that there was something in me radically wrong when heaven had no attraction for me. But anyway, it would be better than hell which I also implicitly believed to be a lake of fire and brimstone, haunted by the devil and all his angels. While I had a vague impression that heaven was spread all over the other side of the blue sky above us hell seemed to me to be situated away off to the southeast!! I was terribly frightened of hell and my fear frequently drove me into trying desperately "to be a Christian."

I had some bitter seasons. I remember that when I was about ten I got it into my head that the Catholic church was the only right one and that outside its pale all were heretics doomed to penal fires! I got these ideas out of a sample copy of a newspaper called "The Catholic World" which had been sent to the postmaster. Its statements were so dogmatic that they impressed me as authoritative. How I suffered because of this! It seems both funny and pitiful to me now. But it was very real and inexorable then. And I was so miserably *alone*—there was no one to whom I could go for help. I would only have been laughed at, or, at best, met with some dogmatic statement which

---

1. A youth movement in evangelical Protestant churches, instituted 1881 in Portland, ME, developed into an interdenominational and international World's Christian Endeavor Union in 1895.

would have been of no help to me at all. In silence and secrecy I had to fight out my own battles and flounder through my quagmires.

Somehow or other I gradually *got* over or outgrew my difficulty about Mother Church only to stumble helplessly into another. The Baptist and Presbyterian girls in school—the "big girls"—were always disputing on doctrinal points, especially on Baptism, and I began to fear that the Baptists, and they only, were right and that I would certainly be "lost" if I were not immersed. I worried over this on many a sleepless pillow and argued fiercely with myself over it for weeks. Finally, however, I passed out from this shadow also.

At intervals—always in winter; I was never troubled with conscience spasms in summer—I "fell under conviction of sin"—that is I remembered about hell and got frightened!—cried, prayed, and determined desperately to be "good"—to like reading the Bible better than story books, not to get tired—that is to say "bored," only I wasn't acquainted with that word then—in church, and *not* to dislike Sunday. Besides, I would rigidly practice a hundred repressions and denials of my childish instincts. For instance, I would, when setting the table, conscientiously put for myself a certain knife which I hated and therefore thought everyone else must also hate. Last winter I read for the first time "The Story of An African Farm."[1] The writer was describing just such experiences of childhood. When I came to the sentence, "We conscientiously put the cracked coffee cup for ourselves at breakfast," I leaned back and laughed. It was as if I had unexpectedly seen my own face peering out at me from a mirror. So this Boer girl, living thousands of miles away in South Africa, had had exactly the same experience as mine! Truly, we are not so different from each other as we like to imagine.

To resume:—the fit would pass in a few weeks and I would lapse back into "wickedness" and indifference again until the next attack.

As I grew up all this ceased. Then came that time in town when B. Faye Mills—he has since gone over to the Unitarians, by the way—turned it upside down. I hardly know what induced me to "join the church" then. The whole air seemed to be thrilling with a kind of magnetism and it was hard for anyone to resist the influence, especially one so extremely sensitive and impressionable as I am. Then there was Mary C. who really wanted to "come out" and wouldn't unless I would, and so, partly for her sake, partly because I was tired of being urged and pestered and harangued every time a revivalist came around, I surrendered and "came out," too. I think it was a mistake, for I put myself in a false position. To "join the church" meant assenting to certain teachings which I did *not* and *could* not accept.

---

1. An influential book (1883) by Olive Schreiner (1855–1920), feminist activist, intellectual, author of the story of a lonely life South Africa; she also wrote *Women and Labour* (1911).

I cannot recall just when I ceased to believe implicitly in those teachings—the process was so gradual. My belief in the fine old hell of literal fire and brimstone went first—it and others seemed to drop away like an outgrown husk, so easily that I knew it not until some day it dawned upon me that they had been gone a long time. I have not yet formulated any working belief to replace that which I have outgrown. Perhaps it will come in time. These things must *grow*, like everything else.

I have written a good deal this summer[1] and had a few acceptances. Had a poem taken by *Munsey*.[2] The latter is quite an encouragement as it is a good magazine.

Yesterday I was reading over Hattie Gordon's old letters. How much I would like to see her! What jolly times we did have when she taught school here! The old school is much changed now and nearly all the old scholars are gone. I am sure the children who go there now do not have half the fun we used to have; but then I have no doubt they learn a great deal more.

I have read several new books lately. "The Gates Ajar"[3] interested me considerably. The author's conception of Heaven seems a helpful and reasonable one. In her idea, we shall keep on being just what we are here, along the lines of higher development and freed from all the clogs and trammels of earth. She does not think that we shall all at once expand into perfect holiness but that our aspirations and wishes will all tend to that, will develop towards it more and more, with every help and hindrance. It is a pleasing conception and I wish I could believe it firmly—for the mere inclination to believe is not enough.

"The Love Letters of a Worldly Woman"[4] was another new book—new to me, I mean. It is a "far cry" from "The Gates." It is the earth, earthy, dealing with earthly passions and appeals strongly to one side of our many faceted nature. It is true to life, and therefore sad and tragical, as all life and all lives are, more or less. But some lives seem to be more essentially tragic than others and I fear mine is one of such. My outlook is indeed gloomy at present, bounded and narrowed in. To quote from the letters, "I feel like a prisoner who has shut the door on all possibilities."

---

1. LMM's scrapbook entitled "Stories and Poems late 1890s" includes sixty-nine items, such as "Old Hector's Dog," "The Tree Lovers," "The Poplars at the Gate," "If Love should Come," "New Fashioned Flavoring," "Margaret Ann's Mother," "Which Dear Charmer," "Kismet," and "A Brave Girl."

2. Magazine founded in 1889, serialized the most popular writers, paying half-a-cent per word; published "If Love Should Come."

3. A long-time bestseller (1868) by Elizabeth Phelps; pious and sentimental treatment of a girl who has lost her lover in the Civil War.

4. Lucy Lane Clifford's popular book (1891), first published in England, went into many American editions (Chicago: Donahue; New York: Harper).

I went in to the Exhibition in September. I stayed at Aunt Mary's of course and in the jolly, *human* society of my girl friends I forgot my cares for the time being, and my unwholesome broodings and speculations.

For my life this summer *has* been unwholesome. It has been spent too much among books and visions and dreams—there has not been enough electrical human interest permeating it to keep me in good mental counterpoise. It has been far too self-centred and analytical.

Aunt Mary's

Mary C. was also in and we had a good time together. We went to the Opera House one evening to see "The Curse of Cain"[1]—a very poor amateur performance. However, the "Rainbow Dance"[2] at the end was really beautiful—to my eyes at least, for I have such a passionate love of *colour*. It seems to me that colour means to me what music means to its devotees.

One day Mary and I called to see Mrs. Macleod who occupies the other half of "Hotel De MacMillan." The "hotel" is vacant now, so Mary and I borrowed Mrs. MacLeod's key and went all through it. Bare and vacant it is now, but peopled for us by many comic memories. We had our troubles and tribulations in that old house certainly, but they have assumed a merely amusing aspect through the mellowing mists of time. And we *had* fun there, too. We explored the old parlour which Jack Whear and Florrie used to haunt, the old sitting room where we studied, the stairs up which we used to race so wildly, regardless of Mother MacMillan's wrath, and, last but *not* least, our old room whose walls had so often re-echoed to our shrieks of mirth, where we wrote and read and entertained our chums and discussed our grievances. But it is all past now and the little colony of roommates is scattered far and wide. Florrie is married to her Jack and lives in town. Poor "Aileck" is in the States somewhere and so is Mary MacMillan—it is to be hoped for peace sake that they aren't within a hundred miles of each other. Bertie Bell is out west, Stewart Simpson is at McGill, Jim Stevenson is in Ch'town, Mrs. MacMillan is at Stanley—and dear knows where old "McMahon" and her fair spouse are. Norman and Mary are teaching and I—well, I am drifting about, tempest-tossed and mocked by fate.

---

1. Perhaps based on Lord Byron's play *Cain* (1821).

2. A spectacular performance in which a dancer, dressed in a flowing white gown with long extended sleeves, was illuminated by coloured lights shining from all sides and from the glass floor on which she moved.

1898

Lower Bedeque, P.E. Island
Jan. 22, 1898

I have been intending ever since New Year's to write up this journal, but alas for good intentions! The road to hell is said to be paved with them and I fear I have contributed not a little to the paving of late. However, I am going to devote this evening solely and exclusively to "journalizing."

When I last wrote I was home, dreaming, analyzing, brooding unwholesomely. Then I came to Bedeque and at once found myself whirled into a life the very antipodes of that which I had been living. The reaction was needed and proved wholesome. And yet—were the life I am living at present carried on too long the effect, I feel sure, would be even more disastrous than that of the former.

I am going to take a good dose of confession regarding my miserable affair with Edwin Simpson. I *could not* say anything about it in my last entry because I was in the worst possible state of mind over it and even to allude to the subject would have hurt me like a rude touch on a raw wound. But I am somewhat calmer now, so I may as well see how my wretched feelings look when written out in cold blood.

It would be useless to try to describe how I suffered over it all summer. I knew perfectly well I could never bring myself to marry Edwin Simpson and yet I shrank from telling him so. I hated and despised myself for my cowardice but I could not overcome it.

Ed wrote regularly and every letter reminded me more hatefully of my bondage. I dreaded the day I expected one, I breathed with a passionate sense of relief when the reading of it was over. Writing to him in return was another exquisite agony. Well, I did not write "love letters." But I tried to write as a friend and Ed did not notice any lack—or did not comment on it if he did. I hate to say anything uncharitable when I am doing him such a wrong, but nevertheless it is the literal truth, which no one who knows him will deny, that Ed is serenely sure that any girl he has honoured with his affection *must* be superlatively happy and enraptured. He betrayed this conviction unconsciously a dozen times during our evening conversations in Belmont.

Ed was in Cavendish for a visit soon after I got home and he and Alf came down to our place Sunday afternoon and had tea. Again that horrible repulsion seized me. I remember excusing myself half an hour after they came and running up to my room where I simply flung myself on the floor and muttered over and over again, "I can never marry him—*never, never, never!*" That outburst helped me. I was able then to go calmly down, get tea, dress and go to church. I did not see Ed again until Christian Endeavor on Thursday night. He came down and after the meeting we went for a drive. It was horrible!

Ed left the next day for a trip to Miramachi,[1] but when he came back it was worse than ever. His attentions to me soon set Cavendish gossip by the ears, he has a host of cousins there, most of whom do not like me, although I have never had anything to do with them—perhaps *that* is the reason—and I'm sure they were ready to tear me in pieces. At last, however, he went back to Belmont and I was comparatively free again.

When I came to Bedeque, after his return to college I had made up my mind that before his return next spring I would tell him the truth. His letters come regularly, as affectionate as ever and consequently as galling. As for mine they have grown colder and colder. It is a wonder to me that he has not noticed this. I have hoped that he would and by asking me the reason open an avenue for me to confess the whole humiliating truth. It would, somehow, be easier for me to open up the subject if he were not quite so complacently sure of his position.

As the Christmas holidays drew near I began to dread them for Ed talked of coming home and of course that would mean a visit to Bedeque. Finally however he wrote that he was not coming and I felt a great relief. The following Thursday Helen Leard and I drove up to Centreville to visit her sister after school and got back at dark. I went upstairs at once. Soon after Helen came up and said,

"Who do you think is in the sitting room?"

The most horrible sort of presentiment swept over me.

"Why, who?" I said, but I knew the answer would be "Ed Simpson." Fortunately Helen could not see my face in the dusk or I think it would have startled her. Quite unsuspiciously, however, she went on to say that he had come to S'side and found no one to meet him, so he concluded to come over and spend the night with them—he used to teach in Bedeque and was a chum of Al Leard's son so that this story sounded quite plausible and Leards had no suspicion of the real state of affairs.

After she had gone down I tried to rally my paralyzed wits. I felt sick at heart. But after a time I regained enough self-control to go down and meet him. Somehow the evening passed. The Leard family, not dreaming that there was anything between us, made no opportunities for leaving us alone and I was inutterably thankful that they did not. I had received a Christmas gift from him a few days before, a pretty silver paper knife with my initials on it. With his accustomed good taste he had written that it had "cost him some self-sacrifice"! Just imagine how it burned my fingers! However, I wrote a brief note of thanks for it and passed it to Ed as I bade him good night.

---

1. A fishing and ship-building region in NB.

I hope I shall never have to live through another such night. I lay there, my hands clenched, biting my lips to keep from screaming aloud. I was denied the relief of tears for Helen slept in the same room. I thought morning would never come; but at last it did and with it my deliverance, for Ed had to leave to catch the morning boat.

But that fearful night confirmed me in the realization that I *must* break my engagement before I saw Ed again. I cannot live this lie any longer. I fear he will take it terribly hard and the thought tortures me. But bad as things are they cannot be bettered by living a lie and I must tell him the truth at all costs. I would make almost any sacrifice if I could blot out '97 from my book of life. It will ever be a nightmare of remembrance to me. Oh, I feel so bitterly ashamed!

Somehow or other, during all this unhappy time I have worn a mask of outward gayety and kept up with my usual pursuits. I have written a good deal and met with some success, having had several acceptances—and of course plenty of rejections.

Whom do you think was married in September? Why, Jessie Fraser, that ancient spinster of the household in Belmont. She married an elderly widower of New Brunswick and as both of them are verging on the sere and yellow leaf it is to be presumed that there is not a great deal of sentiment in the affair. I wonder if the widower in question knew all of Jessie's past—or if he cared. I wonder what a woman *does* feel like who has such a past as hers. Is there any sweetness in the memory of her sin—or is it all bitterness? And what a curious thing marriage is! I never really thought about it before this summer, save in an aloof, abstract way, as if something more or less inevitable some day in the future—always in the future. But during these past six months I have been compelled to look at it in every light, grappling with the perplexing questions of its relationships in an effort to understand them. Marriage is a different thing to me now. I have at least realized what a *hell* it would be with a man I did not love—and yes, what a *heaven* with one I did! Where and how have I learned this last, question you? Ah, I can't tell you that yet!

Since coming to Bedeque I have been having, *on the surface*, the best time I ever had in my life—and *really* enjoying myself when I could succeed momentarily in forgetting my worries and heartaches. The teacher here before me was Al Leard. He wished to get a substitute for six months during his absence at college and my application was accepted. I board at his father's—Mr. Cornelius Leard's.[1] They are a very nice family. Both Mr. and

---

1. The Leard family had been in the Bedeque district since 1823, and were successful farmers. The full story of LMM's relationship with Herman (1872–1899) is covered in Mary Henley Rubio's *Lucy Maud Montgomery: The Gift of Wings* (2008). LMM's account was disputed by the townspeople after the publication of *The Selected Journals of L.M. Montgomery* was first published in 1985.

Mrs. Leard are as kind as they can be. Helen Leard, a girl of my own age, is very nice and jolly. We get along together splendidly and have no end of fun. There are two other little girls, May, aged thirteen, and Feddie, ten, and two boys. The youngest, Calvin, is about eighteen and is staying up at Central Bedeque with his brother-in-law for the winter but comes home often. He is a pretty little chap with big blue eyes and a skin as pink and white as a girl's, and he is as nice as he can be. He and I are excellent friends and I pet and mother him at all times.

The elder boy, Herman, is about 26, slight, rather dark, with magnetic blue eyes. He does not impress one as handsome at first—when I met him I thought he was what might be called insignificant looking—but in the end one thinks him so.

All in all I am very happily situated. The lines of my professional career have been cast in pleasant places this time at least.

As for my school, I am not overburdened with work as there are only *fourteen* children in the district. Imagine the contrast to the large schools I have had! But a couple of advanced pupils give me comfortably enough to do and I simply *love* teaching here. The children are all so nice and intelligent. The school is about 200 yards from here and is a very comfortable one in a grove of spruces. I feel as if I had lived in Bedeque all my life. The people are so nice, friendly, and sociable. It is a lively place with lots of young people and I have had a lively time.

And so '97 is gone! Never before was I glad to see a year go but when '97 went out I was glad with a fearful joy. It was *gone*, that dreadful year, with all its mistakes and suffering. I turned my back on it with a pitiful delight.

Well, this is all—and yet it is "the play of Hamlet with Hamlet left out."[1] Perhaps some day I may write it over again with Hamlet in—and perhaps I shall never feel that I can!

Friday, April 8, 1898
Cavendish, P.E.I.

It is just after dark; the shadows have gathered thickly over the old white hills and around the old quiet trees. The last red stains of the lingering sunset have faded out of the west and

The old quiet trees

---

1. LMM misquotes Walter Scott: "The tragedy of Hamlet, the character of the Prince of Denmark being left out" (*The Talisman*, 1825).

the dull gray clouds have settled down over the horizon again. All is very still and quiet here in the old kitchen and so, with much shrinking and reluctance—for a faithful record of my life during this past half year will be, I fear me, but sorry writing—I have brought out this book and set myself down this dull, chilly spring evening to write out the life— the stormy, passion-wrung life—that has been mine these past months. I am going to write it out fully and completely, even if every word cuts me to the heart. I have always found that the writing out of a pain makes it at least bearable.

The old kitchen

I have grown years older in this past month. Grief and worry and heartbreak have done their work thoroughly. Sometimes I ask myself if the pale, sad-eyed woman I see in my glass can really be the merry girl of olden days or if she be some altogether new creature, born of sorrow and baptized of suffering, who is the sister and companion of regret and hopeless longing.

On March 6th, while in Bedeque, I received a telegram[1] stating that Grandfather Macneill had dropped dead the preceding afternoon!

The shock was terrible. In all truthfulness. I cannot say that I have ever had a very *deep* affection for Grandfather Macneill. I have always been afraid of him; and in his recent years he has been very difficult to live with. Nevertheless, one cannot live all one's life with people and not have a certain love for them—the bond of kin and long association. When death comes this bond is revealed by its being wrenched asunder and we suffer keenly for the time being. Consequently, as I have said, I was shocked and stunned and felt as if everything in life had fallen blackly together. It seemed *impossible* that the news could be true. They had all been in good health at home the last letter I had had from Grandma.

It was Sunday when I got the telegram and I had to wait until Monday morning when Mr. Leard drove me over the ice to S'Side. There I took the train and reached Kensington at 1.30. John C. Clark came to meet me and it was eight o'clock when I finally reached home. Aunt Annie, Aunt Emily and Aunt Mary Lawson were here. It was such a relief to be with them all.

Grandmother was naturally sadly prostrated. Poor grandfather's death had been so terribly sudden. It was presumably caused by heart failure. He had been in good health up to noon on Saturday, then complained

---

1. Telegram service had been established on the Island since 1853; the first trans-Atlantic telegraph message to America, sent from Ireland, was received in Charlottetown in 1858.

of a pain, and in a few minutes dropped from his chair and in a moment passed away.

I went into the parlour with Aunt Annie to look at him. His face was quite unchanged and looked more gentle and tender than in life. I have never, since I learned to *feel*, stood thus by the coffin of one akin to me and it was a new and bitter experience. But *once* before I had looked down on a coffined face in that very room— and that face was the face of my mother.

The old parlor

I was very young at the time—barely twenty months old—but I remember it perfectly. It is *almost* my earliest recollection, clear cut and distinct. My mother was lying there in her coffin. My father was standing by her and holding me in his arms. I remember that I wore a little white dress of embroidered muslin and that father was crying. Women were seated around the room and I recall two in front of me on the sofa who were whispering to each other and looking pityingly at father and me. Behind them, the window was open and green hop vines were trailing across it, while their shadows danced over the floor in a square of sunshine.

I looked down at the dead face of the mother whose love I was to miss so sorely and so often in after years. It was a sweet face, albeit worn and wasted by months of suffering. My mother had been beautiful and Death, so cruel in all else, had spared the delicate outline of feature, the long silken lashes brushing the hollow cheek, and the smooth masses of golden-brown hair.

I did not feel any sorrow for I realized nothing of what it all meant. I was only vaguely troubled. Why was mother so still? And why was father crying? I reached down and laid my baby hand against mother's cheek. Even yet I can feel the peculiar coldness of that touch. The memory of it seems to link me with mother, somehow—the only remembrance I have of actual contact with my mother.

Somebody in the room sobbed and said "Poor child!" I wondered if they meant me—and why? I put my arms about father's neck. He kissed me—I recall one more glance at the calm, unchanging face—and that is all. I remember no more of the girlish mother who has slept for twenty two years over in the old graveyard, lulled by the murmur of the sea.

Grandfather's funeral was very large. I had to return to Bedeque the next day, and there the old heartaches which had been deadened for a time by the newer pain, awoke to gnaw and sting and burn once more.

Of course my miserable affair with Edwin Simpson was one of these. Oh, I know I was guilty of wretched folly in this but have I not expiated it in suffering. For I *have* suffered—what no mortal can know. What a curse feeling is! I never really learned to *feel* before. It takes suffering to teach that and the knowledge is named Marah.[1]

I wonder if there is anywhere in the future real abiding happiness for me. Not the wild, mad rapture of an hour, bitter sweet, such as has been mine now and again this past winter, nor yet the old careless, irresponsible happiness of by-gone days—too well I know *that* is gone beyond recall. But yet happiness, calm, tranquil, lasting—will it ever again be mine? I could lie down tonight and die, unregretfully, nay, gladly, if I were sure that death indeed meant *rest* and was not merely the portal to another life—such a one as this perhaps—or a better—but at all events *life*—and, that means action and thought and feeling—perhaps *memory* as well—anything but the rest I crave.

> I would not if I might be blest,
> I ask no Paradise but rest.[2]

And I think it is Longfellow who says in his *Golden Legend*.

> Rest, rest! Oh, give me rest and peace!
> The thought of life that ne'er shall cease
> Hath in it something of despair,
> A weight I am too weak to bear.
> Sweeter to this afflicted breast
> The thought of never ending rest,
> Sweeter the undisturbed and deep
> Tranquillity of endless sleep!

I must stop this wild wondering—the echo of my confused, troubled thoughts—and begin my story—pick up the dropped threads and go on with it—this miserable life story of mine that can never have a happy ending. But I suppose I am only one of thousands who are living just such unhappy lives—there is no use in protesting against it as if I were the only unhappy atom in the universe. I *don't* protest now—I *did*, but that is past. I have sunk into a sort of apathetic resignation. I have grown *used* to unhappiness—but oh, I am very tired!

I kept up my correspondence with Ed all winter after a fashion, writing stiff, constrained *soulless* letters. He *must* have noticed this—but if he did he gave no sign. The days I expected a letter from him were days of misery. I

---

1. A lake of bitter waters; Exodus 15:22.
2. From Byron's "The Giaour" (1813).

hated to read it. His letters were really tedious, pedantic, involved affairs—but oh, worst of all, so *loving*. His reiterated expressions of affection made me heart-sick. When I had finished the letter I flung it into my trunk and locked it up out of sight, never to be read again.

Matters dragged on thus until they reached a climax. I had intended to wait until I left Bedeque before confessing to him. But there came a day when I felt that I could not endure such a life any longer—it was killing me. So one day early in March I sat down and in a fit of desperation wrote him a letter—a wild, frantic epistle it was, but it made my meaning clear. I told him I had ceased to care for him and could not marry him. I did not mince matters. Neither did I try to excuse myself. I admitted in full my weakness and asked him to give me back my freedom in terms that could leave no possible doubt of my feelings.

I did not know and could not picture what effect it would have on Ed. I knew he was very proud—conceited, if you like—and this gave me a feeble hope that he would release me quickly—that he would not stoop to plead or strive to hold but would simply set me free with the scorn I deserved.

I mailed the letter just before I got the news of grandfather's death and for a few days it was almost driven out of my mind. I knew Ed would get the letter the following Thursday, would probably answer it on Sunday and I would get it the next Thursday. That Thursday came. When we went up to the Y.P. Union that night we called at the P.O. and I got it. But I did not open it that night—I was too frightened of its contents. I knew they would upset me no matter what they were, so I decided not to read it until I came from school the next evening.

The dread of it hung over me all day Friday like a nightmare and even when I did go home—I put off reading it on one pretext or another as long as I could. But read it had to be and so at last, at sunset, I summoned up all my resolution and read it.

It was twenty pages long—and a most frantic epistle. But it was not at all the kind I expected and would have infinitely preferred. I had expected accusation and reproach, contemptuous upbraidings—and if the letter had contained such it would not have cut me to the heart half as deeply as it did. For it was a heart-broken letter and I felt that the mere reading of it was punishment enough.

He declared he could *never* forget—that love with him was eternal. And then he seemed to have taken some very foolish ideas into his head as to the *cause* of my ceasing to love him. Had anyone told me anything about him? Were his letters *too tedious* and so on? As if love could be ended by such things, if it had ever had any real existence!

Now that I have had time to think the matter over a little more calmly some of these queries of his strike me as rather curious. Why should he think anyone had told me things about him? *Is there anything to tell?* And why should he have supposed I found his letters tedious? Tedious they certainly were. But I as certainly never wrote him anything that could imply I found them so—unless any avoidance of any reference to the abstruse subjects he discussed might have suggested it to him. But these speculations are idle.

He went on to say that he *could not* set me free in that letter—he must ask for more information regarding my alleged change. He *could not*, he declared, give up the hope that all might yet be right.

Of course, I had not told him that I had ceased to care—or rather, ceased to *fancy* I cared—for him in the first week of our engagement; I had not said *when* I ceased to care at all; and neither had I told him of the physical repulsion with which he inspired me whenever we came into intimate contact. *That* was something I *could not* tell him.

He did not in this letter ask the one question I dreaded—"Was there *another man?*" It was a question I could not have answered. Because by this time there *was* another man—in one sense, but not, after all, in the sense such a question or admission would have inferred. I knew I would never marry this other man. I did not, with the part of me that *rules*, *want* to marry him. If I had never met him it would have been just the same about Ed. I had turned against him before I ever met or saw the "other man." If I had not, I would have been true to him in spite of everything.

When I had finished that terrible letter I curled myself up on the lounge with my misery and wished again as I had wished a score of times during that awful winter that I had never been born.

I knew he loved me truly—and what a perverse fate it was that I could not return his love! How inutterably happy we might have been if I had only loved him as he loved me—or as I loved—the other man!

But there was only one thing to do and I did it. I wrote again, reiterating all I had said before in even plainer terms, asking for a little pity and consideration although I deserved none and ended by imploring him to set me free from what had become a hateful fetter.

His answer came on the Friday evening before I left Bedeque, but I did not read it then. I did not want to be made miserable my last night there—not with *that* kind of misery anyhow—so I decided I would not read it until I was on the train next day. I took the train at Freetown station about two o'clock Saturday afternoon and as soon as I was seated I grimly opened the letter and read it.

His first letter had made me wretched and remorseful and altogether subdued and humble. But this one made me angry. I had suffered so keenly—I had been so long in the depths of bitter humiliation, that the reaction came with unreasonable force. If I could have thrown his letter to the floor and set my foot on it—if I could have torn it to shreds and scattered it to the winds—if I could have walked savagely through the car—if I could have shrieked aloud—if I could have done any or all of these things it would have been an unutterable relief. But I could not—I had to sit there, outwardly calm, trembling from head to foot with the violence of repressed emotion while the train swayed on over bare bleak fields and through leafless woods.

The letter was long and for the first six pages was pretty much what he had written before. The first sentence that struck me like a blow was "Oh, Maud, I cannot, *cannot* set you free without sufficient reason!"

"Sufficient reason!" When I had told him that I did not and could not love him and that consequently life with him would be "an unbearable martyr-dom"—my very words! Was that not "sufficient reason?"

He went on:—

"Will this do? I will set you free for the next three years—free to do as you please, keep company with anyone you please—yes, and marry anyone you please. If then you belong to another or are of the same mind as at present and the same attitude to me you shall be wholly free."

Then he proceeded to say that we must still be friends and keep up our correspondence.

No, I could not agree to this. My haunting humiliation and sense of bond-age would never be lessened and would wear my life out. Besides, it would be foolish. I *knew* beyond any doubt that I would never change—that I would be of "the same attitude" to the end of my life.

I wrote to him as soon as I arrived home and sent the letter off before I had time to grown calm. It was not such a let-ter as I should have written. It was harsh and unjust and I am now bitterly sorry for sending it. But I felt like a wild creature, caught in a trap and biting savagely at its captor's hand. All things, considered, I daresay it is just as well. It will probably do more than a dozen imploring, self-reproachful letters to convince Ed that I

THE HARBOR AT EVENTIDE   SUMMERSIDE, P.E.I

am desperately, dangerously in earnest, and more than all I hope it will go far towards curing his love for me and opening his eyes to the fact that he is well rid of me. I have not received his reply yet. I suppose it will come soon. That is how the affair stands at present. I am sick of writing about it and am glad to drop the subject, even though the next I must take up will be still more racking.

And it *is*! Yet I am going to write it all down from beginning to end. I suppose this is foolish—but I think it will help me to "write it out." It always does.

If I had known, that evening last fall when I crossed the bay to Bedeque and idly watched the great burnished disk of the sun sink below the violet rim of the water, and the purple shadows clustering over distant shores what was before me I think I would have turned then and there and gone no further—and thus I would have saved myself many a burning tear and bitter heartache, many a sleepless night and wild regret. But oh! then, too, I would never have known the few hours of intense rapture, of unutterably sweet and subtle happiness that were mine also. While they lasted I thought they more than paid for all—and even yet I sometimes think that it was well to have suffered all I have to have known them.

But I knew and feared nothing that October evening and went blindly to my fate.

Now for "Hamlet" with Hamlet in!

Up to the time of my going to Bedeque I had never *loved*. I had never known what it was to love, intensely and passionately and completely. Of course, I have had some attacks, more or less severe, of "calf love," and fleeting, violent fancies for some men, bringing with them sometimes pleasure, sometimes jealousy, sometimes a few romantic day-dreams. But *love*—no, it had never come to me!

Although I had never really loved, still, like every other girl in the world, I suppose, I had an ideal—a visionary dream of the man I thought I *could* love—handsome, of course—did ever a girl dream of a plain lover?—educated, my equal in birth and social position and—most important of all—in intellect. On that last I laid particular stress. Never, so I fancied, could I care for a man who could not meet me on equal ground at least in the matter of mental power!

Well, I have learned the truth of the old proverb—"kissing goes by favour"—and not by rule!

Soon after I arrived at Mr. Leard's that evening tea was announced and the boys came in. Their mother introduced them and I looked them over with tepid interest. Herman came first. At first sight I did not greatly admire his appearance. He was under medium height, slight, and—I thought then—rather

Picture cut from magazine. As much like Herman Leard as if it were his photograph.

insignificant. Calvin impressed me far more favourably. I thought him much better looking than Herman—nevertheless, all through supper I found myself looking again and again at the latter. He was dark-haired and blue-eyed, with lashes as long and silken as a girl's. He was about 27 but looked younger and more boyish. I was not long in concluding that there was something wonderfully fascinating about his face. What it was I could not define. It was elusive, magnetic, haunting; whether it lay in expression or feature could not be told.

It did not take me long to get acquainted with the boys. I found Herman jolly and full of fun. I soon made up my mind concerning him—and I never changed it! He had no trace of intellect, culture, or education—no interest in anything beyond his farm and the circle of young people who composed the society he frequented. In plain, sober truth, he was only a very nice, attractive young animal! And yet!!!

The first three weeks glided by uneventfully. I was too busy with my new duties to have any thought to spare for anything else. Herman and I talked and jested and teased each other continually and kept the house ringing with mirth and laughter.

On Thursday nights we always went up to the Baptist Young People's Union meetings at Central Bedeque. We had no end of fun and jolly chatter on our way there and back, to say nothing of a pleasant drive.

The third evening of Union came the eleventh of November. I am not likely to forget the date—it marked the *first step* on a pathway of passion and pain. When we started home after Union it was a calm moonlit night. I remember every turn of that road—we drove down to Colin Wright's corner at Central Bedeque, thence down the long shadowy Bradshaw hill, over the creek shimmering with the reflections of the stars, up another long hill to Centreville, then down the long slope between Centreville and "Howatt's turn." I was tired and sleepy that night and did not feel like talking so I was very silent. Suddenly Herman leaned over, passed his arm about me and, with a subtly caressing movement, drew my head down on his shoulder.

I was about to straighten up indignantly and say something rather tart but before I could do so there came over me like a *spell* the mysterious, irresistible *influence* which Herman Leard exercised over me from that date—an attraction I could neither escape nor overcome and against which all the resolution and will power in the world didn't weigh a feather's weight. It was indescribable and overwhelming.

So I did not move—I left my head on his shoulder, voiceless, motionless, as we drove home in silence.

When we reached home I sprang from the buggy without a word and ran upstairs. I was overwhelmed by a flood of wholly new and strange emotions which I could neither understand or control. I was aware, in a dim, vague way, that danger of some sort was surely ahead and I resolved that never again would I allow anything of the kind. But the very next night when we were driving home from a party at Centreville it happened again. He drew my head down on his shoulder and pressed his cheek against mine; and as he did so a thrill of delight and rapture rushed over me—I could *not* speak—I could *not* forbid him.

The next Union night Herman went a step further. It was just below James Montgomery's—I recollect the moonlight gleaming on his white house, for every trifling thing seemed to stamp itself indelibly on my memory—Herman suddenly bent his head and his lips touched my face. I cannot tell what possessed me—I seemed swayed by a power utterly beyond my control—I turned my head—our lips met in one long passionate pressure—a kiss of fire and rapture such as I had never in all my life experienced or imagined. *Ed's* kisses at the best left me cold as ice—*Herman's* sent flame through every vein and fibre of my being.

It might have warned me—and it *did*. When I got home and found myself alone I tried to look matters squarely in the face. *This must not go on!* I was engaged. True, it was to a man I did not love and whom I knew I would never marry; true, too, that before I ever saw Herman Leard I had known this. But that made no vital difference. For the sake of my self respect I *must not* stoop to any sort of an affair with another man.

If I had—or rather if I *could* have—kept this resolve I would have saved myself incalculable suffering. For it was but a few days later that I found myself face to face with the burning consciousness that I *loved* Herman Leard with a wild, passionate, unreasoning love that dominated my entire being and possessed me like a flame—a love I could neither quell nor control—a love that in its intensity seemed little short of absolute madness. Madness! Yes! Even if I had been free Herman Leard was impossible, viewed as a husband. It would be the rankest folly to dream of marrying such a man. If I were mad enough to do so—well, I would be deliriously happy for a year or so—and wretched, discontented and unhappy all the rest of my life. I saw this plainly enough—passion, while it mastered my heart, left my brain unclouded. I never for a moment deceived myself into thinking or hoping that any good could come out of this love of mine.

Oh, I *did* try hard to conquer it! But I might as well have tried to stem the rush of a mountain torrent. The very next evening after that fatal kiss we were alone. Mr. and Mrs. Leard were away and Helen was entertaining her own fiancé, Howard McFarlane, in the parlour; the little girls had gone to bed. Herman who had been out goose-shooting came in about 8 and sat down on the sofa to read a novel.

I was sitting by the table, writing; we did not talk but it seemed to me that the whole air was thrilling electrically. After about half an hour Herman threw down his book impatiently and said that his eyes were bothering him too much to read. Whereupon I, having finished my writing and having nothing else to do, offered to read aloud to him. He assented and I took the book.

I don't think I read very well that night—for I had not been reading long before Herman reached out and took my hand in his, holding it in a warm close pressure. I was furious with myself because I could not help trembling like a leaf—he *must* have noticed it. Half a dozen times my voice faltered, my head reeled, the letters danced before my eyes. Finally Herman whispered, "Never mind reading any more," and took the book away. Then he drew me over beside him and held me there, his arms about me, his face pressed against mine. For half an hour we sat there, without word or motion—save that now and then he kissed me. And for me all heaven seemed to open in his kisses. Disgraceful? Oh, yes, I suppose it was! But my love was so intense, so overmastering that it seemed to me at the time to justify my yielding to his caresses.

But regret came—afterwards—oh, how poignantly! When I went upstairs to my room I lay awake for hours to fight over and over again the old unavailing battle with myself.

I knew I was foolish and wicked—and what, too, must Herman think? Of course, he had heard the report that I was engaged to Edwin Simpson. I felt quite sure of that although he never spoke of it. But Helen had, so there was no doubt he had also. So I supposed he was merely flirting for pastime. Yet I certainly had as much power over him as he had over me. Herman burned his fingers at the game of fire as well as myself. Yet there were many things about his attitude I never could understand. Perhaps if I had encouraged him to talk the matter over I should have understood. But I dared not risk *that*. He must have thought me a wild, perplexing creature in very truth, so ready to meet his caresses half way, yet always ruthlessly cutting short any attempt at uttered sentiment. If I never fully understood him I have the sorry satisfaction of feeling that I, too, puzzled him.

When I was alone I suffered everything but when I was with him I forgot all else and was deliriously happy.

The next night—Saturday—we were alone in the evening and it was the same thing over again. Sunday afternoon, too, I was alone in the sitting room, reading on the sofa, when Herman came in and sat down beside me, putting his arms about me and drawing my face close to his. There seemed no need of speech—we hardly ever talked much when alone together—it was enough to sit there in dreamy, rapturous silence. Oh, it all comes back to me as I write—and I long with a wild, sick, *horrible* longing to be back in his arms again—to feel the warm, magnetic pressure of his cheek against mine—to ruffle his brown curls with my fingers—Oh, God!!!

It is a horrible thing to live in the same house with a man you love and ought not to love. There is no respite of temptation and what chance have you to conquer in the struggle?

Things went on thus, with our Union drives and stolen moments of lingering until the 28th of November came. It was Sunday night and Herman drove Helen and me up to the Methodist church at Centreville. I was feeling wretched that evening for I could not help brooding over my troubles—troubles about which I could not speak a word to any living creature but must mask under a smiling face and an assumed gayety—and over my unhappy love which was growing stronger every day.

We drove home in silence for Helen was in no mood to talk, I was too miserable, and Herman was a quiet mortal as a general thing. But when he lifted me out of the buggy he whispered in my ear,

"Will you stay down a little while with me tonight?"

I should have refused—oh, of course I should! We should always do exactly what is right at all times! But unfortunately some of us don't seem able to. The temptation was too strong—I went helplessly down before it and murmured a faint assent.

I went in like a girl in a dream. Helen hurried off to bed—she was in a pretty bad temper just then over Howard's failing to show up—and I sat down in the soft semi-gloom of the firelight to wait for Herman. For the moment I was happy beyond the power of words to express—and yet I was frightened, too—I almost dreaded to hear Herman's step at the door even while I longed for it!

At last he came in, threw off his cap and coat and came to me, pressing his cold face against my burning one. We nestled there together in the gloom and silence. Dangerous? That is too weak a word! I knew that I was tiptoeing on the brink of utter destruction—yet I could not turn back. I could realize nothing except that I was in the arms of the man I loved as I had never dreamed I could love. When we parted and I had gone to my room—then—*then* regret and shame overwhelmed me indeed and I paid the bitter price of my weakness!

The days seemed to me to come and go as in a dream. The only hours I *lived* were when I was with Herman. The rest of the time I was torn by conflicting passions until my life was one long agony and my sleepless night began to tell on my health. But once let Herman's hands or lips touch mine and every other feeling was fused into one of unquestioning happiness.

So the time passed on and I lived my double life—the outward one in which I taught school and wrote and read and went to social functions and talked and laughed and jested, passing the hours in a seemingly pleasant routine—and the unseen, unsuspected inner one, wrung with passion and suffering, whose current flowed on side by side with the other.

Herman and I constantly found or made opportunities to be together. Naturally this new and unforeseen development was an added source of agony as regards Edwin Simpson. My engagement was more nightmare like and unbearable than ever, coupled with my miserable feeling of disloyalty. When, about this time, Ed began writing of his holiday plans, I suffered everything, for in my then state of mind I could not face the thought of meeting him. It is, by the way, a curious twist of the irony of that old jade Fate, that it was Ed's doings that I ever went to Bedeque. He knew Alf Leard and when I applied for the school he asked Alf to use his influence in my behalf, with the result that I got it—which it is not in the least likely I would otherwise have done.

At last, on Saturday the 11th of December, I received a letter from him saying that he had decided not to come. I fairly cried with relief.

That night was gloomy and rainy. I was writing in the sitting room when Herman came in. Helen was at the organ and under cover of the music Herman bent over me and whispered, "Will you stay awhile with me tonight?"

I nodded, and he went out. I went on writing, not knowing a word I was putting down. When all the others had gone to bed I slipped out to the kitchen where Herman was waiting for me. He flung down the book he was reading and came forward to meet me!

When, as I described before, Ed came so unexpectedly to Bedeque my state of mind cannot be described. There was I under the same roof with two men, one of whom I loved and could never marry, the other whom I had promised to marry but could never love! What I suffered that night between horror, shame and dread can never be told. Every dark passion in my nature seemed to have broken loose and run wild riot. I wonder the strife of them all did not kill me.

As to what Herman thought of it I do not know, for he never alluded to Ed's visit—a circumstance suspicious in itself. Yet I can surmise his thoughts for after that Herman was never the same again, save now and then when some passionate impulse seemed to get the better of him. I believe he thought I was engaged to Ed and was merely amusing myself with him. I cannot complain if he thought so. My behaviour certainly gave him the right to think so. Doubtless he regarded me as a girl who was engaged to one man, yet was untrue to him—who could stoop to flirt with another man, yet never commit herself in words. It is a hard thing enough to have to believe that Herman thought this of me, yet it was better than that he should know the truth. Yes in all cold blooded preference I would rather he believed me an unprincipled flirt, going recklessly as far as she dared, than that he should know how madly I loved him, even while I regarded him as my inferior. Anything, says stubborn pride, would be better than *that*!

The Wednesday night before Christmas Herman went to S'Side and was gone all day. I had just gone up to my room when I heard the carriage and when he came into the hall below I ran out to ask him if he had got a magazine I had sent for. He said he had not been able to do so, as the copies were all sold out, so I went back to my room and flung myself moodily down on my sofa. Helen was away and I was in the deeps of the blues. Presently Herman came upstairs and to my door, with a couple of books in his hand. He tossed them down to me, along with a box of chocolates—"Those are for you, Maud," he said, as he turned away before I could thank him.

Christmas Eve came. Helen was still away and during the evening Herman waylaid me in the hall as I came downstairs to ask me to stay awhile with him that night again. I had been tingling with pain over the subtle alteration in his manner since Ed's visit and my heart beat with joy at this return to our old footing, even though clear brain and unrelenting conscience both told me it would have been far better not to.

I have a very uncomfortable blend in my make-up—the passionate Montgomery blood and the Puritan Macneill conscience. Neither is strong enough wholly to control the other. The Puritan conscience can't prevent the hot blood from having its way—in part at least—but it *can* poison all the pleasure and it does. Passion says, "Go on. Take what crumbs of happiness fall in your way." Conscience says, "Do so if you will. Feed your soul on those blood-red husks; but I'll scourge you well for it afterwards."

I listened only to the former voice that might again and had a couple of hours happiness that were worth—yes, that were *well worth*—the afterlash of conscience. I *will* say it, for I think it!

The next day was Sunday. Cal and a cousin of his came down to spend the day and in the evening Herman drove them up to Central Bedeque. It was eleven when he returned. I had been reading in my room but was now sitting moodily on the lounge. When Herman came upstairs he came in. He had for his excuse another book and a box of chocolates. He gave them to me and sat down on a chair at the foot of the sofa.

I was tired and lonely—I dreaded the hours of darkness—and I could not find it in my heart to send him away. He sat there and talked to me while I nibbled candy. Finally he rose and went to the bureau for his lamp; then suddenly he changed his mind, came right over to the chair by my head, sat down, bent over, and laid his head on the cushion beside mine, his cheek against my forehead. I realized that this was going too far and I said—in as careless a tone as I could assume, for I did not wish to give the situation any added seriousness— "You run away. You'll be nice and sleepy tomorrow if you stay up any longer."

Herman seldom disputed or disregarded my expressed wishes; and he knew quite as well as I did that he had no business to be in my room at that hour of the night. He hesitated a moment, said, "I suppose I will," and bent down with a whispered good-night to kiss me. I had exhausted my powers of resistance in sending him away and I could not refuse him that. I flung my arms impulsively about his neck and kissed him. Then, when he had gone, the Macneill conscience said a few things to me!

When '97 went out and '98 came in I roused myself with an effort to look matters squarely in the face. I knew if I let matters drift on as they were drifting one of two things must inevitably happen. My health and it might be my very reason would give way—or I would fall over the brink of the precipice upon which I stood into an abyss of ruin. And I made a desperate vow to break the chain that bound me at any cost—at any suffering.

This resolution was hardly made before it was broken. I was alone in the parlour New Year's night at dusk when Herman came in and began making love to me again—and in the fatal rapture of the hour my resolution was forgotten. Nevertheless in calmer moments it came back to me and I struggled like a drowning man. I tried to keep out of Herman's way—to avoid him whenever possible. But I fear I couldn't have resisted actual temptation had it presented itself. However, it did not; for three weeks Herman left me alone. Possibly he felt and resented my avoidance, possibly it was the influence of Ed's visit. At all events we had no more "scenes," and *brain* said a cold "Thank God," conscience gave approval,—but *heart*—ah!!!

Suddenly another experience broke the bounds again.

It was a stormy Friday night near the last of January. In the evening Helen was writing a letter in the kitchen and I was sitting by the fire waiting till she should be through and ready to go to bed. Herman was lying on the lounge, fooling with Jink, the dog, and we all kept up a triangular chatter of jokes and nonsense. Finally Helen and I began making mysterious remarks to each other about a mutual joke we had and Herman, scenting a mystery, demanded to know what it was. Upon our refusing to tell him he sprang up, came over and sat down beside me, trying to tease me into telling him. But I would not and while we were fooling about the matter Helen in a spirit of mischief sprang up, snatched the lamp, shut the door and ran. I am sure Herman had no intention of asking me to stay down that night and I had as little thought of it. But we were neither of us strong enough to resist the temptation thus thrust upon us. As a result, the hard three week's struggle went for nothing and we were back on our old footing again.

Sunday evening I was feeling blue and headachy, so curled myself up on the sitting room sofa. Herman came in, sat down on the sofa at my feet and pretended to read. May was in the room and while she was in he read religiously holding my hand in his all the while under my shawl. His clasp, the little caressing pats of his fingers, all thrilled me with a delight that flushed my tell-tale face. To meet Herman's eyes was something I could never do. I remember that day, as I was furtively watching *his* flushed cheek, his long dark lashes, and dusky curls, he suddenly looked around and our eyes met—met and locked. What flashed from one to the other I do not know but when I dragged mine from that fascinated gaze he still looked down at me and finding that I would not look up again he shook my wrist until I did; and then—for May had gone out—he flung away his book and with one of his quick, lithe movements snuggled down beside me, his arm thrown around me, his dark head pillowed on my shoulder. I could not move or speak—I was too happy to wish to do either.

Monday and Tuesday were snow-blockaded and we got no mail. Herman went up after it on Tuesday evening. Howard MacFarlane also appeared and he and Helen betook themselves to the parlour. This left me companionless so I went bluely upstairs to my room. Herman came home at eleven. When he came upstairs he brought me in my letters. I was on the lounge, reading. He sat down on the chair beside me, gave me my mail, and a box of chocolates. I was too lonely to send him away. I read my letters, nibbled my creams and chatted to him. But it was not long until we heard Howard going and of course this was the signal for Herman to leave the room before Helen came up.

Friday night Helen and Herman went to a concert practice up at Central Bedeque, where Helen intended to stay for the night. When Herman came home he again came to my room with the mail. He sat down as usual and the first half hour passed harmlessly, looking over the mail and gossiping about Centreville doings. I made a desperate effort to keep the conversation going *all* the time for I had learned to dread nothing so much as those electrical *silences* of ours. But at last I suddenly found that I had nothing more to say. Herman grew silent at the same time. I was trying to summon up enough resolution to tell him to go when he suddenly slipped down beside me and buried his face on my shoulder. Voice almost failed me but I managed to say,

"You must go now."

He made no reply in words—merely raised his head for an instant and looked straight into my eyes. I suppose he saw there the miserable confession of strong wishes struggling with fainting will for he nestled down again, slipping his arms around me and pressing his face against mine.

Madness? I know it was! And I knew it *then* every whit as vividly as I know it now but *that* knowledge didn't help matters any. I knew I was running a fearful risk but I was under the old fatal, paralysing spell, which only those who have experienced it can understand or condone, and I could not send him away. It was *heaven* to be there in his arms and I gave myself up to the delight of it, forgetting all else for the moment. The candle burned low, so as to leave the room in semi-gloom. We did not talk or try to. If he would only go! I could not *tell* him to go—I could *not* send him away—but oh, if he would only *go!*

Then—at last Herman whispered a single sentence in my ear—a request whose veiled meaning it was impossible to misunderstand!

I was not angry—how could I be? I had no right to be for I was as much to blame as he. And besides, I loved him too much to be angry with him for *anything* he might say or do. But his *spoken* words gave me a saving shock of recoil, which was lacking in the more insidious temptation of silent caresses.

"No—no," I gasped bluntly. "Go away to your own room at once. Herman—you ought to have gone long ago. Oh, *go.*"

I fairly sobbed out the last word. Herman did not go at once—he said nothing more for a minute or two. Then he slipped on his knees to the floor, drew my face to his for one long, clinging kiss—and then went.

I cowered down among my cushions in an agony of shame. Oh, what had I done? What had he said? Was it possible that things had come to such a pass with *me* that only a faintly uttered, hysterical "no" had stood between me and dishonour?

I never slept that night. What I suffered makes me shudder even now! When morning dawned my worst punishment came—to go down and face him. I lingered until I thought he would have gone out but when I went down all the family were at breakfast. I had to take my place opposite Herman and never dared to lift my eyes. Neither, I think, did he. Thereafter we ignored the incident and took no open account of it.

For the next week he was away most of the time and I was horribly lonely. The way in which I missed him frightened me. I shut my eyes in shuddering misery when I thought of our final separation.

But that interminable week passed and he came home Saturday. Sunday night he went over to S'Side to church and returned about eleven. I had no fear of him coming to my room that night for there would be no mail and consequently he would have no excuse for coming. So I was startled when he came to my door and asked if he might have Helen's lamp as he could not find one downstairs. I said "Certainly" and he came in and lighted it. But he did not go out. He loitered around the bureau on one excuse or another, trying on my rings, etc. Evidently he did not want to go but realized that he had no plausible excuse for staying. As for me, I had hardly seen him for a week and I was longing madly for his presence, his smile, his caress. After awhile he came and sat down by me and talked aimlessly for a few minutes about his drive to 'S'Side. I leaned back like one in a dream, my face burning, my heart beating so wildly as almost to choke my breath. I knew it was wrong and foolish enough to let him stay there but it was not so dangerous as before, since Helen might be up at any moment and Herman, knowing this, would not make another "scene."

I am not defending myself at all—I am only just telling what happened. I loved Herman Leard madly and, though I knew perfectly well I should be bitterly sorry the next day, his mere presence there brought me such inutterable happiness, so intense and passionate and all-pervading, that I could not thrust it from me at the command of conscience. So Herman stayed—leaned nearer and nearer—took me in his arms—kissed my lips! I gave myself over once again to the rapture of it and harboured only the delight of being in the arms of the man I loved, of pressing my cheek to his, of smoothing his curly hair with a hand that he would snatch and kiss as if every kiss were his last. I feel those kisses now, burning on wrist and fingers.

When twelve o'clock struck I said, "Lad, it's time for you to go." He obeyed me at once, kissing me good-night with that dangerous tenderness of his against which it was so hard to still my heart.

Thursday night of that week came. Helen was again away. Herman went up to a lecture at Centreville, intending to bring Cal home with him. He returned about eleven, came to my room with the mail, and said that Cal had not come home after all.

Of course it was the same thing over again. I was frightened—and yet happy. Yes, I *was* happy. That little room was heaven to me and Herman all the

Myself in 1898

world. He held me in his arms—he kissed me again and again—he pushed the hair away from my forehead and laid his cheek against it. Oh, even as I write I can feel his arms tighten around me, the warm pressure of his dear curly head on my breast. I cannot subdue or endure the sick longing that comes over me for it to be again a reality!

Twelve o'clock came. As the clock struck I said, "Did you hear that?"

"What?"

"The clock striking twelve. It's time for you to go."

He did not reply except by an inarticulate murmur and a closer pressure. As unwilling to send him as he was to go I remained silent for a few minutes. Then I tried to push him away.

"Herman," I whispered, "didn't you hear what I said?"

He lifted his head and looked down into my eyes.

"Are you sleepy?" he said.

"Yes, I am," I forced myself to say, thinking it might induce him to go. It was a lie—and I suppose he knew it. He hesitated for a moment, looked at my clock, and then back again at me. Then, with a long drawn sigh, he slipped down beside me once more.

I gave up trying to send him away then. I sat there in silence—oh God, such a silence. It was eloquent with a thousand tongues. All the women of my race who have loved in the past spoke in me. I felt Herman's burning breath on my face, his burning kisses on my lips. And then I heard him making the same request he had made before, veiled, half inaudible, but unmistakable. For a moment that seemed like a year my whole life reeled in the balance. The most horrible temptation swept over me—I remember to this minute its awful power—to *yield*—to let him stay where he was—to be his body and soul for that one night at least!

What saved me? What held me back? No consideration of right and wrong. I was past caring for *that*. No tradition or training—that had all gone down before the mad sweep of instinctive passion. Not even fear of the price the woman pays. No, that which saved me from Herman Leard's dishonouring love was *the fear of Herman Leard's contempt*. If I yielded—he might despise me! His hatred, his indifference I could bear. But I could not bear his contempt. If it had not been for that I realize that I would have plunged recklessly into that abyss of passion, even if my whole after life were to be one of agonized repentance.

I pushed his clinging arms from me.

"Herman, *go*," I cried. "go—at once—*at once*, I say!"

"Oh, *no*," he murmured—and there is no power in pen to express all the pleading he infused into that one word.

Again that dizzy shock of temptation I had just enough fear, or resolution, or desperation—ay, that's the right word!—to gasp out imploringly,

"Yes, yes, you *must* go. You ought not to be here at all. Nobody ever was before. Now, Herman, *go*!"

For one breathless moment he was silent, with his lips pressed against my bare arm. If he had refused to go—if he had pleaded but once again—but thank God, he did not. At last he murmured in a low voice, "All right, dear. I'll go"—and the next minute he was gone.

From that night Herman was changed. Was it anger—or baffled passion—or what? I thought then and think still that it was partly his distrust of me in regard to Ed, partly that his eyes were opened to the precipice upon which we stood. And he knew, as I did, that safety lay only in putting an end then and there to the mad game of fire at which we had been playing. He never came to my room again—possibly because Cal came home for good and so he could not—and once more we became almost strangers.

What I suffered in the month that followed cannot be told. In a way I was thankful for the change in Herman—I knew it was my only chance of

ever regaining self-control. But that did not make the pain any the less bitter. Oh, that nightmare month. Sometimes, even, a fierce brief temptation
would sweep over me to yield to the love that possessed me—encourage
Herman—marry him. But I never, even in my worst hours, *seriously* contemplated that. Love was a strong passion with me—but pride—and perhaps
rationality—was equally strong. I could not stoop to marry a man so much
my inferior in all the essentials necessary, not to a few hectic months, but to
a long lifetime together.

I had never dreamed that I was capable of such love as possessed me—
ay, *possessed* is the right word. Simply to be under the same roof with him
brought a strange torturing sweetness that nothing could wholly embitter—
a blow from him would have been sweeter than any other man's fondest
caress. Oh, Herman, Herman, you will never, <u>never, never</u> know how I have
loved you!

Of course, all this mental misery, these passion-wrung days and sleepless, tearful nights could not fail of having a destructive effect on my health.
I grew thin and pale. Everyone noticed it but attributed it to fretting over
Grandfather's death. I was thankful that they did for I could not have borne
that anyone should have suspected the real cause. The time dragged away
and the last of March drew near when Al—who came home about the middle of the month—would take the school again and I would return home.
The thought of leaving Herman, of seeing him no more, was agony; and yet
I looked forward with relief to my final departure for I hoped that when I
was once really away from him and from all things connected with him, I
might succeed in forgetting him, might regain—not my old, unquestioning,
care-free happiness for I knew too well and truly that had gone forever—but
peace and tranquillity, cessation of longing and pain. I might find *rest*.

But the thought that Herman might preserve the same coldness towards
me until the last—that I might have to go away and leave him so, after all
that had passed between us was the bitterest drop in an exceeding bitter cup.

But he *did* break through the coldness—thank God for that!

One evening—March 21st—there was a party at Central Bedeque and
Herman drove me up. He was as silent as usual and so was I. Suddenly he said,

"How much longer have you to teach here?"

I was surprised for it was the very first time he had made any allusion to
my approaching departure although it was frequently discussed by the rest
of the family in his presence. But I answered, with the careless unconcern I
always simulated before him when it came to spoken words.

"Just another week and a half, that is all."

He made no other remark for several minutes. Then he said slowly,

"Have you any photos of your own?"

"No, I haven't any just now," I said. He said nothing more, as we were at our destination. But, foolish as it was of me, his question gave me an exaggerated sense of happiness—sufficient to brighten the whole evening for me. And going home that night, under the star-sprinkled violet sky, he once again as of old drew my head down on his shoulder and pressed his face to mine, and for a little space I forgot pain and heartbreak in the shelter of his arms.

It seemed as if that little indulgence brought down all the barriers again and brought us closer together than ever. The next Friday evening we were invited over to Millie Leard's. Coming home under the spruces,—the crowd of us were in the big box sleigh and Cal was driving—Herman slipped his arm about me and drew me close to him. With a little sigh of happiness I nestled there during our drive over the gleaming marsh and through the snowy woods. He held me so closely and tenderly—he had such a dear gentle way of doing everything—and so often his lips met mine in those never-to-be-forgotten kisses that thrilled me "with all the flame of heaven and all the fire of hell."

Sunday Al and Cal were both away. After dinner Mr. Leard and Helen went to church but I had a headache and did not go. Herman and I found ourselves in the room alone all the afternoon. I was curled up on the sofa and he came over, nestling down beside me, his arms around me, his boyish head pillowed on my shoulder.

That last week went by. Friday night came—my last night in Bedeque. Helen, expecting Howard over, had lighted a fire in the parlour and was waiting there in the moonlit dusk for him. She called me in and, nothing loth to leave the kitchen, where the sight of Herman reading by the table, was alternately fascinating me and torturing me, I went and sat down on the sofa by the window. We chatted away until half past eight and Howard had not put in an appearance. We had just concluded he was not coming when Herman came in. Helen did not welcome his advent with a very good grace and gave him some rather plain hints to be off but he would not take them and presently Helen bounced out of the room in a pet. I rose to follow but Herman was at my side in a flash, his arms about me, his head on my shoulder. I was voiceless and motionless for a moment—and then, overcome by a rush of impulsive tenderness I bent and brushed my lips across his hair. Then he drew me down beside him. We stayed there until ten. I was divinely happy. Herman had the power—for me, at least, of blotting out temporarily everything but himself. I feared nothing, cared for nothing, grieved for nothing.

"Life held for me then no enchantment, no charms, no vision of happiness outside his arms."

He asked me to send him a photo when I had some taken and when I promised I would he said,

"You'll be taking the school again after Al is done of it, won't you?"

"I'm afraid not," I said.

"Why not?" he demanded in such a surprised, startled tone.

"I don't suppose I'll be able to teach any more," I said wearily. "I'll probably have to stay home with grandma after this."

He was silent for a moment, then he said in a dismayed way,

"But you'll be up for a visit this summer, won't you?"

"I'd like to if I can arrange it." I said.

Then there was a long silence. Once I said teasingly "Have you fallen asleep?" "No!" he said, "I could sit here forever without talking."

Well, so could I. But when the clock struck ten I said that I must go.

"You won't forget the photograph?" he said.

"No, I'll be sure to send you one," I promised.

He bent over me, and we exchanged some long, passionate kisses. Then he slipped back to his old place but I said quickly,

"Oh, I *must* go."

"When will we have a chance for a chat again," he whispered.

"I don't know," I said chokingly.

He held me to him with my hands crushed in his. I was in a daze of despair and pain. Then somehow we found our way to the door. We paused there in the glimmering radiance of the moonlight for what was our real good-bye. I thought my heart would break.

> Who can conceive who has not proved
> The anguish of a last embrace?[1]

"Who indeed? He held me close—our lips met in that last kiss.

"Good-night," we breathed—and so I left him standing there in the moonlight and went up to my room—alone—*alone*—as I must henceforth be!

In the morning I bade him good-bye on the doorstep and shook hands with him as with the others. He stood on the platform and watched me off. It was all over—and I only longed and wished that life was over too!

Since coming home I have spent a wretched week. I miss Herman heart-breakingly—I long for him—I *cannot*, strive as I will, keep him out of my thoughts day or night. He is dearer to me than ever. There are hours when I am frantic with longing for a glimpse of his face—the sound of his voice—a kiss—a handclasp. But I *will* conquer—I *will* live it down even if my heart is forever crushed in the struggle.

---

1. From Byron's "To Emma" (1804).

It has been a great relief to write this all out. A great pain, too, for it has brought everything back so vividly!

It seems very much of an anti-climax after all these confessions to write of other and lesser matters. But all things are mingled in this life—the most insignificant follow on the heels of the most tragic. All through this terrible winter, when my soul was being wrung with every passion that blesses or curses humanity, I have done all my little duties painstakingly—I have smiled and chattered at home and abroad and done proper homage to all the conventionalities. And so it is only in keeping with this that I turn from these passionate memories to other and lesser things.

I have had some successes in literature[1]—several acceptances, some of them in new places. My work is a great comfort to me in these sad days. I forget all my griefs and perplexities while I am absorbed in it. I am very ambitious—perhaps too ambitious. Herman told me that once—he seemed to hate my ambition—perhaps he felt the truth that it was the real barrier between us. But at least it is all I have to live for now and I may as well hunt it down.

Novels—I have read some—mostly with a new realization of how far short they fall of actual life and what pale reflections even the best of them are. Only two were worth mentioning. "The Quick or the Dead"[2] was striking. It is powerfully written but too morbid and lacks proportion. Moreover, it ends in an exasperating way that makes one conscious of a desire to take the heroine and shake a little common sense into her.

"Night and Morning"[3] by Lord Lytton disappointed me. Lytton used to be my favourite author in old schooldays when Nate—who was also a frenzied admirer of his—and I used to have no end of animated discussions over his books and heroes. But my allegiance has sadly wavered of late years.

Apart from Herman, I was sorry to leave Bedeque and my school. I liked both and I was very successful in the school.

I shall have to give up teaching and remain home for grandma cannot live alone. I confess that my heart sinks at the prospect but it must be faced. Grandfather's exceedingly foolish will[4] has placed Grandma—and

---

1. In 1898 the *Christian Herald* published "A Pastoral Call" (April); the *Philadelphia Times* published "Brother's Queer Ruse," "Real Test of Friendship," "Courage for the Occasion," "A Lesson in Behavior," and "Story of a Ruby Ring." *Golden Days* published three stories; the *Family Herald* published "A Brave Girl" and "Jen's Device." Other work was published during 1898 in the *Sunday Republican, Illustrated Youth and Age, Pilgrim, Congregationalist, Springfield Sunday Republican, New England Farmer, Family Story Paper, Youth and Age,* and *The Churchman.*

2. Amelie Rives's novelette (1888) deals with the hysterical passion of a young widow, fighting against her growing love of a new suitor.

3. Bulwer-Lytton's novel (1841), centred on a lawsuit.

4. Alexander Macneill left his property to his son John with the proviso that the widow could have the use of the house for the rest of her life.

consequently myself since I must stay at home—in a very anomalous position—a position which will I am sure, be extremely awkward and unpleasant, becoming more and more so as time passes.

Then, again, I feel virtually a stranger in Cavendish. I am entirely out of touch with its interests. But of course *this*, at least, is temporary and after a few months all will be as of yore in this respect. But *other* things can *never* be the same, and the knowledge of this confronts me like an unquiet ghost at every turn.

My old room upstairs

In my many long lonely moments I have been passing the time by reading over old letters and the part of my journal written when I was attending P.W.C. How light hearted and merry and nonsensical it was! I have also been weeding out my letters—a process that is always gone through every time I come home, for I generally conclude that some have lost their interest and so I burn them. But there are some I shall never burn—at least it does not seem to me now that I ever will.

I have finished at last and I am glad for I am very tired. It is late and the house is still. I am worn out, for in writing all this down I have seemed to live it over again and that has been hard on me. I must close this book and go away to sleep in my little room upstairs. Oh, I am very tired—so tired of suffering and vain struggle. Perhaps—dare I hope it?—the future will bring balm and healing and nepenthe.

Sunday, July 10, 1898
Cavendish, P.E.I.

These three months seem to have gone quickly—yet it also seems as if a long time had passed since I last wrote in this old book. I have lived through so many phases of feeling that it seems impossible a short three months could embrace them all.

It is Sunday morning—a dull, sultry July morning with a creamy air full of bird trills and sibilant rustlings of poplar and the savor of red clover fields and balsamic fir woods. The house is still, the atmosphere one of dreams.

When I last wrote here I was miserably unhappy. Well, I am unhappy still. Yet life is more placid for me now. The active storm and stress of passion is past—a certain tranquillity is mine—and the surcease of pain is so blessed that it almost seems—by force of contrast—happiness. I have attained to a calm—but I have not attained to it without a bitter struggle.

Which thread shall I take up first? The one interwoven with Ed's life and mine I suppose. Well, thank God, I am free now—utterly and entirely free.

My last entry in this journal was just after I had written that bitter letter to Ed and I had not had a reply. I expected it on Thursday but none came. Saturday—none came—Tuesday and still no letter! But the next day it arrived. The moment I took it I knew that my photograph was inside of it—and *that* meant freedom. I hastened upstairs to my room. Yet I was half afraid to open the letter—for if he still refused to give me unconditional freedom I believe I should have gone distracted. I had endured and suffered until I could endure and suffer no more.

I sat down by the window and opened the letter. The photo fell out and with it a faded spray of apple blossom. That fatal June night last summer I had worn a spray of apple blossom and Ed had taken it as a souvenir.

The first three pages of his letter were very bitter. My last letter had incensed him but it also won me my freedom. He told me I was free—and I dropped the letter in a surge of passionate relief. For a minute every other pain was forgotten and I was happy.

Towards the last of the letter Ed softened and wrote in a more subdued and heart-broken strain. My anger had all gone and I felt bitterly sorry for him. So I wrote a short letter in reply—I thanked him for releasing me from my engagement and asked him to forgive me for all—and for that unkind letter I had written and regretted—and then I bade him good-bye. I hardly expected to hear from him again but on May 7th another letter came.

When Mollie was over here one evening after I came home and we were up here talking in the twilight she told me some queer ins and outs of a visit she had in Belmont last winter; among others that Sophy Simpson had told her that she—Sophy—had read one of my letters to Ed last summer.

I was bitterly annoyed. I had warned Ed so often not to leave my letters where anyone could possibly see them and it made me angry that he *had* been so careless after all. And Sophy, of all people! When he wrote, giving me my freedom, he said that he would burn all my letters except the *first* which he wanted to keep if I would permit him. I did not like the idea but I felt that I ought to give him all the consideration in my power. So when I wrote back I told him he might but added that he must be careful of it because one of my letters to him had been read by a certain person. This it was that caused Ed to write again. He was determined to know who that "person" was and insisted as his right that I should tell him who had done "such a contemptible thing." He wrote another long passionate epistle— said he would "always love me"—that I would always be his "ideal woman" etc. Ah, Ed, poor boy, if you only knew of what common, earthy clay your "ideal" is made!

I was just starting for town when his letter came so did not answer it until I came back. Then I wrote him a brief note and told him it was Sophy who had read his letter. What Sophy's fate has been I don't know—but if Ed came down on her about it it wouldn't be an enviable one.

Finally I burned his letters—they crumbled into ashes—and I was my own woman once more.

So ends it—and thank God, it does! It has been a bitter cup of humiliation and pain and I have drained it to the very dregs. It has leavened my whole life with its poison and blistered the fair page of my girlhood with despair and shame. Yes, shame. I truly feel it a far deeper shame to have been engaged to Edwin Simpson, feeling as I did towards him, than to have given my caresses to Herman Leard whom I loved. It is a memory from which I must always avert my eyes—but it *is* a memory *only* and not a present torment.

For a month or so after I came home my loneliness was almost unbearable. I had been away so long that I felt *outside* of everything. This has worn away; yet there is always a secret aching sense of blankness—nothing *satisfies*—but the worst has gone by. I have got back to my own place again and various duties and simple, unimpassioned pleasures have crept in to fill my life and bring its jangled chords into harmony once more.

Cavendish has been fairly pleasant this summer. I have got around a good deal—there are several boys who seem to enjoy driving me around. But they all bore me terribly. When one has been whirled as I have been into the most tragic passions it is unspeakably palling to be thrown back again on shams and pretences. I imagine that I feel very much as some classic student might who had drunk at the founts of undying genius and revelled in the masterpieces of the ages were he to be suddenly thrust back into the primer class of his childhood's school and forced to con over his A.B.C.'s from day to day again.

But I have a few pleasures which depend not on others and cannot be taken from me. I have books—those unfailing keys to a world of enchantment. I have re-read old favourites and a few new ones. Among the latter was "A Window in Thrums"[1] by Barrie. It has a certain charm and simplicity which hold interest. Barrie touches common places and they blossom out into beauty and pathos. "Opening a Chestnut Burr"[2] by Roe bored me horribly. I outgrew Roe long ago—to be sure, one need not be of a very stately

---

1. An early sentimental novel (1889) by J.M. Barrie (1860–1937) about a young man who sacrifices ambition for the sake of his old mother.
2. An evangelical novel (1874) by the Rev. E.P. Roe, with a shipwreck as a sensational climax.

mental height for *that*. He is too *preachy*. If a book can not point its own moral all the whittling of the best intentioned author in the world can't get it down sufficiently fine to strike home.

I sent for Ella Wheeler Wilcox's "Poems of Passion"[1] this spring. They seem to be written for me. I have *lived* them every word.

Then I have read "Quo Vadis"[2]—the novel of the year. It is immensely powerful—a perfect picture of the splendor and corruption of Imperial Rome and the court of Nero, out of which rises the pure and awful beauty of early Christianity; the which, could it but have retained its primitive simplicity, instead of becoming overgrown with dogma and verbiage would be as potent a force today as it was when the martyrs of the Colosseum sealed their faith with their blood.

x The window of my old room[3]

I have written a good deal since coming home and am slowly but I think surely, climbing up the ladder. I think my recent work is much better than any I have yet done. I study hard and struggle to improve. I like writing verse best but when I get a good prose plot that runs smoothly I enjoy working it out, too.

I am writing here by the window of my dear old room. It is a veritable little haven of rest and dreams to me, and the window opens on a world of wonder and beauty. Winds drift by with clover scent in their breath; the rustle of leaves comes up from the poplars, and birds flit by in joyous vagrance. Below in a bosky old apple orchard and a row of cherry trees along the dyke where the old tamarack stands guard. Beyond it green meadows slope down to a star-dusted valley of buttercups and past that wide fields stretch up again to the purple rim of wooded hills in the background. There is a blue blue sky that at sunset will be curtained with wonderful splendors, and at night will be thick—sown with stars and at dawn will be washed with a silver sheen and radiance.

"Where the old tamarack stands guard."

---

1. Ella Wheeler Wilcox (1850–1919), a popular and prolific writer of sentimental verse; her *Poems of Passion* (1883) was criticized for being "immoral" but was in fact ethereal.

2. This current world bestseller (1897) by the Polish author Henry Sienkiewicz was a trendsetter in historical romance.

3. The "x" has worn off of the original photograph.

I have been skimming around these impersonal subjects and fighting shy of a real life issue. Concerning it, I hardly know what to say or how to say it. I only know and realize with each succeeding day the sense of *loss* in my life—the always existent hunger for what cannot be mine.

When I came home I made a certain wise and prudent and necessary resolution—namely, that since I *must* forget Herman Leard, I would proceed to do so by utterly refusing to think about him at all—that I would put him out of my mind "as a dream that is banished out of the mind when the dreamer awakes"—starve my wild love for him to death by refusing it "any food of glance or word or sigh"—or even of memory. I did not keep this laudable resolution intact—it was broken to fragments many a time and oft, but the failure was not due to any lack of effort or perseverance on my part. I fought with every scrap of determination and commonsense I possessed to forget him. I struggled on through sleepless nights and weary days—and faced each lonely night and each unwelcome morning the consciousness of failure. But I believe I am slowly winning the victory—and I shall fight on till I conquer.

I sent him one of my photographs as I had promised. He wrote to acknowledge the receipt of it. If I had deluded myself into the belief that I was learning to forget him the moment when his letter was handed to me would have undeceived me. I turned icy cold, I shook from head to foot, a mist came before my eyes. I went dizzily upstairs with the letter pressed against my lips and sat down by my window to read it. I suppose it couldn't be called much of a letter. It was not very long, nor at all clever. There were some visible lapses of grammar in it; the writing and expression were rather crude. There was nothing in it that all the world might not have seen.

But never in all my life did I get a letter that was more welcome or that pleased and moved me so. I re-read it until I knew it by heart. I slept with it under my pillow for a week, waking often in the darkness to draw it out and press my lips to it as passionately as I would have done to Herman's had he been there!

Pensie is married and gone—was married last Wednesday evening. The whole affair was kept very close. Pen was up here a week before and never so much as mentioned the fact to me. Considering our old friendship I think this was very shabby treatment. Pen has seemed a bit queer of late years though. She has married Will Bulman and gone to live in New Glasgow so I suppose she has dropped out of my life forever.

Clara

I was over at Park Corner for a short visit about three weeks ago. Clara and Stella are both home and we had one of our old-time rackets with gales of laughter. Clara and I had a long talk one night. She has had an experience very like mine and our mutual suffering has brought us very close together. Cade had her cup of bitterness to drink while she was away and drained it to

Park Corner

the dregs as I did mine—to find at the bottom wormwood and ashes.

Stella

Fannie Wise has also gone. She has taken a clerk-ship in a Ch'Town bookstore. I miss her very much but I am fast learning to take partings such as these very philosophically, as some of the inevitable ills of human existence. They cannot be avoided and it is both foolish and useless to fret over them. "Off with the old love and on with the new" is an excellent maxim—when it *can* be carried into practice. There are some instances where it cannot; these we have to bury and cherish their graves with what tenderness or bitterness we may. In the meanwhile, time goes steadily and remorselessly on and we must go with him no matter what he bears us away from. By and by there will be an end and then we will be at rest forever—or at least long enough to forget the weariness and pain of our old life ere we are required to wake again to some other existence that awaits us—and in which we may perchance find all we miss in this.

Saturday, Oct. 8, 1898

The "moon of falling leaves" again! How swiftly it comes around from year to year, each year seeming swifter than the last. There is always something sorrowful in the fall despite its beauty and charm. I suppose it is because it is emblematic of life's autumn which must also come to us all. But then if we believe—and such a belief, in some shape or form, orthodox or unorthodox, is found in most of us—that after winter comes the spring of another life that ought not to sadden us. Life is a placid, uneventful thing for me just now. I have even learned to laugh again.

But yet I know
Where'er I go
That there hath passed away a glory from the earth[1]

This has been a "lazy" day for me. I wasn't in a mood for work and couldn't even get up energy enough to go on with my new story. I have written a good deal this summer and have gotten into some new periodicals, as well as keeping up with the old. I really think I am improving a great deal. I seem to see more clearly into things somehow. I suppose it would be hard if all I have gone through didn't bring me some compensation. Sometimes I think it has taught me to see *too* clearly—I might be happier if my delusions and illusions were left to me. But yet—one would think blindness could never be considered a beatific state, and possibly when I get over the blinking and shrinking of new vision and accustomed to the fierce white light of reality I may feel as comfortable as of yore in my soothing twilight.

This latter part of the summer has been busy and—in spots—pleasant. Of *Ed*, I have seen nothing and heard little. He came home to Belmont in the spring. I was in dread that he would visit his friends here and that I'd meet

him somewhere. He stayed away, I suppose, as long as he decently could, and when he finally did come on a flying visit, I had been warned in time and was far enough away, suddenly finding it convenient to pay a long promised visit to Bideford. He was gone before I came back.

I spent my Bideford week with Edith England. I had a nice time and enjoyed it all very much, although there was a sorrowful side to it, too. If any person wants to see clearly just how much she is changed—

Edith England

whether for better or worse—let her revisit after some lapse of time any place where she has once lived. She will meet her former self at every turn, with every familiar face, in every old recollection. She will see, in sharp contrast to the present, her old ideals, views, hopes, beliefs, as she would never see them in any other way. Such at least was my experience. I seemed to be *out-side* of life, looking with cool, dispassionate

Edith's home

---

1. From Wordsworth's "Ode: Intimations of Immortality Recollected from Childhood" (1807), on the consolations as well as the losses involved in maturing.

eyes as might a disembodied spirit, on my old self, the Maud Montgomery who used to teach in Bideford school, and who, in some curious manner, seemed to be still living there. And I saw, as I had not before seen, the difference—in ideals and illusions, in estimate of people and things, in capacity for enjoyment and suffering. I saw how much I had gained in some respects, how much I had lost—irretrievably lost—in others. I had at times a curious sense of imposing on the good Bideford people who were so kind to me—because they thought they were welcoming the Maud Montgomery they had known of old, whereas I was not she at all, but a new creature altogether, who bears her name and inhabits her body but is only an impostor after all. That former Maud was so different—she was a happy, light-hearted girl with any amount of ideals and illusions and a comfortable belief in the stability of "things temporal." She had some strong ambitions and aspirations but her main object was to "have a good time" and she had a knack of succeeding with it. She believed in herself and other people, had a good conscience and a whole heart, and did not trouble herself greatly over the perplexities of life. But the girl of today—how different from all that is she! She has no illusions and few ideals; life is flat, stale, and unprofitable, viewed from her old standpoint and full of snares and pitfalls as viewed from her new. She has a "past" and its shadow falls ever across her path. She has looked below the surface and seen strange things. She could no more live that Bideford year over as she lived it then than she could gather up her old illusions and clothe herself in them as in a garment outgrown. And would she if she could? Do you know, that is a question I often ask myself—"If I could would I go back to my old self?"— and I can never answer it. I can never dare to say either "no" or "yes." The fruit of the tree of knowledge may leave a bitter taste in the eater's mouth, but there is something in its flavour that can never be forgotten or counterfeited.

At the end of my Bideford week I went to Bedeque!

Don't you wonder how I dared do it? I wondered not a little myself. But Helen had made me promise to go and I could hardly refuse, or put it off any longer. Besides, I had another reason which I did not proclaim from the housetops.

In the months that had gone by since I left Bedeque I had had a hard fight and, though often worsted, it would have been hard indeed if I had not gained some poor victory in the end. I had really succeeded in a measure in stifling my infatuation for Herman Leard—strangled it into unconsciousness. Was it really dead? That was what I wanted to know. That was why I went to Bedeque. If when I met him it could be without a tremor or a heartbeat then I would gladly realize that I *was* free from the thralldom of that tyrannical passion.

Helen met me at the boat in the evening and we walked up to the house. Herman was building a load of hay in the field by the road and came over to speak to me. The very moment I put my hand in his and looked into his eyes there surged over me the sickening conviction that I loved him as madly as ever. At that moment all the passion I had hoped was dead started with one agonizing throb into trebly convulsive life.

I went into the house as one in a dream. They had company that evening and, as of old, I was forced to mask my pain under smiles and vivacity. It was only when I got away to bed that I could find relief in a passionate fit of tears. When it was over the reactive calm enabled me to look the situation in the face with some degree of firmness. And I made the resolution that I would avoid Herman in every possible way during my visit.

You may not believe that I kept this resolution—but I did, although what it cost me cannot be expressed. The house was full of visitors most of the time and this made it easier. Then Helen and I were much away visiting and while we were home I kept out of Herman's way markedly. Oh, I was merry and unconcerned enough, but I cried myself to sleep every night I was there. On the last evening we were all out in the yard in the twilight. Herman came along, said he was going for the cows, that there was a very pretty lane on the way and "wouldn't I come and see it." I took one step forward—I *wanted* to go more than I have ever wanted anything in the world. Then I stopped. Something—I don't know what—held me back. It would be madness to go and undo the work of months—lose what I had so hardly gained. I said, "I'm afraid it is going to rain," and turned back. It was the wisest thing I ever did in my life—and the hardest.

I wonder what would have happened if I had gone. I shall never know—and to the end of my life I shall go on wondering.

I was so thankful that my visit was at an end. It seemed to me that if I had had to stay one day longer I would have died or gone crazy. I think Herman was angry because I had not gone with him for that walk—at anyrate, he disappeared Saturday morning and did not even come to say good-bye to me. And so it ends—yes, ends. For I will never go back to Bedeque and I expect and *hope* that I will never see Herman Leard again. I feel that no love can ever again be to me what mine for him was—that never again will I meet any man who will have the power to stir my heart and soul to their profoundest depths as did Herman Leard. And, all in all, I think it is best so for I believe that such love is hardly ever the forerunner of happiness—it is a "challenge to fate" and she punishes it surely and severely. I have had my love dream and it is dead—or murdered—and I have buried it very deeply—and now what I have to do is to forget it as utterly as may be.

When I had once left Bedeque I lapsed back into my state of mind before going—a sort of pangless resignation to my lot. I came home—I worked and studied and *thought* hard—and now I am at peace. I feel no active pain.

Sometimes—for instance when I am writing like this—I feel a stab of the old agony and a sudden realization of *all I have missed* comes to me sickeningly. Then I close my eyes and pray to die. But it passes and I am calm once more. I am not unhappy now—at least not with a *positive* unhappiness. There is a certain *negative* unhappiness in my life—the unhappiness not of present pain but of absent joy. But I think there are very few *really* happy people in the world—I can count on my ten fingers all I know whom I believe are really perfectly happy—and I cannot expect to be more favoured than the majority. And, after all, I frankly admit that my suffering was no more than my just punishment—although I don't know that a sense of having merited one's pain alleviates it any—rather aggravates it, I should say.

But I must stop turning myself inside out in this uncanny fashion. For after all, words, even the most felicitous, say either too much or too little. I have much to be thankful for—thankful that I did not wreck my life altogether in that mad passion of last winter. I came perilously near to it.

Oh, thank God, it is all over!!!

I came home by way of Park Corner and Clara came down with me for a week. We had quite a gay time with picnics, drives, etc.

Cavendish is looking very beautiful now, with bloomy mists purpling over its dark spruce hills and all the splendor of crimson and gold among its maples and birches. Cavendish is really the prettiest country place I've ever been in. It is a long, narrow settlement, bordering on and following the outline of the north shore, whose wonderful waters, ever changing in hue and sheen, now silvery gray, now shimmering blue, now darkly azure, now misty with moonrise or purple with sunset, can be seen from any and every point.

Cavendish proper begins at Rob Mckenzie's where the road turns sharply at right angles and runs on through hedges of spruce and fir to Rustico. It is quite a noted "corner," with the McKenzie homestead looking down on it from a windy hill, for it generally marks the limit of "after meeting drives," being a nice distance from anywhere and a convenient place to turn. Down below it, is a short bridge over a brook that has absurdly deep and steep banks for so small a stream. This was the brook to which Pensie and I, in sunny evenings of old schooldays when I would be visiting there, used to bring the cows to water and always contrived to have some funny adventure. At one side of the bridge is a small cow-gate under low-hanging boughs of young spruce and behind it a dim winding path up the brook where we loitered to pick gum before we came out to the dewy clover fields beyond the girdle of spruces.

Away down nearly to the shore on the right, where the waves are always lapping and purring on the beach, is "old Ewen's place," as it is still called,

"Big" George Macneill's house

albeit poor "old Ewen" has long since gone to the reward that awaits the just, and his widow—known by the cheerful sobriquet of "Mrs. Dead Ewen"—hold sovereign sway in the plain, lonely-looking old house down by the shore.

Up on the crest of a gentle hill, quite close to the road is Albert Macneill's establishment, all as painfully clean and whitewashed and spic and span as possible. I have no doubt you could eat a meal off the ground without overbrimming the proverbial peck of dirt; but there isn't a tree about the place and the bareness is painful.

Opposite them, to the left, away up behind a gleaming white birch grove, is "Big" George Macneill's house—not that you can see it, for there is only the gray gable of a barn peering out from one end of the afore-said grove to tell of human habitation, but it is there all the same, smothered in trees as

The Manse

old-fashioned as itself. William A. Macneill's house—"Will Sandy's"—is on the right and then comes Charles Macneill's, looking down over the country side from its little rising. It is a tiny, old-fashioned house, so small that one wonders how the family were ever stowed away in it, when they were all home. They are all gone now except Alec and Russell. Well, we have had some pleasant times in that old house with the enormous willows drooping over it. John Laird's place comes next and is snug and prosperous. Between it and Wm. Laird's is a bit of road I always love to go through, a stretch of spruce wood, always shady and balsamic. When you emerge from it and go up the slope by Wm. Laird's gate Cavendish East drops out of sight behind you and Cavendish Middle flashes up before you, stretching away on the

Geo. R. Macneill's

View in Cavendish, from Church Hill

left to green fields and woods and hills, and on the right sloping down to the shore. There is Murray Robertson's ugly group of buildings and on the other side is "Robertson's Swamp"—a blue, wind-rippled sheet of water, that is rose and gold in the sunset—for it is usually sunset when I am prowling

PRESBYTERIAN CHURCH AND PART OF CEMETERY, CAVENDISH

around thus. Up on the crown of the slope is Uncle John's lane, then the manse in its green square and then "Geo. R." Macneill's snug barns and "handsome new residence"—*a la* 'Cavendish Notes."And from this point the ground falls away again and a panorama of Cavendish West unfolds itself on the opposite hill. We go down past George R.'s to the cross roads at the church corner and the church itself—the big spireless, time-worn building with its oriel windows that flashed back the splendour of the sunset. It is anything but a handsome church, this of ours, but I love it for its memories.

Surrounding the church on two sides is the graveyard for four generations have made it their resting place. There under the shadow of willows and poplars "the rude forefathers of the hamlet sleep" the sleep that knoweth not dreams or waking. Old and young, rich and poor are mingled there in an unquestioned equality. Those old Scotch men and women who lived and loved and suffered when the century was young are resting there. There, too, sleeps my fair young mother, always fair and always young, for time has no empire over the grave. She died when only twenty-three, in the full bloom of her beauty—for I have always been told she was

The graveyard and
Mother's grave

very beautiful, and as sweet and good as beautiful.

Northward from the corner slopes the "Big Lane" down to the shore—a favourite walk of mine in silent summer evenings when the sea is a misty purple and the pond a lake of crimson and gold and the evening star glimmers like a pearl afloat on a crystal sea. There is some charm about that old lane that

Wm. C.'s house

is quite indefinable since it is a bare lonely one with nothing but green, low-lying meadows on either hand.

Westward the road drops down over the "church hill" to the "old mill brook" which runs through a little valley to empty itself into the pond. Pierce

Macneill's grubby homestead looks down on it and on the other side, up against the woods, "far from the madding crowd" is the house where David and Margaret Macneill live—a quaint old pair. Time has passed them by and left them there, the survivors of a forgotten order of things. Then comes another long hill, off which long lanes lead down to homesteads snugly tucked away

The Hall

against a girdle of birch and spruce. There is William C. Macneill's—"Willy Makum's"—old fashioned house down by the pond. It is the oldest house in Cavendish and was considered a fine place in its palmy days—the people of New London and Cavendish used to call it "Government House." It is still a picturesque house, surrounded by its apple orchards and patriarchal willows.

Next in line is John D. Macneill's place and then William Simpson's. On the left hand side of the hill are no homesteads—nothing but wide green meadows reaching to the girdling woods at the back. Up on the crest of the hill is the Baptist parsonage and from it we go down the steep, spruce-shadowed "hall hill" with the hall itself tucked away among its birch half way down. At its foot is another brook and Darnley Clark's lane leads up on the right under arching wild cherry boughs. Next on the right comes the old Clark homestead—the prettiest one in Cavendish to my thinking. Tillie, Jane, and Mary Clark live there, three well-to-do and thrifty maidens of uncertain age, and if their life is not an ideal one it is not the fault of their surroundings.

Opposite this on the left is Alec Stewart's place and then follows a bit of "wild road" sloping gently up until a curve comes where the lane goes down to Charles Simpson's and George Harker's. The next is the forge at Hillman's and there Cavendish ends. There remains yet however a road to be explored—the one that runs out from the church and passes the school a few yards further on. The school is built side to the road, with a bare green playground around it and back of it the dear old "School Woods,"

View of school from woods

"Lairds' Hill"

View from Lairds' Hill

that drop down in a succession of natural terraces to the brook. In my early childhood these woods were simply fairy realms of romance for me and to this day they retain much of their old charm. Beautiful they are, with winding paths and sunny open glades where winds and sunshine come in softly sifted, mossy nooks and corners, "beauty spots" along the brook, where ferns grow in plumy luxuriance. There are hundreds of sweet old memories woven about them.

Opposite the school is our gate and the lane leading up under the birches to the house, which cannot now be seen from the road as it used to be, so hidden is it among trees.

Past the school is the "school hill" and on the other side "Laird's Hill" the prettiest one in C. This is our walk on Sunday evening into Baptist preaching and is always a delightful one in every season. On either side extend sweeps of picturesque meadow, and from the top the finest view in Cavendish is to be had over the whole settlement down to the shore. Just over the crest of the hill is James Laird's house and down past it, snuggled away in a grove of maple and spruce, is the Baptist

Interior of Baptist Church

church. Past it, the road is idyllic, curving through beech and fir woods over brook and hill until we come out at Elton Robertson's. And here, if we are wise, we will stop, for beyond this point is Cavendish road, which is an ugly, commonplace settlement, expressive of anything but the poetry of life.

Saturday, Dec. 31, 1898
Cavendish, P.E.I.

The last day of the old year—it has only five more hours to live—is surely the time of all times for "journalizing." People generally do a little raking over their inner consciousness at this time, as well as making more or less of good resolutions for the coming year. I am going to make just one—later on. At present, I am looking backward and in all truth I cannot say that the record of '98 is one on which it pleases me to look—far from it! I am taking one glance over its blistered pages before I turn my back on it forever.

It is mid-evening. Outside it is chill and frosty and starlit. The little snow that fell today has dusted the old sentinel spruces with white and flung a royal carpet over earth for the New Year's kingly feet to press. Everything is very quiet. Grandma is reading at one side of the table; I am sitting at its end; my cat "Coco" is curled up, a plump, silver-gray creature, at my feet. We are in the old kitchen where we always sit on these long winter evenings that are apt to be a little dull. If the first months of '98 were storm-tossed and passion wrung for me, these closing ones have been as placid and calm as months could be—*too* placid, to tell

Our old kitchen

truth, and I sometimes dare to wish for a little stir and excitement. But then it might not be of an agreeable kind and heaven knows I have had enough excitement of a sort in the earlier months of the year to last me all my life.

I have been writing as steadily as possible, under rather uninspiring conditions and have had a good many acceptances, some of them in new places. How I love my work. I seem to grow more and more wrapped up in it as the days pass and other hopes and interests fail me. Nearly everything I think or do or say is subordinated to a desire to improve in my work. I study people and events for that, I think and speculate and read for that.

In some ways I have been having a rather nice time; and of course there are some worries as usual. I am seldom free from them now.

Cavendish is fairly lively at present. In October the Literary Society reopened and has a good programme prepared. I have enjoyed the meetings. In a quiet life such as mine even so insignificant an outing as a meeting of the Literary is a pleasure. The walk up is nice. We tramp briskly along over the dark fir-fringed road until we reach the hall. Then follows a half-hour's desultory chat with friends and an overhauling of books before we settle down to the particular delectation of the evening—lecture, debate, essay, as it may be. When it is over there is a walk or drive home with some convenient escort with whom you can lightly discuss the sayings and doings of the evening and poke fun at various Simpson idiosyncrasies.

There have been several deaths in Cavendish this fall. One of them was "old Aunt Caroline" who was "old Aunt Caroline" ever since I can remember. In fact, I have my doubts whether she could ever have been young at all. Seriously, she was one of those people whom it is utterly impossible to picture as a dimpled baby or a pink-cheeked, bright-eyed young girl.

She lived at Wm. C.'s and was his unmarried sister and household drudge. Poor old lady, I don't suppose there is a soul in the world who really regretted her or will miss her in any way. She was not an exhilarating person, being one of those unfortunates who are constantly worrying, not only about their own affairs but everybody else's as well, and will not give themselves or others any rest at all. Nevertheless, she was a sort of landmark and one misses her in that

The x marks our pew

respect. Wm. C.'s pew is in front of ours in church and old Aunt Caroline was unfailingly in her place—the corner by the window—year in and year out. I shall never forget her shirred black satin bonnets—or was it always the same bonnet? To my small eyes they were fearfully and wonderfully made. They fitted snugly around her head like a nightcap and framed her wrinkled face closely. (She had more wrinkles than any person I every saw.) There never was anything like those bonnets. I am sure, or like the old black lace shawl that was always laid at precisely the same angle across her thin shoulders, and whose rusty patterns I generally amused myself by tracing out when we stood up to sing. In summer Aunt Caroline would generally carry a big pink "English rose" in her cotton-gloved fingers and hold it to her nose all through the service.

Very conservative indeed was old Aunt Caroline. Anything new her soul abhorred. *Hymns* were antichrist; and *bicycles*,[1] heaven preserve us, were part of the direct equipment of the Prince of Darkness. I used to take an unholy delight in telling her I was going to get one, although I really hadn't any idea of so doing. I couldn't afford one, worse luck! It *was* such fun to see her horror. She couldn't have looked more aghast if I had told her I was going to appear out in trousers.

Well, poor old soul, she has gone, with all her peculiarities and prejudices. It gives me a lonely sensation to look at her old pew corner and find it empty, reflecting that the frail, bent, shrunken old figure in the faded shawl and preposterous bonnet is gone from it forever. It is to be hoped that in the grave poor old Aunt Caroline has found the rest that life denied her and has ceased to worry over the misfortunes and faults of poor humanity.

When I recall my state of mind this time last year and compare it with the present I see how much I have to be thankful for. I *could not* live that dreadful time over again—I do not know how I lived it once. But I did—and

---

1. In the 1890s, the safety bicycle with its rear chain-drive started a craze, especially among women. Susan B. Anthony called the bike "the freedom machine."

it is over—and buried deep! Yet not so deep but that its ghosts haunt me reproachfully, not so deep but that its bitterness is still potent to poison my cup, not so deep but that its cold loathly memory creeps like a snake across hours that might otherwise be happy.

I have been revelling in some new books of late. One of them was "The Christian,"[1] Hall Caine's much talked of new novel. I liked it fairly well although I confess I got heartily out of patience with the hero, *John Storm*, who, judged from a practical standpoint, is really a compound of fool and fanatic. But then I suppose neither the book nor its characters *are* to be judged from a practical standpoint. I have no doubt that there are many just such people in the world as *John* and *Glory*, and that the conflict of their emotions always works out to a tragic issue.

I have also read "The Manxman," an older book of Caine's. It is the only one of his books I really like. I am not easily "moved to tears" over a book, but I *did* cry over "The Manxman."[2]

I got Kipling's "Ballads"[3] for a Christmas present. They are capital—full of virile strength and life. They thrill and pulsate and burn, they carry you along in their rush and swing, till you forget your own petty interests and cares and burst out into a broader soul-world and gain a much clearer realization of all the myriad forms of life that are beating around your own little one. And that is always good for a person even if one does slip back afterwards into the narrow bounds of one's own life. We can never be *quite* so narrow again.

On November 8th I rather regretfully packed up a valise and started to make a long-promised visit to Aunt Emily. I say "regretfully," because Aunt Emily is not exactly a favourite of mine and Malpeque is a place I don't care for.

I went over to Park Corner and stayed there until Saturday. Ever since I can remember "going over to Aunt Annie's" has been a phrase that stood for a delightful jaunt. To begin with, it was such a pretty drive, those winding

Aunt Annie's at Park Corner

---

1. Bestselling novel (1897) by Hall Caine (1853–1931) about an independent young woman's struggles to follow her own religious ideals.

2. Caine's earlier novel (1894), using Isle of Man dialect and folklore and introducing taboo subjects (divorce, illegitimacy) and mockery of evangelical hypocrisy.

3. Rudyard Kipling's *Barrack-room Ballads* (1892 and 1896) included "Gunga Din" and "The Widow at Windsor" (which so offended Queen Victoria that it cost Kipling the Poet Laureateship).

thirteen miles of hill and wood, river and shore. There are first the three miles through Cavendish and Bay View to the Bay View Bridge, spanning the

pretty "Hope River." Three miles further on is Stanley, a pretty village on the banks of another river. There are two or three stores in Stanley and we have always gone there to buy household supplies. Stanley used to seem quite a town to my childish eyes. It

Stanley, coming from Park Corner to Cavendish

was the hub of the universe then—or of our solar system at the very least. Beyond Stanley the road wound on to another little village—Clifton. And here, around a certain corner, is a certain small, yellowish-brown house, close to the road, that I always look at with a kind of fascination, for it is the house where my father and mother lived after their marriage, and where I

was born and spent the first year of my life. The years have passed on and each succeeding one has left the little brown house something shabbier than before, but its enchantment has never faded in my eyes. I always look for it with the same eager interest when I turn the corner. Beyond Clifton is "Clifton Bridge" over which I can never drive without a certain inward, unvoiced shrinking, because long

The house where I was born

ago there were two or three years when it was considered very unsafe and I have never been able to rid myself entirely of the impression, though the bridge has long since been repaired. And then its drawbridge! Do what I will, I have always been horribly afraid of drawbridges and am to this day. I shiver

from the time the horse steps on the bridge until I am safely over the draw. Beyond the bridge is a lovely bit of road, curving around the river shore, with a row of firs fringing the bank, blue river reaches glimmering through them, and afar out the harbour bar, with the gulf surges beating on it. Then comes the big maple grove at Spring

Brook, with the old "Geddie Memorial Church,"[1] the English church and the Springbrook school.

Past this the road dips down to a cluster of little houses we used to call "Stovepipe Town" in the old Park Corner days; then up over another hill

and French River is spread out below, the houses of the village clustered around the head of the river. Beyond French River and the old hall, the road slopes up and down over bare hills to the school, where it turns and runs parallel to the shore, past Uncle Cuthbert's and the old Senator's down to the beautiful pond. Just across the bridge Uncle John Campbell's

Under the beeches [and birches]

lane turns in under overhanging spruces and we drive in over a little brook where blue iris lilies grow thickly, up past the big orchard, under the arch of beeches and birches, and around to the big white house. Here, in other days there was a trio of merry cousins to rush out and drag me in with laughter and mad-cap greetings. But that is changed now. Cade and Frede are away and only Stella is left. However, she is jolly enough for a dozen. Saturday evening Stell and I drove ourselves up to Malpeque.

Stella

It was awfully cold and we would have frozen to death I verily believe if we had not kept up our circulation by laughing all the time.

Lucy came there from Kensington the next morning and we stayed a week. Before Uncle John died it used to be a very jolly house but that is all changed now. Aunt Emily is not a cheerful person to sojourn with. She is too much in the habit of "picking and nagging," and giving you sly "digs." Then the house itself

Aunt Emily's

is at the "jumping-off place," miles from anywhere. To be sure, the scenery is beautiful—but man cannot live by scenery alone, or woman either! The house is built right down on the shore of Richmond Bay and before it extend

---

1. Presbyterian Church at Springbrook, PEI, named for the Rev. John Geddie (1815–1872), Minister of Cavendish and New London from 1838 to 1845, and the first missionary sent out to any foreign field by the Presbyterian Church of Canada.

great sweeps of blue water, dotted with purple islets. On one of these is the lighthouse and every night at twilight its great golden star flashes out through the purple dusk and saffron glow. Some evenings there were the most wonderful sunsets imaginable.

And so '98 ends! I am truly thankful. I turn to '99 with a chastened joy and a trembling hope that I may pass out from the old shadows into the sunshine of its dawning—may throw off the mantle of the past year as an outgrown garment. This night last year I was at the Gardiner's dance and danced the New Year in with *Herman*. We were dancing together as the clock struck twelve. I took it then as a good omen—but it was not. Oh '98, how much I have suffered in you! How much of good and evil you have taught me, stern, cruel, relentless teacher that you were! Yet after all, '98, your harsh discipline has borne good fruit—and bitter as it was, I thank you for it. Thank you and farewell!

1899

Tuesday, April 4, 1899
Cavendish, P.E.I.

This is April—and ought to be spring but isn't! One expects spring in April—expect mud and slush and bare fields and warm sunny days. Cold winds, good sleighing, and as much snow as we have at present seem very unseasonable. However, spring will surely come even if it is late, and it will be doubly welcome for we have had a very severe winter. It has been woefully cold ever since New Year's and much shivering is a weariness to the flesh. The last three months have been busy and not unpleasant but they have not been at all eventful, so that any spice of interest this entry may contain will not arise from a recital of startling or unusual matters. However I'm going to write out the details of my quiet humdrum life this winter simply and solely for my own amusement. I enjoy this writing down my impressions of life and things as I go, even in my narrow orbit, and reading them over afterwards to compare them with newer ones.

It is just a year, almost to the day, since I came home from Bedeque, an unhappy, disillusioned, hopeless girl. Looking back now, I know that nothing in the world could induce me to go through that dreadful time again. Good God, how I suffered! I wonder how I lived through it! Things are changed for the better now. Pain, even the fiercest, wears itself out, even though its *effects* must endure to the end of time—and perhaps through all eternity, if such there be for us as sentient creatures. And so I, someway or other, have come up from the depths, and am not minded to go back to them.

In a way, I have been having quite a nice time this winter. I say "in a way" because in reality the gayety was all on the surface and away down underneath my new inner consciousness was coiled up, brooding like a snake in its den and every once in a while darting a pang into my soul's vitals. But I must not go into self-analysis yet awhile—we will stick to the outside of things if you please.

The Literary Society has been in a flourishing condition this winter and I owe to it the few books that have delighted my soul. I have no doubt that it is a wise ordinance of fate—or Providence?—that I cannot get all the books I want or I should certainly never accomplish much. I am simply a "book drunkard." *Books* have the same irresistible temptation for me that liquor has for its devotee. I *cannot* withstand them. For instance;—the first new story I read in '99 was "Phroso" by Anthony Hope.[1] I brought the book home from the hall one wretchedly cold night and sat up in bed until two

---

1. The pen name of Sir Anthony Hope Hawkins (1863–1933), bestselling author of *The Prisoner of Zenda* (1894), *Rupert of Hentzau* (1898), *The Dolly Dialogues* (1894), and other popular novels.

o'clock, shivering and freezing but quite indifferent to it, and finished the book before I could sleep. It was a glorious yarn—full of life and "go." It was romance pure and simple, without any alloy of realism or philosophy. I like realistic and philosophical novels in spells, but for pure, joyous, undiluted delight give me romance. I always revelled in fairy tales.

But I have read one book recently—heaven send I never have to wade through such another. I cannot imagine a worse "future punishment" than to be condemned to read such books for all eternity. It was an old tale— "The Children of The Abbey"[1] and was the mushiest, slumpiest book I ever read, possessing a most lachrymose heroine who fainted in every chapter and cried quarts of tears if anyone looked sidewise at her. But as for the trials and persecutions which she underwent, their name was Legion and no fair maiden of these degenerate days could endure one-tenth of them—not even the newest of "new" women!

I have been to several concerts and "socials" this winter. I had to recite at most of them and as a rule enjoyed them. But preserve me from "pie socials." They are the abomination of desolation. The programme is only a pretence—the real business of the evening is selling the pies, attended by fearful excitement in the pit. An auctioneer, chosen for strength of lung and ability to crack dollar-coaxing jokes is selected, and the pies are auctioned off to the highest bidder, who shells out his cash, get his pie, and is whisked upstairs by the powers that be to find the fair builder thereof and eat it with her. Those who don't or can't buy pies raise all the disturbance they possibly can and settle old scores by several hand to hand encounters. The Babel is so great that you can't hear yourself think and the scene more nearly resembles the proverbial "bear-garden" than anything you have ever seen.

However, the pies are all sold at last and your escort comes along clinging to a pie with one hand and to the shy little schoolgirl who brought it with the other. He whisks you off to the higher regions where the matrons are dispensing hot coffee. You capture a vacant corner, grasp a knife and attack that pie, cased in sheet armour of frosting. It makes a valiant resistance but is finally overcome and proves, alas, to be but a whited sepulchre. However, by this time you are so hungry you can eat anything, so down goes a generous section of the pie, helped along by gulps of scalding coffee. The whole room is in a buzz, with laughter, conversation and crunching. When you are done, leaving the remnants of the pie behind you on the principle that to the victors belong the spoils, you get on your wraps and start homewards, wondering who first invented a pie social and what was done to him for it.

---

1. A highly coloured gothic romance (1796), by Regina Maria Roche (1764–1845) about young people robbed of an inheritance.

This winter we organized a "sewing circle" in aid for a new church building fund. It has taken a good deal of time I could ill spare and has been no end of a bother. But that is the seamy side. There is another side in our pleasant afternoons of work and gossip—strictly harmless and clarified gossip, of course, patented for the use of church sewing societies!—and our evenings of fun when the boys come in and we play games of the same brand as the gossip. Of course there are some "cranks" in the crowd—is there ever anything free from them?—who try to make things as difficult as possible for all concerned.

We are losing our minister. He has accepted a call to Tryon and Hampton, and is "flitting" today. I do not think he will be much regretted. He was a fairly good preacher but no pastor and his wife and family were certainly fearful and wonderful creatures—whole reams of description could not do them justice. What Cavendish will find to talk about when Mrs. Robertson is gone I really do not know. Her sayings and doings quite usurped the place of the weather in current greetings. "Have you heard Mrs. Robertson's latest?" or "*What* will Mrs. R. do next?" being standard questions. She is really so eccentric as to be abnormal and her escapades have been many and startling, from going to church with boots on but no stockings, to tearing Mr. Robertson's harness to pieces and blaming it on the boys of the congregation. I think and have always thought that the woman is not really sane in some respects. If she *is* sane, there is no excuse for her actions.

May 1, 1899
Cavendish, P.E.I.

There is a magic about the spring—some power that revives half-dead hopes and faiths and thrills numbed souls with the elixir of new life. There is no age in spring—everybody seems young and joyful. Care is in abeyance for a little while and hearts throb with the instinct for immortality.

These days are so beautiful—mellow and breezy and sweet. There are no leaves yet but every little brown bud is swelling and in sunny, sheltered spots there is a hint of greenness. The days are long and the twilights full of a mellow graciousness—and all the snow is gone, gone, gone! There are such lovely blue skies and such faint purple mists over the bare hills; and last Friday night I got some tiny pink-and-white mayflowers—the initial lettering of spring. It is worth while to live through the winter just to have the spring.

April has been such a busy month that there has been time for nothing but work—and if there had been time there were no roads, so one stayed home perforce. Since going out was impossible I filled up my spare evenings reading. The first book I read this month was the "Tower of London,"[1] which is sugar-coated history. I read it once before, long ago when I was a kiddy of ten up at Grandpa Montgomery's. The chapter in which the burning of a martyr at the stake is described made an impression on me that haunted me for weeks. I never saw the book again until this spring and I was half afraid to re-read it, for I thought it wonderful when I first read it and so few of our childish opinions wear. I have in mature life re-read with bitter disappointment so many books that I loved in childhood. It is only a foolish fancy, I suppose, but to me the disillusionment is almost as painful as to meet some old loved childhood chum and find her nothing that your memory had painted. But "The Tower" stood the test fairly well. I found it interesting still and the "terrible chapter" still made my blood freeze with horror.

Among all the flotsam and jetsam of newspaper and magazine stories I have read one that made a powerful impression on my mind. It was a short one in the March *Atlantic*,[2] and dealt with the first experiences of a disembodied spirit after death. It appealed to the curiosity that is in us all regarding the future—a curiosity that can never be satisfied until we are dead—and perhaps not even then. But if not—there will be no curiosity.

My own dear den

I have moved upstairs again to my own dear den and feel as if I had returned from exile. I do not like that downstairs room. Just as soon as it was warm enough I marched up here and began scrubbing and renovating. Then I moved all my Lares and Penates[3] up—and here I am, a queen in my own little independent kingdom. Woe to the poor mortal who has not even one small room to call her own.

Our Literary closed on April 21st with a paper by Mr. Jackson—the new Baptist Minister—on "Religion vs Morality." He *said* it wasn't an old sermon and I suppose we are bound to believe him; otherwise, I should think—but I *won't* think! It is a dangerous habit.

The paper was dry and quite hazy; it is my private belief that the Rev. Jackson was all befogged on the subject himself. But there, he is really a very

1. Another early Victorian novel (1840) by W.H. Ainsworth (1805–82) about Lady Jane Grey, Queen Mary, and Queen Elizabeth.

2. *Atlantic Monthly* (1857–), enduring American magazine of literature, art, and politics. The March issue contained "An Evicted Spirit" by Marguerite Merington, the story of a mourning family, presented from the point of view of the dead child.

3. Household gods (Latin), guardians of cult objects and of domestic possessions.

nice little fellow and it was not his fault that "Religion vs Morality" was not a very enthralling subject.

It is evening while I am writing. The sun has got down behind the trees and their long, lazy shadows are falling over the lane and fields. Beyond, the brown hills are larking in an amber radiance underneath a pale aerial sky of rose and blue. The

A glimpse of hill meadows

firs on the south hill are like burnished bronze and their long shadows are barring the hill meadows. Dear old world, you are very beautiful and I love you well.

May 28, 1899
Cavendish, P.E.I.

This is Sunday evening and there is no preaching. Hence it is that I have come up to my den, where *Coco* is snoozing peacefully on my bed, selected a certain bent, rather rusty little key from my bunch, unlocked a small trunk whole contents are not intended for public circulation, and taken out this book. Having nothing to do, I feel that I would enjoy writing in it for company's sake.

It is 6:15 and the shadows of the trees are getting long and slender. It is the last of May and therefore ought to be mid-spring. But May has been so cold that things are very backward and it is only in these last few days

that the leaves have begun to come out at all.

May has been very busy, Uncle Leander has been here the greater part of it and will be here until July. He is on "sick leave," as his nervous system seems to be badly broken up.

When he came he brought a lot of new books with him and I went on one of my literary "sprees." For a week I simply revelled in books day and night and even read between bites at my meals. The first I plunged into was "The Soul of Lilith" by Marie

Corelli.[1] Judged from a literary standpoint Corelli doesn't amount to much but she can certainly write interesting yarns. "The House of the Wolf" by Weyman[2] was capital. Then came "The Black Douglas" by Crockett.[3] Viewed from a critical standpoint I am afraid Crockett has made a miscue in this instance. The plot lacks unity and is very sensational, but for an exciting and fascinating and blood-curdling yarn, warranted to be finished at one sitting, I can recommend "The Black Douglas." In childhood, when I wasn't afraid to say I liked a book, not caring whether the confession "gave me away" on taste and judgement or not, I would have said it was "simply scrumptious."

I had my semi-annual jaunt to town this month, going in with Mary C. I went up to the station with the mailman. It sounds simple—but it is excruciating. It takes all the pleasure of the trip to counter-balance that dreadful drive up and back. Old Mr. Crewe is no doubt a worthy man but he is the reverse of entertaining and he drives a horse that *may* have been young— once! Then the road he has to follow twists and turns into half a dozen out of the way offices.

I went to Darlington where I spent a couple of days with Mary and had a jolly time. Norman was home and we were all as crazy as ever. Saturday morning Norman drove Mary and me into town and we laughed and jested the whole way in with all the abandon of old P.W.C. days. We stayed in town until Tuesday morning. Sunday morning we went to Zion Church once more. Mr. Sutherland has gone and his place is filled by the Rev. D. MacLeod on whom the mantle of Mr. S. has certainly not descended. But how pleasant it was to sit in that old corner of Aunt Mary's pew again, with Mary C., as jolly and ruddy and fat as ever, sitting beside me.

In the evening we went to the "Big Brick Methodist." We have never been in it since we left town. We recalled the last time we were there together. It was the memorable night of B. Faye Mills' farewell meeting—B. Faye, by the way, has turned Unitarian!—when Jack S. sat across from us in the gallery and walked home with us afterwards, sheltering our new spring hats with his convenient umbrella. Mary and I were two laughing irresponsible college girls then and Jack was—why, just Jack! I wonder if he is "Jack" still and if we were to meet again would we be the good comrades of yore. Jack is living

---

1. Pen name of Mary Mackay (1855–1924), author of hugely popular, high-pitched romances. In *The Sorrows of Satan* (1895) the Devil appears in the guise of a foreign aristocrat, befriending and misleading a young author.

2. A Shropshire writer of historical romances, Stanley Weyman (1855–1928) produced hectic stories such as *Under the Red Robe* (1894) in which a gambler, though under Cardinal Richelieu's patronage, is trapped in his own evil web.

3. S.R. Crockett (1859–1914), Scottish novelist who had shifted from wholesome sentimental novels in the Scottish dialect to historical adventure yarns.

in Ottawa now and it is three years since I saw him. But where on earth am I? Let me get back to my mutton—that is to say, the pew of the Big Brick Methodist. However, there is nothing more to say of it, now I have got back. I came home Tuesday morning, after having an enjoyable outing.

July 24, 1899
My Den 3:30 P.M.
Cavendish, P.E.I.

Haying began today, which means that the best half of the summer is over. And now the field before my window is a sweep of silvery swaths gleaming in the hot afternoon sun and the wind that is rustling in the poplars is bringing up whiffs of the fragrance of ripening grasses.

I am lazy this afternoon—too lazy to carry out a planned photoing expedition. I was down this morning and took a photo of "Victoria Island"—that dear old spot down in the school brook, with the old firs on it, and the water laughing about it, just as it glimmered and rippled and laughed in those dear days gone by when we schoolgirls and boys played there. Nobody ever goes there now but myself—and I not often. Only once and again I stray down and listen to the duet of the brook and wind, and

Victoria Island

watch the sunbeams creeping through the dark boughs, the gossamers glimmering here and there, and the ferns growing up in the shadowy nooks.

We had a Tea here this summer in aid of a new church. It really deserves to be spelled with a capital for the amount of work and worry involved was immense. But it is all over now and everybody up to last reports has survived.

We Sewing Circle folks got it up and bore the burden and heat of the day. Mrs. Albert Macneill and I had to canvass Mayfield[1] as our share of the preliminary operations. It is not a long road—which saving fact accounts for my keeping any semblance of sanity at all. I shall never, as long as I live, be inveigled into canvassing a road again on behalf of a tea! At every house we entered I shrank at least an inch—sometimes two or three—and at the end I

---

1. As in *Anne of Avonlea*, chapter 6, LMM and a friend, as fundraisers, call on each house between Cavendish and Mayfield, the next village on the road to Charlottetown.

Mrs. Albert M.

really believe I must have been invisible to the naked eye. They tore the old church down in June. How badly I felt! I cried the day they began at it.

It was never a handsome church inside or out. It was very large and our pew was the second from the top on the left-hand side. It was right by the window and we could look out over the slope of the long western hill and the blue pond down to the curving rim of the sandhills and the sweep of the blue gulf. William C.'s pew was just ahead of ours. Mollie and Tillie always sat there; the choir used to sit up in the gallery long ago but of late years they have sat in the cross seats in the corner just ahead of us. This was for preaching. For prayer-meeting the highwater mark was lower down, in the middle pews, around the stove and in the seats under the gallery. The gallery itself was seldom used of late years save when Communion service filled even the big church to overflowing. Long ago it was always used and I always hankered to sit there—principally because I couldn't, no doubt—another example of forbidden fruit. Only when the annual Communion Sunday[1] came was I allowed to go up there with the other girls and I considered it a great treat, especially if we were fortunate enough to get in the front

The old church

Old church inside

seat. We could then look down over the whole congregation which always flowered out that day in full bloom of new hats and dresses. "Sacrament Sunday" then was in that respect, what Easter is to the dwellers in cities and harassed dressmakers had worked overtime for weeks getting new frocks finished in readiness for it. So a front gallery seat was very convenient for we could take in all the new costumes and I fear we thought more about them than we did about the solemnity of the service and what it commemorated.

---

1. In the Presbyterian church the sacrament was limited to members of the church who had been given cards in a pre-communion visitation by the elders.

It was always exceedingly long in those days for they adhered to the old custom of a double service with the Communion in between. How dreadfully tired we poor kiddies would get and how we envied the boys and irresponsible people who got up, and went home while the congregation sang, "Twas on that night when doomed to know."[1] *We* dared not stir but we realized acutely that caste has its penalties. And then what a hush fell over the building while the bread and wine was being handed around, the elders tiptoeing reverentially from pew to pew. I used to believe that there was something peculiar about the bread—it could *not* be just ordinary, home-made bread, much as it looked like it. It was a real shock to me when I found out that it was and that the buxom wife of "Elder Jimmy" had made it! I could not understand either why the women always buried their faces in their white handkerchiefs when they had eaten it; but of course I supposed I would understand it all when I grew up. And how glad I was when it was all over and we got down and out under the blue sky once more, where we could drink of the wine of God's sunshine in his eternal communion that knows no restrictions or creeds.

But the old church is gone now, with all its memories and associations. They will put up a modern one which will be merely a combination of wood and plaster and will not be mellowed and hallowed by the memories that permeated and beautified that unbeautiful old church. Churches, like all else, have to be ripened and seasoned before the most perfect beauty becomes theirs.

I have something else to write here yet before I conclude—no less than the "finish" to the most tragic chapter of my life. It is ended forever and the page is turned.

Herman Leard is—*dead*!

I had not heard from Helen since May. On July first when the mail came I was too busy to look at the Island papers for we were fixing up the tea grounds that day. When I came home and sat down to tea grandma said,

"Wasn't there a Herman Leard where you boarded in Bedeque?" I nodded, wonderingly.

> The funeral of the late Herman Leard, Bedeque, took place yesterday to Central Bedeque. It was one of the largest funerals seen in that vicinity for years, there being over 100 carriages in the procession. Rev. W. H. Warren conducted the funeral services. The deceased was a son of Mr. Cornelius Leard, Lower Montague, and a brother of Dr. Alpheus Leard of S'side. He contracted a severe cold not long since and never recovered from its effects. Mr. Leard was 29 years old yesterday, the day of his funeral. It is a remarkable fact that within the last few weeks a funeral has taken place from three adjoining homes in Lower Bedeque. The bereaved parents, relatives and friends of the deceased have the sympathy of the whole community.

> It is with deep regret that we record the death of Mr. Herman Leard, son of Mr. Cornelius Leard, of Lower Bedeque, who was probably the most popular young man in the district. He died on Friday morning, after an illness of seven weeks, during which he had the most skilled medical attendance and the most loving care. His death will be very seriously felt and is deeply mourned in the community. The funeral takes place on Sunday at 2 p.m. The deceased is a brother of Dr. Leard, of Summerside. To the bereaved parents and relatives the PIONEER tenders its deepest sympathy in their affliction.

---

1. This hymn (1781) by the Rev. J. Morison continues, "The saviour of the world took bread."

"Yes. What about him?"

"He is dead."

"Dead!" I stared at her stupidly. "How do you know?"

"It is in the *Pioneer*," she said.

I went and got the paper. There in the local column was the fatal item, coldly brief and concise. He had died the previous day after a seven week's illness brought about by complications of influenza—as I learned later. The funeral was to be Sunday afternoon. That was all.

When Herman Leard and I parted I knew that that chapter of my life was closed forever. So that this death could make no *real* difference to me. And yet when, with one swift pang, there came to me the realization that he was *dead*—gone from me forever into the dim and dread Unknown—and that never again, here, or, as it must seem, hereafter, should we two meet—oh, my God, how awful it was!

I did not shed many tears. I shed too many over Herman long ago to have any left now. There were once nights when I writhed on sleepless pillows until dawn and cried my passionate heart out because he was not worthy of my love. And so now, when he was dead, there was no need of tears for me. No agony could ever equal what I once endured. It is easier to think of him as dead, mine, *all* mine in death, as he never could be in life, mine when no other woman could ever lie on his heart or kiss his lips.

My window

But that night, when all the house was still I knelt down by my window[1] and, looking out into the dim, fragrant summer night, alight with calm stars, tried to realize that at that very moment Herman Leard was lying in his coffin, cold and silent, in the very room where I had kissed him farewell forever, and that if I stood by him and called to him not even my voice could reach him now. There would be no answering smile on his pale cold lips, no tender light in the dark blue eyes whose flash used to stir my heart into stinging life. Oh, kneeling there I thought it all over—that winter in Bedeque with its passion and suffering, all its hours of happiness and sorrow. I lived again in thought every incident of my acquaintance with Herman Leard from first to last—all those mad sweet hours and those sad bitter hours. I thought of that last night before I came home when our real parting was—a parting that was more bitter than

1. Compare *Anne of the Island*, chapter 40.

death. I could stand by Herman's grave and hear the clods rattle on his coffin without half the agony that was my portion that night, when we stood in the moonlight and I felt his arms about me and his lips on mine for the last time, knowing that it *was* the last time.

Yes, I thought it all over unflinchingly—and then I bowed my head on the window sill and wished that I were lying in Herman's arms, as cold in death as he, with all pain and loneliness lost forever in an unending, dreamless sleep, clasped to his heart in one last eternal embrace.

Herman is *dead*. Is *he* dead, or is it only his outer shell and husk that is dead? Does *he* live somewhere yet; and if so does he remember or forget? It is a horrible thought to fancy that he *does* live yet and now *knows* how I loved him and so nearly sinned and so greatly suffered for his sake. I would go mad if I believed *that*. But I do not. And yet it is almost as dreadful to think of him as some chill, impersonal spirit who would pass me coldly by if we met in the shadows of the Hereafter with no warm lips to kiss and no strong hand to clasp in the love of earth. No, no, I prefer to believe that never, never, in any life shall we two meet again—for be the meeting as it would, it could be fraught with nothing save pain and shame on my part—and on his—what?

I cannot answer that question. Herman loved me—or pretended to—with a love passionate and sensual enough, of no very lofty or enduring type; but never, never as I loved him. Well, it is all ended—for this life at least, and as I believe and hope—or *fear*, I cannot tell which—for all and every life to come.

Sunday Morning, Oct. 8, 1899
Cavendish, P.E. Island

We have just been having a regular fall rain. It is over now and today is sunny and crisp and beautiful, as if earth were harking back to her lost summer. But it lasted two days, and what a gloomy world it was—sodden meadows, drenched, mangled leaves, valleys abrim with chill mists and a raw wind that came blowing over "the sea's long level, dim with rain." Night before last I could not sleep for the noise of rain streaming on the roof and the shriek of wind around the old eaves and in the trees outside. It seemed as if all the demon forces of night and storm were in conflict in mid-heaven.

Aunt Mary McIntyre and James called one day not long ago. It was such a surprise for I did not know James was home. How glad I was to see them! They couldn't stay long but our tongues went while they did.

I have always liked my cousins on the Montgomery's side much better than those on the Macneill side—except Aunt Annie's girls, and *they* are half Montgomery on their father's side. I have never cared for any of Uncle Leander's boys or Uncle John's. But the McIntyre and Sutherland boys almost seem to me like brothers, dear, jolly, companionable fellows that they are! I always feel thoroughly at home with them. There are dozens of people, near of kin and association, with whom I am more ill at ease and tongue-tied than with the veriest stranger. I can't explain it but I am painfully conscious that it is so and I cannot overcome it. I am, with them, an utterly different creature

Frederica Campbell

from what I am with others. It is the unwritten law of "like to like" I suppose. If two *souls* do not know each other all the accidents of birth and association will be of no avail to bring them together. They must forever remain strangers, even if one roof were to cover them for half a century.

I was over to Park Corner for a fortnight in August and had a pleasant time, as Stella and Fred were both home. Henry McLure[1] drove me over. He has been driving me about this summer, although he clearly understands that he can have nothing, now or ever, but friendship. He is a crude young farmer of Rustico, whose best point is the possession of a dandy gee-gee and I neither like nor dislike him. He is nil—but convenient.

I took my camera over to Park Corner and got a number of pretty views. There is such a magnificent grove of maple and beech behind Uncle John Campbell's house. I could never tire of rambling through it. The winding paths are bordered thickly with ferns and the light comes softly down sifted through so many emerald screens that it is as flawless as the heart of a diamond. How the girls and I used to scamper through those trees when we were children and race down the long avenues among fallen leaves that rustled under our flying footsteps, while the tall old trees gave back a myriad of echoes to our joyous laughter.

I had a letter from *Ed* in September. What a chill of fear and repulsion went over me as I took it! When I read it I found it rather hard to decide why he had written it. Ed's style is not especially lucid at the best of times. But it

Grove at Park Corner, Frede standing

---

1. Henry Mclure (1872–1910), a friend from North Rustico; married Bessie Schurman in 1907.

seems that he has heard some rumors—though what they are he does not say—about our affair and seems to insinuate that he thinks they originated with me or with something I have told someone. I must say the implied accusation annoyed me. Does Ed imagine that I indulge in talking about him promiscuously—or desire to?

Other parts of the letter were painful. He said he had tried to obey my injunction to forget me, but had not succeeded—"loved me as much as ever"—etc.

I had to reply to the letter. I told him—what was the literal truth—that with the exception of a brief announcement concerning my broken engagement to the few who had known of it, his name had never crossed my lips since the termination of that unhappy affair, and that therefore any rumors that might be afloat could only be the product of surmise and gossip.

I have read only one new book lately—Mark Twain's "More Tramps Abroad."[1] It was delightful. *How* I would love to travel and see all those old world lands and wonders. I wonder if I ever shall! England and Scotland first—then Italy and Greece—then Egypt and the Holy Land—but there, why not include the moon and have done with it? One is about as likely as the other. I expect the greater part of my travels will be on paper and I daresay that is much less trouble—and expense!

Lover's Lane

One cold, rainy, dismal day last week I had nothing to do, so I sat me down and read over Will's old letters. Reading them, it seemed impossible that he should be dead—that there was *no* Will now—on this plane, at least.

Looking back over all the men I've known I think there was not among them a better *comrade* than Will—no, not even Herman. I never *loved* Will, but I thought—and think him still—the *nicest* boy I ever knew. Our friendship was perfect. Those P.A. days seem very far away now—in fact, they *are* far away. But Will's letters carried me back to them once more—the rackets in the old High School where we teased poor Mr. Mustard so dreadfully, our walks home on the crisp winter evenings, our rambles in the summer twilights, the

---

1. *More Tramps Abroad* (1897) described a lecturing trip around the world, as a follow-up to Mark Twain's (1835–1910) other autobiographical travel narrative, *Following the Equator* (1897).

books we read and discussed, and all the thousand and one little incidents of our acquaintanceship. I think I regret the loss of his friendship even more now than when I first knew he was dead—because I see and appreciate its

real value more clearly now. But I know, too, that if he were living, and we were to meet again, it would be no longer possible. It might be the friendship of man and woman with *love* as its finale. But the comradeship of yore would be impossible.

I went for a walk in Lover's Lane yesterday. It is the dearest spot in the world to me and has the greatest influence for good over me. No matter how dark my mood is, no matter how heavy my heart or how vexed my soul, an hour in that beautiful solitude will put me right with myself and the world. Perplexity

The lane uner the birches

and sorrow melt away and the balm of the woods falls on my troubled thoughts like a boon of infinite peace.

It is always the same old way I go—down the lane under the birches and across the old school playground worn bare, and hard by many restless

feet. There in the October sunshine are the old woods where the wind sweeps through the swaying spruce tops with a sound as of surf breaking on a far distant shore. There is a fence to be climbed here and then a winding path to follow, sloping down into the heart of a peaceful hush where now and again a sudden gap in the boughs lets in a glimpse of faraway purple hills or a shining bay of blue sea.

A fence to be climbed

"An autumnal field"

A silvery field beyond

The old spring, deep and clear and icy cold is on our path. The brook purls softly by and the old firs whisper over it as of yore. The ferns are drooping from the banks and the wild vines are running riot over stumps and roots. A maple adown the brook is gloriously gold and crimson and above through the boughs is a glimpse of blue autumn sky. Past the school woods come two autumnal fields rimmed in with golden-hued birches and frosted bracken fern. Beyond them is the dear lane itself, running on along the rim of the woodland, with the maple and birches and wild cherries and spruces meeting overhead and the low murmur of a hidden brook ever in our ears—every step a revelation and a benediction. The air under the firs is purple and the sunshine is as exhilarating as wine. Finally it ends in a bridge over the brook and a silvery field beyond that leads out to the red ribbon of the main road and so, over the crest of the hill home.

The dear lane itself

1900

Sunday Evening
Jan. 14, 1900

How strange it seems to write that date! It really makes me feel homesick for the old 18's. It seems to me as if I belonged back in them.

I don't feel like writing tonight—I feel dull and stupid. I've been very busy of late and that is all there is to it. My life recently has certainly been uneventful. I haven't been anywhere since I last wrote except for a flying visit to town one day in October. I shall grow *mossy* in such an existence!

There, I feel better for that little outburst of discontent. After all, I'm passably contented. I suppose that into everybody's life there come days of depression and discouragement, when all things in life seem to lose savor. The sunniest day has its clouds; but one must not forget that the sun is there all the time.

(Item:—If you are out in a pouring rain does it do you much good, or keep you dry, to remember that the sun is there, just the same?)

Blessings be on the inventors of alphabet, pen and printing press! Life would be—to me at all events—a terrible thing without books. I cannot remember ever learning to read. I suppose there must have been a time when I took my first step into an enchanted world by learning that "A" was "A," but for any recollection of it, I might as well have been born with a capacity for reading just as for breathing or eating. It is fortunate, situated as I am, that I can read books over and over again with never failing interest and zest; otherwise I could never get enough reading matter to satisfy my voracious appetite.

This fall I read all Scott's poems over again. They were one of my child-hood loves that have worn well. In the old "Sixth Royal Reader" was the whole of the "Lady of The Lake." How I always gloried in that poem—its spirited descriptions, its atmosphere of romance, the dramatic situations with which it abounded! What food it was for my eager young mind and fancy! I used to pore over it in the old schoolhouse when I should have been wrestling with fractions—or when the teacher thought I should. But, all the same, it did me more good than the fractions would ever have done. It was nourishment for heart and mind and soul—even for body, too, I verily believe—at least I never was conscious of hunger or thirst while poring over Scott's magic page.

In November I got "Rupert of Hentzau,"[1] by Anthony Hope. It came one day at two o'clock in the afternoon. I sat down and began it, never budging until sunset, when I finished it.

---

1. Anthony Hope's hero in *Rupert of Hentzau* (1898)—as in the book's predecessor, *The Prisoner of Zenda* (1894)—renounces the chance to seize happiness for himself by changing places with his princely double.

It made me *mentally drunk*. I was as thoroughly intoxicated in brain as the most confirmed drunkard ever was in body. For a week after I could read nothing else—nothing else seemed worth reading—everything was tasteless and savorless after that pungent draught. In fact, I think I have hardly got over it yet. Certainly, books like that wouldn't be very healthy for a continuous diet. They would spoil one for everything else. But—once in a while—just for a spree!

At the outbreak of the Transvaal war[1] I re-read "The Story of An African Farm." It is one of my favourites. It is speculative, analytical, rather pessimistic, iconoclastic, daring—and *very* unconventional. But it is powerful and original and fearless, and contains some exquisite ideas. It is like a tonic, bitter but bracing. Also, many people call it a dangerous book. Perhaps it is so, for an unformed mind—but there is more of truth than pleasantness in many of its incisive utterances.

I re-read *Vanity Fair*[2] in December. I read it long ago—back in those enchanted years of early girlhood when one believes in everything. I did not like it then—probably because it hit some of my pet illusions too hard. I was too young. It takes a more mature mind than mine then was to appreciate Thackeray. When I read it this winter I wondered how I failed to see its charm before. Oh, that delightful *Becky*!

I had an unpleasant experience in November. One Sunday evening Mr. Millar preached in the hall. I was sitting on one of the side seats, watching the people come in. Presently the door opened and Edwin Simpson entered!

I was completely taken by surprise for I had not even known he was on the Island. He walked up the aisle and took a seat behind me. When the service was over I hurried out at once for fear I should meet him. But the platform was crowded and I could get no further than the door. And there we met face to face in the glare of the porch light. Well, people *can* meet horrible moments so calmly that no onlooker would dream of the passions let loose. I bowed coldly and said "Good evening." Ed lifted his cap and said good evening in a voice as emotionless as my own. Then he passed on and it was over. Over—yes! But the effects were with me for days.

In October war broke out between England and the Transvaal Republic and has been raging ever since. Canada is in a state of red-hot excitement from shore to shore because several regiments of Canadian boys have volunteered for service in South Africa. Among those who went from the Island

---

1. Canada sent a contingent to South Africa during this conflict (1899–1902).
2. Contrast LMM's earlier comment on this novel in her entry of July 4, 1894.

PRINCE EDWARD ISLAND'S FIRST CONTINGENT FOR SOUTH AFRICA: 1. Herbert Brown 2. Hurdis L. McLean 3. Arthur B. Mellish 4. T. Leslie McBeth 5. Lawrence Gaudet 6. Hedley V. McKinnon 7. Joseph O'Reilly 8. J. Edward Small 9. Frederick Way 10. Frederick B. McRae 11. LeRoy Harris 12. James S. Walker 13. R. Ernest Lord 14. Lorne Stewart 15. Thomas Ambrose Rodd 16. Frederick C. Furze 17. Nelson Brace 18. James Matheson 19. Michael J. McCarthy 20. Joshua T. Leslie 21. Richard Joseph Foley 22. Major Weeks 23. Reginald Cox 24. John Archibald Harris 25. Ernest W [...ness] 26. Artemas R. Dillon 27. John Boudreault 28. Roland D. Taylor 29. Necy Dorion 30. Alfred [....iggs] 31. Walter Lane

was Hedley McKinnon, my old P.W.C. friend and classmate. There is something stirring and exciting and tingling about it all even here in this quiet little Island thousands of miles from the seat of war. Everyone is intensely interested in the news.

May 1. 1900
Cavendish, P.E. Island

On the morning of January 17th I was awakened to receive this telegram:—

"Prince Albert, N.W.T. Jan. 16.

Hugh J. Montgomery died today. Pneumonia. Peacefully happy and painless death."

I have no words to describe how I felt! For weeks I only wished to die.

The news was a thunderbolt from a clear sky. Only a short time before I had had a letter from him written in the best of health and spirits. The next was that brutal telegram.

> WORD was received yesterday of the death at Prince Albert, North West Territory, of Hugh John Montgomery, son of the late Sen tor Montgomery, of Park Corner. The deceased had resided in the North West for a number of years, and died from an attack of pneumonia. A letter was received from Mr. Montgomery about ten days ago, and at time of writing he was in the best of health. The deceased was twice married. His first wife was a daughter of the late Alexander McNeill of Cavendish, and a sister of Mr. Chester B. McNeill of Victoria, B. C., and formerly of Charlottetown. Their daughter now resides with her grandmother, Mrs. McNeill. Mr. Montgomery was married a second time in the North West and leaves four children by the second marriage. His remains will be interred Prince Albert.

Oh, it meant so much to me! Others, losing a father, have still a mother or brothers or sisters left. I have nobody except poor old grandmother. And father and I have always been so much to each other. He was so good and kind and tender. Long, long ago, before he went west, when I was a tiny girl, we were much together, and how we loved each other! Even when he went so far away and for so many years we never grew apart, as some might have done. We always remained near and dear in spirit. Oh father, can it really be true that you are dead? Have you left your "little Maudie" all alone? That was not like you.

Oh, what a long, dreary, dismal winter followed! I have tried so hard to be brave and look out on life courageously but it is hard—hard. I grow tired thinking of it. This is the hour of the evening when I always think of father. The sun has set and the twilight shadows are creeping over the hills. I am all alone and I think of him—oh, I think of him as I used to know him.

Yes, it has been a sad dark winter, but a busy one, too. What a blessing work is! Truly,

"God, in cursing, gives us better gifts
Than men in benediction."[1]

To be sure, in those first dark weeks after father's death I could not work. I had no heart for it. Even my ambition seemed dead within me. What good was it when there would be nobody to care whether I succeeded or not? Father was always so proud of me and of my little talent—and now he could never know or care.

But after a time I roused myself and went to work again. With the effort came strength and the old love, inborn and bred, for my pen came back to me. Oh, as long as we can work we can make life beautiful! And life *is* beautiful in spite of all its sorrow and care. I seem to realize the truth of this afresh every day and to see its beauty more clearly.

1. From Elizabeth Barrett Browning's verse-novel *Aurora Leigh* (1857).

There is so much in the world for us all, if we only have the eyes to see it and the heart to love it and the hand to gather it to ourselves—so much in men and women, so much in art and literature, so much everywhere in even the narrowest, most circumscribed life—so much to enjoy and delight in and be thankful for.

Well, I must henceforth face the world alone. Let me see what my equipment for such a struggle is. I am young; I have a scanty and superficial education, gained in a winter at an academy and another at Dalhousie college; I have three hundred dollars—father left me two hundred in his will and I saved another hundred these last two years. I have no training for anything save teaching, which I cannot at present do; I have no influence of any kind in any quarter. Is that all? It seems a meagre list. Yes, there is something else—my knack of scribbling. Is it a feather's weight—or is it a talent of gold that will eventually weigh down the balance in my favour? Last year I made exactly ninety-six dollars and eighty eight cents by my pen![1] That does not promise extravagantly. But we shall see. I have forgotten to mention another asset and a very valuable one—a belief in my power to succeed. As long as I possess that I shall face the future with an unquailing heart.

The other day I re-read Racine's *Athalie*[2] in the original. It served the double purpose of brushing up my French and recalling bygone days at Dalhousie when Lottie Shatford and I sat at our front desk in Professor Leichti's room and heard him read French with a German accent that might have made Racine turn over in his grave. Poor old professor—what a curiosity he was in the Professorial line! But he was such a perfect gentleman, of the fine, "old school" type you never see nowadays.

I also re-read "King Solomon's Mines"[3] lately. I always liked it because it was so full of adventure and I *do* love that with a love that has outlived childhood. What care I if it be "wild and improbable" and "lacking in literary art"? I refuse to be any longer hampered in my likes and dislikes by such canons of criticism. The one essential thing I demand of a book is that it should interest me. If it does, I forgive it any and every other fault.

In March I read *"The King's Mirror"* by Anthony Hope.[4] It is in quite a different vein from his other books. It purports to be the autobiography of a king from his childhood to his marriage and I found it extremely interesting.

How hard our childish prepossessions die! I have never been quite able to divest myself of my original belief that kings were happy beings—bound

---

1. Half the salary of a second-class teacher in a country school.

2. A classic French tragedy (1691) about the daughter of Jezebel and Ahab.

3. A popular romance (1885) by Rider Haggard set in South Africa.

4. Another of Anthony Hope's annual bestsellers (1899).

by no rules, existing only for their own pleasure, in short, having everything gloriously their own way. When I grew older of course, I understood that this was not so, but the real deathblow to that old delusion was never given until I read *The King's Mirror*. Then I *realized*—a very different thing from believing—that kings were in no respect different from other people—unless it was in that they ran much greater risks of being miserable—and had less freedom in vital things than the veriest serf in their realms. So I don't think I shall ever again dream of being a queen—to be sure, it is long since I did!

Until very lately I have cared most for fiction—history and biography did not attract me. But of late my taste in this respect has changed very much. Fiction no longer satisfies me. I want to read what *real* men and women have done and thought and endured. Lately I have read McCarthy's "Four Georges"[1] and Parkman's "Wolfe and Montcalm"[2] and found them all fascinating. In connection with the latter I re-read "The Last of the Mohicans,"[3] a novel which I first read long ago in schooldays, having borrowed it from Nate. We were both charmed with the story and used to discuss its characters and incidents enthusiastically.

The other night I took the "Ascent of Man" by Drummond[4] out of the hall library, came home, and read it till long after midnight, so absorbing did I find it. It is a remarkably clear and convincing statement of the theory of evolution. Moreover, Drummond makes a good, but not, I think, wholly successful attempt to reconcile science with—so-called—revelation. His analogies seem good as far as they go, but if he followed them out to their logical completion he would be sometimes forced to a conclusion very different from the one he does draw. He stops when it suits him and that is generally the weakness of all such attempts.

At present I am reading "Farthest North" by Nansen.[5] It reads like romance. Besides, it is so recent that one feels as if one had a share in it somehow. To me, it lends a reality to it to remember that during the years Mary and I were at P.W.C., when I was teaching in Bideford, and prowling about Dalhousie library, Nansen was exploring the fastnesses of the polar sea and getting nearer than any other man ever did to that mysterious bourne so many have tried to reach but never have reached. It would be rash to say

---

1. *The Four Georges and William IV*, a four-volume work (1884–1901), begun by Irish historian and novelist Justin M'Carthy and completed by his son Justin Huntly M'Carthy.

2. Actual title *Montcalm and Wolf* (1884), a sweeping history of the Seven Years War and the Conquest, by American historian Francis Parkman (1823–93).

3. The second of Fennimore Cooper's five novels (1826) about American frontier.

4. Scottish evangelical clergyman Henry Drummond (1851–97) produced this popularized and spiritualized version of evolution (1894).

5. Account (1897) of the Arctic by Norwegian explorer and statesman Fridtjof Nansen (1861–1930).

that no one ever will. I certainly think someone will some day. There are few chances for immortality nowadays but this is one of them. Earthly remembrance is assured to the man who reaches the North Pole. It seems odd to think of it, too. It will do nobody any good. But it will satisfy human curiosity on that point and as it is human curiosity that has accomplished almost everything of value it deserves to be indulged in some of its whims.

Sunday Evening, May 20, 1900
Cavendish, P.E. Island.

A pouring rain in a city is an undesirable thing, but in the country—when you don't want to go anywhere—it has charms of its own. We have had a regular rain today, coming down in torrents over hills that are faintly green and woods where the buds are just beginning to open, and valleys where in sunny spots blue violets are pushing up through faded grasses and looking out on the world from under their purple hoods.

But it has cleared up now and tomorrow when the sun comes out, warm and bright, things will grow and the hill meadows will be emerald in a day.

I have something to do this evening that I don't like to do—and that is, write to Edwin Simpson. A fortnight ago I had an unexpected letter from him. It frightened me, as his letters always do; but there was no cause for alarm. He wrote that he had heard I was ill in the winter—as I was for a few weeks after father's death, with influenza and neuralgia—and that it had troubled him; and he asked if I would not write to him and tell him how I was and what I was doing. He put the request in such a way that it would have seemed unkind and ungracious to refuse—and I surely owe him what kindness I can give him. So I will answer his letter this once but if he ever writes again I will not. I made a mistake and paid a heavy penalty for it; but I *did* pay it and have done with it and now I will not have the matter brought up again and again, like the periodical exhuming of a loathsome corpse. My dead past must bury its dead; for me there shall be no assisting at belated obsequies, even if the man I wronged has a fancy for officiating as High Priest. I have put it behind me.

I paid a visit to Darlington last week and went on to town. Mary C. went in with me and it was the last of our Charlottetown jaunts together for in June Mary is to be married. As we knew it would be our last we made the most of it. One evening we went to the opera and saw the "Merchant of Venice." Of course it wasn't Shakespeare! And a very cheap and modern embroidered flannel table cloth on a table in the famous court scenes seemed something of an anachronism; but it was fairly good—the play not the tablecloth—and we felt that we had at least got the worth of our fifty cents. I got a dreadful cold, too, and spent the next day in bed. What a humiliation and disgusting thing sickness is! One day you are strong and well, full of eager, pulsing life, fearless, of the future, ready to grapple with your fate; the next, you are an abject, helpless creature, dependent on others for the merest trifles of service, discouraged, timorous, weak. I hate being ill and I am very glad that as a rule it is my habit to be well.

Mollie was in Friday evening for the mail and I walked part of the way home with her, as I have always done.

In one of his books Oliver Wendell Holmes says,

"There is one very sad thing in old friendship to every mind that is really moving onwards. It is this—that we cannot help using his early friends as the seaman uses the log—to mark his progress. We cannot help measuring our rate of movement by those with whom we have been long in the habit of comparing ourselves; and when they once become stationary we can get our reckoning from them with painful accuracy."[1]

The condition of the friendship existing between Mollie and me has, for some years back, served to point the moral of this quotation; and on this particular evening, as we walked together up the green country road, I realized sharply and finally that Mollie and I have at last reached the point where we have absolutely nothing in common. There did not seem to be *anything* we could talk about. Mollie never reads anything and cares as little for the thought and action of the great world as she knows; she seldom goes anywhere, save to church or a neighbours, so that we cannot even talk much about little local interests and enjoyments; especially as we belong to, or have drifted into, entirely different "sets." Moreover, of late years Mollie has certainly displayed a very ugly spirit of—well, in plain English, *jealousy* of anyone, who in *any* respect, possesses advantages she does not. Our friendship is dead! I regret this bitterly but I honestly feel that I am not in any way to blame for it. I have done my best to keep it alive. I had a very real and warm affection for Mollie once; and now that so many of our old friends are gone or going we ought to be more to each other than ever. I have tried to retain her affection and have repeatedly overlooked behaviour on her part that hurt and annoyed me very much. I did this as long as her friendship seemed worth having in spite of these drawbacks. Now it no longer seems so; she has grown so petty, so resentful, so narrow-minded that she seems incapable of comradeship. Although I feel genuinely sorry over this I realize that I cannot help it. I shall always show myself friendly to her but we

---

1. Modified quotation from *The Autocrat of the Breakfast-Table*, 4 (1858), by Oliver Wendell Holmes (1809–94).

can never again have real companionship—we can never meet on common ground again.

Sunday, May 27, 1900
Cavendish, P.E.I.

One never quite realized that spring has really come until one finds, as I found, today, half a dozen tiny, fragrant white violets growing among sere grasses on the sunny side of a heap of stones in some meadow fence corner. That is the season's autograph lettering in Nature's fairest script.

"Sitting at my window"

On these long, still, evenings, when the night comes down over the greening hills with a benediction known only to springtime we hear the frogs singing down in the swamps and in the quiet pools back in the woods. Sitting here at my window I hear the sweet, sad, silvery chorus floating up through the moist fresh air and it brings back, as always, such dear, elusive memories of old days and long-ago evenings. I can never forget how the frogs used to sing on those spring evenings and how it always made me sad, even when life was new and fresh and although I loved to hear them. I would sit out on the old back porch steps by myself in the long, purple, blossom-scented dusks and listen until the tears filled my eyes. They are singing away now, down in the hollow—"flute-throated voices,"[1] as Lampman calls them—while the light of this calm, rainy evening is fading, always sweet, always sad, as if the voice of the world's sorrow must make itself heard amid all the joy of the young year. But it *is* spring—and I found white violets today—and just now I will not listen to the sorrow.

Thursday, June 7, 1900
Cavendish, P.E.I.

What a perfect day this has been! It is fair mid-spring. The poplars and birches at the foot of the garden have hung out tender green curtains and the cherry trees are white with tufts of milky blossoms. The very wind comes over

---

1. Quotation from "Favorites of Pan" (1895) by Archibald Lampman (1861–99).

At the foot of the garden

the green hills with a benediction in its soft breath and all the pulses of humanity thrill anew with the sweet, passionate impulses of youth and spring and love. And although for me the last is a thing gone by, youth and spring are mine and are sweet and glorious and beautiful.

"Isabel Carnaby"[1] helped me pass a pleasant hour or so yesterday. The book is clever but too "talky." The people in it seem to be so constantly occupied in saying "smart" things and perpetrating epigrams that they haven't time to *do* anything of consequence. Also, after several pages of unalloyed sparkle one feels a little dazzled and wants to look at something green and dull for a rest. However, I really enjoyed the book very much, so it is rather thankless of me to carp at it.

"Janice Meredith,"[2] another "best seller," was fairly good. To be sure, I'm getting very tired of the American Revolution as a background for stories, and *Janice* was spun out much longer than was necessary, but the book is

after all a welcome addition to the rows in my plain little bookcase. I like to look up from my work occasionally and gloat my eyes on them. They are all my pets. I never buy a book unless I have read it before and know that it will wear well, unless it be by an author in whom I have sufficient confidence to buy "sight unseen." There are the poets I love and the Alcott and "Gypsy" stories[3] I read in my teens—and

My bookcase

have a liking for yet—and novels picked up here and there as opportunity offered, and which have been read and re-read, loaned and re-loaned, until they are almost worn out.

We had an eclipse of the sun last week; not quite a total eclipse—only 11/12 of the disc was covered—but even that was something to be thankful

1. The Honourable Ellen Thorneycroft (1861–1930), writing as E.T. Fowler, published *Concerning Isabel Carnaby* (1898), a witty social novel with Methodist sub-themes.

2. A popular novel (1899) set in the American Revolution, by Paul Leicester Ford (1865–1902). Ford's murder was more sensational than his fiction.

3. Some of LMM's stories come very close to Louisa May Alcott's: e.g., in Montgomery's "Her Pretty Golden Hair," published in *Philadelphia Times*, 1898, a girl sacrifices her one beautiful feature to help fan finances, as Jo does in Alcott's *Little Women* (1868).

for. It was very interesting. We smoked glasses and watched it through them. When the eclipse was at its *height* it was almost dark in the house. Outside the light was of the most curious appearance—a pallid, greenish colour— and the shadows were so faint and ghost-like, while the sky was a very strange, dark, livid blue. Through the glass the sun looked like a new moon. I hope that sometime in my life I shall see a total eclipse. But if not—well, perhaps in some future life I shall have all the eclipses I want!

This evening I spent planting seeds in my modest little flower plot. How strange and how wonderful it is to think of the beauty and colour and fragrance hidden away in the tiny brown seeds that I tucked into the dark earth. It is one of the best arguments I know of for immortality—or rather, future *lives*. Immortality means never-endingness and even the brown seeds don't teach *that*, because the flowers they give birth to die in their turn; but a constant *succession* of future *lives* they certainly *do* teach and when, as at present, I am full of life and energy I like the thought. Sometimes, when I am tired, I think it would be better just to rest forever with no awakening.

Sunday, Aug. 5, 1900
Cavendish, P.E.I.

If, as is said, the way to hell is paved with good intentions, then I fear me I have contributed not a little of late to the paving. I have been "intending" for a month to write up this journal but when I had the time I wasn't in the mood and when the mood came there wasn't any time. But for a wonder the mood and the time have come together this lovely Sunday evening and here in "my own old spot" by my open window I sit me down to scribble a bit for my own amusement—something I very rarely do nowadays, for when I write I must write for the purpose of poking some dollars into my slim purse and there is not much fun in that, though there is some profit. Long ago, before my scribbling possessed marketable value I wrote for pure love of it. What an indefatigable little scribbler I was, and what stacks of MSS—now, alas, reduced to ashes, bore testimony to the same! For I was always writing; sometimes prose—and then all the little incidents of my not very exciting life were described. I wrote descriptions of my favourite haunts, biographies of my cats, histories of visits and school affairs, and even critical reviews of the books I had read.

Often, too, I broke into verse—about flowers, mostly, or months. Sometimes I addressed "Lines" to my friends or enthused over a sunset. I remember the very first poetry I ever wrote. I sincerely regret that I haven't a copy of it. I was nine years old and had been reading a little black, curly-covered, atrociously printed book containing a great many quotations from Thomson's "Seasons." So I composed a poem called "Autumn" in blank verse in imitation thereof. I wrote it, I remember, on the blank back of one of the long red "letter bills" then used in post-offices. It was seldom easy for me to get all the paper I wanted and I was often put to devising odd ways and means to obtain the same. Those jolly old "letter bills" were positive boons. Three times a week one of them came my grateful way. The Government was not so economical then as now—at least in the matter of letter bills; they were half a yard long.

As for "Autumn" I remember only the opening lines,

"Now autumn comes laden with peach and pear,
The sportsman's horn is heard throughout the land,
And the poor partridge, fluttering, falls dead."

True, peaches and pears are practically unknown in P.E.I. in any season and I am sure nobody ever heard a "sportsman's horn" here. But in those glorious days my imagination refused to be hampered by facts. Thomson had sportsman's horns and so forth; therefore I must have them, too.

Father came to see me the very day I wrote it and I read it proudly to him. He remarked unenthusiastically that it "didn't sound much like poetry." That squelched me for a time; but of the love of writing is bred in your bones you will be practically non-squelchable. Once I had found out I could write "poetry" I overflowed into verse about everything. I wrote in rhyme after that, though, having concluded that it was because "Autumn" didn't rhyme that father thought it wasn't poetry. What became of it I don't remember. I suppose I must have burned it. But it had many successors. I must have written reams of trash. Yet it was not wasted time or paper either, although the powers that were thought so. I "found my feet" and formed my style on those old letter bills and circulars. My "odes" to June and January, my sunset raptures and florid descriptions of field and shore all served their purpose and deserve to be kindly remembered. Writing came to me as easily and naturally as breathing or eating. I found my dearest delight in creeping away into some lonely corner with a pencil and a "letter bill" and writing stories and verses in my unformed little scrawl, the while I revelled in dreams and visions of the beautiful future when I should be "a famous authoress."

So tonight I hark back to the old ways and write for my own amusement but not with pencil and letter bill now.

Today I was reading Rawlinson's "Ancient Egypt."[1] Egypt has always been a land and an empire that has possessed a strange fascination for me and

---

1. An archaeological study (1881) by George Rawlinson (1892–1902), an Oxford professor and canon of Canterbury.

the volume I have just read has deepened that fascination. Think of it—a civilization that was old, a culture that was marvellous, and an empire that was venerable in the day of Moses! Compared to such antiquity, what mushrooms are the empires of today—what ephemera we who live "in the foremost files of time"! After all, humanity has not progressed a great deal—*yet*. Human nature still seems pretty much the same as it was on the banks of the Nile in the days of the Pharaohs. Men and women loved and hated, drank and feasted, warred and revelled, pretty much as they do today—and were just as happy, too, I have no doubt. In reading the book I think the thing that impressed me most was the wonderful patience and ingenuity of the scholars who out of the maze of hieroglyphics and symbols have spelled out the history of this strange old land. What time and labour and patience it must have involved!

In June Mary Campbell was married. I drove myself up to Darlington on Tuesday afternoon and arrived there at five o'clock to find the bride-elect churning and all the other girls—Donald E. has such a swarm of daughters—flying around doing a dozen things at once. Such fun as we had! And at dusk Mary and I got away in the spare room and had a long talk together—the last talk of mutual girlhood. And we had a bit of a cry, too.

Wednesday was a lovely day and a busy one. After dinner, Archie Beaton, the prospective groom arrived. I had never seen him before. He is a big, quiet, stolid-looking Highlander and seems very much older than Mary. I cannot say I found anything attractive in him, and I could not help wondering a

The wedding guests: 1. Norman C. 2. Archie Beaton. 3. Mary.
4. Laura McIntyre. 5. Bertie McIntyre

little what Mary had seen in him. I have never thought she was very deeply in love with him. I wonder if his Klondike gold—of which he is said to have a store—invested him with any aureole in her eyes. It would doubtless weigh strongly with Donald E. but I can hardly believe that it would influence Mary to that extent.

After his arrival I helped Mary dress; then I went down to help receive guests and unwrap wedding presents. About eighty people came. Norman arrived from town at dusk, bringing Bertie[1] and Laura with him. At eight

Mary and Archie Beaton

o'clock Mary was married. The ceremony was performed out under the trees of the orchard. The pretty wedding group, the bright dresses of the guests, and the glow of the sunset softly fading in the western sky, all made quite a charming picture. Mary was the most composed and matter-of-fact bride I have ever seen. I stood under a cherry tree in the background and tried to feel solemn and romantic as befitted the occasion and scene, but couldn't quite manage it, somehow, because the Campbell dog was having a fit quite close behind me, and making the weirdest, most unearthly noises.

When it was over—the ceremony, not the fit—the girls and I flew in to light up. After supper the minister considerately went home and the rest of us betook ourselves to dancing. They had a splendid big dancing pavilion built out in the garden and roofed over with maple boughs. It made an ideal ballroom, for the night was dewless, and the air kept so cool and pure all the time. We had three fiddlers; there were lots of boys out from town who were dandy dancers, so we had a pretty good time. We danced the night out and the sun was just rising as we finished the last lancers.

Then we had breakfast and a rather fagged looking lot we were in the merciless daylight. But after breakfast I took a picture of all the survivors and then I drove the bridal pair to the station. A lot of the boys turned up with pounds of rice and as I was carrying Mary's parasol Paddy Clarken and I

Bertie

---

1. *Kilmeny of the Orchard* is dedicated to LMM's cousin Beatrice (Bertie) McIntyre (1879–1961), daughter of LMM's Charlottetown aunt Mary Montgomery McIntyre.

sneaked off behind a pile of lumber and filled it with rice. Mary went off with it, never suspecting, and I would have given a plum to have been around when she opened it.

I came home the same day, very tired and sleepy.

Bertie McIntyre spent three weeks of her vacation here with me in July. We had a very nice time, although poor grandmother made it rather unpleasant for me in many respects. I never have much pleasure in entertaining guests under existing circumstances, so I do very little of it. Bertie and I had out pleasantest times when we got away up in my room and talked and read to our hearts content.

Saturday, Aug. 11, 1900
Cavendish, P.E. Island.

Today Myrtle Macneill[1] brought me a bunch of the most exquisite poppies. They are dream-like loveliness—the most delicious crimsons, pinks and whites! I could sit before them and gaze at them by the hour. *Colour* has the most powerful influence over me. It gives me greater pleasures than anything else—it soothes me, it delights me, it uplifts me. A flawless colour symphony gives to me a pleasure so intense as to be half pain. The poppies are lovely—but they do smell abominably! Is there nothing perfect?

Sunday, Oct. 7, 1900
Cavendish, P.E.I.

I have just come in from a walk—a lonely walk some might call it, but not so I, for I walked with good company through the misty purple autumn twilight threaded dimly with the light of the rising moon—the company of old dreams and fantastic fancies, half merry and half sad, now recalling some friend of other days, now quoting in thought some couplet suggested by the rim of a dark hill coming out against the clear crocus sky or the crystal twinkle of an evening star over the fir woods—and now thinking of nothing at all but drifting on, like a shadow among shadows, content simply to open my heart and let the wonderful elusive beauty of the night fill it, as a cup brimmed with a draught of divine enchantment. And so, soul and sense steeped in a languor of ethereal pleasure I wondered on through the glimmer of mingled moonrise and sunset.

---

1. Myrtle Macneill (1883–68) grew up in the house now called Green Gables with her mother Ada Macneill, who tended the elderly David and Margaret Macneill.

This afternoon I was re-reading "Undine"—that exquisite little idyll. I read it years ago in my early teens. Nate had it—a little volume given him by a literary uncle. He brought it to me one day in school and I read it all behind my desk in that delightful, roomy old "back seat" which was so splendidly convenient for such doings. No doubt I should have been studying English History or geography at the time—but then I would soon have forgotten the history and I have never forgotten *Undine*. When I finished it I registered a solemn vow that some day in the bright, beautiful future—I was so sure *then* that it would be bright and beautiful—I would get the book for myself. The other day in Ch'town I was in Carter's bookstore—where the aroma of books and new magazines was as the savour of sweet incense in my nostrils—and I saw the dearest edition of *Undine* bound in white and gold. I paid the price without a murmur, brought it home in triumph and read it, finding to my delight that its charm was every whit as potent as when, years ago, behind that old brown desk in the little white schoolhouse, it lured me into By-path Meadow and opened a world of fancy to my delighted eyes. That is, after all is said—the true test of a classic. It must please every age, from childhood to gray hairs.

Last week I betook myself to Ch'town to attend the Exhibition and get my gray matter stirred up a bit. We would get too mossy if we stayed always in the same place!

But there! I'm getting so horribly tired of my own style that I'm going to stop for tonight.

Monday, October 8, 1900
Cavendish, P.E. Island.

I may be tired of my own style but there is nobody else to write this journal, so here I am back again. But how tired I do get of being myself at times! How delightful it would be to exchange personalities with somebody else for awhile—revel in a new set of opinions, feelings, memories, likes and dislikes. I daresay I'd be very glad to come back to myself again in the end but I do think it's a great pity we can't send our souls off at times for a jaunt as we do our bodies.

Well, I went up to Hunter River and, getting there at 8 o'clock had to wait until eleven at night for the train. I had a rather tedious time. However, the last hour passed rather better, as I fell in with a boy I knew and had some fun. I also met a certain Fred Waye[1] who despite the fact that he is

---

1. Volunteer from Hunter River, awarded medals for service in South Africa.

a rather stolid-looking youth and quite as slow as he looks is yet invested with a certain halo of romance because he went to South Africa last year and was wounded in the famous Paardenburg charge.[1] If I expected any racy accounts of his South African experiences, however, I did not get them since young Waye does not appear to know he has a tongue.

I had a lovely time in town and met so many old friends that I nearly shook my hand off. I shopped, called, larked, read novels, ate candy and ice cream, and dissipated generally. Speaking of ice cream there is a jolly little restaurant uptown at Carter's where we can get that delicacy to perfection. Bert and Laura and I used to trot up there every evening, swarm around a table and have a feast, regardless of shrinking pocket-books. Mine shrank very perceptibly I know. But what difference? I had a good time—and perhaps in other planets they don't have ice cream! And my little outing has heartened me up to face the on-coming winter.

One Saturday early in September I picked up a Ch'town daily and among the "personals" I found this one!—

> "The Rev. Edwin Simpson occupied the pulpit of the Baptist church Sunday evening. He intends leaving for Chicago early in September and will pursue his studies at the University of that city."

I laid down the paper and meditated a bit. If Ed meant to go to Chicago he would probably visit his relatives in Cavendish first; and as it was already "early in September" he might be here at any time. In fact, a sort of presentiment grew upon me that he *was* in Cavendish at that very moment. If he were, he would, of course, be at the Baptist church the next day— and equally, of course, *I* would *not* be there!

The following morning looked so like rain that none of Uncle John's went to church, so I was saved the trouble of manufacturing excuses. But the evening was gloriously fine and—why wasn't I going to church. Well, I had a headache—had had it ever since dinner time—that is to say ever since it had threatened to clear up—and of course, having a headache I couldn't go to church! So all the folks started off and I watched them rather glumly from my

Bert and Laura

window—for it was a perfect evening—and I wanted to go out—and if Ed were not there at all it would be something of a joke on me!

---

1. Volunteers in the Royal Canadian Regiment in 1899 were the first Canadians in overseas service; their charge ended a long siege of Boer forces at Paardeberg in February 1900.

But he *was* there. And he *preached*! This made me doubly thankful that I hadn't gone.

For a week I avoided going out anywhere lest I should meet him. When at last I heard of his departure I drew a long breath of relief. He is gone—and I hope we shall never meet again.

Sometimes I turn back the pages of this journal and read over what I wrote at that wretched time. Heaven knows it isn't for the purpose of refreshing my memory for it is all branded too deeply ever to be effaced. But there is a sort of bitter fascination about it. Poor little wretch that I was! I find myself pitying my old self as I read.

Wednesday, Oct. 10, 1900
Cavendish, P.E.I.

It is a horrible thing to get heart-breakingly, despairingly lonely! It is not often that I do. If I have something to read or some work I like to do I can laugh at solitude. But I *do* get lonely sometimes. And, like all other emotions, when loneliness does come to me it takes possession of me body and soul, and wrings me in its bleak pain until all strength and courage goes out of me. Tonight I am lonely—lonely!

I cannot work for I have worked hard all day and I am too tired to work any more, even if I had the "grit" to do it. I suppose the weather has a good deal to do with my "blues." This is the second day of a heavy, ceaseless autumn rain. The outside world is a dismal one, with drenched and dripping trees and sodden fields. And the damp and gloom have crept into my soul and spirit and sapped out all life and energy.

Then I have nothing to read, for the mailman did not come today. The absence of the mail is a serious loss here, where its daily advent is about all there is to look forward to. There is always something for me—a letter from a friend out in the busy world, a fat parcel woefully eloquent of rejected MS, an envelope so delightfully thin as to be suggestive of no thicker enclosure than a cheque or at least an acceptance, perhaps a book with a whole world and lifetime between its covers, a dainty magazine full of clever scribblings, a weekly paper with an exciting serial—any or all of these may tumble out of the Government's big, ugly canvas bag. But nothing came today and therefore life is flat, stale and unprofitable.

Oh, I am tired! I have no heart for anything. I wish I could creep away into some dark corner and sleep forever. To be sure, this mood will pass. Tomorrow, when the sun comes out, I'll be brave and busy and confident again. But just now I am full of loneliness and pain. You poor patient old journal, it helps me to write this out in you—it half conjures away my dark mood.

I shall laugh at myself tomorrow. This wretched weather! If it would only clear—a fig for my blues!

Thursday, Oct. 11, 1900
Cavendish, P.E. Island.

If weather makes one blue I ought to be of the deepest azure tonight, for it is a terrible storm. I went to the door a few minutes ago and it seemed to me as if all the demon powers of air were battling out there in the wind and rain and darkness! What groans of mighty trees wrung in the tempest, what a thunderous crash of billows on the shore!

But I am not blue—I am not moody. I am tingling with life, for I've just finished a book warranted to produce any number of thrills—"To Have and To Hold."[1] It is one of the year's "hits" and is full of charm and adventure. I have read on and on with never a thought for the dreadful rush of wind and swish of rain outside. Oh, books, books what worlds of pleasure you open! What freedom you offer all prisoners! How do people live who never read or want to read? I cannot understand them—but I pity them.

Thursday, Oct. 18, 1900
Cavendish, P.E. Island.

Ten years ago, when I was a schoolgirl of fifteen, I had a mania for writing "ten year letters"—which being interpreted means a letter, "written, signed, and sealed," to be opened and read ten years from the date of writing. I don't know exactly where I got the idea—I think I'd read something like it in a "Pansy" book. At any rate I adopted it for my own, for it seemed so fine and romantic. And *then* ten years seemed a veritable lifetime and twenty-five a very venerable age indeed.

Now, when the reading of these letters is falling due, it does not bring me the pleasure I once anticipated. Instead, I have an uncanny feeling, as if I were reading a letter from a ghost or across a grave. They give me far more pain than pleasure.

This evening, at eight o'clock, I had to open one of these epistles written ten years ago, in old "Southview" in Prince Albert by Edith Skelton. I

---

1. Bestselling historical romance (1900) of Virginia by Mary Johnston (1870–1936).

remember very clearly the night we wrote them. We had been having a gay time as usual, for Edith was such a jolly girl. And we wrote those letters very light heartedly, never doubting that our friendship would outlive the years. It has not done so—it has just dropped away. I haven't heard from or of Edith for six years. I wonder if she remembered to open my letter tonight.

I opened hers and read it. It was a merry letter, full of our old jokes, some of which I have so entirely forgotten that their significance is quite lost for me. It was not a brilliant epistle at all—Edith's talents did not lie in the direction of letter writing; and all things considered it was not worth keeping for ten years to read it.

Tuesday, October 23, 1900
Cavendish, P.E. Island.

I've been having a book treat—Wallace's "Prince of India."[1] It is a wonderful book—wonderful in plot and conception—wonderful in its grasp of motives and passions. When I read it I felt humbled and insignificant—which is good for me! When I finished it I said to myself,
    "You poor, pitiful little creature, did you ever
    imagine that *you* could write? If so, your delusion
    is now stripped away from you forever and you behold
    yourself in your naked paltriness."
But I do not always trust this state of mind—though I daresay there is too much truth in it. And when I recover from it I shall go cheerfully on writing pot-boilers and investing the proceeds in necessaries—and a *few* luxuries.

Saturday, Nov. 10, 1900
Cavendish, P.E.I.

Today the *November* issue of *Good Housekeeping* came, with some verses of mine in it entitled, "A Pair of Slippers."[2] I consider the occasion worthy of mention because they were given a whole page to themselves and illustrated—the first time ever my verses were so honoured. They are trashy enough little things in themselves I know, but they *did* look so dignified that a careless observer might fancy that there was really something in them.

1. Mystic story (1893) of the wandering Jew, set in ancient Constantinople, by Lew Wallace (1827–1905), author of *Ben Hur* (1880).

2. A sentimental poem about "grandmamma's" young days.

Blessings on the good editor who was inspired to have them illustrated! He has bolstered my self-respect very considerably.

Saturday, Dec. 22, 1900
Cavendish, P.E.I.

We are surely going to have a white Christmas to celebrate the end of the century—the first we have had for years. Winter is here to stay. I hate it because I can't prowl around by myself outside in the evenings. When the dim wintry twilight comes down there is nothing to do but drop my work with a little sigh of weariness and creep away into a dark corner to nurse a bit of a heartache. If it were summer I could get away outside under the trees and the stars and my soul would be so filled with their beauty that pain would have no place.

To be sure, I did start out tonight, grimly resolved to do a constitutional and walked around the square without seeing a soul. It was cold and clear and frosty-white—white, white everywhere, soulless and lifeless, except where a strip of orange ran along the west and far down over the lowlands the sea was black and sullen. I walked around the square and then my resolution gave out and I came in. It was too deadly still and lonesome outside—I wanted to scream out to break the awful silence.

It is not much better inside—just a different kind of loneliness. Grandma sits and sews or reads the papers all the evening. I sit and read—or write—and eat my heart out into the bargain. The monotony is dreadful. I never rebelled against it as I do this winter. To be sure, I keep my rebellion to myself and nobody suspects it. But it is there for all, seething and fermenting.

I love bright, cheerful companionship, laughter, sparkling conversation. I get nothing of them. Grandma has always been a reserved, distant woman, caring less than anyone I ever knew for social intercourse with her kind, and possessed with an odd *resentment* against the liking or desire for it in anyone else. My inner life has, for the most part, been lived entirely alone and those with whom I have had to associate most have been in all times and in all crises the farthest removed from me. The friends who have been a real help and inspiration to me are seldom near me. Sometimes I am conscious of a great *soul loneliness*. Spiritually, and mentally I have always had to stand alone. I suppose it has made for strength and self-reliance—but it is hard.

Well, I'm going to stop growling. But I really do feel discontented by spells. I feel as if I were hemmed in on all sides by a hedge of petty, trivial, unceasing annoyances that prick and sting continually and so "get on the nerves" more than would a great pain.

Tonight, in reading over some old letters I tried to read one of *Herman's*—the only one I ever had from him. Well, I could not do it! I opened it, read the first page and then I had to fold it up and put it away. The pain was intolerable. What an influence that man had over me! His mark is branded on my soul forever. To think that now, two years after his death, I cannot bring myself to read a crude, impersonal letter of his, containing nothing but commonplaces, without feeling as if a brutal hand had twisted itself among my heartstrings and was wrenching them at will. Yet I do not often think of him now and that wild passion is dead and buried with him. It is only when, as tonight, I try to read his letter or the pages of this journal written about him that the old agony wakes and lifts his head and defies me to forget its former power.

After all, in spite of all discouragement and heart-burning I am getting on pretty well[1] in a way. That is to say, I'm beginning to make a livable income for myself by my pen. Oh, *outwardly* I'm getting on all right. It is *inwardly* that all the tumult is. Yes, I *am* getting on and I mean to get on, let come what will of rebuff and discouragement and failure. I have conquered this dismal trio so far and I mean to continue. "What man has done, man may do."

Now, I'm off. This grumble has done me good. I work off all my revolutionary tendencies in this journal. If it were not for this "went"[2] I might fly into a thousand little pieces someday.

---

1. In 1900 LMM published "When the Fishing Boats Come In," "Evening Dream" and other poems, and added *Good Housekeeping, Sports Afield* and *Waverley* to the list of journals that had purchased her short stories.

2. Joking form of *vent*.

Illustrations

Index